Letters from Irish Australia 1825-1929

THE U.H.F. HISTORICAL SERIES

1. *Ulster Emigration to Colonial America 1718-1775* by R. J. Dickson (1966: reprint, 1976).

2. *Essays in Scotch-Irish History,* edited by E. R. R. Green (1969). Essay titles and contributors are as follows:
   - i 'Woodrow Wilson and his Presbyterian Inheritance' by Arthur S. Link.
   - ii 'Education in the American Colonies: The Scottish Impact' by Esmond Wright.
   - iii 'Ulster Emigration 1783-1815' by Maldwyn A. Jones.
   - iv 'The Scotch-Irish: Their Cultural Adaptation and Heritage in the Old West' by E. Estyn Evans.
   - v 'Ulster Emigrants' Letters' by E. R. R. Green.

3. *The Scottish Migration to Ulster in the Reign of James I* by M. Perceval-Maxwell (1973).

4. *Penal Era and Golden Age: Essays in Irish History, 1690-1800,* edited by Thomas Bartlett and D. W. Hayton (1979). Essay titles and contributors are as follows:
   - i 'The Irish Parliament of 1692' by James I. McGuire.
   - ii 'The Beginnings of the "Undertaker System" by David Hayton.
   - iii 'The Money Bill Dispute of 1753' by Declan O'Donovan.
   - iv 'The Townshend Viceroyalty, 1767-72' by Thomas Bartlett.
   - v 'The Volunteers and Parliament, 1779-84' by P. D. H. Smyth.
   - vi ' "The Parliamentary Traffic of this Country" ' by A. P. W. Malcomson.
   - vii 'Middlemen' by David Dickson.
   - viii 'Change in Ulster in the late Eighteenth Century' by W. H. Crawford.
   - ix 'Irish Republicanism in England: the First Phase, 1797-9' by Marianne Elliott.

5. *Scottish Covenanters and Irish Confederates: Scottish-Irish Relations in the Mid-Seventeenth Century* by David Stevenson (1981).

6. *Macartney of Lisanoure, 1737-1806: Essays in Biography,* edited by P. Roebuck with contributions by T. J. Bartlett, J. L. Cranmer-Byng, T. G. Fraser, W. R. Fryer, E. M. Johnston, J. L. McCracken, M. Roberts and P. Roebuck (1983).

7. *Letters from Irish Australia 1825-1929* by P. O'Farrell (1984). Text of letters edited by Brian Trainor.

Letters from Irish Australia 1825-1929

Patrick O'Farrell

Text of letters edited by
Brian Trainor

NEW SOUTH WALES UNIVERSITY PRESS
Sydney, Australia
and
ULSTER HISTORICAL FOUNDATION
Belfast, Northern Ireland
1984

Published jointly by
NEW SOUTH WALES UNIVERSITY PRESS
PO Box 1 Kensington NSW Australia 2033
Telephone (02) 662 3503
and the
ULSTER HISTORICAL FOUNDATION
66 Balmoral Avenue Belfast BT9 6NY
Northern Ireland
Telephone 66 1621

National Library of Australia
Cataloguing-in-Publication entry:

O'Farrell, Patrick, 1933-
Letters from Irish Australia.

Bibliography.
Includes index.
ISBN 0 86840 153 6.

1. Irish — Australia — Correspondence. I. Title.
994'.0049162

Ulster Historical Foundation
ISBN 0 901905 32 1

Printed in Australia by Hogbin Poole (Printers) Pty Ltd

CONTENTS

States and major centres of Australia

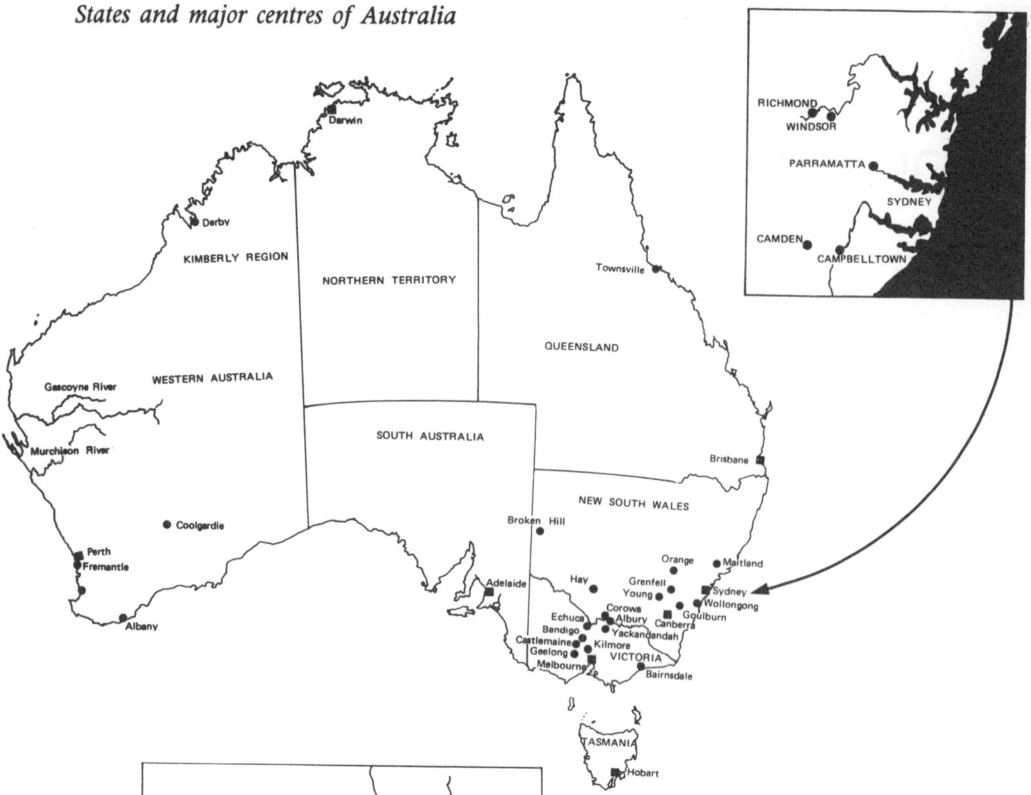

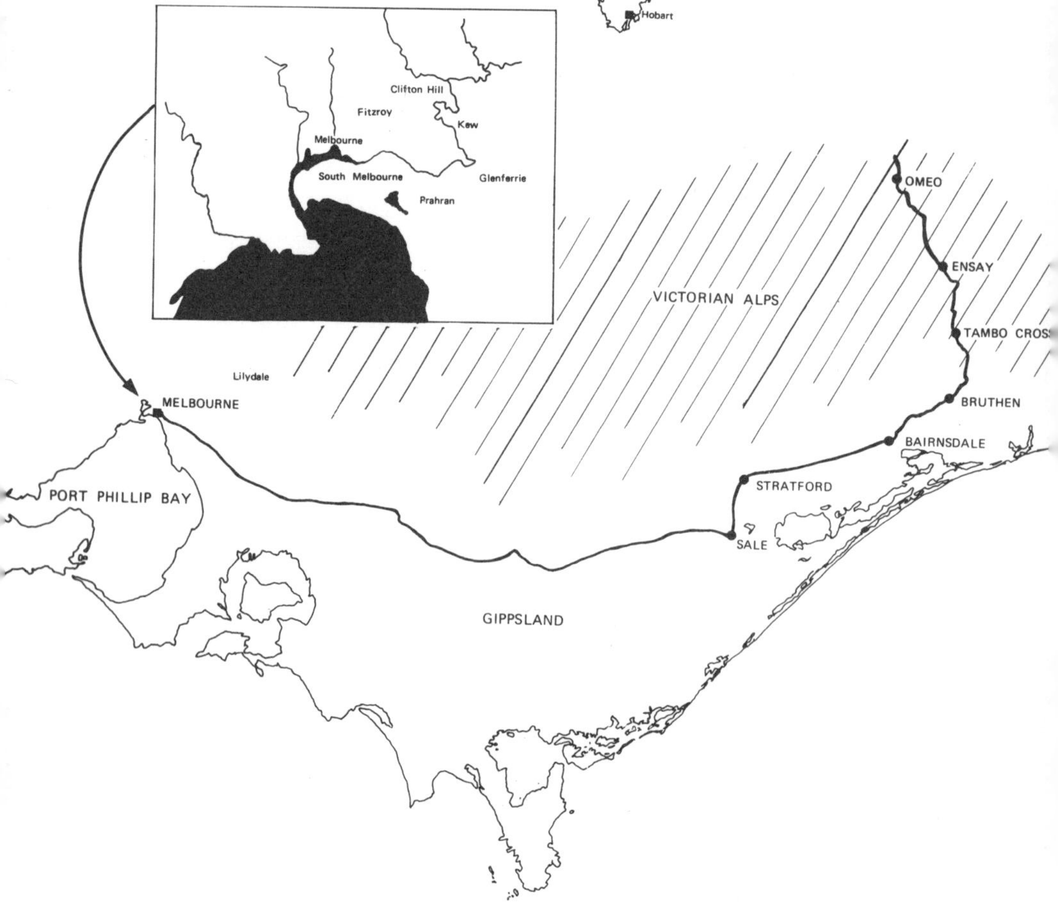

PREFACE

This book, in various forms, has been in progress since 1972. During that time it, and its author, have accumulated more than the usual collection of happy indebtedness. My major and enabling debt is to Brian Trainor, Director of the Public Record Office of Northern Ireland and Administrator of the Ulster Historical Foundation. His name appears on the title page as editing the text of the letters; that is, as responsible for checking against the handwritten originals, the selections I made from the transcript form in which they are available in the Public Record Office of Northern Ireland reading room. But Brian Trainor's role in this book goes well beyond that exacting chore. Not only did he place his Office's resources behind the project, but he gave without stint his own time, energy, enthusiasm, and wide range of professional skills, to the variety of tasks that arise from a complex enterprise conducted in two countries so far apart: it could not have proceeded without him. Of his no less admirable and helpful staff, two deserve particular mention as associated with the book at various stages — Miss Frances McConville and Miss Gertrude Hamilton.

In relation to Chapter 2, the Keeper and staff of the State Paper Office, Dublin merit similar acknowledgement: the recent practical help given by Miss Anne Neary, Archivist, of that office, requires particular mention, as does that of the Keeper personally. I wish to formally acknowledge my indebtedness to the Keeper of the State Paper Office, and to the copyright holder, the Government of Ireland, for permission to use the material in Chapter 2, but also to note, that during 1972-3, when I worked there, the Keeper, Mr Breandan Mac Giolla Choille facilitated my research with generosity and enthusiasm, to the extent of diverting much of his own time and energy, and that of his staff, to Australian explorations relevant to my interests. He also found space to accommodate the work of my then research assistant, Miss Trixie Van Leeuwen, to whom I am also grateful in relation to material in Chapter 2. As mentioned in the Chapter notes, happily Mr Mac Giolla Choille has retained and developed the Australian interests in which we collaborated at that time, despite the enforced hiatus in my own momentum.

That period of hiatus and delay requires its own list of credits. That I am able to complete this book is in no small way due to the care and expertise of medical professionals too numerous to mention, but I single our Dr. J. M. L'Estrange, Professor D. W. Piper, Mrs M. Daly, and others associated with the Royal North Shore Hospital, Sydney. No doubt they might regard as a very remote consequence of their efforts any credit for a work of migrant history: the connection is very real and immediate to me.

Research relating to this book has been funded by grants from the Faculty of Arts, University of New South Wales. To go back to its genesis in Ireland in 1972-3, I am indebted not only to this University, but to University College, Dublin, and Trinity College, Dublin, to which I was then attached.

The book appears as the first in this School of History's historical publication series, an honour for which I thank my colleagues; and also under the auspices of the Ulster Historical Foundation, to which I am also indebted. Its physical production has been an initial test of the capacities and possibilities of this School's new word processor. Special thanks are due to Associate Professor John Ingleson for his tireless and patient devotion to mastering, through the medium of this particular book, the challenges of the new technology. Similar warm thanks should be recorded to the School's word processor operators and secretaries, particularly Sharon Emery who set most of the manuscript, but also Tina Patterson and Susan Jones: their interest in, and good-humoured devotion to, a repetitious and exacting task went well beyond the call of duty.

In order to respect family preference or the sensitivity of descendants, some few of the surnames and place names used are not those of the actual historical individuals, a fictionalising device which will be familiar to readers of sociology: in all such cases replacements are true to the area, period and culture of the originals. This device obviously precludes my mentioning here some persons to whom my debt is very great, all the greater for their generous recognition that the historical worth of this testimony from the past outweighs considerations natural to a sense of family reserve and privacy.

In addition to those I wish to thank but am prevented from naming, may be those that I should thank but of whom I am not aware. Every effort has been made to trace those who have made available the material used, or who have interests or rights in such materials. As far as I am aware, all such persons have been contacted, and I am most grateful for what were usually not so much mere permissions, but enthusiastic cooperation: one of the pleasant bonuses of this project is that I have met or corresponded with a range of delightful people, descendants of the letter writers, whom I would have not otherwise encountered. If there are others inadvertantly overlooked, I trust they will accept my apologies.

A note on spelling and presentation. This always constitutes something of a problem when a writer's literacy and education are minimal or deficient, or when the pressures of time, a casual approach, or carelessness operate — situations common to the human condition then and now. Here, what might be termed a common sense approach has been taken. The flow and flavour of the originals has not been disrupted by the excessive use of obvious editorial interpolations or adjustments, but three conventions used should be noted: double quotation marks indicate misspelling, dialect, or slang terms in the original; words within square brackets represent editorial additions, and, where necessary, guess work; and use of the term [sic] signifies that the peculiarity is in the original.

Many of those who assisted are thanked in the notes at the end of the book, in relation to the section or point on which they were of help. To these I wish to add the following: for comment on the manuscript, the postgraduate seminars of the University of New South Wales and the University of Melbourne, Dr. Mark Finnane, and Mrs. Venetia Nelson; the Irish Ambassador to Australia, His Excellency Mr. Joseph Small for his enthusiasm and encouragement; Virginia O'Farrell of La Trobe University for research assistance on the notes; Mrs Marjorie Morgan of Melbourne for background research in the very early stage of this project, particularly on Alexander Crawford's career; Patrick Morgan of the Gippsland Institute of Advanced Education for help with illustrations; in regard to production and publication, New South Wales University Press, particularly Mr Douglas Howie and Ms Di Quick, and members of the Ulster Historical Foundation.

I am specially indebted to Mr Alexander Crawford of Camberwell, Victoria, and to Chief Superintendent M.A.A. Crawford of Hong Kong in relation to Chapter 5; and in regard to Chapter 6, Mr Stewart Twigg of Cookstown, Co. Tyrone and Mrs Lorna Wolton of Gosford, N.S.W.

In regard to illustrations, I wish to thank — in addition to the Public Record Office of Northern Ireland, Belfast — the National Library of Ireland in Dublin, the State Library of Victoria in Melbourne, the East Gippsland Historical Society, Bairnsdale, the Port Albert Maritime Museum, Victoria, Mr Elliot Wright of Busselton, W. A., Dr. W.H. Crawford and the Ulster Folk and Transport Museum, Holywood, Co. Down, the *Belfast Telegraph*, and Mr John Twigg, grandson of the recipient of the Australian letters.

As always with my books, my wife Deirdre provided an informed testing environment for ideas and approaches. Additionally, in this case, she played a vital role as driver to some of the more distant and inaccessible places from whence these letters were written. Had it not been for her help I would not have been able to wonder, a century later but on those same locations, at what had been achieved, and at the human qualities behind those extraordinary achievements.

Patrick O'Farrell
School of History
University of New South Wales

Counties and major towns of Ireland

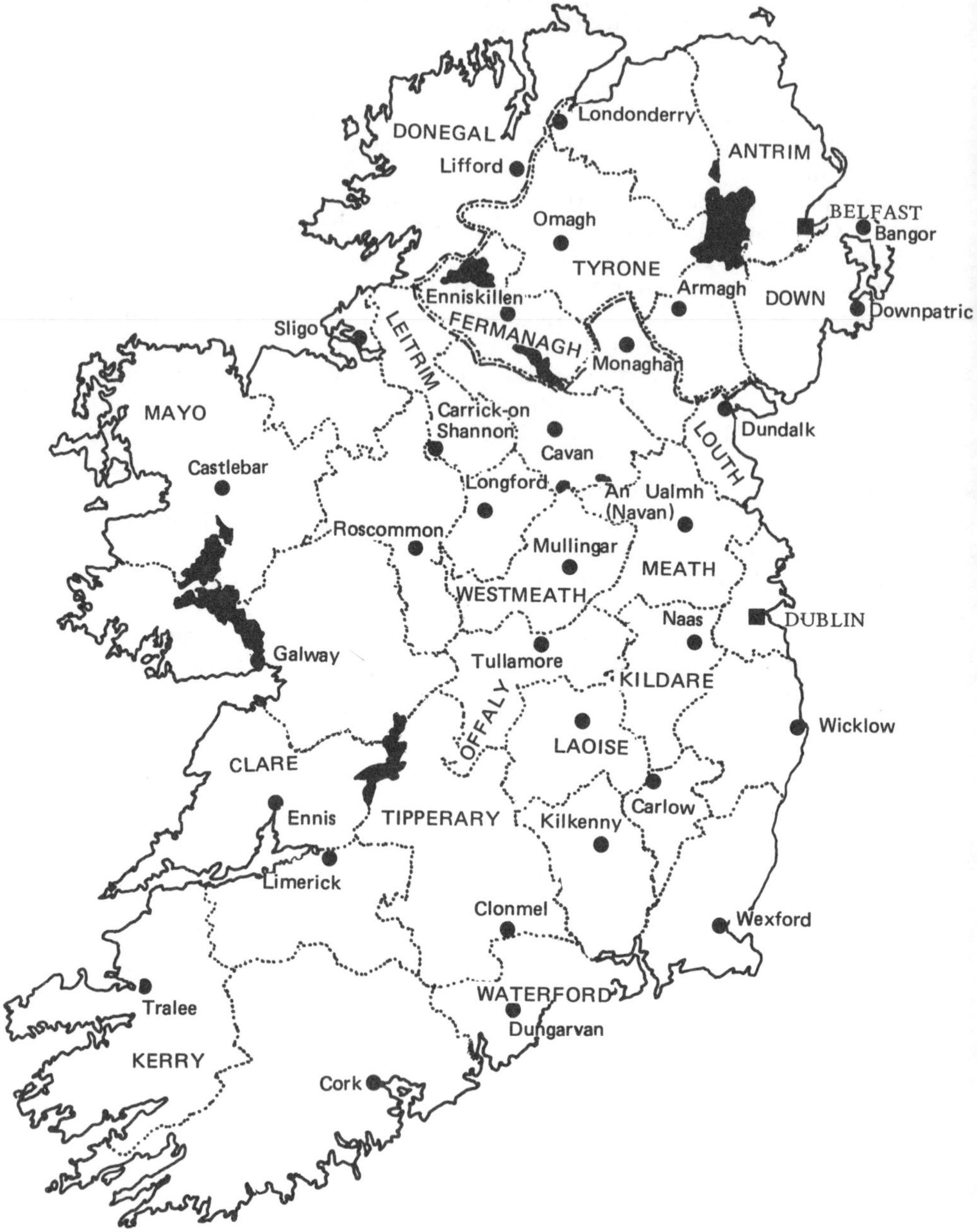

1 INTRODUCTION

Once, people were like this: Irish people — their private letters from their new home to their old, reveal them so. This book is about the experience of Irish immigrants in Australia, seen from the inside through letters they sent back to their families in Ireland. Here is a selection of some of the best of the Australian holdings of two major archives, the Public Record Office of Northern Ireland, Belfast, and the State Paper Office, Dublin. Obviously the selection has been limited by the randomness of what has been preserved, and by the requirements of a manageable book.

These letters are more than informative or entertaining. They take their readers, both then and now, to the heart of the Irish Australian migrant experience: they tell, intimately and particularly, what being a migrant meant. And being both personal and direct, they do this in a unique way, without barriers and across time.

The letters have been chosen and grouped so as to provide a wide variety of angles and standpoints. Six major focal points have been chosen for the organisation and exploration of six different kinds of story. The longest and most complex is the story of the interacting lives of the Maxwell family of Ballygannah, Bangor, Co. Down, five of whom emigrated to Victoria in the 1880s and who conducted a substantial correspondence among themselves and back to Ireland between 1883 and 1929. These family letters illustrate a common form of Irish migration — chain migration of family members and relatives — and touch on salient points of the migrants' experience — work and leisure, friends and society, money making and the acquiring of property, marriage, sickness, birth and death. The Maxwell letters offer a complex family biography intertwining with the daily life of colonial society in a way which is both ordinary and distinctively Irish. The Maxwells are too much themselves to be offered as typical: indeed the lesson of their story of success and disaster, of the differences between the personalities and fates within one family, warns us that the migrant experience is as diverse as the individuals who underwent it.

A different kind of story is that of an individual, James Hamilton Twigg of Cookstown, Co. Tyrone, who at the age of seventeen migrated to Western

Australia in 1891. Like the Maxwell brothers, James Twigg established himself initially with the help of relatives and friends already in Australia, but he increasingly chose a solitary path. His attempts to scrape together enough capital to buy a farm, to improve the quality of his life, to make himself a person of substance, show very clearly the migrant determination to succeed. But the cost of a lonely farming existence, the impact of unrelenting work on health and spirit, was eventually too great. Twigg's pioneering achievement took a sour twist: in 1907 he left a land he had come to hate as one frustrating his ambitions, and migrated to East Africa.

Another way of approaching the Irish Australian disposition is to examine the reactions of a distinctive group with status and prospects in common — convicts and emancipists writing to their wives in Ireland, 1825-1847. These men seek to persuade their wives to join them in Australia and paint a rosy picture of contrast between the constraints and poverty of Ireland and the abundance and comparative affluence of Australia. They also reveal the emotional trauma inflicted by the transportation system on those that were married.

Another way of exploring the migrant mind is through the reaction to an experience common to all immigrants, the voyage out to Australia. The accounts included here of shipboard life, 1838-1884, suggest that the mixing and physical proximity of people on board to some extent dissolved their old social relationships and disposed them to accept more readily the egalitarian and tolerant Australian environment: the ship was, in some important ways, the colony in microcosm. It prefigures the erosion of class and religious barriers, and the length of the voyage disrupted traditional life patterns and hastened the collapse of old practices, particularly in relation to religion and social authority. In contrast with the shorter trip to America, the interminable voyage to Australia wrought subtle sea-changes in the migrant disposition.

The love letters that passed between Alexander Crawford in Western Australia and Elizabeth Mathews in Victoria in the years 1881-1883 are a vignette of intense personal emotion. For Crawford, their background is harsh and remote pioneering life marked by frequent and violent conflict with the aborigines. For his fiancee, the setting is the comparative civilisation of quiet family farming in colonial Victoria. Both long for each other, and for a marriage postponed by the need to win not only approval from parents, but also a hostile land from the grip of drought and its resistant Aboriginal inhabitants.

The last approach adopted is to bring together a variety of brief glimpses of migrant lives in a diverse group of cameo portraits, 1828-1902. These, different as they are from each other, are united in character and treatment by the fragmentary nature of the correspondence that survives, which sets them apart from the large and more continuous collections given in the other chapters. These portraits range from those of the gentry, through small farmers and large, to unionists, goldminers and ballroom decorators; wanderers, men in and out of luck, men happy with their lot, others lonely and distraught; some secure and comfortable, others overtaken by illness or surprised by close deaths.

The principle of selection in all sections has been to try to distil what is distinctively 'Irish' or, more broadly, 'Irish migrant' — the broader term acknowledging that much of the Irish experience and reaction was common to migrants generally. In some contexts the 'Irish' element can be readily separated out: obviously shipboard experiences held much in common for all migrants, but Irish behaviour or reactions were noticeable enough to be distinguished from what was general. In other contexts letter-writers were sufficiently conscious of their Irishness to acknowledge this explicitly as the standpoint from which they made their observations: they saw the world through Irish eyes. In other cases — and here the balance of concern shifts away from the letter-writers and towards the author — an effort is made to appraise the impact of the Australian environment on the Irish migrant, to highlight the reactions he had because he is Irish. This attempt at distilling 'Irishness' cannot be made too precisely or too rigorously, because contact between cultures is an elusive and subtle thing and is not subject to precise description. Therefore 'Irishness' has been treated as an elastic concept, at times clear and firm, but more often shadowy and imprecise, a mood and disposition rather than a list of definitions. For the same reason — that this is a historical area of hints and fleeting glimpses — it has been necessary to draw out from between the lines of this correspondence, material for analysis and meditation. Such meditation is made in the commentary that accompanies and introduces the letters, and is intended as an unobtrusive illumination: the letters and commentary together are meant to generate an impression of, and convey insight into, the lives of these Irish immigrants.

The use of personal correspondence as a vehicle to unearth the essence of the migrant experience requires some explanation, if not defence.[1] In the circumstances of migration, and given the limited communication situation of the day, private letters home came to be of unique importance in the lives of migrants and their families and friends, from the early nineteenth century until the middle of the twentieth. Reforms in the postal rates, such as the penny post introduced in Britain in 1840, were only one of the ways in which postal services were made generally accessible. Growth in the practice of personal letter writing also depended on the extension of literacy and the spread of the habit of correspondence as an expected medium of social exchange and private communication. These developments can be seen clearly in the change in the character of immigrant correspondence from the 1830s to the 1880s: it becomes more frequent, less stilted and stylised, more expressive of the detailed actualities and nuances of experience. But early in the century or late, private letters home are of unequalled historical value: they are authentic, immediate, and peculiarly oriented to the possibility of revealing the central concerns of the migrant condition. Of their nature they are an intimate insight into what the migrant actually thought and felt, expressed without constraint, and with the honesty and candour appropriate to close family situations. A qualification is necessary in regard to one group of correspondence used here. The letters of convicts and emancipists formed part of a bureaucratic process and might be best regarded as semi-private — although those who wrote them were probably inured to invasions of privacy. Certainly for the rest, such letters are authentic, that is, they derive from and express direct personal experience; they are immediate, that is, they report the situation as it then seemed, not overlaid by memory or hindsight: memoirs have not been included, for example, that of Von Stieglitz, who in 1875-76, back in Ireland, wrote his reminiscences of Tasmania and Victoria in the 1830s. And, because such letters are written home to those who are known intimately and whose interest can be assumed, their language and concerns are designed to convey, clarify and make intelligible the key points of the migrant experience.

Is this to claim too much? It has been observed that as emigrant correspondence was, in some circumstances, read aloud — to friends and neighbours grouped together, or by a literate person to an illiterate family — it was often written to some extent for public consumption. Such circumstances were commonly those of an illiterate or at least unlettered society, with notions of privacy not yet extended to the unfamiliar world of communication by letter. In such cases the level of expression was usually in keeping with such simplicity. The letters here do not relate to such a cultural situation. It is quite evident, both from their nature and at times explicit instruction, that these letters are intended to be private, directed to one person or the strict confines of a discreet family, a confidentiality which the Maxwell brothers, for instance, occasionally stressed. What of the conventions that overtook emigrant correspondence to issue in the stereotyped American letter — 'all well and doing well' — that became a standing joke in Ireland itself? How much truth did emigrants tell? The nature of the Maxwell family correspondence, in which four boys wrote back to Ireland, and within Australia to each other, allows a cross checking that suggests an honesty and accuracy close to absolute. Australian circumstances differed from the American.[2] In Australia the immigrant letter seems to have filled needs in the writer other than those of boastful justification of his migration. In settlement patterns very different from those of the American Irish concentration in large cities, isolation within the colonies was added to the separation of the migrant situation, so that letter writing became a substitute for direct human society: it was an affirmation of membership at a vast remove of a valued and familiar kinship and as such could tolerate neither suppression or dishonesty. Besides, the unpredictable casualness and constant mobility of Australian society meant frequent chance meetings with acquaintances tied in with the news systems of Ireland: home would soon know the truth. The inflated expectations characteristic of earlier Irish emigration to America seem not to have attached themselves so strongly to Australia: perhaps some of the lessons of American experience had been learnt before the period of heaviest Australian immigration. It is certainly a fact that many Irish migrants and their families at home had unrealistic visions of fortune awaiting in Australia. Several of the letters included here make clear the migrant response to that situation. Rather than lie, or confess what would be taken as failure, they often did not write at all. They waited to report success — which, if it ever came, might be in ten, twenty years.

So these letters may be taken as truthful. What of their remarkable literary and perceptive qualities? It is an unfortunate truism that popular expectations and images of the Irish have been hitherto anchored to the character of the least advantaged elements of that nation. In fact, Irish migrants represented the whole social range, and there are strong arguments for suggesting that Australia received more than its share of those better off and better educated.[3] Besides, it is an anachronism to assume of the later nineteenth century that comparatively small means and lowly status go together with limited intelligence or lack of verbal facility. Increasingly, the middling and lower ranks of Irish farmers and professional classes provided their sons with both an education and an encouragement to emigrate, a kind of joint investment and endowment enterprise which might pay off in better economic prospects and which also gave young persons a secure view of their own accomplishments.[4] Many of these letter writers have a remarkable assurance that springs from confident mastery of tools basic to the world's work: they believe — and colonial experience proves them right — that they can turn their hands to anything, and do it well. Some have a natural literary flair. But most merely assume that it is among a man's expected accomplishments that he should be able to write a fair letter — or ride a horse, split fence posts, cook, sing or play an instrument, keep books, build a house, and so on. Significantly it was mainly men who wrote these letters: often it was women — their sisters rather than their less well-educated mothers — who replied from home. Those Irishwomen who emigrated seem not to have been from the letter-writing classes.[5]

The letters represented here cannot reflect the weight of immigrant numbers among the Australian Irish: Protestants, and those who came from the Ulster counties generally, are overrepresented. The imbalance is easily explained. Though there were far more immigrants from the Catholic South, they were not so well educated. The Catholic priesthood was the literate and educated class among them, and its considerable Australian correspondence is a separate and professional study, at a tangent to the focus of the present book.[6] The social structures governing the massive emigration from the South and South-west of Ireland were often such that not only whole families but whole districts emigrated: there was no one to write back to, or circumstances of poverty, eviction, or subsequent migration destroyed any continuity with the present that may have allowed the preservation of family correspondence. In the North, a greater locational stability and the fact that some family members more often remained, favoured more likely preservation: it is significant that to this day descendents of the Maxwell family continue to live on the Ballygannah property from which Hugh, John, James, William and David emigrated to Victoria in the 1880s. Deliberate government archive policies and generous resource allocation in Northern Ireland fostered collection: there, repositories existed, and a sense of their value, to a degree not matched in the Republic of Ireland.

Yet if the documentation that survives does not mirror the balance of migrant numbers, in a curious way it moves towards correction of a long-standing error. In Australia, the overwhelming, indeed virtually exclusive image of the Irish immigrant has been that of the stereotyped peasant, Catholic, ignorant, uncivilised, unsophisticated, backward, dirty, drunken and violent. How partial, narrow and incomplete is that view of Australia's Irish heritage will be obvious from a glance at the Irish worlds revealed here, which range from the convict success stories of Dennis Mahony or Peter Fitzgibbon or James Halloran, to the Anglo-Irish affluence of the NSW grazier Thomas Moore, to the ordinary hard-working Presbyterian lives of the Maxwells, James Twigg, the Lawrences, and a host of other non-Gaelic names, with non-Catholic cultural roots — all of which, in their different ways, were firmly and intensely Irish and proud of it.[7]

These letters also balance and enrich the historical record in another way. Usually it is only the correspondence of the prominent or the rich which survives. Here are letters of ordinary people — convicts, small farmers, shop assistants, labourers — people who have no historical reputation and who would not exist for posterity save for what they wrote. They are the rank and file of the migrant army, and, that being so, the weight of their testimony in correspondence follows the graph of heaviest immigration into Australia from the 1850s to the 1890s, with a concentration of Ulster immigration in the 1880s and 1890s.[8]

The historical method of presentation adopted here amounts to orchestration, a procedure designed to arrange and present the material in such a way as to expand and emphasize its essential features, and to contrive from them a satisfying unity — as well as to impart or heighten mood or atmosphere. The very nature of private correspondence is to create a mood of intimacy. It thus needs to be presented in such a way as to draw the reader in as a spy, whose knowledge derives not merely from the content of what is said, but from sharing the feelings exchanged by the correspondents. The emotional tension generated comes not from the information acquired but from caring about the human beings involved. So, mere information widens into knowledge which derives in part from a vicarious participation in what took place in the past. Good history does more than observe, it contrives to share, so that the reader experiences that mixture of embarrassment and involvement that comes from invading the privacy of other people's lives.

With such an intrusive undertaking, care has to be taken to avoid historical inflation. These letters are individual declarations of limited experience: they record a fairly narrow personal circle and their scale of reference is relatively small. Their vantage point in society is neither high nor wide, though arguably it is a position best placed to convey the feel of the ordinary. But because of the intensity and penetration of these encounters with immigrant life, there is a natural tendency to wish to erect on these bases, the widest of generalisations. Some balance has to be achieved between resisting any large claims to typicality and taking advantage of the insights and interpretative angles offered by the cases investigated here. In stopping well short of fabricating new Irish myths — that all Irish were as sensible and as civilised, and in the same way, as the best examples here — one must nevertheless draw out the suggestive historical lessons inherent in these particular lives, even if they cannot be pursued much beyond the status of pointed questions. How these lives fit into the broad and complex picture of the total Irish Australian historical experience which may be assembled from other sources, is a matter to be left to my forthcoming history of the Irish in Australia, to which this book, is, in a sense, an ancillary volume.[9]

Emigration from nineteenth-century Ireland was one of the greatest population movements the world has ever seen — in terms of its size relative to the population that produced it, in terms of its continuance over time, and in relation to the width of its ultimate geographic dispersion. At its peak in the 1880s, when more than a third of those born in Ireland were living outside it,[10] it may be said that Ireland had virtually exploded, disintegrated.

Only such words, with the violent disruptive connotations of a structure which had burst apart, can convey the historical reality with sufficient force, though of course they do not explain it. And only such eruptive concepts can make sense of what Irish emigrants did in relation to their new lives. Blown out and adrift from the centre of the old Irish world, migrants grouped themselves around such fractured fragments of familiarity as they could assemble in their new lands. But essentially they were living in the aftermath of, among the debris of, a social and cultural convulsion of remarkable transformatory power. They sought to find a meaningful coherence to replace that which was lost. Naturally in Australia they built that coherence from what was old, brought with them, and what was new, found here. They added fragments of family and the residue of religion to elements discovered here — sun, freedom, prosperity, each man as good as the other — only to find it a soulless hollow construct. The initially joyful Irish discovery of Australia rested on a wonderful but illusory proposition — that it was possible to have a warm and effective society composed entirely of strangers.[11] Of course, a society of strangers was a contradiction in terms, but this was in fact what Australian immigration had assembled and it was a fact further recommended by considerations of theory: since all men were equal, it ought to be possible to have a society based on principles of common humanity, as distinct from structures of kinship. Like all traditional societies, Irish society had been built around kinship: the division between us and them, between the family construed narrowly or widely, and strangers. The Irish, as these letters make clear, brought their kinship mentality to Australia, where it gradually crumbled and fell apart, declining into a residual social atomism marked by separation, isolation, loneliness and eventual alienation of society's individual parts.

Why did these Irish come to Australia? Assisted passages or the lure of gold played their obvious part, but most came here, rather than elsewhere, because, having determined on emigration, they had relations or friends already in Australia who would meet them, put them up, find them a job. To some it was a matter of indifference whether they went to Australia or North America: it might depend on the immediate availability of a passage, if they had relatives in both. While the length of the Australian passage, and its consequent expense to unassisted migrants, may have been a deterrent to some, to many it was a positive attraction, particularly those who came for their health. By no means all of these were first-class passengers: the medicinal aspects of the voyage and of Australia's climate were rated very highly especially for lung complaints and notably tuberculosis. By the 1880s a significant number of young middling-to lower-class Irish emigrants were coming to Australia in the hope of cure for illness. But by this time emigration itself was becoming very matter of fact, an anticipated and normal aspect of Irish life among the young. Older married persons embarked with trepidation, often impelled by desperation. The young took it for granted, and as an adventure: the emigration questions for them were when and where.[12]

These letters offer other obvious lessons, for instance, that few migrants succeeded in making anything more than a bare living. In this, expectations are crucial. These migrants seemed to have lived with a dual set of economic attitudes — a lottery mentality on the one hand, fed by hopes and dreams, and a clear realism on the other, derived from observation and experience. Migration was not viewed merely as a dull relocation exercise, a translation from one economic world to another: it was also seen as a personal adventure and assumed to have its inescapable costs as such. Ups and downs, hardship, bad luck, discomforts, reverses, were accepted as natural, and weathered as normal, a disposition of acceptance which positively conditioned the way life was experienced and endured: difficulties were seen as obstacles to be overcome, disasters as occurrences to be accepted with equanimity, life as being simply the way things were, not a matter for complaint or disappointment. It is therefore in a sense irrelevant to suggest that their lives were harsh: they seldom thought in those terms. Was this the product of youth, or because failure was the ordinary lot — or at least a constant struggle for survival? In part. It was also because of the intrinsic nature of the Australian economic situation. The experience of the middling migrant confirmed what they constantly contended: that Australia was a paradise for the capitalist and the working man, and hell for anyone in between.

This conclusion did not stop the thrifty, ambitious, enterprising and hard-working attempting to prove they were exceptions to the rule. Such pioneers had constructed a firm image of a pioneer, against which they measured themselves. Above all they knew that they must be willing to work hard, but they also knew they would have to be adaptable, willing to tackle any job, tenacious and resourceful. Clear-sighted esteem for such qualities allowed them to develop self-respect, and it is the pursuit of that secure element of self-regard, rather than any courting of the approval of others which is central to their endeavour. It is easy to see these obvious frontiersman qualities as being a product of the frontier environment. No doubt it fostered them, but young Irish immigrants came to Australia with such attitudes and determination already formed. It was in fact part of the motivation and challenge of the emigration process, by which a man would prove himself, as in some romantic adventure novel. In one of its aspects, the spirit of the migration age, as reflected in these Irish Australian letters, demanded a commitment to proven self-reliance, achieved by discipline.

Mobility is another striking feature of the lives reflected here, striking in itself, and in the contrast it makes with the Irish scene. Once released from the containment of a tiny Irish village, these immigrants became inveterate wanderers. Often they moved in search of betterment, but often it is for the sake of moving. In part it is unsatisfied thirst for adventure and variety, in part the quest for greener grass, in part it is mere pilgrimage, the wish to be on the road. If they cannot have settlement in dear old Ireland (but it is more complex than that: they do not want settlement in Ireland) then they will settle nowhere: they will camp in life where they stop. The break with the kinship-dominated small orbit of place formed by the Irish village is on all fronts, physical and psychological. Self-reliance came to mean not only freedom from the tyranny of the old place, but of any place, from what place means: it will never mean the same again, or be allowed to. This was to divorce the qualities of life encouraged by kinship and stability of place from any precise location in space or time. It reduced such qualities from the power of a network to the compass of the lives of the individual people who inherited them. They tended not to establish their virtues socially by rooting them deep in place and enmeshing them in stable spatial relationships of kin. And so virtue became an individual moral condition, a personal characteristic, rather than what it had once been, a hard-won and clearly regulated location of life, a firm social expectation of the surrounding world.

This is no trivial point, or exercise in pious nostalgia, for a salient feature of the character of the Irish Australians represented here was their integrity and decency. They brought to Australia a strong sense of honour, of obligation, of responsibility, of respect for matters of principle and what they saw as correct moral behaviour. They were not particularly 'religious' persons — indeed they had a healthy suspicion of cant and pretence — but they had a keen sense of how people ought to think and act, according to standards generally Christian and humane. They maintained among themselves a certain style, an approved moral tone. But they did not bequeath it to their environment as their forefathers had done in Ireland. As pilgrim fathers they moved too often, camping on the surface contours of an alien land. Both the letters they wrote, and those they neglected to write, carried the same implied message: no longer was there any such place as home. Writing did not bridge the gap so much as testify to it. These letters embody experiences as intense and as remarkable as they are commonplace: they reveal something of what it was like to be permanently in transit, a pilgrim on an unknown journey, both happy and sad.

2

CONVICTS AND EMANCIPISTS 1825-1847

One of the forgotten human costs of the convict transportation system is the emotional as well as the economic trauma — the loss of the breadwinner — it inflicted on those who were married — about one in five. Early in Macquarie's governorship a few wives and families were allowed, as an 'indulgence', to join such convict husbands as had shown evidence of good conduct and reform, and who were in a position to maintain them in the colony. From 1816 this became a usual practice, with the government soliciting lists from the colony: such wives and families were sent out in female convict ships at public expense.[1]

Such records of the operation of this 'indulgence' as are held with regard to Irish convicts at the State Paper Office, Dublin, include some letters from convicts to their wives.[2] These letters reveal the reality behind the system, husbands who hectored or pleaded, wives who were reluctant or refused to go; husbands frantic for some reply to numerous letters, others confident they had found in New South Wales an earthly paradise to which any wife would be glad to come. Obviously, these letters come from the minority who were literate (although illiterate convicts sometimes asked their masters, or priests, or friends, or professional letter-writers, to write on their behalf) and thus represent the better educated, more mature and advantaged prisoners, those who had been amenable and successful in the colony. The purpose of these letters should also be borne in mind: they sought to persuade their wives to join them, and thus can be expected to depict their own situation and that of the colony in the most favourable light. They are, taking a sceptical view, the letters of a small and relatively privileged minority engaged in special pleading. Yet the fact is that many emancipated Irish convicts did prosper in the early colony: here are some of their testimonies to success — and to the pain of loneliness and separation. Of those many less fortunate, less articulate, trapped permanently in their crime and misery, observers have left ample commentary, of various degrees of worth or prejudice. From the silence of the past, only those with voices can speak out directly: these particular witnesses, for all their personal anguish at separation and despite their convict origins, agreed on one thing — how much better off in Australia they were than they could be in Ireland.

Writing to his wife from Sydney Cove on 17 December 1825, Dennis Mahony was one of the many husbands who sought not only his wife to join him, but for her to plead, before she left Ireland, for a reduction of his sentence.

My Dear Wife, I take the favourable Opportunity of writing these few lines to you hoping they will find you and Family in as good health as I am at present. Thanks be to god for it. I would have written to you Before now but I was not in a Settled way of doing so. My Dear Wife we sailed form the Cove of Cork on the 11th of May 1823 and dropped anchor in Sydney Harbour on September 2nd 1825 [1823] and we had a very favourable passage thanks be to god. I was never sick on the voyage. My Dear wife I have sent a petition for you home signed by the Governor and the Priest of this colony to the Lord Lieutenant of Ireland which I hope you will get yourself in readiness and the said petition is directed to Richard Cox Bowden and Parson McShane and the Parish Priest the Revd. Father Darcy which I hope they will do everything in their power for you to get out to this Colony my dear Wife you will go to Mr. Bowden Esq. and tell my aunt to go along with you and tell him that I expect that his Honour will be so good as to get a mitigation of my sentence as I know that he can do it if he wishes as I have no other gentlemen to depend on but him as it is a poor thing to be a lifer in this colony. He cant have his liberty till he served eight years to Government and a seven years man four years before he can do anything for himself. Therefore I expect his Honour will take it in consideration.

Therefore my dear wife I expect you will be not in any ways daunted in coming to this country for I assure you if you were in this colony we were never happier at home than you would be here as for the passage you need think nothing of it from the first week and I expect as I cant go to you that nothing will keep you from me.

My dear wife you will get your eldest son from the trade as it is a very bad trade in this country and now my dear wife get yourself and your family in readiness and take very good care of them on the voyage and if it be as that your eldest son is not let out along with you leave the second son along with him in the Depot and they will be in Company and together which Mr. Murphy will direct you to do everything that is necessary. Give my best love to my mother and let her know that I am very well and that I hope that I will never die till I see her again. Tell Charles McCarthy that his son has left the place that he was in and removed to Parramata 15 miles from Sydney and is very well in health and I sent him the two letters because that I could not go myself. I live a government servant to Messrs. Berry and Wollstonecraft[3] the two best masters in this colony living within thirty yards of the w[h]arf where you are to land in. If you have an opportunity of writing to me before you come out write three letters and if you can send them out by hand if not direct your letter to the Reverend Father T[h]erry and another to Mr. Connor Debity Superintendant of Government Barracks and another to Messrs. Berry and Wollstonecraft Esqrs . . . tell my dear mother that I am very well and that I can live as well here as people at home that assumes £100 rent. As foı diet I have the best. Remember me to all enquiring friends . . . P.S. . . . when you come ashore go to the priest and he will direct you where to go . . . if you were here with me I could get £50 per year and £25 for Jo[h]nny from any gentleman . . .[4]

No doubt Dennis Mahony's petition for his wife to join him was welcome. He had left Cork in May 1823. By September 1825 the magistrates of Dunmanway,

Co. Cork, where his wife Mary lived, had provided her with a certificate that they knew her to be totally unable to support herself and her family of four boys, and that they were mendicants at present about the country.

The major themes of Mahony's letter are repeated, with variations, in other similar correspondence — prosperity in Australia, shortage of available labour, impatience to gain freedom so as to take advantage of local opportunities, a strong sense of ties to family and friends, the priests as the natural leader and official intermediary. Evident too is the absence from Mahony's letter of any sense of shame, or expectation that family or friends would be embarrassed by his convict situation: obviously transportation for crime, or at least certain sorts of offences, was no social liability within Ireland. Remarkable as well is the fact that Mahony is writing only two years after his arrival in the colony with a life sentence: he is already a favoured prisoner and confident that representations within Ireland will improve his situation further.

From one of John Macarthur's properties at Camden NSW[5] on 8 February 1836 Thomas Made[6] sent his sixth unanswered letter to his wife in Charleville, Co. Cork. He too sought both her company and her efforts in Ireland to get his sentence reduced:

> . . . Don't you fail in keeping yourself in readiness as if you had been here with me I should never see a poor day either yourself or myself and I hope that you will use the utmost of your power in trying to have my sentence mitigated as I expect you won't fail in this request before you come out to this country. This is a very fine country not a finer in the world and a very wholesome climate . . . you need not be any way uneasy of the voyage as it will be the outside of it if you are three months on sea, I am with the best gentlemen in this colony and the wealthiest. I want for nothing . . . The two Egans are here with me on this farm where I am stationed. The two Egans are doing well.[7] They are both in good health and desire to be remembered to their friends. The climate is purty [*sic*] hot. The Blacks are very numerous in this country and are quite savage. This is a very fruitful country. There is three crops in the year growed here so me wife there is nothing troubling me but for want of your presence which I hope I shortly will have. I hope that you wont delay as soon as you receive this that you will answer it . . . the gentlemen I am with they are I assure you very fond of me that whatever I require from them they give it me. We have got only one clergyman in this country which I am sure there would be ten wanted there the country is so large. As soon as you receive this you wont delay in seeing the gentlemen that will have my sentence mitigated . . . Don't be in anyway dismayed we shall be comfortable yet please God . . .

After six unsuccessful letters it may be that this employee of John Macarthur prevailed on his wife to join him. Other convicts — perhaps less sure of their persuasive powers, or less literate, or with more accommodating masters — got help from their employers. Robert Sutter of Lumley in the County of Argyle, Goulburn wrote on 10 November 1834 on behalf of his servant James Brogan. He told Mrs Brogan, in Scarriff, Co. Clare, that:

> . . . I consider that when you are (with your family) fortunate enough to reach this country you have every reason to expect that he will be able (with the exertion of yourself and family) to maintain you respectably. Every person in this colony who is *honest sober* and *industrious cannot fail to do well.*

Sutter also told Mrs. Brogan that her husband had all the relevant permissions and instructed her in the formalities to be followed. He left the last page for Brogan himself to reply to a letter his wife had sent:

> . . . there is nothing in this world grieves me but the delay of you and family . . . my son Thomas cant come in the same ship with you for being of age and the best thing that he can do is to go to the captain of the ship and enter with him as a working hand if he dont engage with the Captain he is sure to come in the next meal ship that leaves Ireland.[8]

Brogan, and Macarthur's employee, had been literate but neither fluent or grammatical. Alexander Boyce who had come from Belfast, and who wrote from the Wollongong district on 25 January 1835, had a literary style whose fulsomeness verged on the poetic. He used it to convey eloquently his deep distress at his wife's years of silence:

> After a silence of nearly three years, that is to say February 1832, at which time I had done myself the pleasure of both writing to you, as also to my beloved children, as well at the same moment of having forwarded to the Home Government a memorial on behalf of having you and my dear children sent to me, and as I am surprised at your neglect and silence, I am now availing myself of the present opportunity of writing to you my dear wife by Doctr. John Osborn, who leaves this Colony for his native country, and which I hope my ever dear belovd. wife, will find you and my ever dear children well in health, as this present leave me for which I thank God, for all his blessings and care of us all and as never hearing further from you respecting my anxious solicitation of your coming to me, or whither you received any account of the application from Government there made by me, and as it appears there has been indifference or wilful neglect in some department which I by no means attach to you my belovd. Eliza but a mind occupied as mine is day and night thinking of you and my fond children that the susceptibility of my feeling at your united absences is indeed indescribable, to think for a moment that hundreds who, at the same time, since forwarded, a similar application for their families now enjoy the felicity of their families' company, while I am left to linger in silent expectation of both you and my beloved children, while my panting bosum and extended arms are every moment open to receive ye, therefore come my dear dear wife, and do not want a wresting [*sic*] place as I will on your arrival have one fit for my dears reception. But should you my love, not have then received it and in any time after they thought it proper to send for you and that any circumstance at the time might have prevented you availing yourself of the opportunity of coming to me, through sickness of your children or any other impediment, you will therefore my dear love on receipt hereof, address a Memorial to His Excellency the Viceroy of Ireland stating the then cause of your not coming and that you are now ready to join your husband, praying His Excellency may admit you to share in his high considerations by granting you and your children a passage and there is no doubt of your ultimate success, there has been many who have been similarly situated, and none ever had been refused. I obtained the indulgence of sending for you at that time from Good Conduct which to the moment I am free to occupy my time as I may think proper having held the indulgence of a Ticket of Leave these two years back and will be as free as air the middle of March next. I will not say more on this subject than that I will look for your coming, which God in his mercy may inspire your heart with equal desire of seeing me where I will now give you some account of

> this Country, N.S.Wales, otherwise named Australia, is for salubrity of climate equal to that garden of the world, Italy, but with this exception, not subject to brain fevers, or European diseases that them countries are, this country the soil of which grows wheat barley oats Rye, Maizes with two crops of that well known vegetable the potatoe, that contributes so much to Irish hospitality. It grows all sorts of fruits, tropical as well as European as well as all kinds of vegetable, that are fit for man or beast, and there is no part of the world where an industrious man can do better, he can earn from 5 shillings to 7s.6d. per day, take one with the other and there are many other indulgencies which a man can avail himself off [*sic*] that he cannot partake of in Ireland such as the following, that is to say, first he can take a piece of land on a clearing lease for 7 years, without any rent, all he grows is his own free from tythes or taxes and all he can accumulate during this time, there is another you can place yourself on a piece of Government Land which you may occupy untill [*sic*] government may require it for sale, and if you bid five shillings per acre, you can get as much as you want and if industrious, you can grow as much on the land as will be able to pay for the purchase of it, which is more than you can get in Ireland, where I will now leave this subject, and turn my pen to the inquiry of my father, my brothers and sisters as also my cousins McCormacks, who I hope this will find well, and to whom I desire particularly to be remembered, having receivd. my father's letter two years ago, I would have answered it before now, but having written a little time before, I waited with the hope of your coming so as to be able to mention your safe arrival. So as that I may no longer labour under suspense, write to me on receipt hereof, as the purport of your letter I will be governed by its dictates, should you be disposed to come write to me and should you not have the candour to say so, but do not deceive me as on receipt of your answer I will send you something for my children . . .

Boyce added a note to this father:

> There is a neighbour of mine here most respectably married named Sarah Cramshee daughter to John Cramshee formerly of Millfield who, at the time of her been transported left a boy child in the year 1825 in the poor house named William Daly in Belfast. You will therefore make all the necessary inquiry of Mr. Thompson after him as she is most anxious to get him out to her if living as she is well off. You will send me these particulars. She [has] been a kind friend to me . . .

This last request — couched in the peculiarly peremptory formalities typical of the style of the time — gives a glimpse into another of the painful dimensions of separation consequent on the transportation system. The flowerly pomposity and convolutions of Alexanders Boyce's letter to his wife overlie and partly disguise the powerful and mixed emotions that seem to impel it — hurt, rage, doubt, confusion, resignation, impatience, wonder and delight at the material benefits and opportunities Australia could offer.[9]

Yet for all that Boyce's suffering is genuine, his ability to express it is also a means of controlling and mastering it, a way to some extent of resolving his predicament. Not so fortunate was Thomas Fallon who wrote on 13 March 1835 from the Goulburn plains to his wife Mary in Athlone. His largely indecipherable phonetic scrawl was not equal to the demands his agony of frustration placed on it to communicate the complexities of the family reuniting regulations:

> . . . dere mary I receivd you loveing letter which wish for long time . . . this

is the forth letter for me Der mary there is nact of Council past since thirty three that know man family cud come out until they wood be eight years in the Colony of new south wales and spesily lifers and when I come into the Cuntry it was onely Foure yeares which greeve me to heer and to say that you wood be so very far from me all my interest cud not get you out to the Cuntry one til the eight years wood be expired der mary do what i am going to explaine to you and there is know fere but you can come out to me by geting petion drew out in proper manner . . . and send it to the lord lieutenent of Irland to come out as an migrant to new south Wales there is good. . . .[?] of men wifes coming out to this cuntry and there is know other way that i know of but that.

Der mary I am not table to do annything in the wourld to help you nor to help my selfe nor anny other man in new south Wales Der mary, I never work one day but fourteen days for myselfe since I been in this cuntry because it is not allowed by Government but if i wonst got my liberty I cud . . . ten shillings per day Der mary let me know in youre next letter is my fathere live or know or did my sister go to meracar or know Der mary this is fine cuntry is there is in the wourld for ateing and drinking Der mary if you wore in this cuntry you cud be worth pound per week but by owne labour and if it be possible that you can come out bring your sister; there is fine girl comeing out as nemigrans [emigrants].

Thomas Fallon added a few lines about a 'cussen' and a friend in the colony, and also that 'Thomas Fallon of Ballyforeen [?] has got life to norfick Iland five hundred miles from this cuntry whear he must . . . for eight years . . .' — no doubt information to avoid any confusion at home in regard to himself.

Fallons' pain and frustration derive not only from inability to communicate: what must have been the plight of the totally illiterate, completely dependent on others to conduct such affairs?[10] and bereft of all privacy? Fallon told his wife to address his letters clearly as he wanted no one to break their seal. No: Fallon's plight was different from that of those convicts whose wives ignored their letters. Fallon's wife was anxious to come but the circumstances of his sentence (apparently life) made him powerless to help her through his own application. The raw emotion just below the surface of this situation is the clearer for the primitive simplicity of his letter.

Yet the distantly polite and polished copperplate hand of Timothy Regan writing from Campbell Town on 9 May 1835 to his wife in Kinsale revealed no less hurt. He had written in November 1832 to tell his wife that she had been granted a government passage but had received no reply:

As so long a period has elapsed I of course imagine you will not, or do not wish to come, but surely you could have answered my letter. I should rather impute your silence to the non receipt of said letter rather than to any other cause. I have now the pleasure of writing again and inform you that God has prospered my industry and exertions and that I have now the means with a continuation of industry to obtain a comfortable living much more so than I could in Ireland — however as you let that favourable opportunity pass, I as I am now a Free Subject can not obtain such another, but if you wish to come you can procure a cheap passage with Female Emigrants whose passage is defrayed by Government . . .

In fact, Timothy Regan's wife Johanna had never received the letter informing her of the free passage in 1832, a malfunction readily understandable as her husband's surname was variously rendered as Egan and Ryan, and her own as Margaret.[11] Many factors besides administrative confusion might frustrate communication. In his May 1835 letter Timothy Regan instructed his wife to 'pay the postage to the Govt. Post Office London, otherwise it will be detained there for want or a neglect of such payment': apart from the problems of coping with the primitive postal arrangements, both wives in Ireland and husbands in Australia frequently changed address. Wives were often fearful of what they regarded as an awesome journey far from people and places known and loved: some joined their husbands only when their Irish circumstances deteriorated, usually as a result of the death of parents or other family circumstances making their home situation intolerable.

Samuel Hammon, who worked for James Atkinson (formerly of Armagh) of Parramatta,[12] felt sorry for himself. By 1835 he had been nearly eight years in the colony. He had written home six times to his wife in Navan, Co. Meath, and received no answer. In 1833 he had applied for permission to have his wife join him. Still no response. In June 1835 the wreck of a female convict ship the *Neva,*[13] in Bass Strait, with great loss of life, preyed on his mind with the possibility that his wife may have been on board. On 11 July 1835 he wrote to Thomas Smith White Esq. of Navan, who had shown kindness to his wife and family, explaining this situation and appealing to him, as one gentleman to another, to understand 'under such circumstances what my feelings must be' and to explain why his wife had not replied. Transported for life, he asked for pity and understanding in an awful situation which he now much repented — 'but to stop short in a course of vice is the greatest effort of nature. There are many like me who if they were allowed their time over again would act quite different . . .' But now '. . . all I want to make me happy is my wife and family which I hope you will cause them to be sent out. Any man that can work can get a good living here provisions are very cheap and wages £2 or £3 and £20 per year board and lodging . . .'[14]

Peter Fitzgibbon worked for William Cox at Hobartville, Richmond, near Sydney.[15] He wrote cheerily on 6 December 1835 to his wife in Kilmore, near Knock, Co. Clare, asking her to try to get a commutation of his sentence *via* a petition of local gentlemen (including the Crown Prosecutor!). If not she must try to persuade a local landlord to send her to the colony, where — if she brought their marriage certificate — he could be assigned into her custody and 'would just be the same as a free man'. He explained to his wife the actual workings of the sentence system, investing it with a kind of impatient wonderment. 'A man that is sentenced for life if he behaves himself he gets his liberty in 8 years after he arrives and 14 years man gets his in 6 years after he arrives and 7 years man for 4 years after he arrives a free man can get £25 per annum and as much as he can eat of everything.' Various people from home were doing well. 'If you and the children could come out I could support you here without 1 shilling better than I could if I had 20 acres of ground at home'. There followed a list of prices of provisions and land — 5/- per acre with plenty of water. The climate was the best in the world.[16] With convicts such as Fitzgibbon in a kind of lyrical daze about their good fortune, it is small wonder that the home authorities were seriously concerned about the deterrent effect of the supposedly terrible punishment of transportation. Moreover, there was certainly an impression abroad — Thomas Connors, a shepherd at Neatsfield, Patricks Plains on the Hunter River, wrote on 27 December 1835 to a clergyman patron in Ireland on this understanding — that mitigations of sentence could be easily secured through the good offices of gentlemen of influence in Ireland.[17]

In fact, the early 1830s saw a further tightening of regulations — and the usual level of administrative delays and confusions, which some convicts and their separated wives bore with more equanimity than others. Early in 1833, William Fitzgerald Esq. of Co. Clare sought from the Dublin Castle administration permission for Honora Moore to join her convict husband, William, in New South Wales. The Lord Lieutenant replied that as previous experience had shown that convicts' wives and families were frequently left dependent in the colony at government expense, a recommendation certificate had to be sent initially from the Governor. Honora Moore continued in her efforts, securing a free pardon for her husband. After eighteen months she wrote to him on 25 May 1835 telling him of this and asking what were his intentions: was he coming home, or should she come out? He was much surprised, not being aware of any pardon. Nor were the colonial authorities from whom he enquired. He wrote to his wife on 7 February 1836 asking her to check the matter in Ireland, but to come out herself immediately, as she had arranged to do with Mr. Fitzgerald's assistance. As to the pardon 'even if was mitigated to seven years I would be as happy as if I got my free pardon'. As to his returning:

> . . . if I had my liberty I would not go home for three or four years so I reques[t] of you to prepare yourself and come out as soon as you can for I can make as much money in three or four years as would support me without working whilst I live . . . I am in a factuary making soap and candles since I came to the Country and as happy as I please.

Then followed what amounted to William Moore's efforts to organise his own family migration scheme:

> I dont expect that my son John will be let with you so send him in the prison man ship . . . fail not to come for you will be as happy as you were in all your life . . . Dont forget bringing Peggy out . . . Tell my brother John to come if he can.[18]

As William Fitzgerald had helped Honora Moore in Ireland, William Lithgow[19] helped Thomas Helion in Sydney. Helion was a shepherd in Lithgow's employ and in 1832 had secured permission to have his wife and family sent out. Helion had been expecting their arrival for four years when he wrote again on 18 February 1836, including a letter from Lithgow guaranteeing Helion's sons 'permanent and advantageous employment' and adding his personal support to Helion's request. Helion begged his wife to come. He had done everything he could; now the matter rested with her. 'From the great want of Farm Laborers in the Colony, I make no doubt of seeing you and my children in comfortable situations as my master is desirous of your coming out and would give you employment and good wages.'

Without questioning Lithgow's beneficence, such an arrangement was obviously in his interest: not only was labour hard to get, but Helion, who had been assigned to him on arrival in the colony, was 'a good and faithful servant' — qualities not unexceptional in the colony — and Lithgow made it clear that he expected Helion's sons to be the same.[20]

W. C. B. Wilson, contract surveyor on the Clarence River, NSW had no such prospect of gain when he wrote to Andrew Byrne of Tulloch, Co. Carlow on 1 June 1842. Wilson had been so impressed by the 'uniform and steady good conduct' of his assigned labourer Patrick Byrne that he wrote to his brother urging him to approach gentlemen in Ireland to seek mitigation of his sentence. Wilson believed that Patrick Byrne had been 'very unfortunate', 'that his conduct and character are highly deserving of encouragement since he has been in this Country and that too frequently under trying circumstances both at my station and in the wild bush', and he hoped some gentlemen who had known Byrne could be induced to intercede for him.[21] Wilson's was an act of gratuitous generosity.

Archibald McIntyre writing from St Patrick's Head, Van Diemens Land, on 9 March 1847 may not have been so disinterested in his kindness. He wrote on behalf of Patrick Mally — who was probably illiterate — to Edmund Corr Esq. of the parish of Kilbride, Co. Roscommon, reminding Coll of his promise to Mally when he left Roscommon to help his wife and family to join him. Mr McIntyre had applied on his behalf to the authorities in the colony and undertook to maintain and support them on their arrival. He asked Corr to inform Mally's wife and facilitate their leaving Ireland. Her husband had saved a little money 'and if his wife is industrious she could maintain herself well by our family washing alone'.[22]

Robert Boyd was working at Dr Anderson's Station at Modbury, County of Murray, New South Wales. He had written many times to his wife without reply, but his whole life was centered on the expectation of her and their children joining him. As soon as he became eligible — after four years in the colony — he petitioned to have her sent out, and on 20 February 1837 wrote again to tell her of this. At first his letter was joyful and enthusiastic:

> I am happy to inform you that I am master of sixteen head of cattle which I have bought at difrent [*sic*] times with money earned after doing my Government work and had you been with me I could have had thrice as many, so that you may very clearly see what an opportunity there is for well conducted persons

But quickly its tone changed to one of pathetic complaint. Her failure to answer letters had made him 'very miserable' and 'most anxious' for her welfare and that of the children. As he did not know what she intended doing, he was 'kept in suspense', 'unhappy', 'and I do assure you, have gone without many necessaries for the purpose of getting a few head of cattle to make you and the dear children comfortable when you arrived'. People he knew were sending to Ireland for their wives. Some from his locality were writing home to ask their friends to call on his wife with news of him. Would she write 'as soon as possible so that I may be eased of the great weight I have been so long labouring under on your account?'[23]

Thomas Montgomery, of Enniskillen Co. Fermanagh, was another prompt applicant for a passage for his wife and children, acting in November 1838 as soon as he got his ticket of leave. Having had no response, he wrote on 16 February 1840 from Maitland NSW to enquire of his wife what was the cause of delay: he expected some administrative malfunction.[24] He passed home news of various friends. He saw Patrick McCaffrey, Dan Murphy and James Keenan every Sunday. Catherine McManus was well ('let her friends know'). Patrick Montgomery had his liberty '. . . labourers wages here is 32 or 34 pound a year with rations.' Cormack McCaffrey should come out: it was a fine country and he would do well in it. The earlier official policy of banishing allegedly dangerous Irish elements to the Maitland area (among others) had produced Irish concentrations which developed a sense of Irish community both within the settlement and in relation to closer contacts with their homeland.

But for outright gratitude for the benefits conferred by transportation the candour of James Halloran writing to his wife Catherine remains unequalled;

We sailed on the 6th of July and landed on the 29th of January eighteen hundred and forty and Dr. Catherine if you can in the world get one pound for yourself and the children, and come to the immigrant office in Dublin and come to this country and if you can bring my brother John with you and he will get out for the same, this is the best country under the sun, for any well behaved person labourer man will get from thirty to forty pounds per year and a servant maid will get twenty pounds p. year and get your certificate bring it to the Rev. Doctor McCabe and he will sign it for you and then there can be nothing to prevent you . . . Thomas Healy, Margt. Healy's brother the pensioner he is cheif over the Police in Sidney Town and he does not know his riches he enquired for me the second day after I landed and he treated me very decently. I am very thankful to my prosecutors for sending me here to the land of liberty and freedom . . . you may let my friends know that in course of six months I expect to have as much as any of my friends at home and if you bring your sister with you . . . she will be paid for service . . .

Halloran asked for a reply to him addressed care of the Governor of the Hyde Park convict barracks. His letter was written to his wife indirectly — perhaps she could not read — and was itself declared to be in the form of a copy — perhaps he could not write and his police friends had provided a copyist. But of his enthusiasm for the colony there remains no doubt.[25]

It would be absurd to erect major generalisations and firm conclusions on the testimony of sixteen convicts over a twenty-year period: the documentation presented here has not been selected (it appears to be all the convict letters presently available[26]) but it was generated with a persuasive purpose, and it came from those convicts or ex-convicts, who were literate, well-behaved, and fortunate enough to be assigned to work with good masters. Perhaps it might be expected that testimony from such a source would be unanimous in Australia's favour — though that is not a necessary conclusion. But what is beyond any reasonable expectation is the warmth and degree of genuine enthusiasm, the absence of any qualification, or doubt among these writers that they were happier and better off than in Ireland. These few convict letters have survived because they related to official applications. Presumably other Irish convicts and ex-convicts wrote home in letters that have not survived. If this lost correspondence expressed, if only in part, sentiments similar to those that have been preserved it is easy to see why transportation from Ireland to Australia could have been seen widely as boon not doom. Perhaps it was only those convicts who succeeded and were happy who wrote home, but it was they who made Australia's image in Ireland. On the evidence of the letters presented here, long before the gold rushes, the picture of Australia being presented to the ordinary Irish through their networks of family and localities, was certainly one of distance, but a remoteness as nothing to its prosperity, productivity, pleasantness and provision of opportunity — 'a fine country', 'the best country under the sun'. Given the brightness of this image, it is small wonder that an increasing number of Irish began to think of Australia in terms very different from that of a distant gaol.

3 THE VOYAGE OUT 1838-1884

The long voyage to Australia in the nineteenth century was a prolific generator of journals, diaries and letters written by passengers on board ship.[1] The Irish — or at least the literate among them — were no exception to this urge to record what was often a hazardous, terrifying and incident-packed venture unique in their experience. Not only were there the perils common to small ships traversing great oceans — gales, the risk of fire, leaks, collision, of running aground or being driven onto rocks — but there were the everyday events and chances that made up shipboard life; sickness, disease, injury, death, drunkenness, insanity, fighting among crew and passengers, exotic foreign ports. Strange sights and experiences of every kind were commonplace in voyages that, in the earlier part of the century, might stretch to half a year. George Hill Adams, employed as a doctor on an emigrant ship, wrote to his brother Thomas in Port Glenone, Co. Antrim, on 28 November 1849; 'I was 5 months and 8 days on board coming home and 5 months and 4 days going out'. Still, he conceded that this was unusual; the ship was 'in a most abominable state for sending on any voyage', sprung a leak in Bass Strait, and had to put into Sydney for repairs which took six weeks. Nevertheless, particularly in the era of the sailing ship, few voyages were without danger or incident of any king. Under such stress, and in the confinement of small ships, the character of migrants was often revealed; diarists and letter writers observed other passengers and in doing so reflected themselves. Such insights give something of a preview of the nature and character of the Irish immigrants to Australia. And what they often make clear, under the pressure of close living, is the existence among immigrants, before arrival, of attitudes and outlooks hitherto assumed to have been generated by the new Australian environment; indifference to or hostility towards religion and clergymen is the main trend illustrated here. But the voyage out must also be understood as a vital part of the immigrant experience and education. The circumstances of being thrown together, largely haphazard, into a packed makeshift community, exposed to common experiences and dangers for three or four months, did much to break down, before arrival in the colonies, the rigid religious and social divisions of the homeland. It is obvious that, in many cases, the voyage to Australia — mixing together closely those whom the old world would have ensured stayed apart — was a direct introduction to, and compulsory lesson in, the operation of an Australian society disposed to be open, tolerant, and egalitarian.

It is not too much to suggest that many shipboard diaries change in social atmosphere and disposition as the voyage progresses; their acceptance of and conformity to the old social order weakens with distance from home. Deference, for instance is evident in the letter of James Dempsey, writing on 18 October 1838 on board an emigrant ship leaving Derry for Sydney, to Captain Stewart Moore, Jnr, Ballydivity, 'Dervock', Co. Antrim. Dempsey was probably a tenant writing to the son of his landlord,[2] who had provided encouragement, passage money, or some other form of assistance towards emigration by gift, subsidy or loan. This practise was not unknown among some Irish landlords; the most prominent such Irish benefactor was Lord Monteagle in the late 1840s. Dempsey's letter reveals an affectionate servant, and one coping well with the finality of leaving home and the whole emotional trauma of emigration, but it also indicates that, at least initially, others were not so settled in the course on which they had embarked.

> . . . I now inform you as it is with us at present: the ship "mooved" down from Derry the south of Culmore on Saturday evening and the weather being unfeavourable, stopped there untill Thursday morning and she is now down the lenth of Movill and intends going off the first oppertunity this evening: it is serious to behold in all corn[er]s of the ship the[re] are sick and women feanting but thank God we are all in good health as yet: the first and second day that we went on board there was a great deal of complaints with the emigrants of their rashions being too small and many of them wishing to go ashore and return home but I endeavred to peasify all that I had any influence with nowing that it was impossable that two hundred and sixty four passingers to be all righted according to there wishes at once: the news reached Capten Ramsys ears and he came on board at Culmore and called all the passengers on deck and give free liberty to all that pleased to go ashore and there was one man from Newtown [Limavady] that went home and this is the reason that I write least the word would be carried home that we are ill treated, and if it does, believe it not. For the hole passingers is put into seventeen messes and there is appointed one man head over each mess and I am appointed over one and it is there business to see the meat eaqully served out according to the number of the mess. We get our breaxfast about eight o'clock, of good tea and one day pork with pea soop for our dinner and the next day beef with flour pudding mexed with suat: there is alsow rum, wine, figs and reasons for those that is sick and everything appears to be carried on in a verry judicious manner. There is six men apointid with the doctor for forseing [?] laws and if any is found pilfering from the other or giving insolence the one to the other or refusing to clean their births or sweeping upper or lower decks, the[y] are reported to the doctor and their names enterd in the registers book and when the[y] arive at Sidney, the[y] will be given up to the goverment and punished in proportion as their crime deservs: therefore I expect good order will be carried on. Now sir be pleased to give my kind love to my master, mistress Miss Ann and Miss Mary and little Stewart and to all the men and let them know that there is no day that the[y] are out of my thoughts and let William Polock know that I wish that he would take word to my people to Bushmills and tell them we are all well. I now sir remain your kind

and affectionate servant till death. (signed) James Dempsey.
P.S. Let William Polock know that I forgot my reazor in the house and I wish him to go to John Mckelly as I think he must have it as he was the last I left in the house and keep it for my sake. Sir excuse the bad writing and blotting as the ship was heaving very hard the time I wrote it.

The hazards and uncertainties of the emigrant sea experience had not much changed fourteen years later, in 1852. Hugh Maguire, waiting to leave for Australia from Liverpool (it was usual to travel across from Belfast or other Irish ports to join ships departing from England) wrote to his mother in Strabane, Co. Tyrone, on 10 July 1852: like other emigrants he had brought from home provisions for the voyage.

[I] expected that the ship would move out of dock into the river before this. She moves out today at 4 o'clock, and will go direct to *sea*, possibly *tomorrow*, but positively on *Monday Morning*. The reason that ships do not sail to Australia upon the advertised day, is that there is no passenger law to that place like what is to America. There are some vessels for Melbourne lying out in the river these past ten days, but the *"Mohill"* in which I go will go to Sea, *positively* on Monday first at the furthest . . . Dear Mother this will be the last letter you will get from me until I reach Australia, and when I get there with the Blessing of God, I will not forget *Home*. The bottles with the milk all *"worked"* and the corks all flew out of them, and of course the milk was lost: but it is better so, as I should have done badly without milk being once accustomed to it on board.

At the end of 1852, a shipboard journal, probably that of one of the Pillow brothers of Mullaghbane, Co. Armagh, makes clear what might be expected on an uneventful voyage — that of the *Digby* of 787 tons — where there were no deaths, little sickness, and few incidents during the four month passage to Melbourne. The *Digby* embarked from Liverpool on 22 December 1852.

There were about 318 souls aboard our ship . . .
On the morning of January the sixth 1853 a tug came alongside and took us in tow: as we proceeded down the river we endeavoured to get the anchors aboard, but this was no easy matter as they had got foul of each other: we got them raised to near the surface of the water but could not disentangle them. When we got to the mouth of the river it begun to blow pretty hard, and as the vessel pitched the anchors struck her under the bows so we were obliged to let them go and so lost them altogether: to add to our misfortune the tow rope broke, the sea being rough the tug dare not approach us again. We now set some sail, braced the yards sharp up (as the wind was foul), and suceeded in getting clear of the sand-banks after touching twice . . .
18th [January 1853] at daylight this morning we found ourselves about 6 miles from the coast of Spain, the wind now became very light, and in a few hours died away altogether: there was a very heavy swell on and our ship was carried broadside on towards the land, about half past nine P.M. we had drifted to within a mile of the shore (near Corunna), a land-breeze now sprung up and carried us out to sea again. Had the calm continued an hour longer we would have been driven ashore, and very probably a good many lives lost . . .
[24 January 1853] — About eleven o'clock P.M. I was in bed, and listening to the watch on deck altering some of the sails, I heard the boatswain sing out 'a sail ahead', coming this way I think, I next heard the mate order the

man at the wheel to luff, I now hastened on deck, on getting there I saw what appeared to be a three masted schooner, on our starboard side, and about 50 yards off: our Captain hailed her but received no reply, neither did she show any light. Many of us now got our guns and pistols ready, as we were afraid that she might make an attempt to board us, however she sheered off and we saw her no more. We lost the S. East Trades in about 24 south latitude. Passed the islands of Tristan De Acunha but without seeing any of them. From this time until our arrival in Australia we had but two quarts of water each per day.

One evening, about the 26th of March we observed a sail right ahead, and very distant as we could only see her royals: next morning we could see all her sails, and in the evening her hull. We overtook her at about eleven o'clock next morning, and found her to be the Barque Sacremento from London with Government Immigrants, chiefly females, and bound for Melbourne. The first thing they did after we came up with them was to lower a boat and despatch it to our ship, with the request that our doctor be allowed to visit their ship for the purpose of seeing two of the immigrants who were sick: they stated that their doctor had died when they were crossing the Bay of Biscay. Their request was granted . . .

[26 April] On our arrival again at the Heads we squared the yards and passed safely through into Port Phillip Bay.[3] Whilst passing through we observed a vessel aground on a ledge of rocks (always covered with water) that runs out towards the middle of the entrance, from Point Lonsdale on the west side. The waves were breaking over her decks, and we could see the passengers and crew huddled together under a cliff on shore. The vessel proved to be our old acquaintance the Sacremento: it appears she made Port Phillip Heads and lay to about the same time that we did, but being in danger of being driven ashore by the squall that came on about two o'clock she attempted to pass through the Heads but with the result mentioned above. The passengers and crew got safely ashore, but lost all their luggage.

One aspect of the role that religion was to play in the Australian colonies is evident in the diary of William Bates, a young Presbyterian minister of Strabane, Co. Tyrone. Rev. Bates travelled on the *Minnehaha* from Glasgow to Melbourne, January to March 1858. He was emigrating because of his health — he had lung trouble — and in the wake of a failed romance — he had been jilted. Well-intentioned, not basically intolerant, and acutely conscious of his inability to fit in with other passengers, Bates nevertheless exemplified the limitations of the narrowly moralistic and scriptural character of the nineteenth-century evangelical revival, and, with the other evangelical clergyman on board, was mercilessly teased and persecuted by his fellow emigrants, particularly the young men. Bates tried to relate to and cope with the larrikin irreligion he found all around him, but his account of the voyage makes clear that many of the immigrants brought with them to Australia the view that religion was irrelevant or a joke, and its ministers wowsers, spoil-sports, or figures of fun. The reception and treatment of Rev. Bates on the *Minnehaha* in 1858 suggests that the indifference and hostility encountered by religion in the Australian colonies was at least as much an imported attitude, a part of the usual migrant baggage, as it was a local-grown product. And it was treatment which made Bates triply lonely; his romance was shattered, he was an emigrant, and his profession of religion distanced him from almost everybody.

[26 January 1858] One feels so lonely, so solitary, as in one step he leaves

> behind all his friends, new and old, and abandons all his prospects and throws down all his airy castles and can sympathize neither with the joys nor the sorrows of his friends so that such a friend with whom one could be intimate who would remain when all these had left us forever would indeed be valuable. But it cannot be. When earthly friendship is thus impossible, would that the friendship of heavenly Father were more eagerly s[ough]t and high prized . . . Our young men seem all to be indifferent to religion. Private prayer is, I doubt, very uncommon. One professes Deism and has never been at any of our services and all of us seem to disregard the fourth commandment far too much. Last evening [sabbath?] was spent very improperly. Altogether the state of matters here in regard to religion is very unsatisfactory. Yesterday the attendance was small, two of the passengers on deck and only four of the crew present . . . Up till now our passage has been on the whole very slow. We might have been at the Equator and at this rate we will not reach it for a fortnight. Captain is downcast and the sailors are now tracing the slowness of our voyage to there being ministers on board. This is a widespread superstition . . . I must again notice the malobservance of the sabbath. The conversation, the action, the books read, all are unbecoming and our young men crowned the sabbath evenings impiety by closing Mr Bowman [the other clergyman] and Mr. R[?] in the two water closets, tying the doors together with rope. Indeed of late they have been playing almost all their pranks on Mr. and Mrs. Bowman and the children. This seems likely to end it, but next day some of them got elevated to the mizzen topmast and began pelting him, as he lay reading, with rotten cabbages and turnips. He is being much annoyed and is compelled to keep now a good deal aloof so as to get rid of their playful incivilities and I have had to stand up in defence of the children who are very roughly treated by the passengers.

As to the character and intentions of the young emigrants, Rev. Bates discovered that several at least were, in their migration to Australia, hardly willing enthusiasts, but rather various kinds of social rejects and misfits being banished to the colonies:

> One has been driven from home by his father in a fit of anger apparently and is not to return till he has succeeded in something or other and has money as the proof. Another was found drunk in the streets of his native town and was brought up before his own father who was, that day, presiding magistrate, fined by him ten shillings and then privately ordered off to Australia. One goes because his friends seem not to know what to do with him. Mr. Bowman and I both go because we must and so all but two of us are like Jacob *driven* from home to a foreign land . . .

The propriety of card playing — a standard shipboard amusement — became a matter for discussion, from which Rev. Bates abstained, being unsure of his ground: only when it led to gambling was he certain he could not countenance it. Blasphemous songs were quite another matter.

> This morning the sailors sung a very wicked song, the chorus, coming in every four lines was (and hell to your soul is it tea you want) I felt shocked and expressed my sentiments freely. Nothing has annoyed me more since I came on shipboard.

Another problem was that of drink. The *Minnehaha* was a temperance ship. But Rev. Bates had two bottles of port wine for medicinal emergency purposes, and he was not a mean man.

> The bottles of port wine lay untouched till yesterday. A young man fell ill, who had been accustomed to free living on shore and said that port wine would benefit him. I offered him some. He took a glass. I then said he might take the bottle with him that, as it had been given to me for medicine and I had hitherto found no need for it, he was welcome to it. It was amusing to see with what avidity he seized it and carried it away to the safest corner of his trunk and the gratitude he felt to me. I could have not gratified him so much any other way . . .
> [10 February] The hard fact become still harder to our young gentlemen that this is a total abstinence ship. Many a time has this been execrated. Songs are sung and published, detailing the miseries of want of beer and it is all the harder to want it since there are upwards of 1,500 barrels of liquors on board and the captain has both wine and brandy for those who need it. Many an onset is made on him for some: many an argument is he drawn into and I am delighted to get seconding him. He is very staunch and has not yet parted with a drop and will not till there is absolute necessity for it. Happily I have concealed the fact of my having still a bottle of port wine and I am sure I would get no rest till I had given it up. The young man to whom I gave the first bottle is the most energetic in his appeals for more [11 February] The chief amusement we have is still ironical laments for the want of beer and petitions for some brandy. But I must say that we are getting a good supply of water and it is a thing to be very thankful for but the extremest unthankfulness characterizes our company. I do not think I have ever heard God really thanked for any blessing he has sent. We ask a blessing at all our meals formally but never publicly return thanks.

And the sabbath observance problem remained, with others, exacerbated for Rev. Bates by his increasing consciousness of his inability to get on with other passengers.

> On the whole we make no progress in sanctifying the sab[bath]. How can we? Perhaps there is not a single truly pious person in the ship, the great majority decidely irreligious. As an instance the wicked song which the sailors sung was caught up by the cabin passengers and frequently sung, and when the captain forbade his crew to sing it one of the best of our passengers condemned the prohibition. It was mere tyranny and would be useless. We passengers, it seems, have been rather too intimate with the men for[w]ard and so tonight he forbade it decidely and ordered us to keep our own end of the ship.
> A gravity natural to me, partly physical ill health, and the many cares I have had and still have, keep both body and spirits down. They are getting up a very little but I have got the character of a grave and melancholy man, very reserved, sympathizing little generally with my fellow passengers, and so perhaps living more solitarily than any other here, or than ever I did. There is none here whom I would take as an intimate friend. The captain is the only one with whom I converse anyway freely . . .
> Monday; we had some music on Saturday night. On sabbath I again rose late (crying but hearing no answer) kept the sabbath only middling, leading often myself into unfit conversation. Mr. Bowman preached a very able sermon from Is.26:3 "thou wilt . . . on thee". The attendance very good. Later in the evening there were two discussions, one on card playing. Is it sinful? Another are certain doings involved in proper observance of sabbath. Little progress in either case towards a conclusion.

> [20 February] This sab[bath] ev[ening] furnished me with a comment on a discussion we had a few weeks ago. The second mate, a young simple straightforward and not very sharp man had stated that on every Saturday night a captain should heave to his vessel so as not to need to work her on sabbath. This view was scouted and laughed to scorn by both the captain and first mate. At first I could not go with either but I could not let the second mate's statement be so kicked and buffeted. I defended it in part and one of my arguments was that it would relieve a number of men of working. But they said no and instanced that sabbath, an unusually quiet one as a proof. But tonight to catch a mere capful of wind all the men were called up and every sail was altered.
> I never have heard of any captain adopting such a course — perhaps it is an extreme [one]. We are quite unaccustomed to the th[ought] but if it is an error it is in the right direction.

Rev. Bates found that as the journey lengthened, human relations grew not closer, but sharply worse, to a degree he outlined in extravagant terms, indicative of the extreme difficulty he found in relating to an environment he found so hostile:

> [13 March] As we draw near the end of our voyage we are giving vent to our tiredness of one and other. One learns a great deal in such circumstances as mine now are — a passenger among strangers — fellow passengers on a long voyage. The character of the intercourse between people, thus violently, as it were, shut up together for three months, illustrates the enmity of man to man. Friendships there are none among us except such as existed before we came together. Kindliness not a great deal but covert dislike, finding frequent vent in backbiting and at length open quarrels are the outgates of the internal fiendish hate.

Nor did he have a high opinion of his fellow countrymen among passengers and crew.

> [26 January] Among our main amusements several auctions deserve notice. This is generally some useless article which the owner simultaneously gets rid of and shows his benevolence by handing the proceeds to the Seaman's Friends Society . . . an old hat has been sold twice. The first time the bids rose to something above £500,000. The bidder actually paid 5d. The second time it was knocked down to me at 6d. But I never got time to enjoy the pleasures of possession. It was immediately seized upon and for half an hour adorned the head of a Paddy . . . . Then it disappeared and I know nothing of it but I expect it will re-appear either for a third auction or to adorn similarly some clownish lout of a would be Hibernian.
> [27 March] For the first time since we sailed a man has been put in irons. He disobeyed the mate and gave impudent talk to the mate and captain. His sentence is to be handcuffed for two days or more till he submits and to be fed on bread and water. If his mates feed him better they must be reduced to the same rations. He is an Irishman, stupid they say and cross. Everywhere it would seem my unfortunate countrymen get into rows and get the worst of it.

Nearing the end of the voyage, the dominant emotion among Rev. Bates' fellow passengers seems not to have been relief, or anticipation, or enthusiasm, but uncertainty, indeed confusion; they did not know what they were going to do in the colony.

[2 April] As was natural one question has occupied the minds of our young men a great deal. What are we to do when we get to Melbourne? Without special aptitude for any kind of work and willing to do anything that would bring support they have been puzzled to guess what they will find to do. Thus my room-mate, who has the most definite views perhaps, yet has four courses before him now: others may be opened up — get work in Melbourne as a compositor or by the aid of letters of introduction some other kind of situation, or join a brother in farming, or try the diggings.
Mr. MacEwan jocularly has always professed a preference for cabdriving and today Mr. B[owman]'s servant, an old, serious, silly creature began to advise him seriously to choose that occupation, promising that her master would always employ him. He bore this, but she went on to give advice that he could not bear "oh Mr MacEwan you smell so bad, you should really take some opening medicine". This acted as opening medicine for one aperture of his body at any rate — he poured on her a torrent of filthly enough stuff advising her to mend her and children's manners and referring to some unclean habits they have got into.
I have pressed him more than any other to become a teetotaller. But tonight he informed that he will not. The current is strong here against that good cause and it may happen that some who are acting as its enemies will find that they have been acting as their own. I rejoice every day that I have been led to occupy my present position though here it has caused me some annoyance. And yet the misery of feeling that one's virtues are rootless. Had mine been real and healthy they would like flowers have been diffusing pleasing and wholesome odours all around: these precious months have been like the withered rose unpleasant to look on and unwholesome to smell.

To cap his own uncertainty and confusion with an implicit repudiation of one of his own central convictions, Rev. Bates ended his diary with an imaginary conversation in which he passed a harsh judgment on the general character of teetotalers:

> I have always found them hard and mean and selfish. They are like Shylock. Give them your bond and there is not one of them that wouldn't exact it, were it to cost you your life. It's their miserliness makes them take the pledge: it will save a few pence now and then and when they do take it, no matter how vicious they have been, they become as proud as a Pharisee, and are lifted up, in their own opinion, to the third heavens of virtue and thence look down, with supreme contempt, on the sinful wretches whose great crime is that they can take a glass when a friend offers it. Then you must submit to be lectured by them on the depravity of your tastes and the duty of joining a "noble band of Total Abstainers".

And to this penetrating insight into how his own teetotal views presented themselves to those who did not share them, he added a quite explicit judgment of himself, depicted in the third person.

> . . . there was a lean bewhiskered son of the church, who was going out to Australia but he wasn't sure to what part, to do he didn't well know what. He was weak in body and not over strong in mind. We found out that some lass had jilted him and hence the voyage.

The voyage out had been a harsh schooling for Rev. Bates and he had learnt a great deal. Yet the impression remaining from this conclusion, with Bates driven to a position of tough self-appraisal, is this; however it may have testified to honesty and perception, it was also a capitulation. Such was the widely unacceptable nature of the social props on which rested Rev. Bates' religious structure — sabbatarianism, teetotalism, opposition to all appearances of the profane or disrespectful — that they had been undermined, weakened, challenged and defeated, even within his own mind, before he landed in the colony itself. The ship was the colony in advance and in miniature, and the effect of that onslaught on what he had taken for granted was to induce in Rev. Bates a profound unsettlement. On arrival, his doubts and confusion were such as to constitute hardly a healthy or promising situation from which a clergyman might enter a happy and effective colonial life. The colony's prefigured irreligious ethos had triumphed at sea, long before the colony had been reached.

Clergy of other denominations — or perhaps of more resilient temperament — were not necessarily unpopular on board ship. Father Patrick Dunne was well liked by his fellow passenger — non-Catholics — when he returned to Australia in 1863. But his description of the behaviour of some members of his former Melbourne flock, given in a shipboard lecture (as reported in the Log of H. Morton, 14 September 1863)[4] indicates that while they had respect (perhaps partly superstitious awe might be more exact) for the forms, rituals and personages of their Irish Catholic religion, they had little comprehension of its meaning, or indeed of the fundamental social structures to which its ceremonies were related.[5] Dunne told his companions on the voyage anecdotes of his country fellows in Melbourne that attested to their extreme simplicity — or stupidity. He had once encountered in the street an Irish servant, sent out with a message, who had lost her way home and could not remember even the appearance of her house of employment in sufficient detail to find it — Dunne had found her another job. But in regard to religion, Dunne's experience in the matter of marriage was most revealing; some Irish he had married, believed — with relentless reverse logic — that as he had married them, he could also unmarry them. 'He mentioned that he had married several couples out there, and about six months afterwards the husband, or perhaps the wife would come back, asking him to undo the marriage knot, and saying they would give anything if it could be done'. Was Father Dunne telling such stories for the purposes of vulgar entertainment? His character apart, it seems unlikely; this was the kind of observation conveyed verbally, in circumstances of some intimacy, to social equals, distant from the place concerned — precisely the shipboard situation. What was unlikely was that such unflattering details would be committed to print or public acknowledgment. Within the Catholic community they could be subsumed in vague general exhortations, because outside it they would provide ammunition for enemies. Dunne knew his shipboard audience; Morton records this account of the strange habits and beliefs of the Australian Catholic Irish not as anything adverse or demeaning, but as an anthropological curiosity.

Other observers were neither so detached nor sympathetic. Charles Elliott of Aughlish House, Scarva, Co. Armagh, who travelled to Melbourne first class on the *Prince of the Seas* in 1861 was a hostile observer of the alien character and habits of the Irish who travelled in the steerage. Perhaps it was one of them who leaped overboard in the middle of the night of 8 September, affected by temporary insanity; the doctor was blamed for not having him under strict watch as he had earlier shown symptoms of derangement. It was certainly a fellow Irishman who was disciplined on 17 September. 'A steerage passenger took up on deck and tied to mast and had 3 buckets of water thrown on him for fighting and raising a row — an *Irish man* "wild".' Both the births on board were the children of Irishwomen in steerage. And, on Elliott's observation, the Papists in steerage could not even kneel down to pray without a fight breaking out. He noted on Sunday 13 October:

> The Papists had what they called prayers in the steerage as usual in the morning and were hardly off knees till they had a hard box among themselves — a most infernal lot of blackguards are the dirty Irish Papists: never had such an opportunity of judging.

Elliott's revealing addendum — implying the distance he usually kept from his Catholic fellow countryman — as well as his sensitivity to the crude doings of the steerage Irish — emphasise the great gulf that existed between his Irish world and that of Catholics; his was a classic case of the intolerant attitudes generated by the separation of the religious communities in Ulster being confirmed and hardened by the shipboard proximity. It was a proximity which compelled neither human contact nor shared experience. Until the end of the voyage the Irish Papists in the steerage persisted with what Elliott called their '*parrot rhyme*' Sunday service. The last month of the voyage was without Protestant religious observance. In contrast with the indifference encountered by Rev. Bates on the *Minnehaha* in 1858, the religious life of the *Prince of the Sea* in 1861 at first promised well. On the first Sunday, fifty or sixty of a complement of about 200 attended service, conducted by the doctor. On the following two Sundays it had risen to ninety or a hundred. But by mid-voyage, as August moved into September, that strange malaise that consistently overtook religion *en route* to the colonies began to show itself. Attendances declined. To Elliott's annoyance, services became erratic, even in calm weather. Then, on Sunday 29 September, the leader in prayer 'the doctor had some 4 buckets of water thrown over him and then the hose applied to him this morning by captain's orders to cool him after 6 bottles claret, 4 sherries, 1 rum, 4 porter'. No further services were held, and the pious Elliott (he commended his spirit into the hands of the Father during a fierce squall a few days out of Melbourne) noted their continued absence with disapproval. Charles Elliott arrived in Australia with his hostile views on Papists reinforced and his distance from them widened. But his disapproval could not alter two religious facts of his voyage; Protestant worship had collapsed *en route*, and the Papists had maintained throughout not only their filth and fighting, but their familiar 'parrot rhymes'.

But there were other ships on which non-Catholic services were held regularly — and where there were very different reactions to the compulsory religious mix imposed by the circumstances of shipboard life. Elliott's observation of Papists was from the distance of the first-class accommodation, from outside the steerage. What of those Protestants who shared the steerage with the Catholics? Samuel Shaw was one of a family of twelve children, on their parents' farm at Oughley, Saintfield, Co. Down. When it was decided on 1877 to give up farming and move to Belfast, Samuel — and a neighbour's son, David — decided to emigrate to Australia, where the Shaws had an uncle living in Sydney. They left Plymouth on 20 November 1877 on the sailing ship *Tyburnia* of 948 tons, with 328 emigrants and thirty crew.[6] Samuel described the shipboard organisation of the emigrants;

> When I was in Plymouth we were divided into messes of 8 or 10 with a Captain to each mess to see that they kept the rules and to go to the store for all the meat. David is the Captain of my mess. There are 10 in it, all of

whom are Roman Catholics but David and I, but we have agreed very well. Each man gets daily half a pound of meat, fresh meat twice and salt meat 5 times a week. We get half a pound of flour daily and bread is baked by the baker four times a week. We get porridge five times a week, and soup five times, cheeses three times, and rashers three, 12ozs. of sugar each, plenty of tea and coffee, and other things such as spices, pickles and molasses, and any amount of biscuits, always plenty of water.

The young men are placed in the fore hatch and the young women in the after hatch. The married people are placed in the 'tween decks. The young girls have the best place in the ship, they have a matron placed over them, who looks after them very attentively, they are not allowed off the poop from the day they get on in Plymouth until they get to Sydney, nor are we allowed to go near them. If they have a father or mother they are permitted to see them, and if no father or mother if they have brothers they could see them. Before the fever broke out we were all allowed to go on the poop on a Sunday morning during Divine Service.

No father or mother need be afraid of sending out their daughter by emigration, as they are better cared for than any class of emigrants, they get plenty of meat, have plenty of room and are very healthy, not one of them has been ill.

We get roaming about where we please except on the poop. In the place where we sleep there are 104 young men. The beds are placed in rows of two from the ground. The number of my bed is 95 and David's is 93, the top beds are the best. The mess is 39, which is the last. We have to be in bed by 10 o'clock and up at 7, which is the rule of the ship.

We get plenty of meat and I must say I never have had anything to complain of. I believe I am stronger and a good bit fatter since I left.

Obviously, Samuel Shaw and his neighbour had not been used to consorting with Roman Catholics, but, as the only Protestants in a mess group of ten, their experience in a situation which compelled close association was that they got on very well with them. This went against their expectations, conditioned as they were to sensitivity to the religious difference, but while maintaining their own beliefs and practices they swiftly adopted a position of practical friendliness and tolerance, and of opposition to any expression of bigotry. On 19 December 1877 Samuel noted;

We nearly had a row in the evening between the Roman Catholics and one of the married men, who was laughing at them at mass. They all came on deck vowing vengeance, but the matter was hushed up.

In fact, such tensions and animosities as existed on the ship were national, not religious, and it was revealed that a common antipathy to the English (generated in Shaw's case by sharing mess arrangements with them) was far stronger in uniting the steerage Irish than any religious division among them. He observed on 14 February 1878;

At tea-time we had the greatest fight yet, between a Scotchman and a Englishman, and as we messed in the same part of the ship as the English, we were all against him. It nearly came to a general row in the end, as all the Irish in the vessel were with the Scotchman, but it was quietened by some who had more sense.

The Anglo-Irish did not share the Celtic sympathy with the Scots. 'Charlie'

Barton, writing to his mother in Ireland from the *Stirlingshire* on 16 October 1884, remarked,' . . . food as a general rule is good, only it is served by *Scotch people,* for it it is a Scotch boat, therefore Scotch crew'. His first-class cabin was excellent save for his having to share it with 'the most selfish suspicious old Scotchman' who 'keeps up to being a Scotchman by his canny movements . . .' Barton's reactions, like those of Charles Elliott, suggest that the socially solvent effects of the close confinement of shipboard life tended to be much less marked among first-class passengers than in the steerage. Barton was adaptable and energetic enough — he often climbed the ship's rigging for fun, and was something of a handyman — but as a first class passenger, the impact of the cosmopolitan and egalitarian flavour of colonial life was delayed for him until the colony itself, not prefigured on the voyage. It seems unlikely that he could have long avoided it; he had introductions, but very little money and had to look for immediate employment in Sydney. Ample money was the only cushion against the onslaughts of the rude colonial world.

Fervour in personal religion did not necessarily produce intolerance, or even the primacy of religious criteria in evaluating one's fellows. Mrs Flemming, who travelled, newly married, from Buncrana, Co. Donegal, to Melbourne on board the *Fearnought,* sometime in the 1870s, was intensely religious, much taken up with Methodism, and addicted to spiritual reading of the emotional kind. Warm and tolerant towards individuals, what irked Mrs Flemming about her fellow immigrants *en masse* was nothing to do with their religion, or lack of it, but their loud Englishness;

> I am thoroughly sick of the English, their abominable jargon sounds hateful to my Celtic ears and whenever I hear the Irish accent, whether North or South, it seems like music after the other.

Mrs Flemming preferred the Irish company available on the ship, in first and second class, irrespective it seems of their religious persuasion — though the Catholics were in a minority in that accommodation;

> There are some very nice Irish people on board and we generally are together in a group on deck chatting reading sewing knitting and enjoying ourselves. Young Walker and his half brother T. Sloane are great friends with us, and there is a Miss Pedlow from Lurgan who is very civil and obliging. I am not fretting as I expected. I hope to go home again sometime and see all the old familiar faces once more. Every night I am with them in my dreams. It is very strange but every time I sleep I am wandering away to the Emerald Isle . . . Our friends on board as a general rule are either Irish or Scotch. We don't mix much with the English.

Mrs Flemming's listing of her Irish acquaintances suggests that some at least were Catholic;

> There is a Mrs. Daly and her 3 children and an old servant all Irish. Mrs D[aly] is a widow and is going out to her sons in Melbourne . . . a Mr. O'Hanlon a great tall fellow 6 feet 3 inches with two thousand pounds per annum to do what he likes with and who would be a nice enough fellow if he did not drink.

The criterion Mrs Flemming adopted in evaluating her Irish friends on board the *Fearnought* was not one of religion, which she does not mention in that regard, but one of social class, construed widely to include matters of refinement, manners, and education. She had been told she was a 'blue stocking', having read most of the authors discussed on board the ship. She spent much of her time sewing, crotcheting and doing muslin work, and enjoyed conversation — and gossip — with 'nice' people. Mrs. Flemming was a genuine and unselfconscious 'lady', kind and without pretence, who obviously prompted liking and respect from others. Her favourite word of character approbation was 'nice'. As a lady she expected men to be gentlemen, and in her company they usually were. She embodied qualities of gentility and civilisation which represented the best elements of the refined Irish world she had left, standards of behaviour and culture which did not blind her to the human reality present in all social gradations; the ship carried Victorian government immigrants in the steerage, and she could hear the migrant women, during the most violent of the storms, 'screaming and praying and confessing their sins and promising how good they would be if ever they would get to land'. Without contempt or distaste Mrs Flemming accepted this, with the illness and death which were a part of shipboard life, as part of the normal range of the human condition. She looked down on the spectacle of the lower orders from the same separated vantage point of privilege and cultivation as did Charles Elliott, but where he saw a narrow world harshly divided according to religious allegiance, Mrs Flemming saw a more complex scene of national and cultural divisions, blurred and complicated by the variety of social groupings and personal idiosyncracies. Her natural gravitation was to people who were culturally familiar and of her own class and kind, but she was open to the diverse individuality of others, and for all her initial dreaming of the 'Emerald Isle' potentially very adaptable to the new social mix to be encountered in Australia.

As to the public shipboard celebration of religion, Mrs Flemming's experience was similar to Charles Elliott's. Early enthusiasm in the emotional atmosphere of leaving home on a strange and hazardous journey, gave way to indifference as the impending approach of the new life in Australia came to dominate the passengers' thoughts to the exclusion of all else. It was as if the hallowed religious aura, and traditional sense of the sacred habitual to the old world, waned with nautical distance. The anticipated secular demands of the new world came to infiltrate immigrants' minds and occupy their concerns long before they had sight of it. So the voyage out became a kind of pilgrimage — away from religion. Its length was sufficient to disrupt the ordered tenor of old established life patterns, an enforced hiatus in which the succession of Sundays gradually merged with every other day, shorn of the reminders of Sunday bells, of Sunday best, of the social event of processing toward some sacred building. The unpredictable encounter with the elements and the perils of the ocean encouraged the spontaneous prayer of fear, but dissolved or weakened the fabric of organised church-oriented religion. The passage to Australia, sharing three or four months of danger and boredom with all kinds and manner of men and women, lay as a strange time-warp across the lives of those who experienced it; they entered as inhabitants of the weekly cycle of an old and rigid world: many emerged already transformed, loosened by the chaos of sea and sky and by the social flux into which they had been drawn. Private religion, and the 'parrot rhymes' of the Catholics seem to have best survived. Why? Perhaps for different reasons, perhaps the same; both had internalised and personalised, in different ways,. individual relationships with a real, wonderful and powerful God whose existence in the world was made obvious — both to the very simple and the serious — by the voyage they had survived. And what when they had arrived? To embark in Australia was to board another strange ship, engage in further unpredictable and uncertain voyages, with an even more various assembly of unfamiliar travelling companions, where Sunday vanished and had to be built again, and where once more the elements and emptyness sought dominion of the earth.

4

CAMEO PORTRAITS 1828-1902

AN IRISH TORY IS UNHAPPY WITH LIBERAL NEW SOUTH WALES, 1838

Henry Cavendish Butler was born on 18 April 1811, at Lanesborough Lodge, Belturbet, Co. Cavan. He arrived in Sydney in 1829 where he became an assistant government surveyor, being engaged in 1838 on surveying the Sydney-Melbourne road for the purpose of constructing a route for mail services. His sister Elizabeth had married Colonel Henry Dumaresq, secretary to Governor Darling, but he died in March 1838. Butler thereupon took over management of his sister's affairs, and in 1841 accompanied her and her children back to the United Kingdom. He returned to Ireland where he married and lived as a prominent landholder in Cavan until his death in 1891.

Writing on 20 August 1838 to John Butler Danvers of Swithland Hall, Leicestershire, Henry Butler was then at St Heliers, on the Hunter River. Rigorously conservative in disposition, he was bitterly critical of the tone of the colony generally and particularly of the governorship (1831-8) of his fellow Irishman Sir Richard Bourke.[1] He felt himself neglected, he was affronted by the egalitarian and selfish spirit of colonial society, and thought the country generally offered little of interest or importance.

> This is a country where *Self* is the 'premium Mobile', the main spring upon which all the actions of it's inhabitants depend. If a man finds it to his advantage to be honest he is honest, but let his own interest be interferred [sic] with and character, friendship, gratitude avail nothing — all are sacrificed and made subservient to the advancement of his own fortunes . . . It is indeed a strange land. The aristocracy of wealth is looked up to with veneration which the most sanguine Parvenue could hardly hope for in other countries. Parties whose birth, parentage and education wd. for ever preclude their being admitted into any society but of the lowest caste at service, thro' its all powerful influence rank here among the Magistrates, and thanks to the liberal sentiments of Genl. Bourke and his 'Whigish clique' have jostled themselves into even being recd. at Govt. House. This was not the case in Genl. Darling's time, and as you may suppose the change that has been wrought in the tone

> of society here in consequence of his successors mistaken notions of equalization, has in no wise improved it or added to its respectability — Party spirit rages also most violently as it must naturally do in a small community. I need hardly tell you that the Tories rank among their number only the respectable class of people here and as a matter of course are far outnumbered. But they nevertheless maintain their position against the united forces of liberals and emancipists and did maintain it with firmness and consistency even when these two bodies were headed and supported by Sir Richd. Bourke and all his patronage; a patronage that was never exercised in favour of any one who differed with him in politics . . . but was lavished with an unsparing hand upon such as wd. support his measures and sacrifice their own principles at the shrine of the 'Irish System of Education' and other oppressive measures that he wished to force upon the Colonists. He is however gone, and I sincerely hope Sir Geo. Gipps will not follow in his footsteps, or imitate the mistaken line of politics he persevered in against the best interests of the Colony. I of course was made to feel the evil consequence of adopting the priviledge of thinking for myself, and was visited with the neglect that awaited all those, who exercised such a prerogative under a despotic Government. But as long as I remained in the Service I did my duty conscientiously . . .

As to his expedition to Port Phillip he remarked:

> The journey overland was interesting enough — but I have already written enough . . . this country affords so few subjects that wd. make a letter worthy of its postage . . .

Butler's harsh judgments and lack of sympathy with the developing character of colonial life betoken a mind much more at home in the closed world of the Anglo-Irish gentry, to which he returned in 1841. In New South Wales he found himself unappreciated, frustrated and out of place.

AN ANGLO-IRISH GENTLEMAN WRITES OF PERSONAL SUCCESS, POLITICS AND THE ANGLICAN RELIGION IN NEW SOUTH WALES, 1845-1866

Thomas Moore was a substantial grazier whose property, Pomeroy, was about sixteen miles from Goulburn, NSW. A native of Derry, he exchanged letters with a friend ('My dear Henry') who was probably Rev. Henry Scott, of Willsborough, Walworth, Limavady and Foyle Hill, Derry, who was also sometime Rector at Inch, Co. Down.

Moore was much concerned with providing his family with suitable and affluent marriages, and it is evident from his letters that his circle was one in which there was a good deal of society 'traffic' back to England and Ireland, by which contact was maintained with relatives and friends. Moore himself remained deeply interested in Londonderry and its doings, and some immigrants from there, now in Australia, he regarded as his personal proteges.

Seeing himself as comfortable rather than rich, Moore took a positive view of colonial development generally, save in matters of religion, of which he was critical. Writing on 15 March 1845 he observed:

> . . . I think I can safely say we are now in a more prosperous state than we have ever been before with our wool tallow oil etc. to England and our horses to India. We have now established a valuable export that must rise more rapidly than any other colony and what is of more consequence our social condition is fast improving; the introduction of so many females into our

> society has had the most beneficial effect and I sincerely trust the exertions now making at home to establish a universal system of emigration will succeed as in most of our colonies there is abundance to supply the wants of your overplus starving population; in this for one there cannot be a finer opening for industrious people. One of our greatest evils is the want of religious instruction a want that is not easily supplied in so widely spreading a population as ours although I think a great deal more might be done than is. The few clergymen of our persuasion are by no means active, at least compared with the Roman Catholics who are fast gaining ground in these colonies. Our bishop Broughton is a talented man but like most of his class eaten up with pride and bigotry and his violent opposition to all other persuasions does our church no good. The clergy are not sufficiently paid and have recourse to keeping schools which occupies the greater portion of their time which ought to be spent in visiting their extensive parishes. We are 16 miles from Goulburn where our nearest church is situated therefore our attendance cannot be very regular. We have become quite settled here now. I feel much more satisfaction in living on my own property than in rented one. Notwithstanding the bad times I have managed to get up a very good stone house or part of a house as it is built with the intention of adding considerably to it with a capital garden and other appurtenances around; the surrounding scenery is very beautiful and capable of great improvement in laying out the ground and planting. In a few years I expect Pomeroy will be the gem of Australia in point of picturesque scenery. I can even have my boat and water sufficient to pull or sail a mile in length on the river Wollondilly which runs through my property nine miles in a direct line. We have Willoughby Dowling his wife and family and Miss Dickson living with us therefore are a strong party and a very Recherche one as they are all good looking and possess considerable accomplishments. We astonished the Argyle County in giving a grand ball a few weeks since at which there were 60 persons quite as refined as you would meet in England; some of them came 40 miles to it; by this you will perceive we are not destitute of society and still we can be as retired as we like.

There followed a long gap in correspondence. When Thomas Moore wrote on 8 March 1858 he blamed the mails: 'a confounded Scotch company having undertaken to convey our mails without means or experience have made a sad mess of it and have caused us great inconvenience'. In giving the news of his daughter's excellent marriage — her husband had £2000 per annum and had settled £5000 on her — he explained his own less affluent situation:

> I have not been one of the lucky ones in a pecuniary point of view. The year before the discovery of the gold mines, not liking the immediate prospects of the colony I determined to reduce my establishment and pay off a mortgage on this property. I therefore sold two outlying leased stations with the stock on them wherein I committed a great error as since the gold has attracted so large a population, property of that description has risen enormously in value . . . those stations which I sold for £3,000 I could since have readily got £50,000, a difference that makes a man rich or poor; in deciding which to part with the leasehold or freehold I naturally held to the latter which no doubt will be the most valuable in the end and is now beginning to improve that the excitement caused by this wonderful discovery is subsiding and people are dropping into the ordinary pursuits of life.
>
> We have had another great cause of excitement that has retarded our prosperity as yet. The change in the form of our Government from irresponsible

> to responsible which has caused so much struggling between two parties to hold the power that the business of the country has been entirely neglected and a system of extravagance been sanctioned that has involved us in a considerable debt. Although the resources of the colony are very great it will take both good judgment and considerable time to set matters to rights again. We have just gone through a General Election, the results of which is that the Liberal Party have gained considerable strength but the country have no confidence in the men that hold the reins of Government and most likely at the meeting of Parliament this month they will be ousted. I take no active part in politics, though strongly inclined to the Liberal side but remain quietly at home witnessing their bickerings and indulging in my favourite philosophical pursuits, though last year I very near committed myself, as a neighbour and friend who I have a very high respect for was nominated one of the Ministers of the Commission of Land and Public Works — who offered me any office in his gift and I was induced to accept his Deputy with a salary of £1,000 per year but fortunately one of the many changes occurred and I was released; he has been again Minister but I would not accept. I have not very long to pass in this world and I prefer spending the time in peace and quietness when I may be better prepared for the next. I take considerable interest in all scientific pursuits going on in the colony and now and then put forth a lecture or launch a shaft against the terrible ignorance and extravagance that has been displayed in making our railroads.

Railway construction was a pet subject of Moore's: he also followed with interest the progress of Irish railways. Another favourite topic was the condition of the Anglican Church. He explained to his Irish clerical friend on 3 January 1859:

> There has been a very interesting conference sitting lately in Sydney and another at Maitland (the two dioceses of this colony) and indeed the same has been going on [in] all these colony somewhat modified — to establish a more effectual system of Church government, one suited to the more liberal views of the present age. The members of the conference are composed of the representatives, three orders, the Bishop, clergy and laity; two of the latter being appointed at public meeting in each parish; the body to meet whenever desirable to establish such laws as they may think desirable — the great point of interest that has lately been under discussion has been the framing of an Act to give the body legal authority in which there has been a very considerable difference of opinion as to whether the Bishop shall have the power of putting his veto on the decision the majority of the other two parties may come to; this point has been carried in favour of the Bishop and the Maitland conference has adopted the same views which I think is the best as I cannot conceive any good government without a supreme head though 'tis really [?] a check should exist as all men are not pure in their motives. As long as the present Bishop (Barker) holds the See we are safe as he is a most excellent man but we may not always be so fortunate. Another point of great interest will be shortly decided in the Parliament i.e. the payment of the clergy. Hitherto there has been about £50,000 granted yearly to support the clergy which sum is now quite insufficient from the increase of the colony and many clergymen are supported by voluntary contributions and as the money is divided between the Episcopalians, Romans, Presbyterians and Wesleyans according to their numbers, other denominations think themselves aggrieved. The general impression is that the whole will be withdrawn as the present

incumbents are removed either by death or otherwise and the whole Church be supported voluntarily and the present Government have promised to bring in a Bill to that effect next session. The oldest incumbents are well paid and comfortably housed say about £500 per annum but [generally?] the clergy are miserably provided for and many cases of real distress exist; therefore a change is much required. In the early days of the colony a large estate composed of the best land dispersed all over the colony was set apart for the purpose of supporting the Church and schools but as from the want of population to render it valuable it did not produce a sufficient annual income it was found necessary the Government should give a grant in lieu and it collects the rent and proceeds from the estate which is carried to the years revenue. It appears to me that this estate (which has now become [valuable?] should be again given up to its legitimate purpose but the great practical diffficulty would be in apportioning it to the different denominations. The matter will afford considerable discussion next year. Hitherto our church government has been under the control of the Archbishop of Canterbury which is found to be very inconvenient.

And then there was some family and personal news.

Two months since young John Moore arrived here from Adelaide in South Australia. He has spent five years at the Victoria diggings without having accumulated any gold having worked very hard all the time. Finding he could do nothing there he went over to his cousin Charles Simeon [?] at Adelaide in the hope of getting employment but not succeeding. Charles wrote to me begging I would give him my countenance or he would have to go to India to enter the army as a private soldier. I paid his passage up here and have given him employment on the farm at sufficient salary to clothe and keep himself respectable while he gains some farming experience, telling him it will entirely depend on the ability he shows at the end of a year what more I can do for him. I would give him a share of the income if he is capable of managing the establishment. He has grown a fine young man and I am happy to say he has come out of that temptation unscathed both in manners and principles which is very much to his credit. I cannot do more for him as I have another gentleman here a son of the late Mr. Dowling of London who is my superintendent, besides a farm overseer. I think you are aware I spent a good deal of time in [planning?] the establishment of railways in this colony and that my services were little appreciated at the time: lately they have been brought before the Parliament and a Select Committee of the House of Assembly have strongly recommended my remuneration by £1,500 which I expect to get next session: irrespective of the money this is very gratifying to me.

It was seven years before Thomas Moore wrote again, a silence for which he blamed himself — 'inadvertence and a dislike to writing'. His letter of 22 July 1866 was written from Edgecliff House, Sydney, the home of his son-in-law Busby.

I had a letter from dear Mary [his married daughter in England] a few months since asking my advice as to her emigrating to this colony with her son which, much as I desire to see her I could not conscientiously encourage. [Her husband] St. John by all accounts is utterly unfit to encounter the roughing of our bush life and there is great difficulty in obtaining situations as there are so many applicants from Colonial youths, when a vacancy occurs:

besides the society is not what would suit Mary: it is generally composed of people that have risen from a low degree by amassing wealth whose manners and habits are not the most agreeable: therefore both William Busby and I strongly advised her not to think more of it . . .
Busby has lately bought this place, [Edgecliff House] the late residence of the late Judge Wise. It is a large and handsome house conveniently situated about a mile and a half from the city in a beautiful garden with splendid views of the harbour all round. He intends to bring his family here every winter that they may enjoy society and be at Cassilis [his grazing property] during the busy months when the sheep require attention: they are now preparing to return there and have already let the house for six months to a nice family for £200 which will save his keeping it. They have been living in great style warranted by his thriving establishments both at Cassilis and in Queensland: in fact there is no one I know that manages his affairs better. We are most especially fortunate in having such a worthy son-in-law who is all kindness to our daughter. I have not been one of the fortunate settlers although I have managed to go on with a fair share of comforts around me, perhaps quite enough, for great success does not improve the character and disposition of man. I made a mistake in the first instance in purchasing so much landed property instead of employing my capital in the cultivation of sheep and cattle on the wild wastes of the interior: this and a disinclination to speculate has keep [*sic*] me just rubbing on with sufficient income to meet our reasonable wants but not enough to go visiting about in the old countries as most of my acquaintances do: however a change is gradually taking place and this landed property is assuming its proper value and will no doubt be the most desirable in the end. Pomeroy is a magnificent estate and will be a principality to the young ones. I have lately changed the character of its management by selling off all the livestock and giving up farming on my own account having leased the land to tenants keeping nothing in my own hands but the house garden and pleasure grounds. I do not get so large an income by these means but it is more certain and free from anxiety and will yearly increase as the district becomes populated: besides it leaves us at liberty to go and come when we like. It is a Derryman and woman that rents the home farm (William Gallagher) who was for seven years foreman in Mr. Watt's brewery. He came to this colony 25 years ago when I employed him and have since had opportunity of befriending them which has caused an unusual degree of attachment in him and his whole family (now consisting of four young women and two sons) to us. He and she have proved themselves to be guided by the strictest integrity and they possess a delicacy of feeling that any gentleman might be proud of. Consequently I have the highest respect for them and notwithstanding their class I estimate them more as friends than otherwise. They have left a valuable farm in Cumberland and came up to live with me, I believe from pure affection: he rents all the enclosures about the house and supplies us with wood, water, dairy produce, vegetables and poultry taking charge of the premises in my absence so that I have none but the indoor servants to look after and they are a family I have had on and off for 18 years so that although I am not so rich in money as my neighbours we are very comfortable and having got rid of farming work I can amuse myself by improving the place which I have done to considerable extent lately. I am voluntarily building a nice stone cottage of fine rooms with detached kitchen and offices as a residence for the Gallaghers as it is both my desire and interest to make them as comfortable as possible for we will probably end our days together: he and

I have many talks of old Derry and would be glad to hear from you of anything that is going on.
Within the last two years we have succeeded in establishing a bishopric in the South-Western part of New South Wales. The Bishop Goulburn (Mesac Thomas) who has for some years been the principal correspondent or secretary of the Society for the Diffusion of the Gospel, living in London, is a very superior man admirably calculated for organising the extensive diocese he has undertaken and not less so by his energetic and amiable wife. They are a strong healthy couple without family, active, devoted to the undertaking and so affable, with a proper proportion of dignity that they secure the goodwill of every person. Within twelve months of his arrival they travelled 2,000 [miles] in their own carriage round the distant parts of the diocese no small undertaking as they have lived nearly all their lives in London. We have managed to collect in money and landed property £20,000 as an endowment which now produces about £1,200 per annum yearly increasing and this entirely from private subscriptions. He is establishing clergymen and schools everywhere so that an immensity of good is being effected.

A SHEEP FARMER MEDITATES ON DEATH AND THE WAYS OF PROVIDENCE, 1845

On 25 December 1845 Thomas Vogan, of Richlands near Goulburn, New South Wales, wrote home to his brother Richard in Armagh a letter of condolence on the death of Richard Vogan's young wife whom Thomas had never met. It was a document of classic Victorian melancholy and fulsome religiosity; a set piece. Yet its setting was utilitarian colonial: Thomas explained to his brother, 'this being a very important and busy time on all large sheep establishments, I found it inconvenient to reply to your letter sooner than the present . . .' Besides, the distance was so great, and the operation of 'the ruthless hand of death' both so usual and so unpredictable, so much the will of 'Him who is the only wise disposer of all events, all whose ways are unsearchable by us and past finding out,' that there was no hurry.

We must remember that our life is as but the vapour and the morning cloud that soon passeth away, that we are but the beings of an hour compared with the years of time much less with those of eternity. this afflictive dispensation of an all wise Providence has, my dear Richard, I feel, been a great trial to you, a severe calamity and heavy stroke indeed. I look upon your loss by this visitation of Providence as in some measure irreparable, and one I fear you will, in a greater or less degree (according to circumstances), continue to feel for perhaps many years yet to come . . .
I feel persuaded that your trial and affliction is one of no ordinary kind indeed, and must, as it were, have borne you down almost to the very earth, and been felt by you with an intensity and keenness to which language fails to give expression, and known only to those who have experienced the like bitter pangs of grief *for departed worth* and that *of one so nearly allied* but from which, if the sincere wishes and fervent prayers of an affectionate but far distant brother could relieve you, or be of any service, they are before a Throne of Grace, and I trust will occasionally continue to be offered up for you and your now double dear to you, motherless little ones. As for myself I am on your account much consoled in consequence of the pious resigned and truly christian manner and spirit in which you have borne and written to me of this distressing event, and in which pious and christian spirit of resignation

to the will of Almighty God I humbly hope and fervently pray His sustaining grace will keep you, and though you will continue to feel in all the relations of life, more particularly those of domestic happiness, the great loss you have sustained, yet your consolation will be the certain knowledge (as I am firmly persuaded it is) that your loss is her great and eternal gain and that you can look forward with cheering hope, and even a bright countenance, amidst all the turmoil, the storms and troubles of this transitory life, to a joyful meeting of redeemed spirits in that happy place where parting will be no more, where the wicket[sic] cease from troubling and the weary are at rest. I trust you are now, by God's dealings with you, and the afflictions you have experienced, often led for consolation to the contemplation of these things, and the happy termination of all the afflictions and troubles of this life, when time as to us here shall cease, through the saving grace and merits of our adorable Redeemer and though that by this heavy stroke and visitation of Providence the beloved and affectionate wife of your bosom, the pious and tender mother of your dear children has been severed from you and them, yet I trust and rejoice to think that you are by grace and with pious resignation to the divine will enabled to say with good old Eli 'it is the Lord: let him do what seemeth him good' and with Job 'the Lord gave and the Lord hath taken away; blessed be the name of the Lord.'

INSIDE AND OUTSIDE VIEWS OF THE PORT PHILLIP SQUATTOCRACY 1847-9

The Adams family of Portglenone, Co. Antrim, was a large one — eight boys and two girls — with considerable means: two of the boys were doctors of medicine, and the family members all had significant income from bequests and investments. One of the daughters, Mary Jane — Mrs Muirhead — was the mistress on a large property in the Grampians district near Geelong; a married brother, Robert, had a property nearby.

Writing home to her brother William in Portglenone on 27 December 1847, Mary Jane took a bright view of their pioneering circumstances, even down to the absence of medical help at the birth of her stillborn son. She wondered why Irish Famine victims were not sent to Australia.

> I humbly trust the famine and distress is quite over now. We cannot understand why Government don't send them out here, as there is plenty of room and plenty of food and to spare. We are giving from £28 to £30 a year to all our men, hut keepers and shepherds; our married couple get £36 a year and all our neighbours are giving from £40 to £50 a year, and cannot even get them at that. We require 13 and 14 men constantly and a man and his wife. . . You would be delighted with this climate. Everything can be grown in the open air, although the winters are generally wet and cold, yet few ever get colds or fevers. Since I last wrote you we have got a very good comfortable house built which has cost £200.

To their existing sheep holding of 9000 — the run would take about 30000 — her husband had recently added fifty cattle.

> He also bought a screw press for to press the wool, which cost £40 in Melbourne. We have 72 bales of fine wool, each bale containing 200 flushes, or 300 lb each. We are expecting £13 this season, as it is not so dear as it has been for the last two years. We have got our shearing over this season five shearers, they shore upwards of 9000 at 16s. per 100 and 4s. a day for washing the sheep . . .

I still have plenty of fowls 24 turkeys 12 ducks and a large flock of geese. I take the credit of having the best poultry in the country. We have plenty of eggs and lots for killing. We can also kill our own beef, pork etc. and a sheep every day, and Muirhead brings up every little thing from town that I require, so we live most comfortably. We have plenty of potatoes, vegetables cheese and milk and butter, so that I have every comfort that this country can afford. You would be delighted with our place. We are surrounded by the fine Grampians and Mount William . . .

And Mary Jane made light of the disadvantages.

You wished to know in your letter if we had any clergymen or doctors. We have no clergyman. The neighbouring settlers are giving £10 each to a Doctor Wilson from Melbourne for three years. It amounts to £300 a year to him. He lives 35 miles from us. Still it is better to have him there as we live 100-120 miles from town. When I required him as I was ill on Sunday night we sent for him on Monday, but he did not come till Wednesday, but my little son was dead. I am now quite well thank God for raising me up from the bed of sickness.

Her brother, Dr George Hill Adams, visited Australia in 1848-9 as a ship's doctor, spending a year there, including four months with his brother and sister on their Grampians property. Writing to their brother Thomas back in Portglenone, on 29 December 1849, George expressed the opinion that the Grampians setting was 'superb' and that Mary Jane's place was 'the nicest and most romantic and picturesque of any place in the entire colony.' But life was nothing like the rural idyll that Mary Jane implied. George's impressions were of appalling heat, little water, economic depression, and ruinous interest rates, as a setting for a colonial life that was vacuous, boring, incredibly insular, materialist and coarse. The first oddity he found among his relatives is that they had not bothered to inspect the surrounding magnificent scenery;

It was rather queer that not one of them had ever visited those ranges till I did, but the truth is, there is nothing almost in any of the settlers' heads but some half dozen things, to wit sheep, wool, bullocks, drays, servants, horses, and occasionally a little about tallow and boiling down and huts and such like. That is the eternal, never ceasing lingo, day and night, summer and winter. It becomes horribly boring, and you can rarely get anyone to talk even for a few minutes on any other possible subject whatever. They shirk it immediately, so that all your previous knowledge and stores of information are perfectly useless and become, as it were, screwed up in one of their screwpresses. As an instance, last year when the most intense interest was prevailing amongst, one would have said, the whole civilized world with regard to the stirring affairs of Europe and the fearful changes and catastrophes occuring so plentifully on the continent, they out in Port Phillip neither read nor cared one fig about the entire matter and never would speak almost on the subject, excepting to curse the French for spoiling the price of their wool, and then they smoke and drink and drink and smoke.

Nor did some of them bother, even when they could well afford it, to build better houses.

As to the huts, in which they lived during the first years of their sojourning on their runs, why no language could almost give you an adequate idea of some of them. Some are still living in those primitive substitutes for houses,

> as Mr. and Mrs. Patterson of Lake Bolak within 9 miles of Robert's place. I stopped twice there and slept, but you never in all your life saw, or perhaps imagined such queer rum places, and another far worse 8 miles from Muirhead's where the Archibald family lived near the base of Mount William, a most strange locality, and as to the hut, it was what they call a slab hut, that you could shoot easily through between every two slabs plenty of fresh air you see.

George Adams admitted that, before going to Australia, he had thought that colonists with an annual wool clip of 1400 would save £400-£500 a year; having seen the reality of the expenses of his relatives' Grampian properties he now wondered how they survived. Of one thing he was utterly sure: it was a young persons' country, an opportunity for the unformed and adaptable, but offering to the older and more cultivated, an unending vista of boredom, crudity and depression;

> Now, as to people going out, I decidedly think *young people* are the right sort, who will have their habits to form and not have to break up old habits or long contracted associations. They will fall into the ways, manners, habits, customs, and so forth of the colony with ease, and get soon to relish the new mode of life, but to older people the change in many respects is excessively unpleasant, miserable and depressing. In fact you would become quite ennuyed unless you drink and smoke etc etc although I must say some do not smoke at all, nor drink much . . . There are many nice people and some highly respectable, but many who are very coarse, and who had come out without a stiver.

WORLDS IN FLUX: ANTRIM AND AUSTRALIA 1853-7

The impact of emigration on some parts of Ireland was profound: there it bred unsettlement, dissatisfaction and confusion among those who remained. John Getty was a small flax farmer from Taughey near Ballymoney, Co. Antrim; in 1852 his brother James emigrated to Australia to join the gold rushes. The Getty's lived in an area and time marked by heavy emigration, not only to Australia, but — more commonly — to America, to Scotland and to other parts of Ireland. Adding to this unsettlement, and facilitating it, was the actual physical disturbance of the district's fields by the building of the Co. Antrim railway, whose arrival wrought a psychological as well as a communications revolution by making it possible to visit Belfast, and for city ways and values to penetrate the countryside. The result of all these changes, and the departure of so many friends and relations, put John Getty in a fever of impatience to leave as well: he was working hard in Ireland for nothing; his brother might also be working hard in Australia, but he was getting something to show for it. On receiving the first letter his brother in Melbourne had written home, John in a letter of 11 July 1853 urgently proffered himself as an Australian partner: he would leave Ireland as soon as James would agree:

> Think ye would I not make as good a partner as any you have got yet? If you think so I will go for it is losing time stopping in Ireland for you can make more money in one month than we can all make in one year. I would not sell the farm. I would only "set" it until I would try Australia. You wish to know how our flax paid us. It paid well. We had 800 and some pounds which we received £30 10s.0d. for; also the grey filly I sold to William John Lamond at £13 a few days after you sailed . . .

> But Ireland is no place to make money though times is very good. Buttar 9d. per lb and pork £2 10s.0d. by the cwt; beef from 2d. to 7d. per lb. Mutton much the same. It is only losing one's time stopping here after all. Mary and my mother would be willing to let me go and it all depends on you. As soon as you get these lines let me know if you would advise me to go . . . As soon as you receive this write and let me or us know if possible what the town and country is like . . . if you cannot find some easier employment I would advise you not kill yourself for big weages. Also let me know what sort of goods to take with me when you advise me to go, whether boots and shoes or neither.

James, apparently, was not encouraging. In Australia he moved around a good deal, shopping around for jobs, staying with friends, and just wandering. He was in and out of work, making and losing money. He wrote seldom. And he fell ill. Meanwhile in Ireland John's enthusiasm waned and became uncertainty — and worry for his brother. This stemmed not only from James' Australian experiences, but from the effect of the reported misfortunes of American emigrants, friends and neighbours. When John wrote from Taughey in September 1855, his tone to his brother was critical, not only of his infrequent writing, but of his lifestyle, and of his fixation on making money. Their mother wanted him home:

> You ought to write often and let us know how you get your health let you get any news from us or not, for dreams by night and thoughts by day are one way [of remembering] him thats far away. We are all in health, much the same as when you left us only a little more worn. We would be glad too see you home again but we are getting on very well. It is only pootting in the time for there is very little contentment . . .
>
> Now as you are about commencing business for yourself I would advise you to lift your money as soon as you win it. But I think I need not advise you for I think you will have need of it as soon as it is "win" but, need it or not, its not a bad plan. I fear you will encumber yourself with houses and work and affairs that you will never get rid of. You talk of coming home some time as soon as you have got what money will keep you easy but I fear that will be a long time, a time some of us will never see, maybe none of us. Life is uncertain. I don't think much of your iron houses. If you had taken care of your money as you "win" it and wrought another year or two you might have had as much as would have done you your time. But what came of your pound or 25s. per day. Sure the half of that was fit to bed and board you. But what right have I to dictate to a man in Australia. He surely knows better than I do . . .
>
> Your mother wants you home that she may see you and bless you before she dies. She says you have money plenty more than ever you will live to see done. She will dream of you sometimes and thinks she hears you at the window and rises to let you in but when she goes to the door and sees you not she finds it's but a dream. She also wants you home to see the fine rode we have made of the gravel lane for in reality it is so and stoned also. By this you would think she was "doating" but there [is] nothing of it. She is so anxious to hear from you and see you if it was possible that [she] so often dreams of you.

But James did not wish to return. He had been to the diggings and failed, and was now working as a wheelwright, sometimes in Melbourne, later in Beechworth and Kilmore. To John's request that he return to Ireland he replied, to the family's puzzlement, that he had been 'colonized'. Seen from Ireland, that word was a mystery in content, but clear enough in its implications: James now inhabited another and different world. So it was that John wrote on 22 February 1857 in the last preserved record of that slow-motion exchange of emotions:

> We received your letter dated July 28th 1856 which informs us that James Love and you were at the digg[ings] which has turned out unprofitable which I suppose was the reason of your not writing for such a length of time. You forget that you told us how glad you were to get a letter from us. We are also as glad to get one from you. You did not tell us what loss you were at nor whether you sold your house or not. We are glad to hear of [your?] doing well also sorry to hear of your losing. I am sorry that you cannot content yourself in one place for you remember the proverb that a rolling stone gathers no moss. If you would take care and settle in one place for a while you might soon have as much money as would do you while you would live, for the times is not so bad with you yet but you might make money and if you had three or four hundred pounds and came home with it to Ireland I think you might li[ve] and [prosper] moreso than you can do in Austra[lia] [Please?] make good your word or promise you will come home. If you remember six years is all the time you said you would stop. I need say no more. We would be glad to see you home again with money or wanting it. The money is no obstacle. We have more than when you went away which you shall be welcome to a share of. You know what we were before that you left us. We are still the same. We would be glad to see you once more in Taughey as you were before you left us. But you say you are coloniz[ed] and say what you think, which puts me to state to know what you mean . . .
>
> We ourselves are like the American letters, well and doing well . . .
>
> My mother cries come home and Mary wishes you were home and I wish you were home. But all our wishes and her crying could not keep you at home and now you are where you are and if you are "contenters" where you are now what you would be at home, stay where you are. If not come home and try to make yourself content at home. You are welcomear to come than to stay.

It was a generous response and an understanding impulse; stay where you are the more content. If only it was so simple. But being 'colonized' meant, at least in part, being permanently unfitted for what both James and John, at opposite ends of the earth, agreed was 'home' — Ireland. As James's Victorian wanderings testified, as did his delight in receiving Irish letters, being 'colonized' did not relate to the concept of contentment in either or any place; it was more a disposition of equilibrium in accepting the occupancy of no-mans-land.

GOLD 1852-77

The very considerable correspondence that survives from Irish migrants on the goldfields confirms overwhelmingly the well-known picture — high expectations, appalling living conditions, little success, disillusionment. The prevailing experience was that of failure. Some few coped with this well enough, moving to other employment when they were eventually convinced that luck would never favour them, finding success and happiness elsewhere. To others, the discovery that goldmining was a gamble in which few won large prizes, came as a crushing blow. On 10 December 1854, Noah Dalway[2] wrote from the Victorian diggings to his mother in Belfast, a homesick, self-pitying letter, regretting the recklessness and dreams of wealth and adventure that had lured him from home, and humiliated by his inability to send money.

> I sometimes feel that I shall never more see you all: I feel as though I were transported for I work hard from 5 in the morning until 9 in the evening. I then sit down in my tent, wearied and tired: hard work little for it. I smoke a few pipes and begin to think of you all at home . . . I say to myself often that I am now suffering for my recklessness at home and I feel that I am justly suffering: it is now that I feel the loss of you all and of a home where, had I been what was required of a son, I might be now happy in that home without any care anxiety or laborious work, all of which are now my only companions. This Australia, dear mother, is most falsely represented: there are ministers in this colony who are working on the roads breaking stones and thousands come thinking to get a fortune in a few months but alas what a mistake they make and the gold fields again which contain *so many thousands*, what are they doing, barely making a living. . .

By 23 February 1857 his situation was no better. He had firmly decided 'it was not my lot to become a fortune finder' and he wanted to return home:

> Will you be glad to see me come home once more for good and never more to roam: it has wrought a great change in me. I am quite changed . . . I am so excited to get out of this degrading country and join again the circle of society of which our home forms a link.

Other unsuccessful miners blamed, not themselves, but their parents and families for not allowing them to come earlier. Had their families not resisted and delayed their emigration, they would have succeeded: now too late all the fortunes had been made, all the golden opportunities taken. William Carlisle wrote on 20 May 1856 from Williamstown, where he had established a successful dairy farm, to his mother, near Dundalk.[3] His letter dutifully reviewed his history — including his marriage and the birth of a son — over the several years that had elapsed since he had come to Victoria, but his account had an underlying tone of bitterness: he had written, not only because his earlier experience in the colony was one of disappointment and failure, but because his mother's letters to him asked for money to pay bills in Ireland, money he did not have until his 1856 letter. The prevailing historical image of remittances to Ireland as being evidence of filial piety, a moving witness to spontaneous generosity and family closeness, is only part of a complex story. In some cases parents solicited such money; indeed badgered their emigrant children with details of various bills and financial requirements, in a way which made such children feel doubly guilty of their lack of adequate achievement. Parental demands were often accompanied, and no doubt frequently occasioned by, incomprehension of the migrant realities. 'Mother' complained William Carlisle, 'I think you knew little about Melbourne when you told George Murphy a lame man would get employment, it's just the reverse . . .' This parental belief that distant fields were littered with gold nuggets placed intolerable strain on family relationships: William Carlisle was not the only Irish emigrant who responded to such expectations by failing to write, but his case illustrates the strength of Irish family bonds in that, despite his resentment, he eventually sent money when he was able to do so.

But to other Irish, less seriously devoted to the pursuit of an elusive fortune, the diggings were a vast entertainment full of society and surprises, an extravaganza they thought should never end. Such a one was John Steele Nicholson, who wrote from the Dimolly diggings in Victoria to his sister Agnes at Balloo

House, Bangor, Co. Down on 24 July 1861. But Nicholson was gentry, from a comfortable background. From his standpoint, the gold diggings were a highly spiced adventure, not a grim struggle to survive while hoping to strike riches:

> I was at a fine kangaroo hunt last week; that's the fun; the devil a ditch or fence but at it as fast as your horse can carry you, sometimes on an open plain, then in low thick scrub, next through a forest of trees . . .
> As to my visiting Europe once more I fear it will be too cold for me to remain. There is fun here in every variety. I visited a Chinese theatre last night. You never saw such a performance.

The spectacular fun, the extravagant spending and wild drinking characteristic of the goldfields towns seem to have generated few direct Irish testimonies. On his way to the diggings in October 1852, Hugh Maguire wrote to his mother in Strabane from his Melbourne hotel (the Crown in Lonsdale Street) of his observing diggers, bearded men in blue shirts, with coarse boots, who spent their money like lords at home: they thought nothing of ordering champagne at 22s.6d. a bottle. Maguire looked on in wonderment — but it did not happen to him: after fourteen months on the diggings he returned with £65 — at a time when common labourers in Melbourne could earn 13s. a day. With keen entreprenurial sense he quit gold digging for commerce on the gold fields: in 1860 his annual salary was £234. All had stories of the big spenders they had seen or heard about: their own experience was invariably very different.

More typical of those Irish who stayed on the Victorian goldfields, while others joined other rushes, or took employment elsewhere, were the Lawrence brothers, Sampson and Charles, from a family of small landlords and mill owners in Coleraine.[4] The brothers appear to have joined the Victorian gold rushes in 1853. Charles had failed to get a cadetship in the army as he had wanted and as his family had attempted to secure. He wrote in 1859 from the Lemplaugh Diggings, Castlemaine, to his sister Sally in Ireland lamenting his failure to gain acceptance by the army: 'If I had been lucky enough to get such, by this time I would either have had I hope an honourable grave or a pretty good pension. Either would have been better than at present . . .' (The sons of genteel Irish families continued to look to the army. In that same year, 1859, John Moore, another Irishman faced by failure on the Victorian diggings, was thinking as a last resort of joining the army as a private soldier in India). Charles Lawrence died in December 1869, a virtual pauper in the Melbourne City Infirmary.

The brothers had drifted apart geographically in the colony. Sampson had stayed in Castlemaine, unmarried like his brother, and supplementing an inadequate income from his gold digging with the interest he received from Ireland following a cousin's bequest. But by 1866 he was so substantially in financial difficulty that he was forced to transfer his Irish capital to Australia in order to settle his debts and take advantage of higher local interest rates. He explained to his sister Sarah on 26 July 1866:

> . . . I must inform you that I have been a miner ever since the year after the gold was first discovered (that is to say 1853) which alone supported me till now. The diggings about where I "resides" is done or deserted almost; only a very few diggers seen at work. There are hundreds of men walking and travelling about looking for employment. Indeed these times it is hard for a man to know what to do to earn an honest living.

In 1869 Sarah died in Ireland, shortly before Charles died in Melbourne. Sampson was devastated, particularly as he had been trying to persuade Charles to come to Castlemaine to live with him: he had become the last surviving member of a family on whom he depended for gossip and newspapers and familiar society — for his sense of place and belonging in the world, a situation exacerbated by the fact that he had been born a deaf mute. He turned to his cousins in Ireland with whom he maintained correspondence — although he became depressed at the constant news of deaths which often dominated his Irish mail: 'I see that our old relatives and friends are fast diminishing. We are born to live and die at the pleasure of our Almighty God, who is the owner of the earth . . .'

As for himself, he was still very much alive, with all the problems and hopes of an unsuccessful digger. He told his cousin Maria Sampson on 31 January 1872:

> I was near to have looked for work when about 3 months ago I caught a chance of finding gold; since I have been making from 3/4 to 1/2 and sometimes 1 dwt. a day for which I am thankful. I am unable to know how long it will take me to work out my claim, should it continue to pay.

Over the years of occasional correspondence until 1880, glimpses of this lonely digger show him content enough, with his energy slowing fading but his hopes of a rich strike still alive. He explained on 15 July 1872:

> I "lives" in a little wooden hut on the near top of a hill in a nice view of Castlemaine and surrounding country about a mile off from town but I have not many neighbours by me. The miners are my *best friends.* One of the wives of one is a good tailoress and dressmaker. She makes suits of clothes for them and me.

Five years later in a series of letters over 1877 and 1878 he gave Maria Sampson and another Irish cousin, Dora Austin, details of his life, and waning fortunes and health:

> [21 February 1877] For 2 weeks I have been cutting firewood in order to have a good supply for winter as I can't afford to pay for a load which the wood cutters charges from 7s. to 8s. each. I am sorry to say that there is no chance of gold now about where I lives yet I hope I will come on a patch some day unexpectedly. I am almost the only alluvial miner seen at work with a *deal of patience.* It is not known, as soon as all the gold is swallowed of these diggings, what the people will do. We must have to work for a living whilst life lasts.
> [20 February 1878] I am glad to tell you that the unpleasant drought is now at an end. For some months the hot weather was so oppressive that I had to sleep outside my hut sometimes at night but I did not feel inclined for a bit of sleep for fear of a snake visiting me. The people made such complaints about the bugs, mosquitoes, fleas in such numbers whilst in bed at night, we had to use the Carbonic acid for their destruction. We have got plenty of bread at last. Before it came the good drinking water was very scarce.
> Since I last wrote telling you how I got on at digging, I am still getting but a good deal less gold; much more poorer than at the beginning. Before I came in sight of a speck I had to draw a few pounds out of the bank [so] as to keep me agoing.
> [19 March 1878] I do all the house works myself except fine shirts which my nearest neighbour a wife of an old Dublin seaman washes for me at a charge of 4d. a piece; a native of near London, she is the one that makes clothes for me and other people; a very good dressmaker and tailoress. I have a nice cat for company for me. She follows me like a dog to where I works. The moment

she sees anyone or dog she runs into holes till she is sure of them being gone out of sight. She sometimes stands a chance of catching rabbits; the hares are becoming plenty. Unfortunately, I have no gun to shoot them.

I am not doing much good at digging just now. There was a heavy fall of rain last Friday all day and night which caused a deal of earth to fall in a new hole I am sinking . . .

Most of my neighbours who cant get gold on these diggings on which I live, looks for work as labourers. I fear I shall take their example when all the gold is swall[ow]ed out of it. [It is] hard to tell what the people will do after. I live by myself in a very good view of Castlemaine, half an hour's walk so that I don't mind being lonely. Last week I got a present of a good lot of grapes and apples and pears from a wealthy gardener. He has a fine large orchard about half hour's walk from my hut. He like a good many miners made lots of money shortly after the gold was first discovered which enabled them to build fine houses on their own land. Castlemaine is beginning to be a fine town, with some fine public buildings (the Post Office particularly) . . .

[5 August 1878] My dear Maria, many thanks for your kind letter of 18th March which was sent to me by my store-keeper whilst lying bad with dysentery with piles at the hospital so I know that you would not accuse me of my negligence in replying to it sooner. I got sick for a time before he recommended me as a member of the committee to go at once to become an in-patient which I found more comfortable with plenty of attendants and attention than my hut. He took me there in his own tax cart. I lost a deal of blood passing till it disappeared on my leaving it, but I *am not quite well yet*. Going up high hills causes me to breathe hard, unlike before. I don't remember having ever been sick of any dangerous disease after or before I left Ireland so I am thankful to God for his kindness in taking the complaint from me. The hospital is a splendid building with a fine view of Castlemaine from the top of a hill about one and a half miles from my hut. Some of the patients were of respectable families at home; amongst was a cousin of the celebrated explorer Bourke of whom you would certainly read in the papers. I had plenty of visitors particularly miners. Some brought me sorts of cakes and jams etc. whilst at the hospital. The surgeon Dr. McGrath is a North of Ireland man, said to be the cleverest doctor in all Castlemaine. From 6 to 8 deaths took place. My diet was such a weak one which consisted of sago "burgoo" porridge, boiled milk, boiled bread, pudding, rice, tea, f[resh?], butter, bread with a good supply of milk and medicines along with a little brandy every day and night till I found myself getting better when the doctor ordered me to live on soup with meat, potatoes, eggs, bread, tea, milk; just before I was fit to come home he put me to the expense of drinking port wine for a month which was pretty hard on me . . .

The weather here has been a bitterly cold one for sometime past with some rains so that I have to make good fires to keep myself warm. I am happy to say that I am now enabled to cut firewood [so] as to save the expense of hiring any more load[s]. Shortly after I came home I had to order 2 loads till I was well enough to start to dig for gold about 4 weeks ago after *getting none since I left the hospital.*

[24 January 1879] You would read the papers I sends you giving accounts of the bushrangers Kellys who I am sorry to say are sons of Irish parents . . . I am sorry to say that my nearest neighbour of whom I spoke in my letters to you is dead — the same woman that made clothes for me and diggers. Since

> her death her husband has been unlucky enough like me at digging; hard times just now with the miners and trade dull. He talks of leaving here and go to near Melbourne to try and get work on the roads for the government. Lots of men can't get any [work] about Castlemaine now. They complain so much of the Chinese men keeping them poor and of the government allowing the emigration of more to "there" colonies. If my neighbour go away I am advised to shift to some place as it would not do for me to be alone.
> [15 April 1879] As to digging for gold I have not done much good like other miners since I came home from the hospital. It is a very difficult task to find gold now about where I "lives" . . .

By this stage Sampson Lawrence was living entirely on the small income produced by the rentals he had inherited in Ireland; these family assets were small, but they sustained his search for Australian gold. He never despaired of finding it, though with failing health and advancing age it became merely the dream and occupation which gave his life some purpose; it was all that he knew. Aside from that, he searched newspapers for news of the success (or failure) of distant relatives; was Sir Samuel Wilson, the wealthy Melbourne squatter, a relative of your uncle. Did you see that the Moody who was inspector of distilleries in Melbourne had lost his £700 a year job? And those bushranger Kellys, too clever for the police, sons of Irish parents. And what was the news of the Canadian relations? From his tiny hut in Castlemaine, Sampson Lawrence surveyed the events of the world, great and small, through his newspapers — Irish, English and Australian — and clung, by the kindness of his cousins, to the remnants of a disintegrated family order.

He had taken the trouble, occasionally, in those early hectic years, to sustain a desultory family correspondence, within Australia with his brother, and back to Ireland. But frequently family members drifted apart, lost each other in the colonies, neglected to write home, failed to receive letters, particularly in the turmoil of the gold rush period. The constant, often frantic mobility of that time, made it very difficult to maintain contact within the colonies: people and settlements came and went. Moreover, the enormous pressures to succeed, to strike it rich, generated by the gold rushes situation, made it difficult for the unlucky miners — the vast majority — to write home; they felt compelled to wait until they had good news to convey, circumstances which often never arose. As the gap in time lengthened and widened, it grew more difficult to bridge.

William and Ezekiel Dysart, with a friend called Noble, had left Derry for Australia during the gold rushes, probably in the late 1850s. Having no luck, William moved on to New Zealand. In 1877, twenty years later, back in Melbourne, knowledge of the accumulated misfortunes and bereavements his family had suffered in the interim descended on him within the space of a few weeks — his mother and a brother dead in Ireland, his brother Ezekiel dead in Australia nearly fifteen years earlier. Shattered by this news, he wrote his first letter home to his remaining brother, Charles, on 31 October 1877;

> I do not know how to begin to write after such a long silence, and the longer one is without writing the more difficult it is to begin, but though so long silent, there was none of you ever forgotten for a single day. The reason I did not write from the first was I had bad luck from the very first and as I was always in the hope of something turning up and then I would have written with some heart. But the news I have heard these last few weeks has stupified me. Mother I could hardly expect to be alive, but as for you James, and poor dear Charles, I thought you were all as I left you. Well if you will

answer me now and let me know what happened poor Charles and when mother and him died, I would take it as a great treat for with what news I have heard lately, I feel downhearted, as I have come to the sad conclusion that I am on this side of the water alone. When we first landed Noble and me went to the digging, done no good: I got fever from which I would have never recovered, had it not been for Mr. Orr wife and family: they are the only friends I have got here and they are friends indeed. Noble and me managed to keep together pretty well for a couple of years or so until I got my back crushed from which I never properly recovered. I was laid up for 12 months: during this time Noble went to the diggings again, promising to write to me as soon as he was settled, but I never got a letter from him nor heard of him but once and then I could not trace him out. But Mr. Orr seen him some years afterwards and told Noble to beware of, I almost said men, but I had better say savages or wild beasts: I mean the men Noble was working with. With what Mr. Orr has told me and Noble disappearing all at once, we can only come to one opinion as to what happened to him and that is too horrible to even think of.

When I was last parted with poor Ezekiel, he was going to Bendigo district; I wanted him to stop about the Melbourne district where I was then, but he fancied he could do better about Bendigo. We parted with the understanding that when we were both settled, we would try and find each other and write, but shortly afterwards, I went to New Zealand and I never seen my kind hearted brother afterwards nor never will in this world. Eating unwholesome food in New Zealand brought on liver complaint, which I never could get rid of, but enough of this.

After I came from New Zealand I had always the hope of bettering my position, before looking for Ezekiel or Noble, so time slipped away until I was told of the advertisement in the paper. Then I set to look for them in good earnest; I advertised for Ezekiel in the up-country papers and "stoped" in town trying all schemes to find either or both. I firmly believed Ezekiel was alive until yesterday when I found he had died at the Melbourne hospital of fever on 16th May 1863. Dying in the hospital here is no disgrace, as it is the only place a single man can go and a man with no money as Ezekiel had, must pay 2 guineas a week and if he dies he is buried in a respectable manner, out of his own money and if there is any left, it is handed to the curator of the estates deceased persons.

Ezekiel had £105 when he died, but William was more interested in finding where he was buried.

And so the gold rushes populated Australia with a diversity of people, a human process alive with wealth and colour, action and movement, a period of extraordinary growth and development. But beneath the surface of this spectacular excitement, the new society of Australia was forming itself most painfully from the wreckage of old worlds torn apart and left behind in pursuit of a mirage of riches. From the pathos of the fragments of intimacy that here remain, the cost of Australian gold to the Irish seems to have been high — innocent greed disappointed, families scattered and fallen apart, loneliness, misery, wretchedness at things done and not done in the realm of warmer human affairs, the reign of a sense of failure. Small wonder that this crucible, this battery, produced human fragments, and hardness of heart.

VARIETIES OF IRISH MIGRANT LIFE, 1866-1902

Despite the heavy weight of assumptions and caricatures, the reality of Irish migrant experience and attitudes resists easy stereotyping. Certainly the human record of migrants from the Northern counties — more of whose testimonies have survived — may be to a degree more various than that of the South, source of much heavier and unlettered emigration. Yet what follows as illustration of the range and diversity of migrant people and their lives offers an inescapably real dimension of what was characteristically Irish in Australia. It expands and makes complex narrow traditional orthodoxies dominated by the generalising image of Catholic peasant. History's anonymous statistics and maps give one view of Irish migration, that which embraces the general trends, the movements of the faceless mass. Here, by the accidental survival of fragmentary letters, tiny windows on migrant life, are some glimpses of faces in the crowd, caught for a tantalising moment before being swallowed again in obscurity.

In 1856, Adair F. Crawford and his sister were sent to Australia by their father, Rev. Thomas Crawford, Drumcliff, Co. Sligo, who had to borrow money from his cousin Alexander in Belfast to meet the expense of their passages. Writing home ten years later from Sydney, on 19 February 1866, Adair Crawford had still failed to find permanent employment and had lost all hope of doing so: he now saw America as the only coming place. He proclaimed that were he home now he would not be so choosy about a career. But how much of this was the self-pity of a failure, or piety for home consumption? He had spent his time recently attending a harbour regatta, and the Criminal Court, where a sensational murder trial was taking place — 'the disclosures were really awful'. Such pastimes were unlikely to have pleased his father, who was much given to the fulsome evangelical rhetoric of the religion of the day.

Young Crawford bore the marks of a genteel wastrel: George McLean writing on 15 April 1870 to William Williamson, Ahory, Richhill, Co. Armagh, had a canny sense of where the money was to be made on the goldfields. He had been in the timber trade and was now storekeeping at Young, in the orbit of new rushes at Grenfell:

> Gold digging is both dangerous and uncertain I do not intend trying my fortune on the gold fields. Store keeping is a much "shurer" game. We have done a very large trade in the wholesale since those new rushes opened.

Sure too was a good farm, far superior to what might be had in Ireland. On 20 February 1871 James Marks told his cousin in Ireland, about his mixed farm at William's Grove, New South Wales:

> . . . We are living on the farm, which is good one, free of rent or taxes of any kind with plenty of wood for the fire and plenty of water. I can grow the very best potatoes and vegetables I ever saw without manure. I have Indian corn growing now sixteen feet high. I have one acre of orange trees four years old loaded with fruit. In another year or so they will be worth a pound a tree annually. Also one acre orchard of all sorts of trees — We have twenty head of cattle and five horses and fifteen large pigs and mother keeps one hundred fowls . . .
> We are doing very well for we have good crops and a good stock and everything we can wish for and a good bit of money in the bank also. We don't regret leaving old Ireland for this is a very good country for steady industrious people though it is not near so good as it was some years ago.

At one extreme of successful farming were the vast speculative sheep-farming enterprizes of the Wilson brothers and Sir Samuel McCaughey.[5] Just how rigorously speculative and business-oriented were these large endeavours is evident in the letter which James Wilson wrote on 4 October 1880 from the Dunlop station (in which he held a fifth share with McCaughey) to a Mr Patrick in Ireland:

> We have just got through the shearing and have now on Dunlop about 150,000 sheep. The station will carry more when it is improved. The great drawback in this country is the want of water. We have one well down 414 feet and not a supply of water and still sinking. It is the intention of the present company to improve the stations and then sell.
> Zoocall [?] has about 185,000 sheep on it. These stations will carry over half a million of sheep. [If] we have a good season there will be that number on the stations.
> It is not likely that I will be home for some time as I have entered into partnership for 5 years to see this speculation carried through. We do not know how we shall come out of it. It is a large undertaking and requires a good deal of capital.

A pioneer gentleman's residence in Victoria in the 1880s: a photograph sent back to Ireland. (Courtesy: P.R.O.N.I. Belfast)

At the other extreme was Matthew Madill, of Undera, Victoria. Writing on 16 April 1874 to his orphan niece Margaret Taylor of Drumsoad, Clones, Co. Monaghan, who was in service, Madill tried to persuade her to emigrate, explaining that he had delayed until he could offer her a home:

> Your aunt and cousins had a letter wrote about 6 months ago. I would not let them send it because they were encouraging you to come out and that was what I did not like because I had not a way that time to keep you from the strangers, but thanks be to God, it is not so now for I have selected 160 acres of land. I have one year's rent paid on it and has got my licence. I am

not labouring it nor won't till November. The rent is only 2s. an acre and in ten years I have it free, so thanks be to god it won't be so bad with you as it is a[t] present if the Lord spares me, for, dear Margaret, I am going to send you £2 now and Ann Jane's husband, Mr. John Sherry is going to send you £1. If you be a wise good girl and stop single. The assistant emigration is stopped for a time; we expect [it] will commence again. Make up your mind and send me word if you will come out to this country and I will pay your passage . . . It is a great deal better out here for a girl than at home.

His daughter Mary Ellen added her plea on 21 January 1875, with an idyllic and exotic picture of colonial life, and assurances of affection:

Dear cousin Margaret, I think long to see you out here till you and I takes a horse each and a kangeroo's dog and has a good hunt after the kangeroos and emus. The girls here does no outside work. It is all housework. If you were in this country you would never see porridge any more. In this country you would have to learn to ride for you cannot go to your next neighbour without riding, it is so far. When I go out always ride on horseback.
If you were here you could not sleep in the mornings for laughing jack asses and cockatoos and parrots and curlews and native companions and a lot of other birds. Father shot some emus and it took three men to lift it into the cart. The old man kangeroo is much about the same weight . . .
I wish you were out here cousin Margaret. We would have such fun. We have our house built in about 10 acres of pine trees. They are about 8 foot high. We have about 100 large trees, father is going to cut down and get sawed for building purposes.
Here is a feather of an emu and one of a cockatoo.
The yellow one is the cockatoo's and the other is the emu's.
My dear cousin I am sorry to hear that you a[re] alone with strangers . . . We would all be so glad to see you.
My kindest and fondest of love to you, dear cousin. I have a lot of cousins but none I think so much of as you from your fond and loving cousin till death.

But Margaret Taylor was obliged to remain in service for another three years: her uncle's offer to pay her passage remained open.

James Milliken was with the police force at Peats Ferry in 1884. He was undecided as to the future: memories of the political domination of Ireland's landlords clouded his view of what was happening in New South Wales; on the other hand he had a mate in New England with whom he might share a lease. On 30 October he explained to this brother in Loughead, Islandmagee, Co. Antrim:

. . . as regards the farming I had a notion of going back to New England about February or March but there has been a land bill "past" that is a great barrier to the "setteler"; it is in favour of the squatter; "their" is a great many of them in power so the[y] make the laws to suit themselves like the landlords of Ireland, but if I went back to New England there is a mate of mine "their", we would have "leaced" a run and put cattle on it but it is very "chancey" for your cattle dying in a dry season.

As a powerful additional complication, his brother had proposed that they might buy a farm coming on the market in the Islandmagee district, and then James could return to Ireland. To this James responded that he 'would like very much to live with my friends', but 'if you thought it would go over its value I don't care "fore" going into much "det". I can make a very good living out here but it is a very wild country . . .'

James stayed in Australia. On 26 April 1887 he wrote to his brother from a farm he had bought at Failford, Lower Walamba River, seeking to borrow money to extend his farm: he wanted to buy an island opposite it. He had a hundred pounds in the bank, but he wanted that to build a house on his farm, to which he now proposed to move permanently; his employment drawing logs had proved profitable, but hard work. His brother sent the money. In his acknowledgement, James made a cautious effort to divert the American emigration process:

> I was thinking you would [have] been married by this time, that you could have sent Doley out to me. Ned Heggan was saying that it was near time I had my "speal" of her; you were saying that Aunt "Marget" is going to America. I wish she would come to me but it is a long way but I could give her a good home. James is married and William will be in lodgings; she would suit me very well; she might not care for so quiet a place as farming in the bush of Australia. I do all my "owen" cooking; it takes up a good deal of my time; she would be comfortable and would like the "climat" very well and I believe her and I would get along very well; if she is not gone away you might see what she would think of it; she will think it rather unkind of me never writing to her.

Farming was only one — although a major — avenue of employment. R. Motherell had fallen on his feet as a ballroom decorator in Sydney. On 9 August 1890 he wrote from 22 Castlereagh Street to a friend in Ireland, telling him of his success, and of the arrival of his wife and some friends, the Beazleys, for whose daughter he had been able to get employment:

> Lilly goes to a nice situation tomorrow morning in a high classed art store, a place I have been able to get here and though she really has had no experience of business she gets a good salary to start with and she is greatly pleased at this.
>
> As to Mr. and Mrs. Beazley they have not quite decided yet what line they will go into, but I fear not that in a very short time I shall be able to locate them safely in some handy place either to manage a small club or boarding house. There are some fine places of that kind here . . .
>
> I have been making considerable headway and have had the doings of some first class ballrooms etc. and all my efforts have met with success and been very much admired by the guests and spoken highly of by the Press, so that is good and I am glad to find that my experience gained in the old country serves me well here and will doubtless stand to me a.1.
>
> I have joined hands with a Portrush chap a Mr. Richardson, better known as the chap who used to win a lot of races at the swimming races at Pickie Rock at Bangor, so is it not really wonderful how people tumble together nowadays. Truly the world is small. He is a very handy sort of fellow and as he was looking out for something of the line we are in, we tumbled together and took a place which so far suits us well and are kept very busy and your new nurios [?] that I have introduced for ballroom decoration and sale take well, so that we never know what results may come yet.

William Quinn was doing well as a miner in Broken Hill, sending his mother in Falls Road, Belfast, quite frequent bank drafts, perhaps £10 every three or four months. The 1890 strike was a major event, as he explained on 7 October 1890:

We had a great strike all over the country, New Zealand as well as all the mines were stopped for five weeks and all the coasting steamers are still stopped as the men are still out on strike. It was with the shipping that the strike first started as the sailors were all union men so then the ship owners got blackleg labour to run the boats, so the coal miners would not let the boats get coal, so steam boats and railways have been stopped. The Government sent large forces of police and volunteers to shoot the men down but the men all turned out to a man and were well armed and drove the police and volunteers back and took some of the cannons of[f] them that the Government sent to shoot the miners with, so now the miners will shoot them with them; the men are sti[c]king well together and the Government can't do nothing with them, so I think the strike will soon be settled.[6]

But in writing to his mother on 28 October 1892 he described how he had come to be directly affected by the industrial turmoil which had begun in 1890:

I have been away from Broken Hill for a short time, as we have all been out on strike for the last 17 weeks and no telling when we will go to work again. The mine owners was wanting to lower the wages, so the men all struck to a man; there is 7,000 men on strike; we struck on the 4th July last, so things are in a very bad state in Broken Hill, as there is no other work but "minen" in this part of New South Wales so all the men are walking about the streets. There has been about 1,500 men left the Hill since the strike. There has been some "ruff" work here since the strike as the mine owners have been fetching miners from other parts so the government have sent large bodies of police to keep law and order; there has been some shots fired but no lives lost as yet; there are 8 of our leaders in jail; their trial is going on at present; we all thought that they would get about five years but I think the way the trial is going that they will get off with a short term; they are all married but three.

He added a complaint about the attitude of his brother John who was unable to get work in Belfast.

Why don't he try his hand at something else. If I was out of work like that I would try any kind of work rather than be idle. Since the strike took place myself and four other men went out prospecting; we walk[ed] 100 miles out and in and carried our "swagges". So if a man was to sit down in this country he would starve here just the same as he would in the home country; "they nothing got" here but what a man works for.

He was still in Broken Hill in 1893, with his money in the Commercial Bank, which had stopped payment. By 1895, either by choice or because he had lost his job in Broken Hill, he was on Hannans goldfield, Western Australia, still sending money to his mother, having by 1897 progressed from labouring at £3 10s.0d. a week to underground manager at £7 10s.0d. In 1905, after injuring his leg, he was out of work in New Zealand, living on what appears to be substantial assets: in 1906 he sent his brother in Ireland £110 in gifts to the family. And he had become a little embarrassed by his family and friends. His brother Patrick was gum digging in New Zealand, but addicted to drink and thus no social asset. Some of the mail he got from Ireland was primitively addressed and written: it might do for Ireland, William observed, but it was unacceptable in the colonies.

Writing on 4 February 1887 from South Melbourne John Sayers[7] was perplexed as to how to advise his brother, a Methodist clergyman in Ireland, on the question of emigration. He was comfortable enough himself: he was in commerce, his wife kept a small shop and they rented out two cottages. But the matter of full time employment in the service of colonial religion was another problem entirely, particularly as support for a family in the style to which they were accustomed was involved.

> I feel in a difficulty when I try to tell you everything in the way of advice. In the first place I fear you should not feel at home or happy in any other calling then the one you are in, so long as you are able to discharge the duties pertaining to it.
>
> And I also see the difficulty of combining it with any other so as to make both contribute to your support and that of your family. Then again supposing that you decided that it is your duty to abandon the work of the Ministry in order to make better provision for your family, the most promising thing for you, and that which you could best do, would be to go back into the country and purchase or select a block of land 2 or 3,000 acres or more, on which you could do a little cultivation and graze on the remainder. But would that be the kind of life you would chose for your family or would they like it.
>
> You might be within an hour's ride of your nearest neighbour and 3 or 4 times that distance from the nearest school, and that not much good if there was one in the district at all. You might have no church unless you made it in your own house and as to society you can judge.
>
> Accepting these *drawbacks* (as most people would reckon them) and have a fair amount of capital to start with, success financially is pretty certain.
>
> I have often thought such a life much more natural than the way we do live packed together in large towns. It is certainly more patriarchal.
>
> But are there no other modes of living open to a man like me beside going and getting buried alive in the bush? There are, and some of our ministers here who have become unfit for the active work but who have physical strength and mental energy are going well as insurance agents and in business . . . that sort of thing would allow you to live in the heart of the community near to the best schools and colleges and where you could preach as often as you liked *for nothing*. And you might get something for preaching too; it often happens that a new district wants developing and a circuit does not wish to take the responsibility of going to conference for a young man which means a married man after 4 years but to pay £100 or £150 to a good local man or superannuated man for doing the work. And besides there would be opportunities for the young ladies, if so disposed, to earn some money by teaching either privately or in some of the schools or colleges. Or another way which I suppose most people would call best of all if you had sufficient money to invest you could live on the profits and just do as much good as you could and in any way you pleased.
>
> There is a very much better return for money invested or lent here than in your country. Banks give from 5 to 6 per cent and building societies which are as safe as banks give 7 per cent for money deposited for 12 months. But capitalists can often find customers for money at 10 or 12 per cent with ample security.
>
> I do not know if I can say anything more that might assist in deciding as to your course. I do not know what amount of capital you could bring with you nor do I know if you have any right conception of the character of a new country like this or America. I know that the whole thing was a surprise to me . . .
>
> I am glad I came for several reasons and I still believe it to be in many

respects the best country under the sun. Yet when all that is said many come here and are disappointed, not finding a niche into which they can fit themselves and where they have the means, sometimes after wasting time and money, return to the old land.

In 1892 Isaac Sloane, then an elderly man, left Ireland to live with his married daughter Elizabeth and son-in-law in the small town of Orange in New South Wales. A keen and humorous observer and something of a 'character', Sloane wrote home frequently of his Australian impressions to another married daughter back in Ireland. On 31 July 1892 he assured her that 'All the colonists wishes you home rule [and] think it would be so good for you'. He was much struck by the riding habits of the locals. 'The postman rides telegraph [boys] rides, labourers ride town boys and girls ride from the cradle to the grave. I wonder they don't ride to bed. The horse in general is neither groomed nor cared for, saddle taken off and let go. Race horses is the only cared for animal'. In this he was much struck by the priorities of the locals. 'There is a lot of Irish papests in and about Orange but polliticks is at a very low eb. It seems that if there was an election and a race meeting on the same day there would be few at the pole'. Later he was to note 'no open bigots here': in July 1892 he observed 'You won't be ast what you are at least I haven't yet' a strange experience for one used to a society which revolved around religious division. But then the colonies were remarkable in other ways too. It was said the economy was in bad shape. No wonder, if a man would not work for less than five bob for eight hours, tradesmen 10 shillings. They do everything slovenly. Indeed they didn't like to farm at all: some farmers bought their spuds sooner than hire labour. And they seemed to think nothing of money when they got it. And you could not get a man to dig: they ploughed the ground, scratched in the seed and left it to providence. As a consequence 'the chinamen raises nearly all the vegetables and know how to charge for them'. He would see to it that this was changed. He began digging, and fencing a garden, digging deep in the half hope that he might find gold. In a few months he had set up a fowl run, and had a cat with kittens. Soon he added a horse, a cow and a calf, geese, parrots, a talking magpie, two tom cats and a fox terrier. And he had become indispensible: 'I am everything here Cow boy foul Boy Coach man gardiner house steward'. Children liked him. He gambled a little — a building society lottery in Brisbane — and had enough money for drink when he wanted it. His loins and legs never seemed to get quite well, but he had the best vegetable garden in Orange, beating the chinamen. He dreamt a lot, sleeping and waking, of Ireland, market day, distant and dead friends whose faces he saw daily in his mind's clear eye. If he had won that lottery he would have paid his Irish relatives a visit — 'not that I would care for living in Ireland though I had very happy times in it. No man had better times than I have that is for eating drinking and wearing yet I am not fully contented at the same time I will never be fit for the rough life of Australia too old for that nor can I fall [out?] with the old friend . . .' And there was the climate. Another of his married daughters lived at Hay, where they 'are all but roasted . . . not a green blade of grass a bad place for an Irishman and he wants something green to look at . . .'

Isaac Sloane had made himself 'a man of all works' around his daughter's house. She was moving up in the world; they shifted to a new and larger house in April 1893, to the annoyance of her old father who disliked 'flitting': he thought his daughter had 'house property on the brain', believed it involved needless expense, and hated the disruption of moving. His daughter's elevated social aspirations required of him appropriate adjustments of social role. The expected performance was that of the venerable patriarch, a role which he obligingly attempted but found very exhausting to sustain: 'I am killed trying to do the grand old man', he complained to his daughter in Ireland on 2 September 1893. A role much more to his liking (and no doubt to his Australian daughter's fury) was that of 'the rough Irish man', in which he exaggerated his own origins for the purpose of debunking the pretensions of visitors he chose to believe had descended from convict ancestors. He described the essentials of his performances in a letter to Ireland on 15 April 1893:

> She [his daughter Elizabeth] has great times paying and receiving visits as she "mooves" in the upper ten, as I call them, the[y] are all so fine. I do the rough Irish man, by the way, and takes "sum" of the[m] down about their language. The[y] seem to know so much in one generation by their forefathers as they were clumsey allowing themselves to be "catched" thieving and then getting a free passage and "rashings". The[y] don't like it for the[y] are "realy" good looking and smart.

Nevertheless, Isaac Sloane was a convert to colonial ways — or most of them: he didn't care for the distance that seemed to separate neighbours and keep secret their beliefs and Sunday observances. But of the superiority of the colonial political situation he had no doubt whatever. Australia had home rule to a far fuller extent than Ireland ever would: 'all we have british is a governor and the country gets on first rate.' On 26 May 1893 he wrote to Ireland: 'the Queen's Birthday is over, it is a general holiday and all classes seem to be loyal and rejoice alike. I suppose you will be that way in dear old *Ireland* after you have turned your 'speers" into plough and your swords into "prooning" hooks but very likely you may use them a little first more fools you'.

Of course not all families stayed close: they wandered, quarrelled, fragmented, to the pain of those at home. On 22 April 1893 Daniel Quigley in Seralba, replied to his married sister, Mrs Susanna Bell, in Belfast, who was enquiring about the whereabouts of her son William:

> I am sorry that I am not in a position to give you the desired information as to Willy['s] whereabouts. About 5 years ago I heard from him; he was at a place in the north west of Queensland about 2,000 miles from here. If I remember right it was the Seatopa gold fields he was on at the time he wrote me. I have not heard from him since nor of him from anyone.
>
> I often see the Joseph of our family in the form of our oldest brother Patrick, but as he and the writer has not spoken for the past 13 years, any information that he could give me on the subject I am not likely to get, but in this case I will get a friend of mine to interview him on the subject of Willy's whereabouts. I will write to my friends in the different Queensland gold fields and see if I can find him; as soon as I can get any trace of him I will let you know at once. There is very little doubt but he is all right in some of the colonies; I suppose by this he is hitched to some of the banana women in the north or west of Queensland with a family of his own and quite forgotten that he left an old mother in the Emerald Isle to mourn his loss or to dream about his death or otherwise. However old gairl you can make yourself quite easy in your mind for he will turn up some day all right, perhaps with a big nugget in his fob[?] and half a dozen of young Bells with him and Mrs. Bell but let us hope that she won't be black as I was very near getting hitched up to a black myself. There is nothing impossible for a colonial in the back blocks to be up to, but for fear you should think that I married a black princess or an old jin for to colonize myself, I will get Mrs. D. Quigley to

send you her photo and that of my gairl, Doris Bell Quigley who was 2 and a half years and my son, so she say, Charles Banister who was 1 year and 6 months at the time the pictures were taken. I got married in June 1889 and of course those two are the result of that union. Do you think that I got hitched up too young; of course they say that the older we get the foolisher we become.
I have been all over the country where Willy is now, some nineteen years ago and I may be able to find him out: to advertise for him might be useless, for I have been in places where we never seen a newspaper from Christmas to the next Christmas. I am sorry to hear that you have been troubled but Burns said that man was made to mourn and I suppose he meant woman too.

In fact William had written to his mother a month previously from Back Creek, Wellington Road, New South Wales. He had been in Queensland but had not seen Daniel, only his other uncle Patrick who alleged that, as trustee, Daniel had maladministered their mother's estate — wills and legacies were a prolific cause of family disputes. William explained to his mother why he had not written:

You will think that I have forgotten you all but no, I never can do that but things has been very bad out here and I kept waiting for a turn but none has come as yet but I hope that you will forgive me for the way I have neglected of writing to you years ago, but dear mother, I have been knocked about a great deal since I wrote last. I have been at death['s] door in Queensland twice with the fever but thank God I pulled through, but it was touch and go with me the last time for when I got over the fever I had no money and I was among strangers, and far away back in Queensland and as weak as a child, so it was pretty hard lines but I thank God I pulled through. I left Queensland soon after and came to N[ew] S[outh] W[ales]. A man, an old mate of mine, paid my way down to Sydney, and from there up the country 300 miles and we both got work on a new railway that was "a making". So, dear mother, things were so bad I did not care about writing as I had no good news to send but I hope that the[y] will soon take a change for the better.

While some immigrants thought in terms of survival, and lived from day to day, others planned — or dreamt — for the future. Robert Gass who lived in North Goulburn told his sister on 5 April 1896:

I am laying out my plans to be able [to] cease work when I am 50 years of age, but man proposes and God disposes, and none of us knows what the future has in store for us. However we can only do our best.
Today I am 33 years of age being born on the 5th April 1863 so that in 17 years more I intend to return home for good, that is if God wills it so. No doubt 17 years is a long time to look forward to, but it is a short time to look back . . .

Reversals, the collapse of plans, were the rule rather than the exception. What was unusual was the fairy-tale twist to the story of Joseph Witherow in Townsville, North Queensland. On Christmas Day 1898, he wrote to his uncle and aunt in Coolban, Garvaghy, Co. Londonderry: they had not answered previous letters.

Well Uncle and Aunt I have been a bit unfortunate this last eleven months past, I had a good situation in the leading Shipping Firm here as (Wharfinger & Delivery Clerk) until we got two New Managers from Sydney up here, they both are Roman Catholics Mr. Doyle was my boss as Shipping Manager & Mr. Condell as Merchandise Manager. Whenever they found out that I was an Irish Protestant they both had a set on me, with the result I had to leave my Billet to make room for a man who owed the firm a lot of money.[8] The rumour went round that I would have to leave to let this man get my situation so I wrote out my resignation to give them, as I had another better situation offered to me if I would take it, in the Shipping line too, but I was advised to not give in my resignation until I first asked this *Mr. Doyle* if there were any truth in the rumour that was going. He said to me no there are no truth in it Witherow & dont believe any lying reports, so I took his word as truth & did not give him my resignation & one week after that he came to me & said Witherow your time will finish in a week so what do you think of an old scoundrel like that. I lost the other situation through his telling me lies, so I have never dropped into a good permanent situation since.

Joseph Witherow was married with three young children. On 28 November 1899 — nearly a year had elapsed — his uncle replied:

> Well I may say that I am not as young as I once was nor yet as I was when you and I last parted. The years are telling on me and although I cannot complain of health yet I feel that my business is getting rather heavy for me and that before long I will have to get the load lightened some way. Thinking over latterly what would be the best thing to do as you are aware I have not many relations who would suit to carry out the ideas which I want carried out, and I have come to the conclusion to put before you the following proposal;—
>
> As you are aware I have two farms of land at home and the other in Upper Coolban which you know. Now that upper farm consists of about 80 acres or thereabouts some of it rough but a large portion of it level and arable with fences gates and in the best of order. It is bought out for ever the interest to be paid annually is about £15 for 49 years and of these 7 years are already paid so that about 40 years would remain when it would be free for ever. There is a big farm house on it which could easily be made comfortable or rather two houses and the whole has been valued at about £1,000. Now I want to say and do now say that wishing to keep some one of my name to represent me in the neighbourhood where I spent my life, if you and your wife and children agree to come home and take the said farm free of any debt or incumbrance and settle down and live on it I will make it over to you as a free gift as soon as you come. I also wish to add that in the event of your coming home and doing as I offer there are several things which would be of advantage in addition. My house here is open to you and your family until the upper one could be put in order. Farming implements are here which would not have to be bought and I may say that the Creamery system of which there is a branch at Garvagh has made the butter & Cattle trade the best paying business we have and the farm is admirably adapted for that particular branch of farming.
> Your aunt joins in hoping that you will see your way to accept this offer and that if you do so she will be glad to see yourself and wife and family and to do what she can to make you comfortable until you get settled down and to lend a helping hand in starting on your new place.

It was a dream offer which Joseph in Townsville accepted with exhilarated alacrity and fulsome professions of undying gratitude. He could hardly believe his good fortune. By March 1900 he and his family had begun the voyage back to 'Old Ireland' — after borrowing a necessary £10 against his uncle's name, permission presumed.

The fairy tale lacked a happy ending. The Witherow correspondence survives because of its inclusion as evidence with the briefs relating to the legal action taken in 1902 by Uncle John against his nephew Joseph in relation to their dispute over ownership of the farm.

5

LOVE STORY 1880-1883

Alexander Crawford was born in Belfast on 5 May 1857, the older son of James Wright Crawford and Madge Crawford, nee Mathews. The Crawford family had settled in Ireland in the seventeenth century, and by the nineteenth had become a virtual epitome of Ulster history. Its earlier members were Presbyterian ministers, but the nineteenth century saw them prominent in science and manufacturing, through the discovery of a formula for chlorine bleach. By the time of Alexander's birth the family had converted to devout Methodism, lived in a mansion aptly named 'Chlorine', and was involved in a range of chemical manufacturing, centred on a bleachworks and starch making.[1]

Alexander—Alick—Crawford was educated at Queen's College, Belfast, and at Albert Agricultural College in Dublin. Various relatives had emigrated to Australia, notably Mrs Crawford's brother; the Mathews family had a farm at Linton near Ballarat in Victoria. Early in 1880, when he was twenty-two, Alick came to Australia to visit these relations,[2] eventually arriving at the Linton farm where he helped with the work, felling trees, mending fences, working in the garden and helping with the cattle. He got to know the three Mathews girls, his cousins, who had been born in Ireland but emigrated as children with their parents; Mattie was the youngest, aged fifteen: Mary Bell was the oldest — his own age: and Elizabeth Jane — Lillie — was eighteen, and described by Alick to his parents as 'my girl . . . she sits on my knee in the evenings and gets me to tell her of home . . . '

Alick was strongly attracted to his cousin Lillie, and when he left Linton, first to work on a station at Gunnedah in New South Wales, later on gold diggings, he tentatively began a correspondence with her. He was keenly aware that there would be family opposition to the development of anything more than a friendly relationship between cousins, and also unsure of Lillie's reaction to his writing. She responded warmly, and when, after a year in Australia, he was about to return to Ireland, he did so after a further stay at the Linton property, at which time they quietly became engaged. On his way to Melbourne in April 1881 to board the *Lusitania,* he stayed with other relations at Ballan. They probed and teased, but he kept his love to himself, sensitive to the possible reaction to the

The Crawford's family home 'Chlorine' (later 'Cloreen'), Malone Road, Belfast. The front door, and a back view, prior to demolition in 1953 to provide a site for Queen's University extensions. (Courtesy: Belfast Telegraph*)*

Front door of Cloreen, Malone Rd. Demolished in 1953 to provide the site for University's new Engineering College.

idea of cousins marrying, and to the expectation of some of the family that he was returning home to secure an Irish wife. His relations attributed his preoccupation and mooning about to the excitement of going home; to Lillie he confided in the first of his love letters (20 April 1881); 'You have no idea my own darling how I miss you. I feel as if there was a something put on my spirits that was crushing me and all my spirits out.'

The dining room in the Crawford family home in Belfast, prior to the 1953 demolition. A portrait of Alexander's mother is above the fireplace. (Courtesy: Belfast Telegraph*)*

Alexander Crawford did not stay long in Ireland. By October 1881 he had arrived back in Melbourne, wishing that he had stayed in Australia, married Lillie, and returned home with her to confront his parents with his marriage as an accomplished fact. As it happened, his father in particular was strongly opposed to the marriage of cousins, a stance no doubt taken on principle, but complicated by what appears to have been his anticipation that his son would follow him in the Belfast business. The outcome was a row over the question of money to help Alick set himself up in Australia; whether his father refused to give it or Alick refused to accept it is uncertain, but it was not given — and Alick made it clear to his parents that they could not expect him to return to a house where his wife would not be welcome. The breach was neither complete nor final — more a stand-off between a stern father and a determined son — but their relations thereafter remained cool and distant.[3] His father appears to have hoped it was a passing infatuation, and was anxious that relatives in Ireland not know of the engagement; aware of this, Alick wrote to as many as he could — fifteen letters in one day — publicising it. To Lillie, he wrote in anticipation of seeing her again, and in recollection of their happiness:

> O how I did enjoy those happy happy hours, and how I keep counting and thinking that in two clear days more I shall clasp my own darling once more to my heart and have her chat to me, smooth my hair, and now and again muster up enough courage to give me a loving kiss. O how those kisses do thrill me, the recollection of them is sweet for weeks after. Sometimes I almost feel as though you were present with me. O my own darling, how I do long for the time when you shall be my own in very deed and these bitter "partins" and separations over, and all uncertainty shall have ceased.

The longest separation was about to begin. A month later, in November 1881, Alexander Crawford was on his way to Western Australia, a lock of Lillie's hair with him in a black enamelled locket. At first they thought he would be compelled to seek his fortune in America, that distant El Dorado where all things were still possible; with this prospect in view, Lillie dramatically released him from their engagement. But there was a nearer land of hope. In a decision taken after prayer and a committal of his ways to the Lord — in keeping with his firm Methodist convictions — he accepted the proposal of a Dr Hope of Perth that he take the management of a jointly purchased sheep station in the remotest area of outback Western Australia. The property, 'Erridabubba', was in the Murchison River district and carried about 9000 sheep. It had cost £12000, of which £6000 was borrowed from a bank; Crawford held a fourth share, apparently in recognition of his managership. Seeing himself as partly estranged from his parents, denied their assistance, and cast on his own energies and resources to make his way in the world, he looked on his fate with stoicism, as a kind of balance to an excess of happiness and as an ordeal through which their love must pass. He told Lillie (18 November 1881):

> I do so miss your dear kind loving arm so round my neck so much and I miss your soft warm cheek on mine. But we were too happy for it to last long I suppose, but I shall comfort myself with the thoughts of the past, knowing that there are brighter and greater joys to come when we shall be united, not part as we have had to.

He also sent her the words of Thomas Moore's popular sentimental ballad 'Oft, in the Stilly Night',[4] a packet of Sturt's desert pea seeds for her mother, and the pious wish that 'may He who never slumbers or sleeps watch over and keep you my precious one until in his own good time we meet again'.

At first, it was merely the financial hazards of his new employment that concerned Crawford. On 13 April 1882 he wrote to Lillie from Geraldton in Western Australia, where he had stopped to buy horses and provisions for the three week journey inland to his station:

> I do hope I will be successful in this station. The last manager lost nearly £500 a year on it but everyone says it was through bad management. When I come to think of it it seems a risky undertaking for one with so little experience as myself to undertake to manage and bring a station, in a state of utter disorder, into good order. I have scarcely had one year's experience but if close attention to it and hard work will do anything towards making it pay it shall not be lacking on my part. And I am the more encouraged when I think it is not myself alone I am working for but for the *dearest girl living.* Oh Lillie *my own true love* I would undergo anything for your sweet sake and count it but pleasure if I but brought you the nearer to me. I often think what would life be to me now without the *love of my Lillie.* I managed to get along in a kind of a way before but now it would be misery indeed. Tis the

sweetest thought I have that before long I hope to take you to myself for better, there will be no worse in it. Sure there won't. Do tell me more about yourself in your letters. Fill them up about Lillie, commence with Lillie, end with Lillie, and fill the space between with the same subject, and you may add a postscript about her too, it will not be too much. It is a subject I never weary reading about, writing about, or speaking about, so satisfy me in this respect my little girl. I am looking as if I had just escaped from prison, my hair cut close and my beard also. I do wish I could make my mustache grow a bit longer. It sticks at the one length much to my disgust. Is not this vanity worse than a girl, I fancy I can hear you say. Perhaps by the time you see me next it may have stretched a little and you may not be able to get at my lips. How will that do?

But when, over a month later, on 24 May, he wrote to describe his journey, and conditions on his station, more immediate problems and hazards had become evident. He had travelled inland with a small party which became separated, Crawford becoming lost when crossing seventy miles of bare sandy plain. He found water several times and eventually tracks, but had great difficulty in making himself understood to an Aboriginal shepherd before being led to an outstation. He told Lillie:

. . . it was all I could do to drag myself along. I was stiff and sore in every joint. At last I reached the hut and found the hutkeeper and he immediately set about getting something to eat. I was now 72 hours without having anything at all to eat. I thought a good wash all over would revive me so I went down to the river and it looked so tempting I undressed and jumped into a deep hole. I was scarcely in until I was paralysed all over and could not move my legs or hands at all. I came to the top, then went down again, then up and I saw a branch of a tree hanging over my head and with a great effort I managed to move my hand up and catch it and I slowly drew myself to shore. After some difficulty I got out and then I began to come to and was soon alright and went up to have a good tuck in but at the first mouthful I was sick and could scarcely eat anything. A few hours after, I managed to eat a good substantial meal.

Nor was becoming lost, with attendant hunger and thirst, the only source of danger and difficulty. Crawford also encountered torrential rain and floods on his journey, and arrived to be confronted by housing which was primitive and miserable in the extreme. The homestead was one room, twenty feet by twelve, made of poles, with walls and roof of rushes. There were two beds, each made of four forked sticks driven into the earth, with two rails in the notches and then barrel staves laid across. The station community consisted of about thirty men, ten white. The nearest neighbour was sixty-eight miles south-west. And there was what the white men regarded as a serious Aboriginal problem, which Crawford outlined to Lillie on 25 May 1882.

The natives up here are very troublesome, one of the men has just come and told me one shepherd had three killed last night, and for the past week scarcely a day has passed without some being killed in one or other of the flocks. We never go a couple of hundred yards from the hut without our revolvers or a gun. I am the farthest back, most remote from civilisation in Western Australia. It is about 80 miles to my nearest neighbour in one direction, that is north west. South west it is 68 miles, east a couple of thousand, and south about 800, so I am pretty well isolated. I have nine

> white men on the station and about 20 niggers, some I only keep and feed to keep them from killing the sheep. They are the most primitive lot I have seen. They wear no dress nor covering of any kind. Some of the men have a string tied round their waist to stick their boomerang or Corvak in and some a string round their foreheads through which they stick kangaroo bones as ornaments. They are good natured among themselves and share all their food in common. They will never eat anything if there are others about without sharing it, sometimes giving it all away and going without himself. They have no religion nor idea of God they are afraid of an evil spirit they called 'Gingie' and they have long flat pieces of wood with a hole at one end for a string this they whirl round their head and it makes a curious moaning sound and they think it keeps off the 'Gingie'.
>
> The women are not allowed to see them; if they do and a man gets to know about it he will kill her. Some odd times they indulge in cannibalism, but not often, and they only eat black fellows that's one consolation.[5]

To Crawford, Aboriginal sheep-stealing represented a serious threat, one, at least in his case, more complex than offered by the killing of his livestock, the challenge to white authority, and the dangers of attempting to catch the culprits. There were nearly 9000 sheep on the station, but his immediate assessment of its prospects, virtually on arrival, was that despite excellent rains and feed, it would not pay even working expenses for several years. As Crawford saw the situation, the question of selling out, at profit, was present from the beginning, greatly sharpened for him by his impatience at his enforced separation from Lillie, and by his dependence on this venture to set him up for marriage as soon as possible. In addition, he was under constant and annoying pressure from his mother to renounce his Australian life and ambitions and return home to what she saw as his proper position as elder son. Native sheep-stealing was thus to him more than a direct erosion of his assets, it amounted to an assault on the realisation of his ambition and dreams, a challenge to his determination to succeed, and a factor frustrating his plans to prove himself to his parents and fiancee. This led him to vigorous efforts to defend his property — and all it symbolised. And it was part of his necessary self-image that he should cut a fine figure while doing so. On 29 May he described a 'nigger hunt' to Lillie, with himself in a swashbuckling central role:

> The natives are killing the sheep here wholesale. On Friday I had four killed and a black fellow came in and told me about it and where he thought they were camped, so I got a couple of horses up and put him on one and although it was almost dark, still the moon was up and it would not be very dark and I went off to try and catch the thieves. Would you like to know how your Big Boy looked, well I will try and describe him. Medium height and fair with some beard and whiskers of a duckety mud colour, a soft hat with a veil hanging on it, a flannel shirt open in front, no buttons or studs and sleeves rolled up to elbows, a pair of mole skin trousers kept up by a leather belt with a leather watch pouch on the left-hand side and a silver chain running from it to one of the studholes in the shirt, on the right-hand side a leather pouch with some string, matches and a knife (I hardly ever smoke now), in front a Colt 6 chambered revolver just where you can put your hand on it at a moment's notice. A pair of top boots and spurs and a double-barrelled gun in a leather gun bucket suspended from the saddle, the whole mounted on a fine coal black mare . . . I rode on until about half-past eight p.m. when we came to a waterhole about where the native with me thought they were

camped. We found the camp but they had gone somewhere else that morning. I rode up towards the range for about three hours and then as we came to a waterhole I thought we had better camp, so I hobbled the two horses with my stirrup leathers and lit a fire and lay down beside it and slept until morning. I had expected to be home by 10 or 11 the same night and had brought nothing to eat, so I told the black who goes by the name of Monkey to look for some colias, a kind of root not unlike the potato in appearance and sweet and some Bardies a kind of grub that is about 2 inches long. He soon found some and we cooked both in the ashes and made our breakfasts of them and then we went on looking for blacks. About 11 o'clock we came on some tracks which we followed up and soon Monkey pointed out something but I could see nothing. He said gallop which I did in the direction he pointed and I saw a black fellow run and try to hide under a bush. I made straight for him and all at once my mare jumped over a bush and as she did so I saw two black fellows under it so I pulled her up as quickly as possible and wheeled round just in time to see one of them fitting a spear in his Womera to throw at me, I had not a moment to lose so I pulled out my revolver and shot him in the leg. This frightened the others and I managed to take three and broke all the weapons I found about. One of them on the way back, picked up a stick and tried to hit me with it, but I had my eyes too sharp on them to give him a chance, so all he got was a crack with the butt end of my revolver on the head for his trouble. The one I shot was not much the worse, only a flesh wound through the fleshy part of his leg; it will be alright in a day or two. I did not like firing at his body for fear of seriously injuring him. With a good deal of difficulty I chained them up by the neck and made them fast to a tree. I told one of the other black fellows to make a fire beside them and gave them some supper and left to this morning. I made enquiries as to whose they were and found two were strangers and the other had killed a sheep some months before. The first two I let go and the other I gave half a dozen cracks with a whip and told them if I ever knew them to kill a sheep again I would beat them well and send them to jail.
I found that there was no difference made here between Sunday and any other but I have stopped all kinds of work except what is absolutely necessary so that at least we have the quiet of that day.
You ought to see me morning and evening feeding the blacks. There are about a dozen round the station who do anything that is wanted — I give them damper and meat and boil our tealeaves over again for them and put some sugar in it for them. They are very generous, divide all they get with all present, no matter how many. One who gets it given to him will go without himself rather than let another who got none go without. They get it made up to them by the others who bring in bush food and divide just the same. I gave a couple of the best of them a shirt and trousers to keep them warm these cold nights but to my surprise when they were going to sleep they took all off them and lay down in the cold absolutely naked.

A few days later (2 June 1882), he described a similar incident, in which he had caught, during a casual night-time inspection, one of his own native shepherds playing host to an Aboriginal sheep-roasting. Later, approaching in stockinged feet, he had apprehended several Aborigines at gunpoint while they slept: one he had chained around the neck shook so much with fear, that the rattling of his chains warned others, who escaped. Crawford apologised to Lillie for the monotony of his letters: 'the only incidents that occur are nigger hunts'. Certainly these were frequent and arduous. On 2 November he complained that the aftermath of one had cost him two sleepless nights: he had a black prisoner to bring sixty miles, but as he was alone, and had no chain, all he could do was sit up and watch him all night. The strain of his total situation was immense. On this particular occasion, when he arrived back at his hut he found mail had arrived, but nothing from his beloved Lillie: he promptly burst into tears of sheer vexation. Any gap in her correspondence threw him into frantic worry and self-doubt.

The other side of this intense personality was evident to his assistant, Frank Monger. Monger had been reading Charles Kingsley's fictionalised story of the exploits of the gallant Anglo-Saxon hero *Hereward the Wake* who had defended England against the Norman invasion. He told Crawford (who reported it to Lillie) that 'when he sees me riding and going about he always fancies that Hereward must have been very like me. Am I to take that as a compliment or not?' Crawford obviously took it as such — it was one of his favourite books — — and extended it to Lillie by comparing her to the learned and noble-hearted heroine Torfrida.

Crawford not only pined for Lillie's letters but dreamt of her constantly:

> I have told some of the natives to get me a young parrot and I will teach it to say 'Lillie pretty Lillie' etc. so that I will hear your name constantly and be ever thinking about you. What is come over you for the past two or three weeks, you have not come to see me just before I go to sleep as you generally do, is it because I go to bed so early about 7 or 8 sometimes or what is the reason? Be what it may, I miss you very much and wish you would maintain your loving visits, the only drawback to them is just as I fancy it is really yourself and can almost feel you and clasp you in my arms, either you fade away or I sink into the arms of death's twin sister. Oh my little girl how I long to have you with me never to leave me again. How I long to have you stroke my hair once more, to smooth the furrows in my brow and as you turn your face up toward mine and display that tempting little rosebuds to press it again and again . . .

He had adopted the practice of calling her 'Wifie', but was increasingly unsure if he could reasonably ask her to join him on the station. It was a crucial matter on which his opinion vacillated. His partnership was for seven years, but he could dissolve it at six months notice. He had a standing plan of saving his salary as manager (£100 a year) and selling the property in a couple of years at a few hundred pounds profit. Later, when arrangements were made for police and a magistrate to be in the area, he thought it might be safe for Lillie. For the moment, in 1882, it was too dangerous. Asked for a description of the interior of the primitive hut he shared with his workmate Frank, Alick supplied a detailed list of what came to his eye. It read — unconsciously — like that of an armoury, an outpost under heavy seige: against the wall, in the boxes that served as shelves, there was food of course, but also 'powder, shot caps, 2 or 3 pistols, half a dozen revolvers, 6 guns', and on the table on which he was writing, 'a couple of revolvers' as well. There were only two white women — squatter's wives — within two or three hundred miles. As to social life, this consisted of assemblages occasioned by the need to give evidence at the occasional trial of natives accused of sheep-stealing: the one Crawford described on 18 June 1882 at a neighbour's property, saw twenty natives tried, all convicted, with sentences of two to three years. The assembled whites stayed on for a week trying to catch some more, but failed. Crawford enjoyed the food, and the opportunity to make music — he on the harmonium, Mr Smith and his son on violin and flute: the repertoire was of the 'Swanee River' and popular hymns kind. Mrs Smith occasionally sent Crawford cake and scones. The Smiths were Scots. Crawford confessed that although some people found the Scots aloof, standoffish, he got along with them 'first rate'.

But Alexander Crawford wrote not to convey news, but love — page after page of it; how they would eventually hug and kiss, how she would look in her sleep, her 'little white throat is lost sight of in the pretty trimming of a night-gown', how they would sleep in each others arms (he would gladly renounce the blanket on the earth where he usually slept to share a mattress with his dearest Lillie), how their love made the estrangement from his parents as nothing. Then there were the incidents of their courtship — moonlight walks, playful kisses stolen during tussels in the pantry, fun at being caught with her on his knee, the little miseries of jealousy, and exasperation at older people's goose-berrying — all these details were recited and reiterated. 'What do I think of my future wife' he asked in a letter which began on 12 October and meandered on over various dates, to 2 November:

> I think she is the most loving tender hearted purest girl I have ever seen or known, that she has a winning loving face that makes you want to love her as soon as seen and, once knowing her, are content to be her slave forever. I think I know no-one can know her and not love her and that she is sure to be a favourite wherever she goes. I think she is a darling and the dearest girl on earth, I think she has two lovely eyes that look more lovingly at me than at anyone else, that her mouth is so sweet and delicious that when I am near it I want a continual feast ever enjoying yet never satieted or satisfied. I think it is one of the most delightful sensations that I can have to have her arms round my neck and her head on my shoulder and wish I could keep them there forever. I think she is like an angel of mercy who takes pity on poor mortals and turns their earth to a paradise, I think the kiss she gave me in the kitchen sitting on the table nearly 3 years ago fixed my destiny. I never got over that. It thrilled through me and when I left Linton and did leave her behind and went to New South Wales that kiss seemed to grow more and more in significance and it assumed immense proportions until the image of Lillie used to be constantly before me . . . to me it seems as if our souls met and refused to be separated again . . .

Crawford saw himself as 'morose'. He was hardly that. But he was introspective and intense, something of the 'hot headed Irishman' he also believed himself to be. Yet on balance he emerges as Hereward the Wake, the confident if complex adventurer. Basically he remained an optimist. He believed his father would come to approve of their marriage, and that his initial doubts about the success of his hazardous sheep-farming venture were misplaced:

> I think this will turn out better than I thought. It would be a pity to throw away a good chance. This may be the tide which if taken on the flow will lead to fortune but if missed I may be borne back on the ebb to struggle in vain forever to regain lost ground — 'hope and be undismayed' — I would be quite content if I had you with me my whole soul longs for your society, to have you with me, to be near me — when you are near I have a feeling that I cannot go wrong — goodnight my loved one . . .

As his optimism flowed, he began more often to picture her with him in the wilderness: her presence would make the desert bloom. He stayed there only for her sake. Why not marry? It would transform the world.

Not that he neglected his job for want of her. Dressing up the natives — skirts and bodices for the women, red jumpers and white duck trousers for the men — afforded him immense amusement, but there were some matters he treated very seriously indeed — and which made him unpopular with his white labour. He explained to Lillie (25 November 1882):

> I will tell you the principal reason for being called a tyrant, because I will not allow any of the men to keep black women which on nearly all the other stations both masters and men do. I may be guilty of what you say, being too fond of bossing, but I do not think so, but I dare say I am but a partial judge and I should think you were even more so. I know at least in most things you are. I never did profess to be a gentleman.[6] I have got rid of all the bad men I had and the ones I have now are all rather decent.

So dedicated was his application to his work that Lillie was caused to wonder if he was not being seduced by the pursuit of wealth. He defended himself reasonably:

> I do not want you to treat me with reverence only with love and that you always do: it is not in your nature to do otherwise. I quite agree with you that happiness is not at all dependent upon wealth. In fact I have rarely known very wealthy people what I would call happy. On the other hand I do not consider poverty conducive to happiness either. It may have the effect of drawing a family closer together but there are many things connected with it not calculated to give happiness. Should it ever become my lot to be possessed of wealth I do not think I should live in a grand style. I prefer quietness, I hope you do too but I do not think I am likely ever to be troubled with that, I have no ambition to be a so-called wealthy man. So long as I have you to love and cherish I shall consider myself rich in the true sense of the word. Yet for your sake I would like to have a fair competence. Did I not hope to have a house of my own sometime and you with me I should be content if I got enough each day to pull me through. That saving young man I wrote about and whose photo you wear in your locket never saved a penny scarcely in his life until within the last year and now he saves all he possibly can and then thinks he does not save near enough, and all that is through you so you see what an influence even a little woman can have on a person whom she loves and who loves her although separated by thousands of miles.

Loneliness and introspection were certainly conductive to self-knowledge, but not all of that was positive and healthy:

> I hate to receive anything and not to be able to return the compliment. I do not mind how much people are indebted to me but I cannot bear to be indebted to anyone if I can at all avoid it. It worries and annoys me. Sometimes I even feel so about you and wish I could do something that would in some measure make up for all I owe you but I can only wait and hope to be able to do so by and by. Then my darling I shall do all I can to prove how much I value you.

He even came to the point of regarding it as his misfortune to have been born an Irishman, an affliction puzzling to Lillie and unexplained by him: she sensibly brushed aside such self-pity.

But the main topic of his concern was the quite practical one of whether it would be possible or not for Lillie to join him on the station. On the answer to that rested both marriage and future career. Lillie had reported her brother Stewart as saying that it would kill their mother with worry if Lillie went there. What if Alick were away for two or three days and the natives were to break into the store? It would kill Lillie with fright. Crawford responded:

> So that is the extent of your confidence in me that you think I would bring [you] up 300 miles in the bush and when I got there, go away for several days at a time and leave you alone. That is the first thing you have ever written that has really hurt me. I don't feel it from Stewart so much . . . But that Lillie, my loved Lillie should thus think of me I did not think possible. With reference to what aunt may have said and what you say about one or two inevitable obstacles that cannot be got over you do not say what they are. If you had, I might have been able to answer or remove them. So you had better let me know what insurmountable difficulties [there] are and if they are really such I must take other measures to make you a home. You see it just comes to this. I am in this for seven years, I may make a good thing out of it by that time. If I leave sooner I have no money to start myself as you know well. If things go on as they are I would feel free to marry soon. If you cannot live up here why I will not stay up here seven years to live a lonely hermit's life and perhaps at the end of that time be delayed again through my not getting something else to do at once. It just comes to this: if the difficulty is considered insurmountable by aunt I will give up this place at once and go and try my hand at something else and either come back and claim for you for my bride in 3 or 4 years time with enough to settle down in comfort, or if I find that I am one of *fortune's fools* I will not ask you to bind yourself to one who may selfishly keep you bound to him and after having thus held out hope to you year after year, perhaps never be in a position to marry you and the best portion of your life gone. I shall think no more on this subject until I get your letter in reply then I shall take steps accordingly.

On 8 December 1882 he made even clearer the strength of his love — and dependence;

> Ah! Lil my darling little wiffie I wish I could hear these magical words 'my Alick my own' from your own dear lips, that would be happiness indeed. I am afraid my 'wiffie' has been a little downhearted when writing to me or you would not think of melancholy things as the future without me. Why my darling I dare not think of the future without you in it. It would give [me] the blues for a month. Oh Lil the very thought of such a thing being possible makes me shudder. As for you bearing it if I were single, I think if you did not marry me and married anyone else I think if ever I met him I would kill him. I would go mad, the idea of another man clasping you my darling loved one in his arms would drive me really mad, the thought of it now makes the blood rush to my face. Lillie I could not bear it. If I could not get you myself I could not let anyone else. It is selfish but I could not help it. I do not feel wounded but I think you must have been in a despondent state and I would not like my little girl to be downhearted, it does not make much matter about me as I am alone but my Lillie must keep a brave heart for she knows her Alick loves her and her alone and those about would feel to see my little one sad. Yes I do love you far better than anyone else in the world and with you alone is bound up my life's happiness.

He had now convinced himself that there were no obstacles to her coming up to live with him on the station after their marriage. He had seen what the place was like, was building a suitable house, and he believed that he understood the natives. But ominously, he had continued to report throughout 1882, punitive expeditions against the Aborigines. On 22 November he reported the taking of twenty-two prisoners by a force of police. The trial had taken place at his station. All were convicted, and sentenced from three to nine years hard labour.

In May 1883 Alexander Crawford was lucky to survive a native attack — or rather, survive their defence against his efforts to apprehend them. His letter to his parents (20 May 1883) describing this serious incident made clear the substantial size of his sheep losses from Aboriginal depredations. It also reflected his fierce determination to strike back with armed violence:

> Having no overseer now I have a great deal of extra work and in fact I am going to try and do without one and save the expense as I have had some heavy losses, nearly seven hundred sheep killed by the natives, most of them ewes heavy in lamb, besides several other severe losses of horses, and about £350 expense my late overseer put the station to during my absence so that altogether things are not looking very promising just now. It is not all prosperity a squatter's life in Australia, any more than in any business elsewhere, and there is far more trouble and anxiety than in almost any other business I know, but such as it is we must bear it. I am labouring under a considerable difficulty in writing having sore eyes. They have been very bad for over a week, so bad that I cannot bear a candle in the hut after sundown and can do nothing but lie on my rug and think or practise on my flute and make all kinds of hideous noises but that does not matter much as there is no one to hear and be annoyed at them.
>
> I had rather a serious encounter with 13 natives the other night I had my left arm rendered useless for days and my left knee badly hurt. It has swollen up considerably and gives me a good deal of pain, besides sundry odd knocks on the back and head. I had to fire 6 shots at them wounding some severely and then I had to fight them with my revolver which I had by the barrel and knocked two down with it when it broke although a strong Colt. I would have been finished I think outright had not my native boy, hearing the firing, come galloping up shouting as he came and the others I suppose thought help was coming and cleared off. It was all I could do to keep in the saddle riding home but I am getting all right again. I have sent a report of it to the Colonial Secretary and the Governor demanding police protection . . . The natives sent in word with one of my shepherds, first spearing him, to say that they would come down altogether and kill all the white men on the place. It may be only an idle threat but I have given out all the revolvers and guns I have to the men, and told them in case of an attack if possible to come into the station and tell me, and I will go and meet them. I have two or three rifles that none of the men can use and with them in daylight I consider myself a match for thirty or more niggers. If they do attack us I'll teach them a lesson once for all that they will remember to the end of their days.

His father saw in this the faults of his son: his letter of 9 August was hardly sympathetic;

> I hope you are getting on with the natives better, your Aunt Matty says kindness goes far with them. Probably if you tried some of this you might do better. But I am sure you are kind naturally, yet you are too much inclined to drive men more than lead. But most likely your views on this point may

> have been modified before now. My mother used to say never use the broken reed if love will do the deed.
>
> I have often shut my eyes to what I see for I know no man is perfect. Then again if I turn fellows off possibly [the need may be worse]. *There is a great deal in the way* we take with men. How we get on. Too exacting is as bad as too careless with them. I do hope you are being used by the Most High in giving out his precious truth and light to those around you. You may do a real *mission* work. May the Lord keep you. I hope we may have good news from you soon.

Critical too was the reaction of his fiancee. Elizabeth Mathews was a person of strong principles and opinions, willing to speak her mind in judgment which was both tempered and pointed by the language of love. Her involvement in Alick's life was committed and constructive — and highly intelligent: she knew his shortcomings and how best to persuade him to change, or think again. She had long urged him to try to heal the breach with his father, although quick to concede that his father was both difficult and depressing to deal with. Given the close family situation of cousins — and with a realistic eye to financial matters — she was anxious that Alick not completely alienate his father through his tendency to harshness. She was determined also that her future husband's soul and moral good be not damaged in his remote pagan world without Sunday. He kept whiskey in his hut for guests, and a casual reference to this led her to think he had broken his practice of abstinence. In her letter of 2 May 1883 she apologized for her misunderstanding.

> What a dreadful set the Gascoyne [River] lot are. Its dreadful to know in this the time of so much gospel knowledge that they have no regard for the Sabbath. Surely they need missionaries and ministers there as much as in the heathen lands . . . Now darling I want you to give me a good scolding for something I wrote to you in my last letter about total abstinence. On reading over your diary I can see my darling is as strict as ever, and I am very sorry I ever wrote about it to you, for I am afraid you will think I have not sufficient trust in you. I am very sorry if I have pained you and I am afraid I have. Tell me I am a very naughty girl for writing such a thing and try and forgive your penitent little girl.

The idea of Sunday without observance of a day of rest, or church service worried her a great deal. She believed that this corrupted goodness and undermined Christian duty: would her future husband remain unchanged and unsullied by this ungodly environment? She was very much in love. Her letter of 1 June 1883 began:

> I wonder what my Alick is doing now. This is Thursday afternoon. I have got 1st June but it is 31st May. They always tell me here if I do anything wrong or stupid that I am in love. So there's an excuse. So you must take it that I am in love if I write down anything wrong or stupid. I expect if you were here you would tell me that you 'hoped I *was* in love'. Well I scarcely need to tell you I am in love, or the person I am in love with need I. My Alick knows that don't you? . . . The best part is yet to come, the purest happiest joy is yet in store for us darling. The time we are both looking forward to so eagerly, when we shall be to each other what we have yet never been, the sharing together of mutual joys, sorrows and the different experiences that come to all homes. Oh darling with what joy we look forward to the fulfilment of our hopes don't we?

Playfully, she suggested that the Australian climate had thawed his northern resolve not to marry:

> Oh dear me love is a queer thing. What made you do such a thing, you a young man who tried to convince us you would never do such a stupid thing as fall in love or get married, why you hooted the very idea of such a thing. Surely there must be some magic at work, or has Australia the effect on cold Northerners of making them hot and rash so that they fall in love, get such fervour unstilled in them that they get quite hot. What is it? Australia must be a funny place, especially Victoria. At any rate you have changed and shall I give the credit to Victoria. Now don't you think you are going to have a very respectful little girl for a wife? If she makes such fun of you now, what will she do by and by? Do as you tell me! Eh!!! Now don't you be thinking you're going to tame me up in the wilds of W.A. Why I'll be as wild as a March hare. Don't you feel afraid of this little monkey's naughtiness? . . . I am in a wicked mood I think this afternoon, I would just like a good piece of fun. I feel I would like to tease you if I were near you. Do you remember I used to tease you when you wanted a kiss and I would just touch your lips with the very point of mine and you would look as though you would shake me, especially if I repeated it several times. You must teach me good manners when you are the veritable lord and master. Oh don't I quake at the thought of the treatment you'll subject me to!!!

By the time of her letter of 29 June 1883, the matter of whether she would join him, after their marriage, on the station, had been resolved — positively and generously on her part. She made light of the difficulties and shortcomings and urged him not to worry about what was lacking in their accommodation:

> I am so glad darling you like the station life and can be happy in it. I am sure that I will like it and be very happy there too with my Alick. Of course it will seem strange to me at first to have no shops etc. but I will soon be used to that. It is a good thing I have not been brought up with dainty ways for it would be a very strange change to one who has been used to life with only its easy and delicate side. You see, if we do not make a very nice and pleasant home there, don't you think we will as time goes on? It will be very awkward to bring furniture so far, it would need to be very carefully packed. You make your mind quite easy about the furnishing of our home, it will please me just the very way my Alick has it, and I do not expect to see in it what you would have if you lived near a town, so don't please trouble yourself that 'you do not think Lillie will like this or be satisfied with that', just because it is bush fashion.

By 13 July — she noted that 'yesterday was the famous 12th July' — Lillie was enquiring if the house had a clothes line and pegs, and if mud bricks made substantial dwellings. The long years of waiting would soon be over;

> I feel though as if I could never love you enough. You are very dear to me my darling, and you know your little girl does love you so much and longs so much to be with you darling, I do get so tired of the waiting especially when no letter comes and it seems as though the time would never pass. But I suppose it will come some day and then we will be so happy, I shall have my own Alick and won't your little girl be proud of her big handsome husband, so proud and happy that I will not know what to do to express my joy.

Into the quiet excitement of these domestic plans and romantic anticipations dropped the violent news, carried in the West Australian columns of the Victorian newspapers, of Alexander Crawford's encounter with the Aborigines, a lurid report which had him speared while gallantly in pursuit of cannibals.[7] This, in addition to the shock it brought Lillie over Alick's safety, transformed the prospect of joining him on the property. She wrote on 20 July;

> Oh my darling what a cheerless world it would seem to me without your precious love and the hope in prospect of being your little wife. And I, although I love you so dearly I don't idolise you darling. I don't love you or think more highly of you than I *know* you deserve and I have no fear of ever being disappointed in you Alick dear. I know what a dear good man I am going to love for a husband, but I know you are not perfect, I know you have feelings, but they do not hinder you being a dear good noble man my darling, and I don't praise you my Alick unless I think you deserve it. I let you know sometimes what I don't like now don't I? It does seem very tantilising not to be able to get men to work at the house, but my darling things seem scarcely fit yet to bring a young wife to the station. In a year's time the blacks may be quieter and more settled and if you sell a [out] station it will take you less from home. I would be willing to go tomorrow, but darling we must do what is best and nothing rashly. At present a young wife there would be a great anxiety. You must be a good deal away and you would not like to leave me and yet the station cannot be neglected, so darling putting to one side the house not being ready, perhaps it is best you are not tempted to come this year. I know it is hard and gladly would I be with you if it were possible my darling, and I know another year of waiting will be hard to bear, but my darling knows a higher hand overrules it all and if He knows that it is not to be this year it will not be. Oh Alick you know it does not cost me no effort to write this. It is a long time to wait and I know we will often feel very lonely without each other. I would it could have been this year my darling. It would have been joy indeed and happiness to have had you sooner and I will try to wait patiently my own. Your little wiffie does love her own Alick so much and does long for the time when I shall be yours indeed.

Moreover, she was most unhappy about the morality of the situation in which he now found himself. In the same letter, in a section written two days later — fittingly a Sunday — she put to him the essence of the problem, seen from her Christian viewpoint;

> I do wish you had not so much to do with the blacks. It is a dreadful thing to be continually hunting down ones fellow creatures, for they are our fellow creatures and have precious and immortal souls. Oh my darling keep your hands free from your fellow creature's blood. For you to need to fire on them makes me feel miserable. It seems dreadful when really in your heart you cannot blame them for taking the sheep. They don't know right from wrong. They only fear the punishment that may be inflicted if the white men catch them. Be very careful in your use of firearms my darling, poor degraded wretches though they are, yet in God's sight they are precious, Christ died for them as well as us, and for this reason we should protect them as far as lies in our power.
>
> We are, I know, apt to look down on them as something little better than beasts, but remember darling they have souls as well as we, and don't let them rise up in judgement against us in the last great day. Keep your hands free from human creatures' blood, or how can we expect God's blessing to rest on us my Alick? We will not prosper if we disregard his commandments.

I know my boy tries to follow his divine master, but we need grace every day darling and we need to fight against our own inclinations else we will sadly go astray.

Crawford's inclinations in the matter were very clear in his letter to his parents — vengeance, and resort to the lesson of slaughter.

But he was not to be allowed, if his fiancee could help it, to follow such inclinations: she was to return later to the matter of treatment of the Aborigines. For the present there were other aspects of his behaviour and lifestyle which she thought demanded correction, which she undertook on 27 July, setting her remarks in the context of an outburst of love:

> You ask me if I forget the 'loves' we used to have. I'll forget I am in existence as soon as forget that darling. How I dwell on the happy times we passed together and look forward to brighter and happier days. Nor do I forget the one on the kitchen table. You remember it so vividly can you remember the *first* you gave me. I think it's time you blushed, please don't give the excuse that there is something red in the room. Dear me what an impudent cousin we had those days. To think of the liberties he took, shocking!!! But I suppose you will be telling me we were just as naughty to permit such things. Ah well, perhaps we *were*. I remember the last kiss you gave me, the last real one in Aunt Mattie's parlour, you said 'we'll say goodbye now before any other others come in' and we gave each other such a real love that it's fresh yet darling. I got another kiss after, but that was when we were all standing in the hall. Oh darling how vividly that day rises before me, how mechanically I went through every thing and tried to talk and laugh as usual, but Oh that I could have been alone, how I missed the one dear face so tenderly loved and the voice that thrilled through me. Your letters are all I could wish letters to be, but I miss the reality, the writer, a blank is here, which only you darling can fill. I want the loving substance, my heart craves for something that will not be satisfied without you. There's a continual unrest an eager expectation, a looking forward to hopes fulfilled, which will not be at rest till I feel I have you by me not to be separated. It's a very queer feeling, intense love for someone. It may be wrong, but I cannot help it that home does not satisfy me as it did a few years ago. I keep longing for something not in the home, a continual yearning to know how you are, whether you are well or not. But I do not wish you to think I am fretting darling, for I am not. I know how that would grieve you and do no good but perhaps harm. But you alone know the feelings I have and understand what the heart longs for and to you only would I thus write . . .
>
> I have been going over your letter and now come to something I would like to speak to you about, but first try and think your little wife is on your knee with her arms round your neck and my head on your shoulder and you with your arm round my waist holding me to yourself and I tell you I want to say something and please give me your serious attention for a few minutes. It's this darling, in some places in your journal it grieved me to read that several times on Sunday you were out laying poisoned baits and riding some distance after sheep and one place firing at some birds in the garden. Now darling you may think I am making a fuss over very small things but darling may they not lead to larger things. I don't want to vex you but I do want my Alick to keep the Sabbath a holy day. These may be small things now, but unless you watch over yourself and pray, they may lead to larger inroads on the Sabbath. O my precious one, my own dear husband guard against the very appearance

of evil. Your little girl prays for you darling and don't forget to pray for yourself my Alick. Don't neglect your study of God's word, my own, do not neglect your precious soul's welfare, it needs daily nourishing and watering or it will go back and not forward. It is easy for me to write and advise easier far than to act I know, but darling it is for your good I write, but I love you very tenderly, you know this don't you, that I do not mean to be fault finding, but I write in love to you, Alick my own.

The skirmish with the Aborigines on his property greatly complicated all their plans. Lillie's mother was frantic with worry at the prospect of her daughter ever going there. Lillie herself taxed Alick with imprudence in pursuing the Aborigines without gathering enough support. And she made it very clear that she would not expect him to bring her there unless there was another white woman already on the station: Alick had been trying for some time to employ a married couple. It was a situation whose difficulties and frustrations turned his mind again to selling the property, and to his various other troubles — such as the rift with his father. On 10 August 1883, Lillie consoled him, counselled perseverance, and put it to him — obviously in response to his dwelling on Irish might-have-beens — that they were better off in Australia:

I know my love is doing his very best. To do the best is all you can do, and I am sure you'll make a good thing out of it. It must take time. You are a very short time there and must expect it to be uphill work for some time but I feel assured you will make it profitable in time if it is possible to do so, my Alick. I was indeed pleased to read your mother's letter my darling. We'll hope in time your father will write as cheerfully too. Maybe my darling your father *unknowingly* has done what is the kindest thing to both you and me. He has prevented us living in Ireland and it may be that Ireland was not the place for either of us; it did not suit your health, that had been proved. I was untried and very young as well. I have been brought up in a warm climate and though not delicate, yet not strong, and it might have brought back the tendency to a weak chest which I am outgrown quite. And Australia agrees with you, my husband dear, you know it does, and once the pecuniary trouble is removed from the station a comfortable happy home can be made, and a happy life enjoyed, and time will bring more population. The land must in time become private property and it will be impossible for people to have such enormous runs. So looking at it in this light only, yours and my health, we see *one* good coming from your father's opposition. There are other blessings too, but I have spoken of them before to you. The waiting is hard, the trial of separation severe we both know, but *all* trial *all* troubles are for wise purpose and I think we should look at it as such.

On 22 August she mused to him on the strange nature of love, a passion within the Christian design for them both:

How strange it seems that two people should be so dependent on one another for happiness. I so often wonder at it all, other people seem so little to us. Its 'you and I' all over the world. Such is love, strange mystic passion!. We do not feel that we are satisfied until the solemn vows are spoken and we are one. There is a deep craving while we are separate that feels it's not satisfied until our lives are joined in one. Life now with its various duties cares and joys to be equally shared together. It's a very responsible position one takes when married life is begun. Each should help the other onward, upward, ever growing more united more as one, and if our lives are sanctified ones, this will be the issue. We each hold a sacred trust and happy indeed will be life together spent if Christ is the Head of our home. Sorrows and trial may come but they cannot take away the peace He gives if we are His alone. How we are both looking forward with joy to the end of the waiting time.

And, as her letter of 21 September shows, Lillie could balance such Christian seriousness with playful references to the physical, with teasing, and with ordinary wondering about the behaviour and affections of others:

> Why you are a cool young gentleman to ask me how it was I allowed you to be so familiar with me as to allow you to take me on your knee and into the kitchen and pantry? Why for the simple reason I could not stop you. Do you forget how I used to struggle to get free? But I was held as in a vice, so finding struggles useless I submitted, but I suppose I might as well be honest and confess that it was not always disagreeable to be fondled, but I did not always deem it prudent, you naughty boy. Ah well that's all gone and past, it's your love I have now and I have given you mine without reserve, Alick is mine and I am his, I love you fully and freely and I am so happy in the possession of your love darling, I can afford now to laugh at the past when we were 'cousins' together and to me at least nothing more than cousins.
> Nor can I understand how anyone can go on being in love one week with one girl and next week with another. It's not love, it can't be, maybe they fancy it is but its mere fascination, and the spell is soon broken, it's not in human nature to be always changing one's affections. The person who does so has never been really in love, for if love for a girl or reverse the case if a girl loves any young man, all her feelings raise against making believe she is in love, week after with someone else and just the same with a man don't you think so? I think you know enough about the marriage ceremony without my teaching you, of course you don't know that I have to promise to obey you? And I won't satisfy you by having a string of pretty bridesmaids either.

On 4 September her long compendium of news, endearments, teasings (he was *not* ugly), criticism of his father's constant gloom (the starch trade was bad in Belfast), wedding plans, and an assortment of dreams, took her eventually back to the shadow which lay at the edge of their lives. Her mother simply hoped he would keep clear of those niggers. Lillie's dread was deeper, and more than particular to him: she knew, with the clarity of Christian principle, that some fearful day the whole white world would be called to account for what it had done to those black others:

> Do you know we laugh at your ideas of the native language, there being no words tenses etc. Why Alick, how do you know they haven't? You know very little of their language, [that] they have one of their own is certain, for see how they will talk to one another quite volubly. It's because you know so little of their language you cannot make them understand you, now isn't it? I hope you have not had much trouble with the natives lately. I do hate to hear of any hostility between them and you, to me it seems dreadful to fire at them, and the poor prisoners that are sent to Bathurst, they have a fearful time of it from what has been coming to light lately, poor miserable degraded wretches. The whites will have a deal to be answerable for someday I fear, so called Christians. Oh my darling keep yourself free from any stain of these poor creatures, I know how very annoying the attacks on the sheep must be but we should strive to 'do unto others as we would have them do to us'.

The love letters of Alexander Crawford and Elizabeth Jane Mathews are not preserved past the end of 1883. They were married on 3 March 1885 at Linton in Victoria: he was twenty-seven, she was twenty-three. He had left the station property in 1884 and at first took labouring work. In 1886 he went to Europe to study dairying — perhaps his Lillie went too — and on his return became a government lecturer on that subject in Victoria. In 1887 they were back in 'the wilds of W.A.' at Madura. Alick had been seriously injured in an accident (a camel fell on him) and their financial fortunes had been up and down — mainly down. Of the success of their marriage there was no doubt. Writing on 7 January 1889 from Buln Buln in Victoria, Alick confided to his brother:

> I am almost four years married now and I think I can truly say that Lillie has never cost me one minute, one second of unhappiness. She makes my interest in everything hers. If she sees I take pleasure in anything she tries to also, to have our pleasure mutual. A wife is something more than a beautiful . . . figure. A wife ought to be a "helpmeet" not only for this world but for the world to come. Again if you see a girl that you think would suit you and be slow to make up your mind on that point, be very sure of it, try and calmly and dispassionately weigh both your own and her disposition and see if they will balance but having done so and come to the conclusion that they will, do not let any false feeling of pride keep you from getting married because you cannot start where your or her parents leave off. We have to crawl before we can walk and no girl is worth marrying who is not willing to start with her husband at the foot of the ladder and help him to climb it rung by rung until he is in a position to give her many things that she has had to do without but against his will. It is a mistake I think for men or women to delay marrying. The longer the delay the more fixed and formed the habits of life are and the more difficult it is to form a real amalgamation. Like two young trees when young, you can twine them round and round each other but in a few years if not united they will grow nearer and nearer but they will never unite like they would in their young days. Again you cannot know the happiness that is to be enjoyed in knowing that there is one being dependent upon you who loves you better than all the world beside and whose interest is yours and yours is hers. I wish I had married five years sooner.

Two years later, in 1891, Lillie was dead, at twenty-nine. On 6 December 1891 Alick wrote to his brother from the new house in Melbourne into which they had been about to move: he was utterly desolated, wishing he was dead:

> Lillie planned it all herself and I am constantly reminded of her in every turn in it and it makes me very very sad to think that after all she cannot share it with me. Often since my wee wife was taken from me I have wished that I were dead and laid beside her. I have nothing to live for now no interest to work for. Before I did not mind how hard the work was or how long the hours, so long as I was earning something that would help to make my Lillie more comfortable or provide for her future in case anything happened to me. I sometimes feel as if I could not bear to stay in Melbourne, there are so many associations that continually remind me of the past. If I see an opening on a station in some of the other Colonies I think I will try for it and go there.
>
> . . . I have nothing more to write about now. I think in fact I wrote more for the sake of having someone to talk to than that I had anything to write, but I am lonely and I have not what I could call a friend here and I do feel so lonely, so completely isolated at times that I wish all were ended.

Alexander Crawford in his mid seventies, at his home in South Perth W.A. (Courtesy: His son, Alexander Crawford)

On 5 April 1893 Alexander Crawford married Mattie (Martha) Mathews, his deceased wife's younger sister, the fifteen-year-old of 1880, that large girl, very quiet, with quaint sayings: he had sometimes flirted with her, just a little, via his letters to Lillie. In 1896 he joined the West Australian Bureau of Agriculture, eventually becoming chief inspector under the Rabbit Act. Mattie died of consumption on 22 April 1921: they had three children. When he was young he had favoured Home Rule for Ireland, but as he got older (and got more sense, as he put it) he concluded that it would mean Rome rule. By 1922 he was out of patience with the whole Irish situation. He told his brother (24 June 1922): 'For the atrocities that have been committed not only now but all along I think Lloyd George should be tried and hung. He seems to have shirked his reponsibility all along'. He held a similarly low opinion of Australia's Prime Minister, W. M. Hughes, 'also a Welshman and seems to be emulating his countrymen in his worst features . . . it is to be hoped that Hughes will be sent into the obscurity he deserves'. He held compromise and concessions to be the mark of weakness in politics. But his main concern in Irish affairs was the question of the survival of his brother, who, as a prominent Unionist was an obvious target: Alick told Frederick in 1922 he was almost afraid to read the Irish cable news for fear of seeing his brother's name among the victims. He wished — on grounds of affection rather than principle — he could come to Belfast to help, or better still, that Frederick might find some employment in Australia, where he could live in peace and comfort.

Crawford married a third time — Mrs Gladys Greenham, a much younger woman (he was then sixty-six) — on 4 July 1923. They had one child — a daughter. Both Crawford's neuritis and financial problems were by then constant. He died on 8 November 1935, aged seventy-eight.

Crawford's greatest friend, Rev. J. Grove, told his oldest son Alexander that Crawford's third marriage, and his subsequent family life was one of the lovelist things he had ever known. Crawford's son wrote to his uncle Frederick on 12 November 1935, 'Father was exceedingly happy and so were those about him — a strange mixture of ages seeming to add to and not detract from the charm of their home life'.

6 SUCCESS AND DEFEAT IN WESTERN AUSTRALIA 1891-1907

In mid 1891, when he was seventeen, James Hamilton Twigg left his home in Cookstown, Co. Tyrone, to emigrate to Australia, travelling second class on the *Lusitania.* When he landed in Western Australia,[1] he travelled from Albany to Bunbury ('both are miserable holes') to stay with his cousins, the Wright family. They had a station called 'Wormup' on the Blackwood Road about forty miles from Bunbury. Geoffrey Wright (of Grouse Lodge near Lough Fea) was travelling first class on the same ship as James Twigg: if James was something of the poor cousin, he refused to accept any inferior role.

For a seventeen-year-old,[2] James Twigg was remarkably mature, self-reliant and perceptive. He wrote home regularly to his solicitor father, John B. Twigg, to his brother Richard — also a solicitor in Cookstown — and to his sister Carrie (Caroline) and was very much dependent on them for replies. Emigrants wrote home for a variety of reasons. Some wanted to keep in touch with a known and supportive family structure: it is notable that correspondence became less frequent after the emigrant became better related to local society, and particularly after marriage. Others wrote letters so as to get letters. Particularly for remote selectors,[3] receiving mail — and the visit of the mailman who brought it — was some respite from sheer loneliness, and writing letters was their only chance to express themselves, to formulate their thoughts and to communicate them: it was both a necessity and a recreation. Still other emigrants wrote as a type of hard-headed insurance: there were often legal ties remaining with Ireland and one never knew when it might be necessary to borrow money or perhaps receive some legacy; the image of the emigrant sending money back to povery-stricken parents is only one facet of a complex financial inter-relationship. While in Australia James Twigg received two legacies, one from his mother, another from an aunt, as well as payments and loans from other Irish sources.

Glimpses of all these motivations can be found in the Twigg correspondence, but the atmosphere overall is one of extraordinary family solidity and warmth — and honesty. James often wished that his father (who hated writing) would write to him more frequently, as, particularly when staying with friends, the absence of mail was an embarrassment: 'It looks bad for me to never get a letter

The Twigg house in Loy Hill, Cookstown, Co. Tyrone. The old residence was the entire building shown here in January 1984, including what are now shops. The old stable door is at far right. (Courtesy: John Twigg, grandson of the recipient of the Australian letters)

from any other one only you . . .' he complained to his brother. Mail from parents was an important matter of prestige and status among emigrants, at least some of whom had broken with their parents and been consigned to the colonies in disgrace. But for James Twigg the matter was much more than one of appearances. As his life became solitary, when alone, riding or walking, his thoughts turned to his father, whose letters, when they did come, affected him greatly.

From the beginning in Western Australia, James was intensely homesick, in a manner difficult to describe. Religion offered no consolation: he was not much of a churchgoer, and as to parsons, 'we get some awful rotters here, the cast-off dregs of the old country'. Nor did he care much for politics, save confessing annoyance at the way colonials lumped together all Irish as disloyal. He was himself a moderate loyalist and was irked by the disruptive reputation which spilled over from the activities of Irish nationalists to affect all Irishmen. Spectacular Irish nationalist agitation prompted the non-Irish to identify all those of obvious Irish origin or accent with the nationalist stereotype. This angered those, like Twigg, who supported the political *status quo*. 'Those damned Nationalists give Irishmen a bad name for loyalty all the world over but it is all bark': such was his comment on the anti-Boer War agitation in Ireland, although he had some sympathy with the Boers. It was not so much that he was antagonistic to Irish nationalism, or that his loyalism was fervent, as that he resented being embarrassed by being linked in the colonies with a disposition of political discontent he did not share.

Twigg's discontents were much more personal and elusive, a sense of loss, of disjunction, an ache in his heart beyond remedy. He asked for a photograph of his father. But family photographs, when they arrived, made him homesick: they came at a stage when he had only a cat for company and the cat often rambled, deserting him. Receiving photographs over the years became an ambivalent experience, the joy of recognition competing with the shock of the passage of time, age and new life, baldness and babies. 'I can notice no change in you at all' was an observation that revealed more than it said. James liked to keep up with local Irish news and gossip. The family sent the northern *Irish Times* and *Answers.* He also got *Pearson's Magazine* and *Budget.* They were refreshingly familiar. And he asked his sister for some 'coloured pictures all you can get to decorate my little cabin. It makes it seem less lonely and I can get none here'. He sent back seeds, coloured bird's feathers.

Yet, as for returning, however powerful the nostalgia, James was realist enough to feed his imagination with the thought of only a visit, not permanent return. In 1901, after ten years in Australia, he was quite firm. 'I often feel a great longing to see the cliffs of old Ireland and the river I used to fish in, but that awful climate makes me feel content again. No.' But it was more than the climate that he feared, it was change itself. He confided to his sister in December 1903 that 'I would like one more day's fishing in the river before I join the majority but don't think I could live long in Ireland. Dick says places have changed so and then the climate'.

Places have changed so: the familiar phrase of letters from home triggered an emigrant's warning systems. The threat was of change itself, a process like an unguarded blow which would forcibly remind the emigrant that home was no longer home, not the place he or she had left: it was another, different place, sufficiently reminiscent of its former self as to inflict the greatest pain. It was warm and interesting to hear from afar reports of change, new buildings and people, old deaths and disasters, but to risk actually seeing and experiencing it was to hazard too much. Perhaps it might be too much to be borne. Whatever of the head, the heart said the new 'home' was never really home. If the old one did not exist any longer, there was no home, and the emigrant's life a lonely pilgrimage indeed. All of this James Twigg sensed and knew. Like many emigrants, he knew how best to cope with home truths — and how best to dispense them: of his own fortunes and feelings, his brother got the unvarnished facts, his father the brighter version.

All of these complications and subtleties lay in the future. At first, life in the West Australian bush at the Wright's station was a great adventure. Writing to his brother in September-October 1891, James was bursting with vitality and enthusiasm:

> I have been doing everything since I came, riding, shooting, cutting timber. Frank (Geoff's brother) and I rode 30 miles through the bush to a man called Brockman to get the shooting of his paddock. We can have the shooting if we ring-bark some of his trees. We rode around to see if it was worth it and we think we can make a £20 note out of it as we saw plenty of kangaroos but it was a windy day and they are always wild on a windy one. Though we came up the wind they never let us nearer than 1000 yards. We had rifles of course. I had a 10 shot Winchester . . .
>
> . . . We will build a hut in the paddock while at it. I can ride like a bush-whacker and jump my horse over fallen timber. Geoff rides a buckjumper. He is a toff at riding and has never been thrown. He is the best rifle shot ever I

saw: never misses. I shot some cockatoos (3) they are good eating. Frank got a small doe kangaroo yesterday. We have soup and roast ever since I came. It is the best grub ever I tasted.
I can't write at all and as I cut my finger with an axe half an hour ago. I wish you all were out here, nothing but big gum trees everywhere you go. I have never seen 30 yards of clear ground since I came . . .
You wouldn't know me now with a big hat and a Winchester on a fiery mare and a big knife for skinning in my belt . . . Frank and I run together now (he is older than Geoff) as Geoff has been away prospecting. He is going again on Monday. Frank thinks to get the ring-barking of Brockman's place (6s.0d. to 9s.0d. each a day) after we shoot the kangaroos . . .
We passed several parties of kangaroo hunters when coming out here. All of them have blacks with them. I wish I had brought a rifle with me. I will have to buy one soon. We are going tamar hunting this evening. It is a small animal of the kangaroo species and very numerous. I will send Carrie some possum skins when they dry. The girls trap them by the dozen and sell the skins.

Kangaroo hunting had become popular employment. James Twigg soon met a commercial traveller whom he had known as such back home in Cookstown, who had also taken to kangaroo shooting. So had many others, with the result that Twigg quickly found it barely profitable. He turned to fencing and also applied for police work. On 23 November 1891, his enthusiasm undimmed, he explained to his sister:

I have been miles away in the bush camped for the last three weeks. It is simply glorious. I was out in a paddock shooting kangaroos but we (cousin Frank and I) only made out expenses. The fellows from the tin fields poached them all out of it. I have to pay £5 for the use of the paddock for one year and when we paid our £5 each we found we had just cleared ourselves. But you see we can go in the paddock now anytime in the year and will make pounds if the skins still keep going up in price. We have given them a rest just now for a month or two as I am going fencing as jackaroo or man of all works to two other fellows . . .
My first kangaroo I shot off hand at 150 yards. He stood nearly 6 feet high. I shot a brush or silver grey kangaroo before I shot this one but we don't reckon them as being kangaroos they are so small.
I am going on peelers (mounted) but won't be called for a bit yet (pay up to £10 per month) for a common peeler. Mr. Wright when he was on got £15 a month and would have been a judge by this time if he hadn't took to liquor.

Whatever of Mr Wright's drinking problems, the Wrights were a lively and sociable family: James liked the girls. He was now 'stout and brown', sported a moustache, and signed himself 'the Bushwacker'. He was getting 'some niggers' to make him some spears to send home. And he was soon pronouncing authoritatively on the best guns and ammunition for kangaroo shooting, and giving advice to his brother (2 January 1892) on the question of emigrating. But his position as a working guest of the Wrights was becoming less than satisfactory and he was most grateful for the prospect of independence conferred by his receiving £100 from Ireland, a substantial sum when labouring wages were £3 to £4 a week.

The best rifle to use here is the ordinary Snider, a sporting Snider (1,000 yards) by Hollis to take a 577 boxer ammunition is the best rifle for kangaroos.

A Martini is very good but too long to carry on horse back in the bush and it drives the bullet so quick that it does them no harm unless it hits a bone whereas the boxer 577 which is hollow fronted turns inside out when it hits anything and the wound bleeds freely. I was surprised to see the damage it does. A Snider gets leaded very fast and for accurate shooting must be sponged well every third shot . . .

I am glad to hear about the business doing so well and that £100 is a veritable Godsend. It will start me. I would not advise you to come here till I look around a bit. You see you and I are totally different. I am only fit for roughing it and take delight in so doing. Some rough fellows some days ago were trying to disgust me by eating the grubs out of the black boys but I at once asked for one and it really went fine. For nearly a week I was camped with some niggers and they having taken a fancy to me gave me a grand corroberie a thing few of the colonials have seen.

I would not advise you to come here on mere spec[ulation]. You no doubt would get a situation in Perth and be one of the first in the place on account of your education. If you can see young Stewart's father he might write to his son who is aide-de-camp to the Governor in Perth (Claud Stewart). He could do a lot for you. You can be sure of a living anyhow.

I expect to be with the surveyors soon. I have not earned a penny only on an odd "boomer" [kangaroo] skin. As for being a burden to the Wright's I work very hard for them as Geoff is so lazy and Mr. Wright is too old for work so Frank and I do the most of it. Geoff can shoot, ride and reap and this is all. Frank who owns the stock and land is a hard worker and very decent. He is making £3 a week shooting at kangaroos but he uses two horses a day. I tried but could not manage on foot. They are much tamer when you are mounted with a bell on the horse. He has made £3 a day with his bullocks hauling timber at the saw mills. Geoff was too proud to do such work but goes shooting and then never gives his parents anything and never bought any stock. I have persuaded him to apply with me for a job with the surveyors but he only wrote today. Elyjah and Harry [Wright] are in comfort but have to work hard.

When I got here I could not sleep; the house is full of bugs. It is made of split mahogany slabs and mud and has 4 rooms.

Christmas was spent shooting, a sweepstake and athletic sports and then we danced till daylight. I can dance a bit *colonial* still. The girls here are a fine lot and can work like horses. I don't see why you put Mr. on my letters. Excuse dirt as I have been out with the rifle.

James Twigg's first effort to get employment outside the orbit of the Wrights was as an axeman to railway surveyors. He told his father (January 1892):

There is a new line starting from Bunbury to the Vasse, a small seaport 32 miles from Bunbury. I went down yesterday and being out of work applied to the contractor for an axe at 1s.0d. an hour. I am going down again with my kit on Tuesday. The line will last about 9 months and I ought to pull at least 60 pounds off it. I can make plenty of money here, but only by "hard graft".

But this was excessive optimism, the talk of youth and inexperience. May 1892 found him 'at the Preston on the Blackwood River working for £1 a month and my tucker. I had no money so took this poor job in despair'. His hopes for a rosier future now lay with the police force, as he explained to his brother:

> I told you long ago I had sent in my name and I then thought they would send for me when wanted (I wrote to the Commissioner, Perth). A fortnight ago he wrote the inspector Bunbury and he wrote to me. I went in and passed a rough exam and a stiff medical one. I had to pay the medical myself 10s.6d. for the certificate. The Inspector said I would probably have to go to Perth and get sworn in almost immediately but I have not got orders yet. The pay is about £7 per month but you have to grub yourself (£1 a week out here). I wish I was on the force. I am about sick of here . . .
>
> I am sure to be sent North where the niggers are committing great depredations. They chained up a copper the other day and sacked the station.

His application failed: perhaps at nineteen he was deemed too young and inexperienced. But he decided to go North anyhow, with Geoffrey Wright, to try for work on a station — a plan to which he harnessed dreams of eventual land ownership. He told his sister on 20 November 1892:

> Geoff sends his love. He and I are going to try our fortunes up in the North (Derby) among the wild niggers. We start next month sometime after Christmas. We ought each to get £100 per annum up there on one of the stations. You see sheep and cattle with a few horses constitute a station. It is too hot for anything to grow so no actual farming is carried on. The country up there is sparsely settled but a lot of men are wanted on the stations and high wages are given as men are scarce and the gold fields draw them all off so if we can keep steady and save a little there is nothing to stop us having a station of our own eventually; sheep increase so and land only 10s.0d. per 1,000 acres (lease perpetual) and good feeding land too . . .
>
> By the way I cut my knee on the edge of the kneecap so badly that although done a month and over I am lame still and I'm in doubts whether I won't always be a bit rickety. I cut one of the sinews badly. It had to be sewn up.

The knee injury was sustained in his tree-felling job, whose hazards and difficulties he described to his brother on 10 April 1893:

> They are making a continuation of the railway from Bunbury out in this direction, bringing it now within 14 miles of Wright's. I have been felling timber on the line. It is reckoned the hardest work a man can go at out here. I got 1s.0d. per hour 8 hours a day. I did well and was saving fast when the weather broke and the Australian winter came on rendering work by the hour or day no good as one could only make tucker (3 bob a day).
>
> You can see by this that I am a better man by twice than when I left home and a passable axeman as you have to be to get on a felling gang. But had the weather not broke up I would have had to gone home as I caught a severe cold and a terrible attack of dysentery of which I am afraid it will cost me something to get rid of. All the evacuations are mucus and blood in large quantities and at very short intervals.
>
> It is just possible I will go to the gold fields this winter if this disease don't put me under. In the bush one can't get medicine and only the most local and cheap remedies are all I can obtain such as warmth, rest, castor oil, laudanum and chlorodyne.[4] I have been a week now and no improvement. I wish I was well as I think I see my chance of making £40 or £50 in a few months. My knee is not painful nor am I lame as expected but it feels stiff in wet weather or when I squat down etc.

As to the plans for going North, all was in flux.

> I cannot make up my mind here for more than a month at a time. I mean that Geoff and I talk now of going fencing, then off gold seeking, then off Kimberley and God knows what next. He was grubbing trees on the line and Elyjah and I felling. Where the rails and embankments and cuttings go the trees must be grubbed up by the roots but 22 yards each side can be chopped and felled as they more commonly call it.

From this arduous work, James turned to the hardly less taxing employment of log-splitting, all the time keeping a keen eye on the possibilities of taking up some cheap land grant. On 7 November (1893) he wrote to his sister in his usual cheerful and self-confident vein:

> I am getting on extremely well, that is I am making a living which means in its turn that I have always enough tough damper and salt mutton to eat. I am still on the extreme head of the Preston River and about 50 miles from Wright's.
>
> I have been out over some of the back country looking for land. We rode day after day over a barren wilderness of sand and iron-stone gravel and saw (what would delight your eyes) herds of wild horses as we neared the better land on the other side of the said wilderness. We saw kangaroos in one place like flocks of sheep and emus too. Should the price of kangaroos skin rise I could make about £500 in about 12 months out there. The place has been seldom explored by whites. A few shepherds etc. are about the only ones. This country is covered by a plant or rather shrub which has a very pretty flower of a passionate red colour but it is a deadly poison to all stock. Sheep must be shepherded and kept out of the poison except horses (which don't chew the cud and of course kangaroos[5] etc) so that you see settlement has been afraid to venture out. But the present responsible Government have recently made some very lenient acts relating to the purchase of this Poison Land as it is called. In fact they all but give it away only charging a £1 per 1,000 acres per annum for 21 years, when if you have the poison cleared off it and have it stocked and fenced you get a "grant" or the land becomes yours for "ever and ever amen". I thought on reading up the Poison Act that as the terms were so lenient I would go out and see the country and I went and liked it very well. I could take up 3,000 or 4,000 acres and in a few years if I picked (as you may bet I would) a place where the plant grew thin I could have a fine living and place. But before taking up any of it I am about to start out again to see more about it.
>
> At present I am splitting a few thousand slabs and a few hundred posts and rails for a settler on the river here. I can tell you 9 feet rails (mahogany) take belting out with a heavy maul or beetle and a dozen or so steel wedges. I am as strong as a wild bull and my heart is stout so I don't care a curse and never get down on my luck. Somehow I feel as if I must come out right. I have done so well all along. I have got a grand name for being a good worker. When I was navvying the navvies used to call me Jimmy the pony I was such a little stickler.

James Twigg's active interest in seeking favourable land was probably influenced by the fact that his cousin Geoff Wright had taken up '400 acres of miserable hungry cold clay land near his father's place'. But early in 1894 he was offered a job too good to refuse. In explaining his decision to his brother on 12 March, James revealed not only his exuberant satisfaction with his own success, but also his sense of superiority among a people he believed to be mostly of convict descent — a mistake, but one which evidently helped to put him at his ease by reducing his sensitivity to his own shortcomings: he thought of himself a rough, uneducated fellow and his ready acceptance in colonial society was a source of great wonderment and pleasure to him:

> I am to manage a store at some big saw mills which have just been started some miles from this place. When I say manage I mean that I will only have to manage myself, the store and a horse, no under-hands. My wages for a start are £1 per week and myself and horse found in all but clothes (the horse clothes himself).
>
> When I said I was going farming I really intended to do so and did in fact put in a fortnight ring-barking and felling. But this job which is permanent and out here a gentleman's billet was too good to be lost so as I had only paid £6 or £7 on the land in work and cash I let it go to Government. If the store should be a failure I will go to the fields (Gold). A fellow never knows what his luck is going to be till he tries and anything is better than knocking about at contract work or navvying on railways.
>
> When I come to think over it all, I can see that it is the best thing that could have happened to me my coming out here. I always succeed everywhere I go and as I have never let liquor cross my lips nor done anything mean or ungentlemanlike I am well liked and get into the elites of society. You would not believe the offers I get of employment of all sorts. I can't go wrong. It would open your optics to see me falling, all sweat and charcoal and the next day mounted on my thoroughbred (Rainbow) on a £6 6s.0d. saddle togged up to the nines going to a ball or cricket match. I am invited down to the coast to some very nice people for a fortnight's duck and swan shooting and sea fishing not to mention a little flirtation with the pretty daughters. As far as money goes I have enough and to spare though I want more like everybody else . . .
>
> I was offered £150 and found !! a year to go up to the Murchison district (North) to keep a store but my life would not be worth a kangaroo's owing to the fever and ague. You will wonder at my getting this offer and my present billet but you must bear in mind the illiterate state of a people without schools and descended for the most part from *convicts.*

But again reality failed to live up to expectations, and within a year James was off to the Coolgardie diggings, this time with the standard gold seeker's dream of making a quick fortune, as he explained to his brother on 23 January 1895:

> Well, old man, I am getting tired of this hard life and I can see nothing for it but hard work till the end of my life if I continue on in the present way. So I am going to stake all and even my life in a big venture. "Never venture, never win" you know. I am off to Coolgardie Gold Fields as soon as the rain starts. I am at present engaged getting three other fellows to join me, all men I know to be honest and sober and above all men inured to hardships and bush life and good bushmen. There are dozens of parties which have never been heard of which have gone out prospecting and, never having been accustomed to bushing it, have got lost. If a man makes one mistake it is his last, so one wants to be careful. I think one of my *mates* has something good already. He went up last year and found a chain of fresh lakes evidently permanent and close by found some specks or colours in a reef. He had no rations and his mate was sick so he had to return.

The intermediate country is utterly devoid of water except at certain times so we must wait for the rain which may come anytime now but most likely about April or May. The man who found this is named Bussell and is from a very old Colonial family who founded one of our principal towns Busselton. His estate is highly mortgaged and he is on his last legs. His brother went up with a chap I know well named Dawson and they have made their fortunes. Dawson's brother, J. Bussell, A Heppingstone and I are the four, if nothing happens. Bussell and Heppingstone are related and Lancey Dawson and I are old chums and might be related someday. All three are good honest *gentlemen.*

Clogher Cottage, Clogher, Co. Tyrone, where J.H. Twigg lived as a child, with his grandparents and aunts. (Courtesy: Mrs L. Wolton, Gosford, N.S.W.)

Gentlemen they may have been, but the party soon split up, and by September 1896 James — now with Geoff Wright as an unsatisfactory partner — was reporting from the Princess Alix mine, via Niagara, North Coolgardie, about seven months of failure:

> We have been here now close on 7 months and have had no luck as yet. When I say no luck I mean we have not made a pile but as for finding reefs we or at least I have had no trouble whatever. I found one the third day and we thought ourselves made men but Geoff wouldn't stick to it when the gold cut out and another party with more perseverance have struck it rich. It has been the same all through and I am so sick of it that I intend leaving him to pick up with someone else and I will take a job at £4 10s.0d. per week which are the current wages up here. I can save £3 5s.0d. or £3 10s.0d. of that and the work is interesting and besides I would like to get a little more insight into it. I can save a little and wait a chance to join some decent party looking out for a mate . . .

It is such a game of chance this reef hunting and when you find one and test it to 50 or 60 feet and it is a good strong payable reef at that depth, you have a job to dispose of it without interest among the buyers and bribing judiciously in certain quarters (chiefly the experts). Still I don't know of any better way of making a rise or a better place to do it than W[estern] A[ustralia] miserable as it is to live in. There are thousands on these fields now and many have made enough to give them a good start in life but few have made more. It is not a bad life, plenty of excitement and risk and plenty of decent fellows always about. I never was in such a place in my life for books and papers so that a fellow has amusement as well as hard work besides always knowing how the world wags.

Two months later his story was unchanged, in reply to a query from his brother Richard about the possible emigration of their younger brother Lewis[6]. A couple of years earlier, James had thought this a good idea for the future, and suggested that in the meantime Lewis learn some trade, horse-shoeing etc. Now, in 1896, James made it very clear that he was unable to help if Lewis came. He was short of money and had no intention of settling down until he had made some. And evidently the wandering instability of James' life was a mystery and source of impatient irritation to his respectable solicitor brother. James explained:

The reason I threw up the survey job was because I had saved up sufficient to give me a start on the fields and good accounts as to rain and feed being to hand, thought it best to go up at once. I have spent 7 months prospecting and it has cost me all out over £10 per month. The country is so hard that dynamite has to be used besides you must have a portable forge to point your tools, shoe your horses etc. I got into the knack of blacksmithing immediately and was smith to the camp as I am here.

Well, my money being nearly exhausted I thought it best to take a job till I can save up a bit more. So here I am saving £3 a week (getting £4). The price of things has come down so much that I can live on £1 or nearly so a week. Water, of course, is thrown in. I rank as a practical miner now and am getting the highest wages, £3 10s.0d. being the lowest . . .

Re Lewis: I have given this, as you say, my best consideration, which means about 40 pipes of tobacco and the following:

At present I can do nothing but if I was down South I feel sure I could get him apprenticed, as it were, to a station. I am nearly certain of this as the owner is a friend. He would be treated as one of the family but would have to work for 6 months for nothing but his board in lieu of a premium not being paid. After that he might get 30s.0d. a month or even a bit better and so on on up to £4 a month but after he had the new chumminess knocked out of him I would take him with me if he were so disposed and we could knock around and battle together.

There is no mistake the gold fields are the place to make money and spend it too. As for the Wrights you have no idea how poor they are and altogether without influence. They could do nothing for Lewis and I wouldn't ask them. I consider myself as being in their debt now morally speaking and mean to pay it off too when I strike it rich.

By jove, old man, I killed a big snake under my bunk last night. He skeared 6 months growth out of me.

I would advise Lewis to work at different things that would be use out here. Let him learn to *milk*. That is the first question he would be asked on a W[est]

A[ustralian] station and he can learn at Clogher. Next let him learn to ride and saddle and groom his own nag etc. also to plough. If possible he might rub up his figures a bit and book-keeping also as he would have to keep the station books (a simple matter).

I can only repeat I can do nothing up here. Wait a while and if he learns the above he can command wages as soon as he lands.

However, to James's relief, it was decided that Lewis would go to New Zeland where an uncle had settled. When he wrote to his father on 27 December 1896, James also revealed both his underlying current of home sickness and his philosophy of meeting life as it came.

I am very glad Lewis is satisfactorily disposed of. He is going to a better country than this can ever be.

Geoff has gone home for Christmas and a few month's rest, he says, but I don't think he will show his nose up here again. It is truly a God-forsaken hole. I have been laid on my back in a boiling tent with my old enemy dysentery since the 23rd inst. and so have not spent a very enjoyable Christmas but I suppose I'll get over it all right. It is frightfully hot, night and day, and a tent is like an oven. There is no natural shade at all owing to the almost total absence of timber.

When I leave here I think I'll take a run over and see you all once again. I'll reckon up the cost and see. A fellow should do the trip there and back for £100 comfortably, third class return of course. After being out here for 5 and a half years pretty well one wants a spell . . .

I suppose Lewis goes out to N(ew) Z(ealand) as a cadet. Let me know his terms and future prospects and send me his address I might be on the Thames diggings this time next year. But I've found that there is no good laying plans for the future in this kind of life one being entirely guided by circumstances. The market is very dull now at home and the outlook for prospectors bad. If we had public batteries[7] on the out fields like these, a man could do well enough during a slump, and we won't have those for another 5 or 10 years, there being no alluvial to speak of, the poor man has no show. The middleman i.e. the development companies make all the beans, and the prospector getting next to nothing. I found the mine I am at present on and showed it to the present owners and I think they will be pretty decent if they dispose of her all right. At any rate I'll have a spell down south when she's floated whether or not.

I shot some pigeons at a water hole last week. They were a treat too. With March we get cool weather again, 3 months! and the two coming are the hottest of the year. It seems funny to be boiling here at Christmas while you are freezing over there.

I must have lost over half a stone in the last 4 or 5 days. It's a terrible place to be the least bit sick. You can get nothing to eat that you'd like and when you do by chance get it the cooking of it yourself takes away your appetite. Every camp round here has gone to the pub to spend Christmas and all their spare cash. I got a present of a bottle of whiskey some days before Christmas and the seal isn't broken yet.

Six months later (July 1897) he wrote from 'Lake Way' East Murchison to describe a major prospecting journey:

My dear father, this is the first place I have got a show of sending mail since soon after leaving Princess Alix. Three of us started out from there with three big horses and a strong cart and about 5 months supply of flour etc. for the Earlstown Creek via "Mount Margaret", "Hawk's Nest" and "British Flag". Not finding any good country about the Earlstown we took the bush for it and got into the desert. We steered north-west and as we had no map we didn't know where we would hit out but after travelling for over 200 miles we have just struck Lake Way. We were lucky enough to get water and only did a perish twice and then only for the horses. We saw no blacks but could see their tracks fresh sometimes in the morning. We had a dog and she kept them off in the night as unless a nigger can make a dead certainty he won't tackle you. We had 3 revolvers, 2 rifles and a 12 bore shot gun. We found water by ranging out 5 or 6 miles from the line the dray took, one on each side and sent up smoke signals when we noticed signs of Blacks or found water, which latter were usually got on flat granite rocks and unless one tumbled right bang on top of it he might miss it. The sand was up the spokes half-way to the "nave" and as we always kept our 100 gallon tank full (half a ton) you can imagine that we had a job.

We are at present on a small patch of alluvial and are making tucker. As for wages it is impossible to get work; the country is flooded with men out of employment.

Do not write to me as I may be on my way to the Territory or Kimberley in a month.

We have been the furthest east of any dray and I expect the police will be sent out to look for us from Princess Alix as only three months before we left a man I knew called Reison was killed by the niggers on the Earlstown Creek . . . .

This country will be in a bad state shortly. The mines are going bung but you wouldn't hear about that as the papers make such a noise about the few good mines in W[estern] A[ustralia]. Anyone in England would naturally think it was a grand place for the working man but it takes a very few men to work even a mine like the Boulder until they get down to 2,000 or 3,000 feet which won't be for 15 or 20 years at the present rate and there are thousands in the country who can't get out of it.

I will drop you a line now and again from such points of civilisation as we may touch in our travels. There are about 500 niggers here always cadging tucker . . . When I see any prospects of our being anytime in once place I will write to the Alix for my mail, and if you people have acted up to my expectations I should get a good budget.

There are lots of ducks, swans, and geese on the lake but without a canoe one stands no show of getting them. I've got a lot of native weapons but goodness knows if I'll ever be able to take them home.

This time James's party had some success, which he reported to his brother on 11 September 1897, having returned to the Bunbury district. It was not without personal cost. He returned not merely with a bad cold and hungry for months of waiting mail, but with severe indigestion and — at the age of twenty-three — hair turning grey.

We got 276 ozs. of gold and sent it round to the Sydney mint to be smelted as it had some of the matrix with it. The largest piece was 7 lbs. (avoirdupoids) the others being two of 6 lbs. . . . and one of 14 ozs. (troy). They are the finest nuggets that have brought in from Murchison for sometime. I will invest my share in a block of land and build a house on it in Bunbury. I can get £40 a year rent and this on any outlay of £250 is good interest.

I was nearly going home for a spell but it would cost me £100 and I've earned it too hard to sling it away to gratify a pleasure. I may go back to the fields and I may start in some business in a small way in Bunbury which by the way is going ahead wonderfully.
We got all the gold by dry-blowing and all in about 8 weeks.
I am going into Bunbury on Wednesday next to have a look at the fishing banks as there is a big population and no one to supply the demand . . .. I will get my photo taken in Perth in a few weeks when I get all right. I had no clothes when I was coming down from Cue or I would have got it done then. I think you will find me little changed in appearance, but a few more years of the life I've led on the back blocks would make an old man of me. I am turning grey already like all the young men in the fields. Isn't that strange. I think it must be the tinned stuff. I know it has ruined my stomach . . .
I was quite bashful talking to the first white girl. I hadn't seen one for so long but it soon wore off.
One of my mates has gone to England and one to South Australia. There is great talk of British Columbia out here and lots are going. It is too jolly cold for me. You people have been having a fine time over Her Majesty lately. What a lot of rot it all is. I see Dublin didn't altogether approve. I may come home in the summer *if I've luck* but don't expect me.

In November he gave his brother further details: his share of the gold would be about £250. His intention was still to invest it in land, but he was also having a boat built in Fremantle with the idea of combining sport and a summer living in deep-sea fishing. The state of his kidneys and liver was such as to counsel no heavy work for a while. Meanwhile he was staying with his friends the Wrights. He had given up all idea of going to New Guinea — too fever stricken — or British Columbia — too cold — concentrating on improving his health and getting his weight up to 11 stone so that he could be photographed in Perth, to send his portrait home.

Modest success, a little leisure, and the need to recoup his health, gave James the opportunity to take stock of his situation. After six years of wandering and a variety of exhausting jobs, he was determined to try to settle down, an idea bound up in his mind with a complex of plans and ambitions — the wish to create a permanent home, the desire to get his brother Lewis across from New Zealand to join him, the intention of building some secure capital, and the determination to escape from the coarseness and crudity of colonial life into some higher level of refinement and civilisation. Some of this is evident in a letter of 2 December 1897 to his newly married sister Carrie, who had become Mrs Wallace, living in Downpatrick, Co. Down. James was trying to rent a large property, with the idea of then sending for Lewis. Having become very much the Australian colonial, James was critical of the New Zealand scene

You see in New Zealand things are much like the old country too civilised and as a natural consequence wages are down to zero and as Lewis says the highest wage he can possibly obtain is £1 a week and found. I have given half as much again to a nigger and a stray hiding now and again thrown in gratis.

At the same time, he was critical of himself — or at least not satisfied with merely a comfortable labouring performance:

Out here on the fields I can save £10 a month and when I say save I mean I can put that much in the bank and have plenty of pocket money besides for clothes, boots, tobacco, etc. . . .

I am doing all right but cannot get settled down. My sole ambition is to make a place I can call home and I can assure you it is through no fault of mine that I haven't done so. I am trying to rent this place I spoke about with the right of purchase for £1900 when my lease is up by instalments of course and I think I could manage all right when I have the place in working order.

Twigg's growing preoccupation with the idea of acquiring land does not fall within the Irish stereotype category of 'land hunger'. He came from a town and his family background was professional: his father was a solicitor, his grandfather a doctor. And his landholding ambitions were large-scale: not for him some tiny plot. Land appealed to James as both an investment — financial security in a highly unpredictable world — and a personal challenge. It was also, in a generalised way, both a stake in a country he had come to like if not to love, a tangible commitment, and an adventure. And it promised a respectable living with social status. Once he had mastered the land, and when it showed itself to have ceased to promise the kind of living he sought, he showed little affection for it, no abiding loyalty: it was a means, not an end in itself. Merely possessing land was not enough; it had to justify its keep on his standards.

This disposition chimed in with the social aspirations James revealed to his brother in a letter of 5 January 1898. Two years earlier he had impressed on Richard both the strength of his affection for the Wright family — and their poverty and powerlessness. Now he linked his plans to acquire land of his own with his determination to get away from these very kind but embarrassing cousins:

I am going to look at some land 20 miles from here as soon as I get maps down from Perth so that I can make a home for myself and I think Louis [Lewis] couldn't do a better thing in the event of my getting suitable blocks than join me. I can keep him with me all right and he can take up some land when he comes of age as he has a few pounds then and would have half the increase of my stock while helping me and I could help with the rough work in return for his work while with me. I really believe he would do better that way than in N[ew] Z[ealand] where he will sink to the level of a labouring man[8] as I nearly did here but have since risen a bit socially and don't ever mean to work for wages down here again.

I want to get away from Wright's if I can and make a home for myself . . . I am getting to know some very nice people round about and frequently stay away for a few days which breaks the monotony a bit. It is so nice to hear a piano again. You wouldn't believe how I enjoyed it. A branch of the Edgerton-Warburton's are among the earliest settlers here and have kept themselves very select. However I am admitted into the charmed circle and I can tell you I am glad to see a little refinement after so much roughness.

James wanted to break his nexus with his earlier associates so that he would achieve a higher social level of respectability and refinment and enjoy the arts of civilisation. This growing sense of divergence of lifestyle and expectation was a common outgrowth of the colonial experience. Some migrants were at ease with, indeed revelled in, the roughest colonial ways: they lived in a kind of expansive squalor, in which old-country habits of poverty were sustained unthinkingly in an environment of plenty, by virtue of laziness, ignorance and waste. To others, such as James Twigg, the liberty and opportunities of colonial life were a pressing personal invitation to seek the better things of life, to rise in the world and to make it a more pleasant and more cultivated place for him to live in. These divergencies operated not only between families that had known each other on terms of equality in Ireland, but occasionally even within families;[9] their development is not readily ascribable to variations of social status, or 'class', or of background and education. Perhaps their operation reflects basic idiosyncratic peculiarities of temperament and taste, suppressed or at least minimised by the stagnant Irish socio-economic world, but liberated by the free possibilities of Australia: 'bog Irish' became a term of opprobrium even within the Irish Australian community itself, to denote those deemed of lesser cultivation and cleanliness — and of low ambition.

By 15 August 1898 James Twigg had a grant of one thousand acres at Powalup, Balingup, near Bunbury. He told his brother:

> I am getting along slowly as I am by myself, Geoff [Wright] being on his own place. I am still fencing, but the land not being as yet surveyed, I am at a standstill until it is . . . I expect the surveyors any day. The weather is very wet, the river being in a flood . . .
> I could do well if I had enough to stock my paddock when it is fenced and ring-barked as meat is 8d. and 9d. a lb. in the towns now owing to the duty on imported stock and the dread cattle tick (ixodes bovis) has made its appearance in the North. Kangaroos are plentiful now and I can get one anytime in an hour or two. But ducks are breeding and I won't shoot them . . .
> I have the makings of a very pretty place if I can only get over the first three years I will be all right. I am getting a bit scared. I have to raise £25 a year rent. I would have only taken up half the quantity of land but was afraid of its being selected all round me and I was right too, as it has been taken up on three sides already and a man can't make a living off less than 1,000 acres that is grazing. If I can get other people's stock to fatten in my paddock I can raise the rent that way as they are giving good rent for paddocks. But I suppose I'll get through all ok so won't despair.
> Carrie is going to send me out some papers regularly and I wish you would try and do the same. If you were here for a week you would know what it was to be without anything to read in the evenings and no one to talk to.

By the end of the year he was settling in, but none too happily. As he told his brother on 16 December 1898, money worries were already beginning. With the financial commitment and the constant physical burden of coping with the demands of his land, the tone of his letters was changing from his customary optimism to worry and concern. He was over-extended not only financially, but, more important, emotionally: the challenge and the risks were enormous, the work lonely and unrelenting.

> I have been so busy that I have not had a rest for this last 6 months, Sundays included. I have been helping Geoff but have finished with him now and am back in my own little "humpy", running the wire round my block. The weather is very warm now about 112 degrees in the shade today and the sun is fearful. I am in good health but thin and could do with a spell very well, but must keep at it while my money lasts which won't be much longer now. Rent in March means £25 and I have just paid £50 for fencing wire freight and carting from station to here.
> . . . when I can get stocked and farm implements I will be right. I will have a very nice place in a few years and I hope with good management profitable

one. I have only £50 in the bank now and when I pay rent in March and for the young fruit trees in June, ordered from Victoria at 2s. 0d. a piece, I will have nil and must work for wages again. I won't go back to the fields unless it is for wages or other surety. I can't afford any more wild trips through the back country, much as I would like. I have spent my all on the block and am convinced it will pay me to stick to it. In fact it is Hobson's choice.

I have never got a paper of any kind from you but Carrie sends me a budget of penny papers weekly or thereabouts which keeps me fairly sane.

There are plenty of young ducks about and I anticipate good sport when the season opens in January. Everywhere people are looking for land but as I foresaw when I selected, it is all taken up that is any good. I wish you could come over for a spell. I can promise you good rifle shooting. I shot two kangaroos at daylight the other morning in sight of the house. Their tails make grand soup . . .

I heard from Lewis sometime ago. He talks of coming over here. I am not very keen on it. He says he has no money and I think has fooled all his inheritance away. The New Zealanders are a bad lot, they bear a bad name in all the Colonies. The place seems to be the resort of all the nere-do-wells and broken down Johnnies in the old country and he would be better out here. I could get him a good billet on a survey party in a few months at 30s. 0d. a week and found which is better than being groom for a sharper at 10s. 0d.

He had a welcome holiday at the end of the year, but a letter to his father on 16 January 1899 was gloomy:

I am still on the place although just about done now financially. It seems so hard when I have been getting on so well, to have to leave and work for someone else. A little capital now would make me independent of work off the place . . .

I have been on a three weeks holiday to the seaside to one of the oldest places in the Colony Lockeville the residence of the Locke's a highly respectable family one of them being M.L.A. for this district. They keep race horses and a few stallions of their own and have a fine old place all through. Plenty of tennis parties, etc. and boating, fishing and bathing, besides balls and riding parties and the best duck shooting on the estate of any place in the South-West. It did me the world of good as I was quite run down but I found that work when I got back was very irksome. However I am fairly into harness again and I suppose it will be a year before I go on the spree again . . .

I find the kangaroos scarce here now but ducks seem plentiful. I am still fencing; it is slow work by oneself. The ground is so hilly that the wire has to be packed on horseback for miles and if you ever meet a man who has packed any barbed wire, keep out of his way. Still on the whole I have got a lot done in the 9 months I have been living here but I badly want a little money now.

Work is hard to get and, when got pay is poor. The reaction which always follows a boom has set in and things are flat now in W[estern] A[ustralia]. A steady boom in land has however been going on but the selectors are a poor lot and will never stick. They are chiefly store-keepers etc from the fields and don't know how to work, much less farm, as one has to here to make it pay. While their money lasts they may do all right but, in three or four years, partly improved places will be going cheap.

Potato growing pays better than anything as they bring from £8 to £22 per

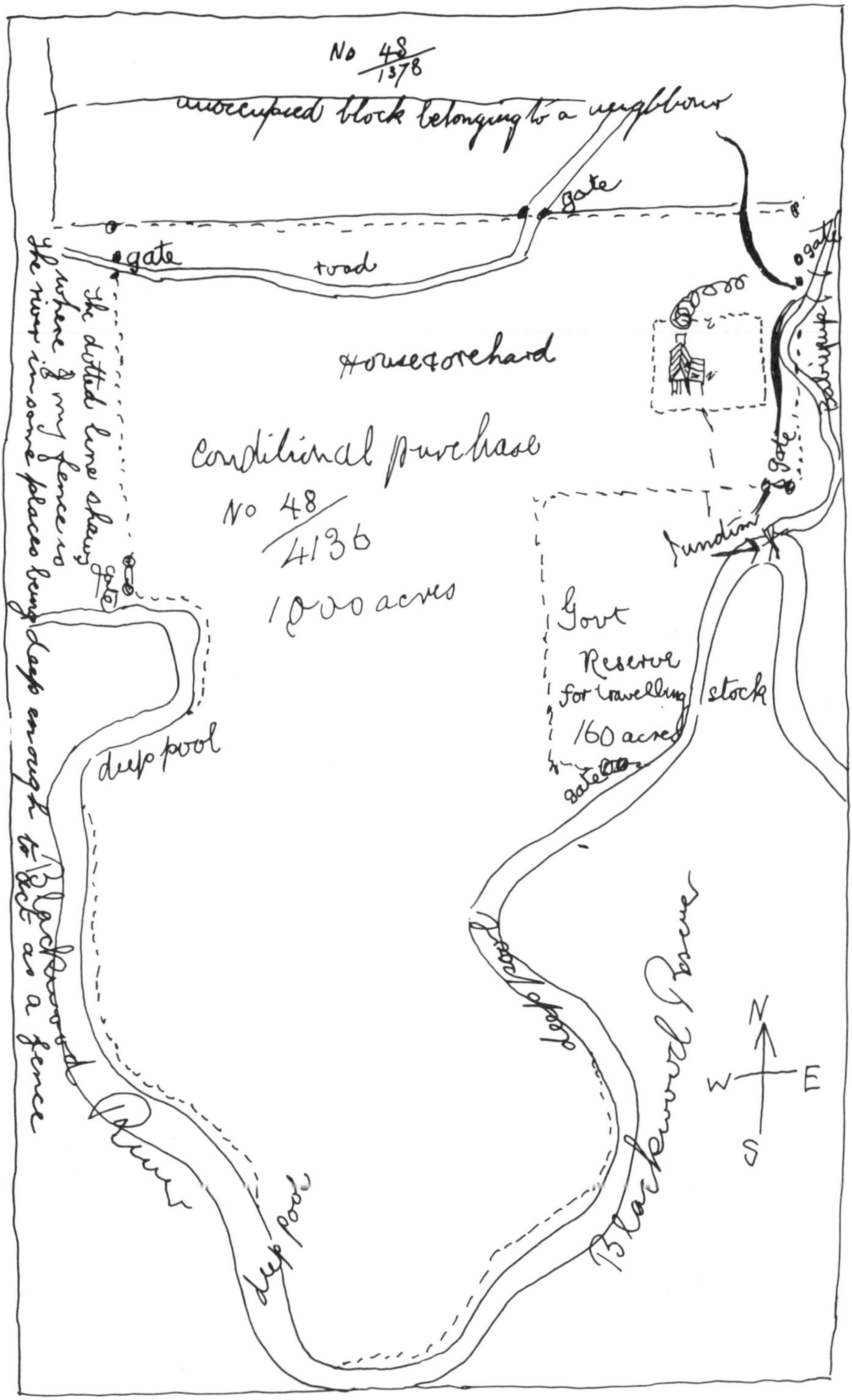

J.H. Twigg's sketchmap of his property at Powalup, which he sent to his aunt Jane in February 1899. (Courtesy: P.R.O.N.I. Belfast)

ton, about £12 being the common price. I have no implements and so am stuck in the mud.

On 26 February 1899 James wrote to his aunt Jane Twigg of Clogher, Co. Tyrone, giving details of his block of land and his fruit-tree planting and commenting on the misadventures of his brother Lewis in New Zealand:

> He says that on his arrival at Auckland his box, with all his money, was stolen and so he was left stranded there and had to find a job as best he could. But as you remark his letters are never very explicit and show great indecision. Of course he is young, and soft, and all these little things will sharpen his wits. You doubtless know that his partner was broken and that poor Lewis was swamped in the flood to the tune of all his little fortune. I think myself he got into the hands of sharpers at Auckland as surely he would never leave his money in his box and how is it he didn't come on to Albany, W[estern] A[ustralia] as he must have had a through ticket. Of course he might explain these things, but in his letter he gives no explanations at all. He has saved £5 where he is and when he makes it up to £10 he will come on. I am afraid he has been in bad hands all through.
>
> The Balingup brook is a tributary of the Blackwood and the town site and station are called Balingup too. Powalup is the black's name for the junction of the two. I enclose a map showing position of block and how I was enabled to get so much river frontage. Water being scarce in W[estern] A[ustralia] the Government only give a certain frontage running you back till you have the quantity of land applied for in a long narrow block but by taking a big block in the bend and there being a block at the back they had no help for it.
>
> I have finished the fence and am getting the ground clear for my fruit trees coming in June from Melbourne. . . . I am very fond of fruit growing. The pruning etc is very interesting, if carried out scientifically and the profits, just now, are enormous. Apples in the winter go up to 1s.6d. per lb. as there are no foreign or inter-colonial apples allowed into Western Australia for fear of disease, etc. The importation of vines is disallowed but anyone will give you the cuttings. One or two trellised round the house are all I will require for jam and eating.
>
> The "rosella" is the parrot you mean. They are worse than the rook at home for corn and I have shot hundreds. Snakes are only thick in the damp places. An Irish rush meadow like the one in front of Clogher cottage would be the very place for them. Of course we often kill them about the houses but a snake as a rule will always scoot when he hears you coming.
>
> I enclose a bit of the black cockatoo tail feather, peculiar I believe to W[estern] A[ustralian], untameable and nearly extinct.

As to his brother Lewis, James had been somewhat restrained in writing to his aunt. In a letter to his brother Richard on 13 March 1899 he expressed much more forthright criticism, sharpened no doubt by his own financial situation:

> I am getting rather sick of Lewis. He is an awful fool and I am afraid a liar as well. He left Napier to come to me with a few pounds he had saved from the wreck of his legacy and on reaching Auckland (says) he had his box stolen with his money in [it] and after a hard struggle got work as groom in some racing stables at 15s. 0d. per week and find himself and winds up by asking me to send him a fiver. However James is 'nothing green' and I wrote and

told him to sue the company under the Carrier's Act if the box was stolen while in their charge as it must have been.

Now from your letter I should say you had heard a totally different story, and from Aunt's letters to me he tells them some awful crammers. He was in debt to a fair amount before he got his pile on the expectation system, chiefly for subs to golf clubs etc. and then went in partner with his boss (poultry) who went broke and Lewis lost all. This is from what he has told me. He had £5 when he wrote and I think he had been cleaned out by sharpers. His box, unless very green, would not be the place to keep his boodle in and by his own showing prior to his departure he only had enough to come comfortably and then again he must have booked right through to Albany to save fare in which case why not come on, on his ticket and wire me for train fare from Albany.

I am stiff now myself and just about to take over a fencing contract 2 miles at £14 and Lewis could have helped me through with it. It is hard to have to leave the place when I am getting on so well. I want £40 to make my paddock sheep proof and £110 to stock it with sheep. I would in two years from then have a very decent living of say £150 to £200 per annum, as of course I can work at home and grow spuds, onions, fruit etc. But money is very scarce here now even the Government have over-reached themselves and are forced to retrench in the various departments pretty considerably.

Writing to his father towards the end of 1899 (23 October) he put a cheerful and confident complexion on his difficulties, placing them in the context of better times to come:

Gold has been found within one mile of old T Wright's on the *road* to his house, a fine big micaceous schist formation and some 12 miles further good reefs are crushing 3 ozs. regular. My place is just off the line (north and south) of the same belt of country and I am so tied down that I can't get off to prospect. One must have a little capital to take up a lease and develop it.

Of course land is going up like smoke and, *if I can*, I mean to stick to the farm. I will have a tight squeeze for the next twelve months and if I can wriggle through, I can then manage. My fruit trees are all in and making growth. Tomorrow I am going to ring bark for a neighbour about 8 weeks solid slogging with the axe 200 acres at £16 by myself camped out 3 miles from a human being.

Of course if I can let the big paddock next year I will be much better off as I won't have to save £25 for Government rent . . .

This is going to be a wonderful country. The mineral wealth is only just being tapped and in 5 years the output of gold will mean three times what it is now. This country down here will be harder to prospect, it is so thick and rough, very like the Welsh country with giant trees added, but once found, mines should be easily worked as all the needful, barring the battery, would be on the lease.

Towns spring up here like mushrooms in a night and the first thing one thinks is how they all live. About 5 pubs and 20 stores in a mining town of 1,000 about 400 in the town and the residue scattered in tents over say 5 miles square coming in to get drunk every night. The Boer War is now on. I pity the Boers and in fact a number here sympathize with them.

Horses are very dear here now, that is the draught stamp. Of course ponies of 14.2 or 15.2 are still cheap say from £5 to £15. Some of these bush reared things make excellent hacks and as hard as nails doing better far on grass

then chaff and oats. Medium draughts fetch now from £20 to £25, in fact can't be had. Heavies are very little more, being unsuitable for the majority of the farmers, there is no demand. You see a farmer likes something he can turn out when not in work and the heavy horses being all imported can't get their own living except when the feed is at its best.
Prices generally are coming down for farm produce and should we be forced to federate on the present terms it will just about ruin us around here, all the newly started industries for a certainty such as vineyards, orchards, etc.

In reality, as he explained to his brother on 22 December, his financial affairs were in desperate crisis and he had barely scraped through by getting a job ring-barking for four frantic weeks. Nor was the tenor of his ordinary life much better — 'one day work, eat, sleep, all the others ditto':

Prices are down to zero now and I am very much surprised at labour keeping up so well. Wages have never altered since I've been here but must soon as men can live very cheaply here now. I did my 200 acre job of ringing in 4 weeks making £4 a week. This is a record for the district, 8 weeks being the average time. Tucker cost 10s. 0d. a week as I shot my own meat. I worked like a nigger as it was life or death with me. I have *I think* another job coming off after Christmas 100 (acres) at £8 10s. 0d. the lot and I am sure I can do it in a fortnight if the weather keeps cool. It is 104 degrees in the shade now and has been for weeks. We generally work from 6 to 11, have dinner and a siesta, work again at 2 and knock off [at] half six then bathe, tea, smoke and bed. It is black as a dungeon at quarter past eight.
I feel the want of some stock badly and cannot really make anything off the place till I get some of my own. The £25 rent is what takes making up and a fellow can't always get work.
My trees look very well considering the heat. It must be 140 degrees in the sun as we often have it 160 degrees a little later and such a fierce heat too, if your sleeves are rolled up a bit higher than usual you will have all the skin peel off in 10 minutes and the ground is like a brick. I shot a large emu this morning running over 200 yards, broke his leg but flukes count you know every time.

By March 1900 he had taken employment prospecting for tin. His letter to his brother informing him of this (20 March) found time to take pride in Irish success against the Boers and to question Australian military suitability:

I am at present prospecting for tin some 8 miles from "Powalup" for a person named Gilbert at a wage of 9s. 0d. per day and all tools found and dynamite. I will stick at it for 6 months if possible.
I am glad to see the Irish soldiers fought so well and that all our best Generals are Irish. It makes one feel proud to think he hails from the same country. The Australian are, as you say, no doubt useful as scouts, etc but don't take kindly to discipline.

In a letter to his sister a few weeks later (8 April 1900) he explained that his work, which was very heavy, would enable him to pay some debts for farm stores, and then perhaps buy a cow or two. He was anxious to get some familiar clothing:

I would greatly appreciate any kindness in the way of *woollen* socks and brown flannel shirts. The former *cannot* be had in Australia; I mean such as I wore at home and I find the wool is unobtainable in that heavy quality. Perhaps

> you had better only send socks as I wear under flannel and cotton shirts. The former are from 4s.6d. to 6s.6d. and the shirts from 3s.6d. to 6s.6d. or even less. I would rather, if you still knit, have one of those white woollen sweaters like Dick used to wear for cricket. I play tennis a good deal and have to pay 12s.6d. for a flannel shirt and it shrinks when washed so that I cannot button the neck. Be sure and put the Ad Valorem duty as low as your conscience will allow. I will get photoed again when I go up to Perth next. Be sure and send me one of yours.
>
> I expect no more fruit than I can eat myself for four years as we prune hard back for three years after planting to get a stout stem and encourage root growth. A seven year's tree here is the shape of a wine glass and low. Apples are 7d. a lb. here now. I have had very little fruit this year.
>
> Everything is dear here. Look at wages nothing less than 8s.0d. a day and of course stores are in proportion.
>
> The Boers hold out well.

Obviously James Twigg — like many Irishmen, and Australians — was ambivalent about the fate of the Boers.

And also about farming. Far from being settled on his land, James had put it up for sale at a reserve which had not yet been reached. He explained this, and other news, to Richard on 8 July 1900:

> I have been seriously thinking of selling "Powalup" and have actually had it under offer at £600 for the last 4 months. I got a reply yesterday. I refused by wire. The intending purchaser would give £500 in 12 months. I would have bought a store here in the mining town I am now in situated about 13 miles from Powalup as the crow flies. I am getting now 10s.0d. per day of eight hours. I get the extra 1s.0d. to camp with the tin down on the washing site with a gun to keep tin thieves off at night.
>
> I don't think I ever told you I was robbed myself at the farm and caught the thief who had stolen my horse and saddle and all my belongings. I had my rifle with me of course and laid him out with the butt end. He has been in the asylum ever since from the effects of the blow.
>
> Since I've been here I was robbed again but the police caught the thief and I recovered one article, the revolver which I had marked and could swear to.

How he had been pushed into attempting to sell, he explained to his sister on 28 August. A winter of exceptionally heavy rain had flooded out the tin mine, depriving him of the extra money he needed to stock his farm. Without sufficient stock, his farm hardly provided enough to meet basic expenses. This induced a sense of extreme frustration, as he dreamt of what he might do with a little development capital. As it was, all he could make was a survival living, which would never enable him to get married. The future of West Australian fruit farming under Federation would be disastrous. He was lonely, worn out, old before his time.

> I am trying hard to borrow enough money to make my place sheep-proof and get sheep. If I fail I will sell out and go to South Africa. I am sick of working off the place for wages. One can just earn enough to keep the place without ever being able to stock it. I can earn at the lowest estimation £200 per year from my place, had I it stocked. It would carry 450 ewes and I would make this, and more, out of the increase and wool, besides what I could grow in the way of fruit and corn and potatoes, etc. For security I have the place

> itself worth £500 which I have refused from two people. I can get money but at 8% which is too high. I am trying for 6 or 5 if I can get it.
>
> If I had the farm so that I could make a living off it I could get a wife and things wouldn't be quite so lonely. Fancy seeing people only when you ride from 3 to 9 miles for I am separated from the Wright's by a roaring river and in any case it is only Geoff I care to keep acquaintanced with.
>
> I nearly lost my foal which is rather a valuable animal through poison not long ago but I roped it and bled it and it is all right now. This is the wettest winter in the memory of man . . .
>
> The Colonies, as you doubtless are aware, have all Federated which means among other things that there will be no inter-colonial duty on anything so that farmers and especially fruit growers will suffer. Instead of 10d., 1s.0d. and 1s.6d. per lb. it will (fruit) be 2d. and up to 4d. as they can send fruit from the older colonies cheaper than we can grow it. The benefits we derive in W[estern] A[ustralia] will be chiefly of the sentimental order, one Nation, one Flag and one destiny etc. We are getting along very nicely and could have held our own with any of them in another 10 years but it will cripple a lot of young industries on which thousands have been spent.
>
> Stock are dearer in the colonies than ever they have been before, meat 8d. a lb. in Adelaide and up to 1s.1d. here in Perth. I have never since heard from Lewis. My fruit trees are just starting to sprout out some being in blossom (plums and peaches) and I expect one or two on each tree will set.
>
> The constant hard living and hard work is making me stiff already. A man here of 30 is to all appearance as old as a man of 45 in the old country. Somehow one gets careless of cooking and often when one comes home wet and tired at night one hasn't got heart to cook an edible supper and just has some bread and butter (if he has butter) and goes to bed.

But for all this, as he explained to his brother on 4 October, depressed or not, he was not prepared to sell for less than his asking price. Besides, Spring had come and the bush was blooming. And he had been able to borrow money — albeit expensively — and to make an arrangement regarding some stock. His confidence was returning:

> I am getting sheep (200 ewes) on the following terms: a friend finds the sheep, I the paddocks and sole management and two-thirds of the increase and two-thirds of the wool, he of course the remaining third of each.
>
> I am paying 8% for £75 to fence it with and believe it will pay well, if I only have luck and no dingoes come around. It is, I can assure you, nothing to lose £30 or £40 in a single night by dingoes. The Government give 10s.0d. reward for every dingo destroyed, the proof being the scalp and tail . . .
>
> I have refused another (cash) offer of £500 for my place but will battle along now. The weather is glorious here now and the bush simply goregous with colour, blue, yellow and white flowers, creepers, etc mixed in one dense mass as far as one can see. If you ever pay me a visit come in September as from then till Christmas is the pick of all the year.
>
> Carrie sent me some woollen socks which were very acceptable I can assure you. I suffered with indigestion from the same cause as you and went under chloroform and had the lot (back teeth) yanked out and although I have had no others instead still I suffer no toothache and the other trouble a little Siegle's syrup always cures. A teaspoonful neat after meals and before going to bed will shift old Nick.

Ten days later (14 October 1900) he responded to his sister's Irish wonderment as to why he did not grow potatoes:

> We cannot get sufficient per ton here to make the growing of them profitable unless close to town, so that a big source of income is now removed from the bush farmer and he has to depend mainly on wool and meat to fetch him a living as the country down in this district is not adapted for the growth of corn, being too hilly and wet not to mention the cost of clearing the land in the first instance which does away with five year's profits at least.
> I am busy making my paddocks sheep-proof in hopes of getting sheep this season and should they do well, and the dingoes keep away, I may pull along all right. It is strange that since I wrote to Dick the said dingoes got into Geoff's paddocks and in two nights killed 36 ewes and lambs and more are so badly bitten that the blow flies will kill them too. He has poisoned one dog and other baits have disappeared so it may be sometime before he gets another visit. The blow-flies are a kind of big blue bottle and are so bad at the beginning of the winter and summer that they blow the sheep's wool and the maggots, unless constantly attended to, will eat the sheep alive. So you see a farmer fights nature out here in all forms. As the land gets opened up these things get less as the fly likes the dense bush . . .

The following month he explained to his sister (25 November 1900) that not only had he borrowed privately for fencing, he had also borrowed 'from the Government Land Bank a new institution and one I have great faith in'. He enclosed details of his loan, on the back of a printed prospectus of the Agricultural Bank set up under the Act of 1894, with 1896 Amendment.

> I have borrowed £200 for which in accordance with rules I have to do £400 worth of work. As I put a good valuation on the work the half value obtained from the bank will pay me well and give a profit from each completed piece of work to carry on the next.

Clearing 5 acres entirely at £10	£50		
Cutting black boys and ring-barking 950 acres at 5s.0d.	£237	10s.	0d.
Fencing 22 miles wire netting at 10s.0d. per chain	£80	0s.	0d.
Shed with lean-to 30 foot long 14 feet wide 12 foot high	£32	10s.	0d.
Total	£400	0s.	0d.

And he added:

> I feel the want of a little capital awfully as I have any amount of grass going to waste and could buy stock and fatten at an average profit of £2 per head at least. I am also stuck for a house. I could build a very decent four-room cottage (one storey of course) for £100, chiefly of timber. Matrimony might then be considered and the kids you mention duly counted before they were hatched. There is very little trouble here in bringing up youngsters. They earn their tucker I can assure you, as soon as they can ride and muster stock. I am afraid no Clogher money will come our way; those Dungannon sharks will take care of that. However, with help and luck I should be a prosperous man in ten years.
> Could you not send me out a nice little Irish girl with a small fortune? The life is a glorious one. A man can grow all he wants and a woman has little to do and no "conventionalities" to study. It would have suited a wild little monkey like you to rights.
> My orchard looks well and I expect some few apples next year. I have ripe

> cherries now! Working horses are very dear here and horse and cart costs, the horse £25 and the cart and harness £22; these are the lowest. At present I borrow from my neighbours. I am working now harder than ever in my life before ring-barking.

James's reference to the prospect of marriage prompted a swift reaction from his brother, who feared that James might marry a colonial, or at least, someone beneath his station. James — who, for all his colonial labouring, had no doubt of his status as a gentleman, derived from his Irish professional origins — was at pains to put his matter at rest, not without a touch of male crudity: family exchanges, including that with his sister, were devoid of prudery or embarrassment, while at the same time respecting the privacy of others. James wrote to Richard on 23 February 1901:

> You need never be afraid about my marrying other than a lady but how can I ask one to share poverty with me? In four or six years with God's help, which means literally by hard graft and luck I should be comfortably off and then "who knows" what may happen . . .
>
> I am getting very well known and I think at the risk of being considered egotistical I may add respected now. I am certain I have no enemies as I owe no money my credit is good for anything.
>
> A great many of the old country gentry came out here 60 or 70 years ago but they were all with few exceptions single young men and had to marry emigrant girls of no birth. The country was then boomed by the Australind [?] company. Father might remember it. A gentleman farmer here, if well married, has not such a lonely time as you might think. Visitors from the cities are dying for invitations in the summer etc and again there is so much in the little known fauna and flora of W[estern] A[ustralia] to interest an educated refined woman that the fact of her being educated is a host in itself. Besides it won't be for want of trying if my old woman hasn't visitors of her own shortly after marriage.

James was conscious of the sensitivity of his family to what they might regard as deficiencies in colonial manners and habits. In recommending to his brother an Australian friend who was visiting Ireland in 1902 and who proposed to call on the family, he remarked, 'You may find him wanting in little matters of etiquette. Most Colonials are, as this is a free and easy life. Still he is a gentleman and no fool.'

James's more immediate concerns were toothache, bushfires, kangaroos and the unwelcome prospect of the arrival of his brother Lewis. He told his father on 20 March 1901:

> I am working away on the place but am thinking seriously about going into town to get my teeth out. I went under chloroform 3 years ago and got all the double back teeth in the upper jaw removed and will now get the lot out. I have suffered more this last week than ever I did before or mean to again. The bush fires have been giving me fits this year. I wanted my own paddock burnt but had by law to get my neighbour's secure first. However, I've got it safely accomplished at last . . .
>
> The kangaroos are coming in more now as the back country is all burnt this year but I never care for the meat in summer somehow. It has very little nourishment in it and has to be fried with bacon to give it a flavour. Of course the tail soup is very rich. The tail is a mass of sinews and fat. An old boomer will stand about 7 feet and is very strong both in muscle and scent.

> In fact you can in the season (early summer) easily smell one before you can see him. In running shooting I frequently break their leg and have great fun when killing him with a waddy. They fight like steam and even with the leg broken can make nasty little rushes . . .
> Lewis wrote me from Queensland re coming over here. He wants a billet in some gentleman's house as lackey or coachman as he says he doesn't like hard work. If he takes my advice he certainly won't come here.

To his brother Richard he wrote on 6 May 1901 about his usual problems — hard work, bad luck, shortage of money — this time with a tinge of envy of those young men — English — better placed than himself:

> I am working away as usual and the outlook is far from cheerful. You have no idea what heart a man wants to tackle the making of a home here with only his hands. He literally carves it out of the forest. There are some young fellows out from England, remittance men we call them. As a rule they get £100 to £200 a year and are supposed to be doing great things in the way of farming. They booze all they get and when that is gone loaf on the settlers. The exceptions are few, but give a man £100 a year who is willing to work and it is wonderful what a nice place he has in a few years. I have a friend (Lethbridge) who failed for the army and who has the above allowance. He paid £700 for a nice little farm on the instalment system and lately his father sent him out £400 to pay off. He is doing really well and now makes quite a snug income dealing in stock.
> I've had a bit of bad luck. Geoff[rey Wright] and I tendered £40 for a small bridge across the Balingup brook but the rains are early this year and the brook is now flooded so we can't get our piles in. We could have earned the £40 in four weeks and I was rather depending on my £20 to meet some coming debts. As it is I will buck in and get some more work done for the Agricultural Bank but as I only get half the value of work done it means a lot of graft for a little money. Meat is going to be a snorting figure this year. My dog-proof fence is worth £60 a mile 2 foot 6 inches netting and 3 wires. Dingoes won't jump wire in this Colony yet.

But this time the problems were more than usual, and quickly worsening. Although the farm was worth substantially more than when he had tried to sell it two years before, by the end of 1901 his stock and financial arrangements had degenerated to the point of crisis. The arrangement to secure sheep to stock the station had fallen through. He could borrow no money. Bankruptcy threatened. He told his brother on 2 December 1901:

> My dear Dick I am in a rather critical position just now and was waiting to see what the outcome would be before I wrote. However I'm no further from a solution than before.
> I think I told you that a friend was going to lease me some ewes this season (by season in W[estern] A[ustralia] in relation to sheep I mean shearing time November as this is the only time after the wool is off that one can buy ewes at reachable prices). When the time came he wanted so much more rent than he had previously asked that it not only left me no margin of profit at the year's end but if I had chanced to have many losses I could easily have been out of pocket.
> I am trying now to come to terms with another man but am afraid I will not do much. I have now a fine place, fenced, sheep-proof and sub-divided into 6 paddocks and could make £300 a year easily, had I only stock of my own.

> For 3 months now I can purchase young tegs (2 tooth ewes) at 12s.6d. per head or by going a long way for 10s.0d. and I want 400. The wool from 400 sheep one can put down at £50 and the lambs at say £20 per year and then your increase you can sell at Christmas to the butcher fat at 10s.0d. easy and in good country like mine, well sub-divided, one should get at least 300 lambs from 400 ewes. This is putting in a margin of 100 less for losses and the other prices are also well in bounds so you see I could make £220 at this rate per year and in a few years when I get grasses established I can carry double the stock.
> As the Government hold my security I cannot borrow so am in a fix and cannot possibly get out of it. If I could borrow on P[romissory] N[ote] I could give 8% and repay in instalments and it would simply be a case of luck with the stock whether I got through or not. Dogs and poison weed are our curses here, but good supervision etc. can do a lot. I would not now voluntarily sell my place under £1,000 although if I was sold up it would probably only fetch £800.

By early in 1902 he was desperate and on 8 February wrote to his brother asking for financial help:

> If I cannot raise £150 before the 1st October I will have to sell everything and join some contingent or something of that sort.
> You can have no idea of the hard life this is or how lonely . . .
> I had saved up £35 from the bank money and bought 60 ewes lambs with it but will have to sell these by 1st October to meet my p[romissory] n[ote] for £75. They will with luck be worth £45 by then. If I only had £150 I could save these and pay my other debts and buy a few more but I am afraid I am buggered to use a forcible expression. However I have made a brave fight although I say it myself and I've never turned cur yet. When my horses and sheep go I will try and find a buyer for the place as without my four neddies I would be useless and when the bank gets their £200 out of the purchase money I won't have much left I expect but if I have over £400 I'll take a run home and see you all for the last time.

Richard responded with the offer of a £100 loan from their sister Carrie,[10] to which James replied on 28 April 1902 that this was not enough, setting out his assets and liabilities in some detail — and with the news that Lewis had joined him:

> My dear Dick, I got your welcome letter on Saturday. Louis [Lewis] is with me now, been here about a fortnight without any notice at all. I am breaking him in by degrees. He is easily influenced, I think, and does not seem to be over-burdened with gumption and I will find him very handy. He got 60 traps by my advice as possum skins are a snorting price and by having them all round my boundary fence he can kill two birds with one stone by looking after the fence and sheep and so save me two days a week. He only had £6. His grammar and style all round is something awful and I dare not take him anywhere . . .[11]
> Re the £100. I will first explain my exact position. First 1,000 acres ring-barked (all) and blackboys cut down, sub-divided into 6 paddocks, 5 of which are sheep-proof altogether 9 miles 75 chains of fence. 3 acres of orchard coming into bearing.
> A shed valued at £100 (with yards) a plough, harrows and scarifier; 4 horses and 200 sheep (lambs all). No cart but a fair kit of tools.

Government rent £25 a year.
Interest on agricultural bank loan of £200 at 5% = £10 a year and loan from Gilbert £75 with 8% interest £81. Total £111 besides living expenses.
Now, to meet these I have nothing but 200 lambs and only 64 of these are paid for. The balance were sold me by a friend who gave me 12 months to pay for them in. In order to pay him I will have to sell about 100 after shearing as they will be worth a third more then than when I bought them. Mr. Brockman who is an old friend and a rich man sold me the lambs at a shilling a head less than I got the 64 for and I paid cash for those too. But there are few like him. Now what I want is to keep these lambs and breed from them next year and in order to do that I must have more than £100. I will pay Carrie whatever you consider fair interest. The only thing she need be afraid of is my death and I will make my will in her favour. As the place is worth, with the sheep etc, £1200 at Geoff's [Wright] valuation but we'll say £800 which is a big drop as I've spent £500 in actual cash she ought to get a fair balance after the Western Australian Government Bank get their £200. There is not much chance of my marrying for years to come but in such event I would give her a second mortgage on the place.
Farming is no good. The land is too hilly and I am too far from market besides clearing is too heavy, but out of sheep, with the start I have, I could do well but I must be able to buy 200 more ewes after shearing. They would cost for cross-bred prime roughly a £1 a head and I must be able to keep what I've got.
I am very thankful to you indeed for what you have done but £100 will only prolong the agony. I cannot leave the place to work and I can make nothing off it for want of capital to work with.
What I have done has opened Lewis's eyes and Geoff [Wright's] who is much in the same fix, can tell you too. I don't want anything given. I am able and willing to pay fair interest but if you want to do me any good you must give me something to work on and I can repay in instalments when I get on my feet.
When I started with £200 my idea was to improve the place and sell when land rose but I have since got to like my little home and it is nice to see things you have planted growing and bearing fruit and I would dearly like to stick to it and die on it.
I have never made a will and often wondered who I'd leave it to. Geoff[frey Wright] made a will in my favour when he went to Adelaide to Dr. Hamilton but he came back all right and is thinking of getting married and I often thought I'd leave all to him. This is a risky life and many's the narrow shave I've had from falling trees and flooded gullies and a man never knows what may happen but I know the place would pay a good dividend after my debts were taken out and I will make a will in Carrie's favour if she will let me have enough to pay debts and buy some sheep.
Thanks to my good boundary fence I've had no dogs in yet but they are in my neighbour's now. Geoff's sheep are in my home paddock as the dingoes have taken possession of his and he is after them day and night. They killed 13 in one night and next morning we mustered the flock and I let him put them in mine. He has a poor fence, thinking careful supervision and poison would be enough but I differed from him.

A letter to Richard on 8 July told of his continuing fight to maintain a subsistence living:

> . . . Lewis is turning out all right and works well and hard but can't do much. He has a great liking for the garden and I encourage him to grow all the vegetables he can as it helps the tucker bill.
> I had to sell my horse the other day to buy food and pay the half yearly interest to Government. Rice is 3½d. a lb., sugar ditto, and butter is 1s.10d. flour 28s.0d. a bag (200 lbs). This is since federation but can't last long.
> Aunt Jane says you suffer from your teeth. Take my advice do as I did: go under chloroform and have all out and get a set. I have never had indigestion since to any extent and Siegles syrup cures it then. The teeth are the primary cause of the thing and of course in my case rough food.

In September he received a £200 draft from Carrie, and wrote to both his brother and sister on the 22nd. In acknowledging the money, he explained to his sister that he would also get paid for some contract fencing he had undertaken: Lewis had been trapping, shooting kangaroos, and doing the cooking.

> . . . I will have £25 in about a fortnight for a fencing contact I am doing for a neighbour and so I will have a little for my wool this year and may get another contract in the summer. I will now be able to worry along. I will have to pay for a paddock for my sheep at the end of summer as I must burn my own paddocks this year, the ground is so choked by leaves and twigs from the dying trees. In about 3 years all the rubbish is down and only the trunks and main limbs left and they stand for 50 to 100 years and during those 3 years the ground must be cleansed by fire or the grass can't grow and besides the ashes manure the land as long as the fires are not fierce enough to burn the roots of the grass.

To Richard he wrote about their brother Lewis — quiet, industrious, but helpless at anything requiring skill — and of his determination to improve his intolerable housing situation:

> I must try and improve my hut this summer for which it is adapted but I cannot stand another winter in it. I think I can build an adobe one myself. Anyhow I mean to try. Sawn timber is hard to get and a long way to cart it and Loo and I could make the big mud bricks in a week for a small hut. Aunt Jane is sending Loo out a bible and me two pair of socks. I reckon I'm getting the best of the deal and he seems to think so too. She is also sending us out some illuminated texts to hang on the shanty walls!! Some of the boys will think it's a church.

In fact James still attended church, but the trappings of religion were low on a list of colonial priorities where death might be casually encountered by accident and the immediate utility of a pair of socks was much more obvious in, and apposite to, the parlous pioneering situation than an irrelevant bible there was no time to read. James knew what he needed most. He told his brother on 5 November 1902:

> What I want now is a house. My debts came in all to £198 10s.0d. but the bill for P[romissory] N[ote] for the sheep I won't meet till due on 4th January next. The other one I paid or met on 1st October last and I will get about £18 or £20 for my wool this year. If I had a few more sheep and a four-roomed cottage furnished I would not be a bit afraid of matrimony and would be a lot better off and contented.

The obvious solution to the housing problem was to build one, although by this time Lewis had left him to work in Queensland and James would have to construct it by himself, with a boy to help. He described progress on 15 February 1903:

> I am awfully busy making bricks for the adobe house. They are 17 [inches] by 9 [inches] by 6 [inches] and weigh 44 lbs. on average and it will take 2,500 to make what I want. I have nearly finished the bats and start on the foundations this week. Of course I will only complete one room for my own use this winter. The others can wait till I am in better circumstances but the iron roof *must* be on and soon too or I will have the winter on me and be ruined. I am going to do everything on my own with a boy to hand mortar and bricks etc. I will send you a photo of it when finished if I can capture a Kodaker anywhere.
>
> I am working all the hours the Lord sends and at top speed. The brick making is heavy work and slow. I could easily make and burn the ordinary brick, but when it came to building, although I could lay them all right, it would take me a long time and I would want a lot of lime and there is the chance that the kiln would be a failure. I will plaster the mud bricks outside with a cement wash to protect, in addition to verandah, and the whole should be a very comfortable four-roomed cottage "bungalow" style of roof. The roof is the only thing that costs anything but time, if we except doors, windows and sawn timber.
>
> 9 March: I am awfully sorry old man but I was called away to help a neighbour fight a big bush fire and I have never had time to finish this till now and I am writing this after tea by lantern light on a makeshift table. I have been, and am still, most awfully busy with the house. I am, I am glad to say, making a first rate job of it so far. The bricks are splendid and I am laying them well and true. The house is four rooms two 18 by 12 and two 14 by 12 with ten foot walls. I am now building in the window frames and have the chimneys and partitions up about 7 feet from floor level.

Winter and the demands of the farming round soon stopped building, as James reported to his brother on 1 August 1903, but not before he had completed sufficient of the roof to keep him snug and dry.

> I am busy at the lambing now and by this time have 84 lambs of which number only 32 are rams. Ear marking, castrating and tail cutting are all jobs I am now an expert at. I suppose you know a good hand can cut and tail about 1,000 ram lambs a day keeping 2 men very busy catching for him. One slash cuts off the end of the purse; the testicles are then squeezed out with thumb and finger, dragged out with the *teeth* with one back jerk of the head, another slash at the ear, then the tail and next please. One gets covered with blood from the tail as it squirts out from the two big veins for about 3 feet and for a couple of minutes in a day they are skipping about as well as ever but must suffer a lot as the testicles are dragged right off the kidneys.
>
> Having such a small percentage of wether lambs will materially effect my future income for this year as of course I must stock up with the ewes. . .
>
> I am in a hole through losing my big cart horse. He got poisoned weed and lost the use of his hind quarters. I took chaff etc. to him in the paddock till he got down to it, and went home to fetch the Martini; came back and found him dead so saved a cartridge. Swore an awful lot and vowed (different to swearing) that I would buy a lot of arsenic and soda, borrow a syringe and kill every blade of it on the place. It would be a gigantic undertaking but could be done in time and with an awful lot of really hard work in carrying water up the hills etc.

When Lewis was here I took in 300 wethers (store) to fatten on half the profits. I lost 130 in no time but fattened the balance and got such a good price that they fetched me clear of my liabilities but I had a big gain in experience.

Financially, James was beginning to get a little ahead. He sold fourteen cases of his apples at 17s. a case, and a little wool. But the unfinished state of his house and the missed opportunities of his underdeveloped and undercapitalised farm continued to depress and frustrate him, as he told his brother on 25 October 1903:

> The rain has been so universal that the north-west stations have any amounts of fats [fat cattle] to sell this year and sheep are selling in Perth now at 4½d. per lb. Last week they were 6d. which is a rattling price. Had I the cash to *buy* now and the grass to *hold* I could nett hundreds in March but the country necessary to carry the sheep is the clause that sticks. One wants a lot, and good too as the Nor West sheep too, can't stand poor feed.
>
> Wool promises well this year which is some consolation, though my little bit won't flood the Bradford market. It is very galling to a man to see good chances of turning over money and having to let them slip through want of cash.

The real news of this letter was of his plans to marry Alice Bradshaw. The decision required him to overcome his pride, for his circumstances were not the affluence he would have wished.

> She is the first girl I ever met that improved on nearer acquaintance and we have made up our minds to get married by next spring (August). She says she can help me so much in hundreds of ways by keeping fowls etc. and house-keeping and I have been looking thin lately and she thinks I'm starving myself etc. that I have resolved to make a big effort, put pride in my pocket and as others have done, make a humble start in the way of furniture etc. and get married. You would say I was wise if you knew how awful this solitary life is, week after week and only the mail on Saturday.[12]

Perhaps it was this news — with its connotations of 'settling down' and the pursuit of security — that prompted his brother to ask if James belonged to any Orange Lodge. He replied:

> Re Orangeism I believe there are lodges in the larger towns certainly in Perth and Bunbury, but I live so far from either, and money is all their cry, that I seldom pass myself as an Orangeman, and doubt whether I remember enough to get admitted to a lodge.
>
> Benefit societies are all the go here, where all men are dependent on their hands to fill their stomachs but I belong to nothing. I am putting the money into something better; though I may never see it back, those I leave it to may know my work was not for nothing. Land is ever increasing in value, as it must, where there is such a small portion suitable for home making out of all this big desert. People who make money in the north or east come down here in this "Sou West" corner to make a home and now the good land is all taken up, they have to pay big prices and this must go on, up and up, as the population increases.

Writing to his father on 28 November 1903, he was able to report progress on various fronts: house building, shearing, the farm generally. Yet his social unease was growing. Despite his manifold pioneering achievements, despite his obvious enjoyment of them, he still did not feel at home: something in him stood apart from and above the common colonial norm. After twelve years in the colony — all his adult life — after turning his hand to the roughest and most demanding labouring pursuits, he still felt different and alone, and that his neighbours were objectionable and ignorant. Their sensitivity was of a very different kind from his: where his represented an educated and articulate refinement, their's was crude touchiness.

> I may be able to get the boards, doors and windows by end of January with a bit of luck, but I can get no work of a payable nature close to home and I daren't go far away as bush fire time is due after Christmas till April. I found shearing very hard work indeed. It made me so stiff that I could hardly get out of bed the first four mornings. We shear here in a totally different way to you old country people, your methods of holding the sheep being found too slow. It is simply marvellous the way some of these constant shearers get the wool off a sheep under two minutes, and do them well, while it takes me 18 to 20. However one has to learn and I want to do everything myself, that I can, in order to keep down expenses.
>
> I am all alone now and have been for sometime. I am going to strive hard to have the wife here by next August. She is full of pluck and doesn't think it fair for me to do all the work and a women out here isn't the costly and useless thing she is at home. These women can turn their hands to everything and Alice says she can keep the house with fowls etc. if I'll grow the corn to feed them on.
>
> I made £12 out of my fruit last year and may make nearly that this [year], but prices are falling fast as indeed they need do. Land is fast rising in value and when the house is finished I will have no difficulty in selling, if I wished, for £2,000. For many reasons I would like to leave this part of the country. Where a man has made himself by the work of his hands he has unavoidably made many acquaintances of an objectionable character that it is snobbish to cut and yet that he cannot associate with. And yet I wouldn't like to leave the place I've toiled on so. And new country means new experience which is generally expensive, so perhaps, as Alice says, it is best to live it down. In this wild land one must keep in with one's neighbours for many vital reasons and these ignorant people here are very touchy indeed.

And yet he was locally popular. It was a painful ambivalence in which he was now permanently trapped: he pined for the jolly Irish Christmases but loved the solitude of the bush. On 4 December 1903 he wrote to his sister about his approaching marriage and of his own health:

> I am a thin ghoul-like looking creature with hollow cheeks etc. owing to bad food and no back teeth, indigestion, liver, etc. But Alice says she'll soon fatten me up. I am better as regards the heart trouble, more so, I think, since giving up smoking. It was a hard fight. For 15 years I have smoked constantly but scarcely miss it now. You have no idea how awfully lonely it is even with all the farm work to do, no one to talk to, and I only can spare time to go and see Alice every 6 weeks or so. We want to get married next August if I can possibly manage but although I keep a stiff upper lip and talk hopefully in my letters to her I often feel very dubious about being able to have things fixed up by then. We are both fairly popular and may expect a lot of the usual "rot" in the present line and, of course her people find all house linen,

> but furniture even of the humblest kind, costs much boodle however sparing one may be . . .
> There are no singing birds here and the bush is as silent as the tomb except when one disturbs some cockatoos and they make an awful row, and the trees are all the same colour, a sombre black green, like a yew. You will always find bushmen very quiet men who rarely laugh and I suppose it must be the effect, and solitude, of the bush.

On 16 January 1904 his tale was the same as usual — unrelenting work.

> I have so much to do on this big place that I have no time to go anywhere. Even my Sundays are spent, by way of rest, by going round the sheep and I was butchering one last night at 11 o'clock and up this morning at 5 to get the carcass in before the flies got at it. I am very thin now but feel in very good health. This hot weather a man can't be bothered cooking and the eternal salt mutton and damper and jam is, I assure you, nothing to look forward to after a hard day's work and it requires no small amount of pluck to keep on. The orchard looks promising this year but being away so much from home the birds get the best of the fruit. One blessing here is that the nights are always cool even chilly after the great heat and so one always gets a good night's sleep. I haven't shot anything, barring a snake or two, for ever so long. Every year one has narrow escapes from snake bite, and it is a wonder people are not more often bitten. I do so much more walking than most Australians that I have far more escapes than most people.

It was the same story on 18 February, though James was taking great pride in the progress of his house:

> I have been awfully busy at the house etc. Sundays and all. There is truly no rest for the wicked (and poor). The season is one of the hottest on record. I am busy plastering the house and find it, without help, a slow job as I have to mix, carry, and put on all on my dead own. I am now quite an adept and can slap it on true and level and quick. At first I found it rather hard as, of course, it is a trade of itself but I've surprised everyone and the house is going to be a credit to "Ould Ireland".
> I expect to have house finished by end of April with lots of luck and must then buckle round after a contract to earn enough to furnish by August.
> Alice is working away at shadow work etc. She says she is going to have one decent room at any rate . . .
> I am so hard put that I have had no show of sending you the interest on the £200 but I have left the principal, with 5% per annum added, to Carrie in my will so you can look on it as an investment. Fruit is falling now in price, as you can see, by the Western mail and I am not in a position to grow crops yet and, as I am only one-third stocked, my income is very limited indeed. I would dearly like to go to New Zealand but my capital is too small should I realise. I want to plant 10 acres of fruit trees in the next few years which should make the place very valuable . . .

Obviously, from the reference to his wish to go to New Zealand — a country of which he had formerly been highly critical, but where he had relatives — he was still by no means settled on his farm: not sentiment or success kept him there, only his financial situation and the building of his house:

> I am very proud of my house but it wants a lot done to it yet. The timber will cost about £30. Just as I get a nice few pounds together, rent day comes

> round or tucker bills come in and knock me down again and so it goes on. There is a lot to be made here with fowls and Alice talks very big about what she will do. Some of my neighbour's women make £2 a week with eggs in the winter.
>
> I am working on Sundays now, and have never had a whole day's rest for months. Sheep seem to take a lot of attention and kangaroos keep breaking the wires. You know a big boomer in full jump at night would knock a house down and I have to be constantly going round mending or the wild dingoes would soon play old scratch with my flock. The Government have stopped the kangaroo shooting but I bang the brutes over every show I get. They are increasing too in this district but ducks are getting very scarce on the river now.

On 14 March 1904 he reported to his sister further progress on the house, now almost complete:

> I will soon have the house finished now as I have ordered the timber for the floors and the first coat of plaster is all on. You wouldn't believe all there is to do and I have to plot and plan how to do them by myself. The rooms are drawing room 18 feet by 12 feet, dining room 18 feet by 12 feet and two bedrooms 14 feet by 12 feet, kitchen and store rooms each 15 feet by 10 feet and bathroom 8 by 10. The latter building is only in my head at present and as the bath fixings [fittings?] cost a pound or two but I can erect the room in verandah corner in a very short time. It will make a very cool comfortable house and is strong, so much so, indeed that most people laugh. An architect from Perth gave me many valuable hints the other day re plastering but was kind enough to say I ought to be very proud, indeed, to think I had built it all on my own.
>
> My sheep are looking very well indeed but the hard time of the year is on us now when they have to live on dead grass, bleached snow white with sun and rain. Indeed it would puzzle you to see what they do live on in the winter.
>
> The birds are worse this year, than they have ever been known, owing to the scarcity of their native food and my fruit suffers in consequence. I am like a jumping jack first thing after day light out with the rook rifle shooting parrots. They sit in the trees and turn their heads sideways at you and when the rifle cracks the others only stop eating for a second or watch the fluttering one on the ground. I feel so angry with them sometimes that I can hardly load the rifle and feel like throwing it at them.
>
> Can you advise me re furniture? How about bamboo pith or cane? We only want one decent room in the house as few people will see the other.
>
> I can furnish on time payment but don't like "over loading the cart". I am quite satisfied that I'll never do any good till I am married. This deadly loneliness and hard work and hard food is just about killing me by inches and I am really more fit for the hospital than the church. Alice is staying at the coast in a swell hotel and having a fine time while I've been fighting bush fires. All the hair is burnt off my arms and eye lashes etc. but I got it under.

This style and pace of work and life was sustainable only so long as James's health held good. But what if it did not? Just how precarious was his mode of existence became obvious, as he wrote to his sister on 19 April 1904.

> I am down with influenza and being all alone it is rather rough on a fellow.

> Luckily I have baked a big batch of bread and carted some small wood and the rain gave me water off the roof, before I got ill, or I should have had a still rougher time. Anyone passing would think I wasn't at home as my present abode is back of the house. I heard someone crack a stockwhip once and once someone cooee'd but I couldn't answer. This is my first day up for nearly a week. The pains in my head and chest seemed hardest to bear.

He gave his brother further details on 26 May:

> Things haven't been progressing favourably at all with poor me. I've been having a rough time with influenza and no one to wait on me. It hit me while I was rather down too, being underfed and over-worked trying to run too many things at once. I didn't want to keep any sheep for my own use as I wanted them all to sell (wethers) when the price rose a bit and consequently was living on bread and jam, rice, spuds, etc. and so was weak. However I'm all right once more and hard at it though very thin. I suffer a lot from indigestion having no back teeth to chew with and no time or means to get a set.
>
> The house is very slowly nearing completion but one man makes slow work of this sort of job. I am very proud of it and am finishing it off in style. Two rooms are now finished bar the colouring on the walls and painting. I made a real good job of the plastering for an amateur and put nice architraving round doors and windows, borrowing beading planes for the purpose and getting a real good book on house-building but I made many bloomers and so the work was slow . . . .

However, his major worries for the future were not so much personal, as general threats to the West Australian farmer: he feared the imminent depradations of Labor parliaments,[13] bush fires, and the advancing rabbit plague, as coming scourges of roughly equal proportions:

> I am afraid the colonies and W[estern] A[ustralia] in particular are going to have a hard time of depression soon. The labour men are getting into the State Parliaments in big majorities and their aim seems to be big wages and cheap food two things dead against the farmer. Fruit is now let in free from any where and this has let prices down with a run, apples being very cheap all the year round now. Clearing the land out here is an awful item and when chaff and wheat are down the poor farmer has only his stock to live on. If I could only stock my place to its full capacity I could easily clear £400 a year but I was nearly burnt out this year and I *must* be next so I will have to arrange with someone for a paddock for a few months. You see the bush burns every second year the fire starting out with the timber mills, though the law is very severe if anyone is caught setting it alight in summer time. We settlers make breaks and stop these fires but next year all the country to the east, north and south of me hasn't been burnt for so long (3 years) that the fires will be so fierce no break will stop them. All alone I made a break 3 miles long on my west side 8 feet wide with rake and spade and when the fire came I met and burnt against it. It will be to my own advantage to burn next year . . .
>
> The rabbits are coming nearer and nearer now. It is a very vexed question whether they will live in the "Sou West" it is so very wet here for 4 months in the year 10 inches (of rainfall a month) and little or no ground for dry burrows back from the sea hills. I will finish the house now in three weeks. From careful perusals of catalogues we have come to the conclusion it will

> cost £40 to furnish with just the bare necessaries. The sitting room with Jap matting and some pith or bamboo chairs and a couch and Alice has curtains made, and a picture or two. I for my part don't care so long as its home. I've lived a dog's life now for over 12 years and it's had its effect on me. A man can't live on sodden bread, black tea, bacon and salted junk etc and camp in all places in weathers for so long without feeling it. I will be 31 next August . . .

Taking stock of his age, health, and the looming threat to his already uncertain livelihood, James issued his brother with a request for information and notice that, come the rabbits as a last back-breaking straw, he was about to quit: 'find out what B[ritish] C[olumbia] is like. When the rabbits come we'll be off'.

Still, there were his plans for an August marriage. On 30 October he wrote to this brother explaining why that had been postponed, and would be delayed further.

> I don't think there is much hope of our early marriage, as my sole source of income is my sheep and my lambing this year was so very bad that I will not be able to realise any sum now for some months. The blow flies kill some of my best ewes, through my now being unable to attend to them. When they get blown they wander off by themselves and in these rough hills and thick bush and bracken, take a lot of finding. The main loss was through being compelled to use old rams as being so much cheaper. It takes all my wool money to pay my store bills. Just now the butchers are getting big supplies from the Nor' West and turn up their noses at lambs that are not prime . . .
> There is not the slightest chance of our ever being able to get home. This life is not at all a money making one. I am simply "existing" on bread and jam and now and then some kangaroo and am as thin as a post. It requires a lot of determination to live alone and on such tucker for 6 years and working hard too. One has such nasty set backs too. Just as one is getting a bit ahead, a horse dies or dogs get into the paddocks. This year the eagles were very bad and are hard to kill. They seem to simply kill the lambs for sport as you rarely find one eaten. I always carry a bottle of poison and when I shoot wallaby or a kangaroo, poison portion of it. Louis shot a lot for me when he was here. He used to get them watching the possums in his traps.
> Not enough breeding ewes is my great draw back and in order to live and get married I just sell my ewe lambs so I am getting no forrarder. Potatoes here fetch from £4 to £14, the market depending on supplies from Eastern States. When a ship comes in with spuds the price drops.

By now Alice had become a decisive factor in his life, and virtually the only force keeping him tied to what had become a nightmare existence in a situation he had come to hate. His rage against the imprisonment of his farming circumstances boiled over in his letter to his brother:

> I haven't seen Alice for 6 weeks as she is now at home doing some sewing for the home. She will neither let me sell the place as I wish or borrow money to get married on as she says it's a bad start. Had it not been for her cheering letters I would have sold out and taken her to Canada or anywhere away from this cursed hole.

And all the time the idle, the fun-seekers, the incompetent wastrels continued to enjoy themselves and apparently prosper: it was only human to wish to predict — indeed to secretly hope — that it would not be for long. James wrote to his father on 22 November 1904:

> The Wrights are still pottering along on their very badly managed little farm. Every building is propped up and all fences in ruins, too indolent to do anything, only thinking of shows, races, dances, etc. Having plenty of stock they get their money too easily to value it but it can't last long.[14]

James was clearly out of sorts, and the news and observations conveyed in the rest of that letter show a similar souring of tone:

> The Labour Party being in power now, are making things very hard for the "pioneer". So far the "beef" ring has proved too strong for them and they have failed in pulling down the prices. They aim at high wages and cheap living.
>
> I am carting my few bales of wool to the station today. The "clip" is a poor one in this part this year, "earthy backs" prevailing, caused by too much wet in thick country. The wool goes like Astrachan all down the back causing a broken fleece. My lambs are very fine this year however.
>
> I think it probable that we will be married at Christmas but I will have to cut things down very fine indeed. We will be unable to have any little trip to Perth, just a simple wedding and then home. Not much for a girl to look forward to is it? . . .
>
> I am glad Lewis is doing well [in Queensland] but rabbiting is not the game it used to be and if he earns 7s.0d. a day on average I am told he is doing well. Years ago the rabbiters in the other States earned far more than the biggest squatters and had imported English horses and carriages to drive round and inspect their men. They gave swell dances and picnics etc.
>
> This is a great year for grass in all the colonies, the rains keeping on so late and the big stock owners should be able to breed up to what they held before the drought. We have no big stations here and no droughts. Our biggest sheep station only runs 12,000 while the ones up North run 50,000 to four times that. They train the Blacks to shear etc. so the labour question is nothing up there and good managers and foremen, teamsters etc. are easily got while they get their runs for 2s.6d. per 1,000 acres and less and run 10 sheep to the 1,000 or more in some parts. Imagine the expense of fencing sheep proof. In good seasons the country is like a grass sea but soon blows away in dust when the sun parches it. Three good seasons in succession makes a man a rich one and he retires but mostly with broken constitution so where is the good?

James Hamilton Twigg married Alice Bradshaw on 10 January 1905.

In February-March 1905 James sent his father some of his observations on Western Australia in the form of what he described as an article. Much traversed the same ground as his letters, but there were comments which were new. He had no respect for Australian sporting attitudes — or honesty in that area:

> Hunting the kangaroo with dogs I never cared for; it is not sport at all. Very few Australians are genuine sports. They love horse racing and crooked running at that and will never work for their sport as we do.

Nor did he think much of local wine — though a boy who left Ireland at seventeen might not be thought a connoisseur:

> The class of wine made out here strikes me as being very poor. They think it must be heady and strong. I have never tasted anything in the way of light table wine that I thought anything of but some of the wine of a port nature is very palatable.

The matters which most attracted his attention and interest were worker dominance of the political system at the expense of landowners like himself — a topic to which he always warmed as a pet complaint[15] — the silence of the bush, and the customs of the Aborigines, which he had long viewed with fascination:

> This is an ideal home for the working man as distinguished from the settler. The working man comes from the other colonies, leaving his family behind as living is so dear over here and earning from 25s.0d. per week on the farm and his keep or 10s. per day at the mills, down to 8s.0d. and keep himself or if he takes out a timber license and goes hewing sleepers at 1s.0d. to 1s.6d. each for either the Government or a big contractor he can earn from 10s.0d. to £1 a day and his outlay for tools is only about 50s.0d. Also if he has £100 or so when he lands he can invest it in two horses and a dray and go sleeper carting for the hewers and earn splendid money, say on an average 30s. per day. All this money is sent out of the colony to keep the aforesaid wife and family so although these men have an equal vote with the land owner they don't care a button for the State and are doing the State no lasting good. Their union keeps up the price of wages and controls the hours of labour and they now are in full power in our local parliament. Their policy is high wages and cheap food, the direct opposite to the farmers. By taking off the duties on imported food stuff etc. they can keep down the prices to a great extent but owing to the great distance by sea and the shipping combine's high rates, prices still keep so that we can grow stuff at a profit. The day these men, who only live a few months or weeks on one place and in a tent got an *equal* say in the affairs of the State Government with the land owner, it was a fatal day for us as they soon put into the Legislative Assembly their own men chosen by the Union and the first thing they passed was the Payment of Member's Bill! £200 a year and now they propose raising it to £300:
>
> The first thing that strikes a newcomer to W[estern] A[ustralia] is the dullness of the bush, the sombre hues and the silence. Unless the wind is blowing the latter strikes one at once. You feel, as one used to, in a very big church with the organ rumbling away up in the roof somewhere. Now and then a bird chirps to its mate or some parrots or cockatoos make their harsh noise, and then one may ride miles without hearing a sound. A kangaroo or wallaby jumps off like a shadow making, after the first startled rush, no sound at all and soon lost in the scrub. Before and after Christmas, for a few weeks, the bush in places does look pretty to us, as the wild flowers are out then, some of them being very beautiful in their construction when examined carefully. Of the Aborigines no trace is left now in the South West, beyond a very few round the towns and country villages and a sprinkling of half castes and very smart fellows they are, very athletic and mostly splendid horsemen and crack shots, quick with the gloves and generally pulling off most of the events at the country sports unless squared to lose . . .
>
> The much read-about "boomerang" all over W[estern] A[ustralia] called "kylie"is more a toy than anything. I remember reading how a traveller saw a black throw one at a flock of cockatoos and how in its erratic flight it killed first one and then another and then came back to its owner. This is all tommy rot. I've seen some of the best throwers in a mob [?] of 500 blacks throwing their "kylies" on the shore of Lake Way and not a dozen of them could speak any more than a few words of English, and understand that its not every black can throw a "kylie" just as some of us are better shots than others; it

> was simply wonderful the way they can make the thing go . . . When one hits anything, ever so slight, it simply falls fluttering to the ground but the blow it strikes is immense and the noise it makes considerable. They are rarely used for anything except fighting or amusement. In a fight it's first spears, then kylies, then sticks. The combatants begin by calling one and other names (presumably) the women helping. Then they get their weapons but are at once held by their friends and struggle like mad in the "let me at him style". The women keep in the background exciting their men by shrill cries and walloping bushes with their "wanas" [?] or digging sticks. Presently the men are loosed and whiz goes a spear the distance being just 22 yards or so. The spear goes like lightening and as straight as a bullet but the other fellow just seems to lean a little one way or the other and it just grazes his naked body. He then lets fly, each coming gradually nearer till you wonder how they miss but the little shield taps off the point of the spear nearly always. When the spears are thrown, they are at once picked up by the women and broken, and when one or other is speared the fight ends. An old man comes up and spits on the ground making a little mud and plasters the spear hole with it and the "buck" is walking round in a day or two as proud as Punch. Of course this is only in the case of a thigh wound etc. and the spear generally has to be cut and pulled through owing to the barb and if he gets it through the body with a glass spear it's a case. The "kylies" make ghastly wounds. I've seen a whole camp at it hammer and tongs, but little harm was done, a few broken wrists and one man speared through both thighs (high up). They are wonderfully clever at dodging. I could go on writing for a week about them and their customs etc as I loved studying them and hunting with them. They are the best hunters in the world and the most patient.

The long-expected bush fires arrived in June 1905; on the 20th James reported the damage to his brother:

> The bush fires came on me from every side and all I could do was get the bulk of the sheep mustered and away to a paddock some 12 miles north west of here which I had bespoken previously and the best I could get. A few got burnt. All attempts to keep out the fires here are unavailing unless greatly favoured with wind etc. The country is too rough to plough breaks and they would be no good as the burning pieces of bark and bracken travel for 300 or 400 yards and burning logs break loose and roll down the hills firing the dead grass as they go, smashing one's fences and raising Cain generally. I have lost 38 sheep (ewes) all told and it is a very serious loss to me too.
> I have just recovered from influenza, thanks to Alice's good nursing, and now my foal has got poisoned and I am afraid will die or be a cripple. Such is luck.

He concluded this letter with a remark that pointed the direction of his future

> I saw in the "Times" an account of British East Africa that attracted a lot of attention and I am writing to Downing Street to get particulars from the Agent for the Crown Colonies.

Writing to his father on 4 February 1906 he explained why he was considering moving to British East Africa. Basically the reason was the same as had unsettled him since he had taken up his land seven years before: he felt trapped by lack of capital into a life where the future promised only poverty and unremitting hard work and he was determined to escape.

J.H. Twigg with his horse, in front of his house at Powalup, about 1906. (Courtesy: Mr Elliot Wright of Busselton W.A.)

We expect a little one about the end of March and Alice is away for a week at her mother's making clothes and things. I am all alone and miss her sorely. She is wonderfully well but, poor girl, doesn't realise what is before her . . .
I am seriously thinking of selling out and, either shifting to a less thickly timbered part of the State, or of going to British East Africa. It is nothing here but a bare existence, no sport of any kind and the hardest of manual labour from early dawn till dark. There is not one settler in this part, who makes more than a living, even those who have big families of sons like the Wrights and have no wages to pay, are poor.
If one could enlarge one's holding it would be all right as one could increase one's flock but all the good grass land was selected 7 years ago. It costs, in this portion of the State where the very heavy rainfall is, from £10 to £80 per acre to clear the land and the £10 land would be poor, either stiff clay, stones or sand. It can be cleared 100 miles north east from here for 30s.0d. and is better land, but the poison has to be cleared off it before stocking, say another 10s.0d. per acre. I don't want to be a drudge all my life and I have a big asset in a varied experience if I go to a new country where there is black labour.

On the table land of B[ritish] E[ast] A[frica] the climate is lovely, owing to the altitude and many are going there. Australian merinos have been imported too and I am watching the result with interest and am getting all the information from Downing Street that I can, from the Emigrants Information Office . . .

There is no doubt this is a splendid country for a working man but for the same obvious reasons it is no good for the man with small capital. If I got a decent price I should be able to land in B[ritish] E[ast] A[frica] with £2,000, after paying all debts etc and with my experience and ability, I would not be a bit afraid.

Canada is too cold and the Argentine I know nothing about. Besides there are mineral possibilities in E[ast] A[frica] of a very promising nature.

There are openings in the "Nor West" of this Colony and the Northern Territory of S[outh] A[ustralia] but only for men with from £8,000 to £10,000 capital, to start on stations but the life would be too rough for a woman.

By 25 July 1906 James Twigg had firmly decided to go to British East Africa. As he saw them, the attractions were that it had an excellent climate, cheap land, and cheap black labour. More powerful still was that it seemed a land of vast possibilities, new, exotic and strange — or at least different, and it was not Western Australia. Much of the impetus to move sprang from those old social discontents, from James's feeling of unease in his Australian world, from his belief that he could do better, could climb higher than his present circumstances and surroundings would ever allow.

I want to get right away from this place. I am dragged down by old associations and one can't get away from it here where the population is so thin. Another reason is I am ambitious and know I can never educate my kids on this place and as all the land is taken up now, there will be nothing for them to do but work with their hands at trades etc. Alice is quite of my way of thinking too, so you may hear at any moment we are all en route.

East Africa had become to him the emigrant's dream reborn. As that dream took on more glowing substance, with emigrant literature and the reports of friends and acquaintances who were there, the contrast between the limitless possibilities of East Africa and the constricting realities of Western Australia became more stark and dominant in James's mind, as was evident in a letter to his brother on 1 October 1906.

Alice and Carol have both bad colds. We are having such a late and wet winter, quite unprecedented, and consequently an unusually bad year for grass. The sheep are everywhere looking miserable and butchers giving 7d per lb. for carcases. Most settlers have had heavy losses not only here but in all the colonies. Some years ago the Government withdrew the 2/- per head on eagles and the result is only sheep owners trouble to destroy them and so a big increase. I have lost between 40 and 50 lambs this year by them. I found 7 dead on a little patch of ground no bigger than a cricket pitch and only the eyes taken and disembowelled; just killed for sport. They drop on the lamb and only seem to touch it and it is dead. They meet the talons through and through behind the shoulder. To make matters worse I haven't even got one bird the whole season and I can assure you it hasn't been for want of trying. So far I have not succeeded in selling the place. Cash buyers are scarce and the new Government's land tax will make them still scarcer. Nearly every farm in this district is for sale!!! The clearing is so fearfully heavy

and labour so high. . .
The policy of "one man one vote" adopted by this colony some 5 years ago has done a lot of harm. The tramp on the roads has an equal vote with the owner of 10,000 acres. Coupled with the payment of members (£200 per annum) it has resulted in a lot of "gab gifted" adventurers getting into parliament and doing a deadly lot of harm to the settlers by lowering duties on imported stuff to bring down living prices and putting the wages at a high standard.
If I can find a buyer I certainly intend going to B[ritish] E[ast] A[frica] to have a look at the country. The best land here will only run a sheep to 3 acres and that after years of improvements. English grasses won't stand the long dry summer. B[ritish] E[ast] A[frica] will carry on the high escarpments 4 sheep to the acre and *is* doing it now with native hairy sheep so why not with merinos?
. . . a young chap left here this year for there, from whom I am also expecting a report. Lord Delamere wife and children are living there and their stock flourishing.

The problem was, to sell what he had at the price he wanted. As he explained on 21 January 1907:

Selling out is not too easy. Buyers are many, but few have capital, and the hills frighten them, and they want too long to pay in. We are making a living here and in no way forced to sell and will simply wait patiently till I get my price. There is absolutely no future to this place. The land is far too patchy to support any population. The settlers sons even cannot get land to settle on and people, deluded here from home, are going back again disgusted.
People come here, take up the land, and then, and not till then find out that they must grub the poison plant up before they can stock. Some English farmers took up some heavily timbered and ferny land without poison south east from here. They fenced it and found that it wouldn't run their horses all the year round (they only had 3) until it was ring-barked and the trees dead (3 years). They went home again. In the eastern districts where clearing is light (30/- to £3 per acre) on some of the areas those who selected 4 to 5 years ago are doing well. They grow wheat, and that alone, and run no stock except for working purposes. These are the people set up as examples by the W[estern] A[ustralian] Government but all that land is gone and the remainder is sand plain etc or held by big land companies and sold at exorbitant prices. Wheat growing is debarred from us down here in these hills. Out of my 1,000 acres, I could perhaps plough 100, that is taking patches here and there level enough but these patches would cost from £12 to £24 per acre to clear and the poor returns would never pay.
If you *can* get me any information of B[ritish] E[ast] A[frica] from returned sportsmen or anyone else I will be glad of it. We expect No. 2 in April or early May and I want to get out of this before I am hampered by too many kids.

On 25 March 1907 James wrote to his father to tell him that he had sold the property. It, and two other adjoining properties, had been bought by a Mr Sharpe, a wealthy Presbyterian Irishman from Cootehill, Co. Cavan, who had been in Australia since he was eighteen: he was now sixty. Sharpe had a station in the North-West, and property in Perth. As James had constantly insisted, large-scale holdings and substantial capital were the only means to successful

Happier days; J.H. Twigg in East Africa, after he had left Australia. (Courtesy: Mr Stewart Twigg)

farming in his area: Sharpe had bought the three adjoining properties for his son, who would consolidate them into 3000 acres to carry 1000 ewes.

James's letter to his father told him he would have £2000 clear to start in British East Africa. He wanted more information on the area if his father could get it, and some letters of introduction to someone there, if that was possible. But in fact his father was dead, even before the letter was written.

Leaving his wife and two children behind, James went to East Africa to prepare the way. He was glad to leave. As he told his brother on 31 March 1907:

> I want to get away as much from my surroundings as anything. We don't like our neighbours. The few with money are such snobs.

On 13 December 1907 he wrote from Nairobi, to report the safe arrival of his wife and family. He liked the climate and the country: he would probably go sisal growing in the Kedong Valley. At thirty-four, after sixteen years of arduous pioneering in Australia, he was no longer young. But he was still hopeful, vigorous, self-confessedly ambitious, an enthusiast. There was something in James Hamilton Twigg's aspirations and character that Australia never seemed to satisfy, a need that it failed to meet. In part this may have derived from the erosion of his dream of personal empire and leisured wealth, but there was much more to it than that. It was not so much a matter of a sense of superiority (though that was present) as a feeling of difference, of separation, of being an outsider, of not being fully at ease. Why that should be so in a country in which he had spent half his life, and where other migrants felt fully satisfied, must remain something of a mystery. Who can explain why one man more than another feels more sharply the restlessness, dissatisfaction and sense of being incomplete, to which all are heir? Versatile, adaptable and tenacious pioneer though he was, James Twigg in Australia remained the essential pilgrim — perhaps nothing mysterious, for the condition of migration most closely resembles that of pilgrimage.

7 THE FORTUNES OF A FAMILY 1883-1929

The brothers Hugh and John Colven Maxwell were two of a family of five sons and two daughters, children of a moderately prosperous small tenant farmer, who had some grazing, land for crops, and good horses.[1] The family was Presbyterian, and also Orangemen, but not enthusiasts in that cause. The two brothers left London for Australia on the *Liguria* in October 1883, travelling third class, which they detested, complaining of poor food, rough usage, and having to sleep too close together. Hugh was aged twenty-five; John twenty-two. While Hugh's emigration seems to have been part of a general process stimulated by large families, lack of opportunity, the search for adventure, and established patterns of behaviour, John's situation was specific. He was suffering from consumption, and was one of the many who emigrated to Australia for their health, seeking a cure in a dry sunny climate — and in the voyage out.[2] On the basis of his experience he passed home advice to another consumptive:

> I believe the sea voyage will do John Newel good provided he comes second class but if he does not it will probably kill him as many who are far on in consumption die on the voyage.

This was sound advice, confirmed by the deaths recorded on board ship, and John was to repeat it often in the years that followed, in relation to other Irish sufferers who thought of Australia as offering a cure. For John Maxwell it seems to have worked: he ceased spitting blood and his cough diminished.

From the *Liguria* Hugh Maxwell reported (27 November 1883):

> There are a great many old "collonians" on board and they say that most money is to be made in the "bush" as the[y] always call the country. Melbourne and great cities like it are mostly pretty well supplied, while more inland it is hard sometimes to get hands.

The experience of travelling to Australia with successful earlier Irish migrants returning from visiting their former homes, was shared by his brother William Maxwell when he emigrated four years later in October 1887, on the *Ormuz;*

> . . . there is a great many people going back to the colonies by this boat. They

seem to have done very well as when they went out 14 years ago one party had only 4 1/2d in their pocket and another party 1s. 7 1/2d. so you see there is more money to be made in the colonies than in poor old Ireland, if you have only a little to start upon.

A typical Ulster village about 1910: Laghey near Moy, Co. Tyrone. (Courtesy: P.R.O.N.I. Belfast)

Obviously, at least by the 1880s, there was two-way traffic between Ireland and Australia: as in the case of America, affluent migrants returning on visits disseminated in Ireland information about Australia and an image of sun and success.

Hugh and John Maxwell emigrated with a group from their own Bangor district, which included their friends Sam Jelly, Hugh Sheils and William McBride. They had direct Australian contacts in the Reid family,[3] earlier migrants known to the Maxwell family, who had established themselves with substantial business and farming interests in and around the Victorian township of Yackandandah, fifteen miles or so from Beechworth, itself 150 miles inland from the port of Melbourne.

On arrival in Melbourne, the group was met by and introduced into a network of earlier Irish arrivals, relatives and friends. To Hugh, Melbourne seemed a very fine town, all the streets at right angles, with electric lighting as well as gas.[4] The group first stayed at a Temperance Hotel, where they contracted diarrhoea. George and Hugh Reid came down from Yackandandah, asking John to go back to their farm with them: he was 'not to attempt any heavy work for a little, only what will amuse him'. The Reids were only one of a number of Ulster Irish families settled around Yackandandah: the day after their arrival in Melbourne, Jelly, Sheils and McBride went up there and got work on the harvest. They were binding wheat at 7s a day, plus board, which they reckoned good wages.

In Ireland, Hugh Maxwell had been a shop assistant. After walking around Melbourne for a week, applying in a great many shops, he got employment (a "crib" as he put it) in a large draper's shop in Elizabeth St, at 30s a week. This was through the kind offices of another family friend, a Mr Andrew Agnew,[5] known from Ireland. Agnew was an established businessman, and, to help towards securing employment, he also added hospitality. Hugh explained (12 December 1883)

> Mr Agnew invited John and I down the first Sunday to his place where we met Mr Crickard who of course we saw the day we arrived. Mr Agnew was very kind. Mrs Agnew showed us much friendship. We saw Miss Aicken. She looks in very good health. We have a good feed of strawberries and other fruit. I commenced on Friday last 7th December and when I was leaving Mr Agnew in the street he again invited us to go out a second Sunday, also a Mr Brown from Co. Down who he was also trying to get into a situation but Brown went to a situation in a country town about 200 miles from here so John and I went ourselves and enjoyed a pleasant evening. We also went to his pew in the church he goes to in Melbourne. His residence minds me of some of the house[s] you would see up in the Malone Road [Belfast][6] with their lawn before the door and nicely laid out ground but in the Australian fashion with veranda etc. He has four nice little cobs or rather ponies. He drives one of them in town when going about business to the bank etc. His business is a "Coach builders Ironmonger" not coach builder and ironmonger. He proposed to give John a letter of introduction to a farmer he knows if John does not like to stay where he is gone.

Yackandandah about the time of the Maxwell's arrival. (Courtesy: State Library of Victoria)

From Yackandandah, (11 and 12 January 1884) John Maxwell described meeting a wide range of various degrees of cousins, friends of the family in Ireland and numerous Irish acquaintances, who provided instant social acceptance, and contacts for initial employment. Letters of introduction and the clergy also helped. So did Irish migrants on the same ship. John was optimistic:

> Mr George Reid is going to try and get me on as a coach driver between

Beechworth and Yack[andandah] . . . The situation will be worth a pound or 25s. per week. Each driver has only to drive a few hours every day and was[h] his coach twice a week (I will have my board too). If I do not get this "crib" I will likely get on a sheep station after a little.
There is a Mr Finlay who I got an introduction to by the Rev. Robinson who said he would try and get me a "crib" on a station but he advised me to take a month or six weeks before commencing work. I went to Dr. Bird of Mel[bourne] before coming up here and he examined my chest and give me a recipe. He also weighed me, I was only 11st 3lbs without coat and vest. My light weight was owing to my having diarrhoea for a week which greatly weakened me. However I have not [had] it since.

The Esplanade, Bangor, about the time of the Maxwell's departure. (Courtesy: P.R.O.N.I. Belfast)

Within a few weeks of arrival, opinion among the Bangor group was divided on the respective merits of their old and new worlds. John reported home (12 January 1884) of Hugh Sheils:

> He is getting along nicely but is always talking about how much can be made at home and how a man who has a farm could make money. My advice to such people would be to stay at home and content themselves and not be running of[f] to Australia away from their relations and society. Yet he says he is content. If money is to be made at home how many men can get 7s. a day for harvesting and £1 a week and board as a ploughman. I know a young fellow named Brown who has £1 and board for attending to horses and doing a little farm work and another named McBride who is employed with a Mr Henry over beside James Reid's here who has 15s. per week and board. His work is not hard and he eat[s] at the table with his master and mistress of everything of the best. I know for I have been often over there and has stopped nearly two days with them.

> Hugh Sheils is working to Alexander Perry at ringing trees. I suppose you would not know what ringing trees is if I did not tell you. It is to take about 6″ broad of bark and the last spring's growth off right round its circumference. Young Jelly is going to Albury about a situation next week.

John approved of a country where work was much easier to get, wages higher, and a man could sit down with his master. Besides, he liked the heat, his health had much improved, he had put on weight, and his cough seldom troubled him. His only cause for annoyance — and he was furious — was he had found that his family in Ireland had been discussing his letters (or alleged lack of them) with the neighbours: this came back to Australia in distorted or erroneous forms which reflected badly on him and Hugh. He demanded that his letters be treated *en famille;*

> H. Reid has a letter by last mail from his brother giving all particulars and among the rest that the Maxwells had not written from Plymouth (that was a mistake). You know it looks careless not to write from these places where the ship calls at. And I felt it greatly when it was read out in my hearing that we did not write. There were none of whole party who wrote more than us. You must not be saying anything I said, to any of the neighbours. You know it might go to Watson's or Sheil's and then come back here and if it does I will promise you that all the news you get will be little from me. Remember that.

Hugh and John Maxwell devised a system whereby they wrote to each other within Australia and then sent such letters on as enclosures in letters to family members in Ireland. And they sent each other the family replies. Thus was formed a regular interchange of family information and opinions between Ireland and Australia.

John did not stay long with the Reids at Yackandandah. In February 1884 he went North to central Queensland, to work for Ebb Smith Esquire, at Werribone station at Surat, 350 miles inland from Brisbane. Hugh, then living in Napier St, Fitzroy, in Melbourne, reported home on 27 February:

> John was only one day there when he wrote but he was likely to like his billet pretty well. He has a little bedroom to himself and eats with the overseer of the station and his wife. He was helping to put up some fences as he must know how to tighten the wire before he can be a boundary-rider. He says that Queensland is much "ruffer" country than Victoria as much as Victoria is "ruffer" than home, some of the roads in the bush being very bad and no stones on them. He describes them as like the moss roads.

John Maxwell was not the only one of the Ulster migrants who had come to Melbourne on the *Liguria* in November 1883 who was restless and mobile within a couple of months. Frequent changes of location and employment were the rule, not the exception among the newly arrived. Hugh remarked on 27 February and again on 26 March that those who had gone to the country were drifting back to the city (and vice versa), or simply moving around from job to job. Some were dissatisfied, others just footloose and unsettled. They changed addresses constantly, moving between relations and friends, or sharing houses or boarding together. They began various ventures — usually short-lived — dreamt about others, craved action and change, thought about home and missed the structured social life and occasions for fun they had left behind. It seems likely that this unsettlement and mobility was, if not new, relatively enhanced in the 1880s. A buoyant Victorian economy was one factor helping it. So was the number and wide dispersal of earlier Irish migrants, known from Ireland by the parents of the new younger migrants, providing a range and dispersal of employment possibilities, people to see and places to visit not available earlier. There was also, by the 1880s, a new type of Irish migrant, one habituated to the migration process as a central feature of Irish life — and, perhaps, with extravagant expectations. John Maxwell conceded (27 March 1884) that Mr Agnew's Melbourne house was 'a beautiful place' but 'not nearly so extensive a place as we were made to believe on leaving home'. Commenting in April 1885 on the Australian fortunes of a Mr McVicker, well known to the Irish family, John observed:

> I don't think he . . . has made much of it in Australia although he has £2 a week and every opportunity of getting an advance but he seems not satisfied and the country is, I believe, behind his estimate of it at home. People come here and think they will get money almost for the lifting and are disappointed when they arrive.

In subtler, less fanciful forms, the myth of colonial, as well as American streets paved with gold was long dying.

In the midst of all this movement and dissatisfaction, Hugh Maxwell was a paragon of stability and sense, patient and frugal, very sure that the single man travelled lightest, a realist among those with ambitious hopes. All expenditure was carefully controlled. Washing cost about 9d. a week: at the rate of 4d. for a shirt, a collar, a pair of socks or a handkerchief, this suggests very infrequent changes. Hugh did his own darning. He wrote home (27 February 1884):

> I saw S. Jelley on Sunday. He is down in St. Kilda with a cousin of his there (a butcher) where he is going to stop until he gets a crib. His cousin says there is a good chance of him getting one soon. Jelley seems to think that H. Sheils is not too well made up with the country; perhaps his expectations were too great or he may have jumped at the thing without thinking seriously. However he has had his £1 a week and found up to the present. He was not working to Perry lately but was helping a young farmer to split timber at £1. I think there is not enough of sport for him and he may be troubled a little with homesickness. If he had the first 6 months over he might come round. However *do not* say anything about this to anyone for you know how soon it would spread. Be especially careful about this and let it be his own pen that shall make known the fact. Indeed it is a very common thing to find people grumbling when they are well enough. A young man from near Lisburn the name of McBride is a little tarred with the same stick. He was up in the Yack[andandah] district also but has left it and gone to a place south of Melbourne and is going to try his hand as a missionary. He had never been from home until he came out here so I suppose that is how he takes it so hard.
>
> There is another Co. Antrim young man that was up in the district about Ballarat about 50 miles from here. He liked the country very well and had constant harvest work and 5s. a day found. He could have got £1 a week the year round on a farm there but he thought he would see what he could get about Melbourne first. He has got a job at pick and shovel work at 7s. a day and is stopping with a neighbour of his who came out in the Liguria also. This said neighbour has bought a horse and dray and can earn nearly £4 a week at drawing rubbish or stuff somewhere about Melbourne. Mr McNight

was thinking of starting something of the same but I do not know whether he has or not. Of course people cannot expect fortune to shine on them all at once and it requires a little patience.
John was making me laugh when he was in Mel[bourne] that H. S[heils] was saying that there was no markets or fairs and seems to look on this as hard indeed. His time for that sort of thing has not come yet and it would be a very poor way of making money or saving any if there was many markets and fairs.
I consider that I can keep myself on 17s. or 18s. a week including washing, never speaking about the beer or tobacco, cigars etc which does not happen to form an important item. I do buy a few apples occasionally to help digestion but the habit of eating apples can be left off at any time.
. . . if Harry has any notion of coming to any of the colonies of Australia I would recommend him not to have a burthen where with to regale his shoulders, in the shape of a wife with him as he will be far lighter without one . . .

At the Maxwells' home near Bangor it had been a sad Christmas without John and Hugh. John wrote from Queensland on 22 March 1884 to console his mother:

. . . she need not mourn for as soon as my chest gets better I will surely give Old Ireland a visit again. Although the climate of Queensland is well suited for a [we]ak chest yet it is not well suited for the liver. I am greatly troubled with my liver now and then. I think so much mutton and beef and the warm climate is the cause of it. If I had plenty of buttermilk I would not be troubled with it. I never have seen buttermilk since I came to Queensland but Mrs Smith the manager's wife is going to get three or four cows and make butter so I will get buttermilk then but Australian milk is not so well tasted as the home milk because it [is] only the cream that is churned. . .
You will be surprised when you hear of my being in Queensland. I got a letter of introduction from Mr Agnew to Dr Rowan whose brother and himself owns a good part of this station, Smith the manager having also an interest in it. The Doctor's brother gave me a letter of introduction to Mr Smith and sent me up to Queensland. The letter said that I was a new arrival who had chosen the squatting as my profession and that I was to receive exactly what pay I was worth. Mr Rowan said he would write a private letter to Mr Smith telling him I was to have a little room or cabin separate from the other men. I have my meals with Mr and Mrs Smith and I have a nice little bedroom where I am now writing but as regards pay I don't know what I will have. I would be content with 15s. per week. If I don't get that I will try something else. I intend putting over winter here if I can and next spring to get a job at sheep or cattle driving down to Victoria and there begin harvesting and afterwards either to return with a drove of sheep or employ with a farmer. There is always sheep going south and others going north which you will think strange. Sheep can be reared cheaper in Queensland and are driven south to a better market and good breeds of sheep are driven north."

In Melbourne, Hugh tried to help new arrivals from his home locality and responded to one of the numerous queries from prospective migrants passed on by his family in Ireland. He wrote on 2 June 1884:

. . . I suppose Mr. McVicker will be in Melbourne in little over a week. I will do any little thing I can for him but it is indeed very little that I can do. Of course I can introduce him to Mr. Agnew and I suppose that is the best I can. I hope he may be fortunate in getting a situation but as far as I can understand things are a little dull just now.

There is a young man from Belfast, a grocer, who came out in the Liguria with us, and went to a situation up country shortly after we came, but about three weeks ago he left his situation to try and get one in Melbourne. He has been looking about a good deal and has not been successful yet. I see him very often; indeed he often calls on me to have a walk and a talk; of course he is likely to fall in before long, but not so quickly as he would like. John says that "times are bad" in Queensland owing to the drought. I believe Mr. Gowan would be better to come to Victoria. Queensland is very warm and rough. Victoria is quite hot enough for anyone to work in. There is not much land to be taken up now but he has plenty of money and could buy a farm. Up the Goulburn improved farms sell from £6 to £10 pounds an acre [freehold]. There are other districts where farms can be rented but I can pretend to say very little about it as I know very little. The climate of Victoria is well suited for any person with chest complaint. . .

There is some talk about unemployed labourers and scarcity of work yet I see by the papers that farmers in some districts cannot get a sufficient number of hands to get their crop in. These said unemployed turn up their noses if they do not get a high rate of wages and will not work for low wages so they are not so much to be pitied.

A fortnight later, John joined Hugh in Melbourne, explaining to his parents (17 June 1884):

> . . . . you will wonder when you get this why I left the station so soon. I would not have left so soon had the food been good enough to afford healthful nourishment. The first seven or eight weeks the food was pretty good as I got plenty of milk for my tea and sometimes a bit of rice pudding for dinner but the two cows which we had on the out station went dry consequently there was no milk to be had and all my meals consisted of bread and salt meat and tea without milk. I would have put up with it for a bit had I not got a cold which started my cough so Hugh wrote for me to come down to Melbourne and I did so and got here yesterday morning and was quite long enough on the station. Hugh was greatly uplifted when he saw that I looked so well for he was very uneasy when he knew of me getting cold. Hugh Sheils was telling me yesterday that there was never a bit of life in him when I was away and whenever he heard of my coming back his spirits rose and he [Hugh Maxwell] got quite cheery. I was quite long enough on the station . . . all I got for 15 weeks work was £8 so my trip to Queensland was pretty dear. It cost more than twice as much to take me there and bring me back again so you see I have not made a pile yet but I hope my fortune will change by and by.

On 10 July the brothers wrote a joint letter in thanks for a post office order sent from home. Such remittances point to the responsibility Irish families felt towards those members who emigrated, helping them financially if they had the means to do so, particularly to get established on arrival: the traditional picture of Irish migrants sending money home to support aged parents is only one facet of a complex set of two-way financial relationships in which money was given, inherited, bequeathed, lent, borrowed and transferred. On this occasion John observed:

I was not in such great need as you expected but at the same time the order was acceptable as I am now out of work and do not intend doing anything till I am quite rid of my cough. Had I remained another three weeks among Mr. Reid's people I would have been earning something instead of being idle. I could, provided my chest was strong, be earning 6s.6d. a day for very little work on the police. They have only eight hours duty. However I have to content myself with the thought that the summer will make me all right. At present I can eat and sleep well and scarce ever feels ache or pain except on a very wet day or a cloudy day before rain. (I always mention myself first because I know you will want to know how I am first and then you will read or listen to what I have to say, afterwards, better.) I believe that Hugh has had his health as well if not better than when at business at home. Of course he is sometimes troubled with his stomach but you could hardly expect any person who is confined in a draper's shop all day to be as strong as any one who gets the fresh air and plenty of outdoor exercise.

Hugh told his brother William that he had moved to a new address in Market Street, South Melbourne, the house of an Ulster friend:

. . . we are now lodging with Mrs. McDonnell. We can manage to live cheaper at least my bill is more reasonable than when I was stopping in the other place. John and I have taken to porridge in the evening and find a great benefit from it. Mr. McVicker had a walk out with us on Sunday, indeed the last two Sundays. He has been here several times in the evening. Of course he is a little lonely and we are great company to him. He is getting along nicely in his situation. He got the same salary as myself to start with but he thinks he will never have such fine times again as when in J. R[iddell?]'s . . . Mr George Reid called with me a fortnight ago. His father and Hugh [Reid] were "pegging" out some land for "selection"[7] but do not know if they will get it, as some others were "pegging out" too . . .

John has improved a good deal since he came to Melbourne. He is much heavier. I don't think Queensland is much of a place to go to as there are a great lot of immigrants continually arriving there and can't all get work; besides black labour cheapens white. You see the farmers and squatters return the members of Parliament and they only return those who will vote for free immigration so that they can get their work done cheaper. There is a good deal in the papers about the unemployed in Brisbane as well as the capitals of the other colonies.

John took a keen interest in the land and farming matters. He was observant and quick to offer opinions (8 August 1884):

The land about Yack[andandah] is more of a red colour and better adapted for vine growing. I think Mr. Reid's people should go into vine growing as they have some land admirably suited for it. Wine being a smaller commodity in proportion to the bulk of land planted, could be raised at a greater distance from a market or railway which would convey it to the market than grain or any other root crop whose cost of carriage would be great. Indeed it seems to me that vine culture will be the prevailing industry in the drier parts of Victoria as the dryness of the climate is greatly against all other agricultural industries.

Meat has risen to a very high price this winter mutton being as high as 5½d. and beef as high as 7½d. for steak.

I observed in the paper a few days ago where some bullocks were sold at £21 each. I believe the rise in meat is owing to the very dry season which has been in a great portion of New South Wales. Sheep and cattle have died in thousands from want of feed and water. I knew of a man who started from New South Wales with 22,000 (thousands not hundreds — he was a drover and of course had a lot of men) to travel through Queensland for grass. He passed Talavera when I was there with about 400 the rest having died from hunger. When a squatter chances to have no feed for his sheep he often employs a drover to drive his sheep to another part of the country still keeping driving on from place to place till he hears from home the station to which they belong that feed is beginning to rise and that by the time the sheep gets back the grass will be good enough to sustain them. Thus they keep travelling at the rate of 5 miles a day which is the rate that law will compel sheep to travel but if often happens that sheep like these I have been speaking about do not travel so fast and only do so when urged by the squatters and "selecters" whose runs they pass through (a day) during the time they are absent from their own station. Sheep when travelling are allowed half a mile on each side of the road.

Farming in the Dividing Ranges between Victoria and New South Wales; a photograph sent back to Ireland. (Courtesy: P.R.O.N.I. Belfast)

In matters of judgment and opinion, Hugh was much more cautious. Soon after they had arrived their brother James had mentioned he was thinking of emigrating. In mid-1884, so was their brother William. Hugh's advice (12 August 1884) was to wait. He also broke the news of what was a comparatively rare occurrence — a migrant who intended to return to Ireland permanently:

. . . Hugh Sheils's opinion about farming in this country is not very great. Of course he has only been in one district and cannot form a very correct opinion. He still seems to be in the notion of going home in about April next although he is now getting very good wages £2 a week. I think now that he is here he should try it out for a while longer. You will please to remember that the above is not to be spoken of to *anyone* not even his own people. Let himself be the first to give such information as I do not want my name mixed up with it in any way . . .

. . . as he cannot see a good prospect in farming he thinks it not worthwhile to stay. If he does go home in April he will be able to give you a description of the "bush" and "bush life".

There is only one district where there is any good land for "selection" that is called Gippsland but I believe it is very heavily timbered although the land is said to be good when it is cleared. A selector of Government land has not to pay all the money at first but pays in instalments — the paying it is not so heavy as the getting the right kind of land and in the right place not too far from railway or good market I mean. On the whole I cannot advise you to come this year and you must not hold too high an opinion of a place until you have seen it.

When John grows a little stronger and the weather gets warmer he will be giving it a trial up country and in the course of another twelve months we will be better able to give you an idea of the state of things as we find them ourselves and not by the report of others. It is a very fine climate; the winter is very mild only a little cold in the mornings when there is a white frost. This winter for so far has not been wet. The worst in my opinion is the heat in the middle of summer.

As far as I am concerned I have rather better prospect than in Belfast and by no means regret the change although in some ways it is *very different* you know. John is certainly better in this climate than home . . .

It was indeed very different. John remarked (25 August 1884) on one of the most striking social differences: the common migrant experience, the sense of solidarity in being new and different in the colony, was rapidly breaking down the rigid social distinctions that had existed in Ireland:

. . . I saw M. Hawthorn today. He was telling me he had got a situation. (I think he said in Launceston. If so it is in Tasmania. It is an out of the world place to my mind. Tasmania is very slow going place and not at all energetic like the rest of the colonies) in a hardware house. As I am not quite sure don't say much about it lest I made a blunder. He (Mr. Hawthorn) is very sociable here and stops and shakes hands with either Hugh or I when he meets us but Australia and the crossing of the line makes a great change on people's sociability.

The brothers' letters are full of Ulster names in Australia, people they had known in Ireland, or whose families they knew, who were now in Australia, people living in or passing through Melbourne (calling on friends of friends was common and accepted), familiar names heard of as being up-country, or spoken of as possible employers. Their letters suggest a closed and heavily populated Irish-Australian world. Yet it is obvious from their references to the letters they received from home that their district was no exclusive well-spring of emigration to Australia alone: local people known to the Maxwell family frequently emigrated to the United States, both East and West Coasts, to California and Chicago. In the early months — and years — of their Australian experience, the world of Hugh and John Maxwell was, in structure, still essentially the old one transported,[8] consisting of an Irish network radiating outward from a core of established and known family friends, relations and neighbours, gradually broadening to impinge on a wider world of those who came from adjacent Irish counties. Identity and acceptance in this world was defined not so much by name — though with immediate contacts it was 'Jack' or 'Lowry' or 'Robert Barron' or 'Mr. Hawthorn', the various name forms reflecting the perceived social gradations and relationships — but rather by place of origin: so and so was a 'County Antrim man' or a 'Ballyback man'. They belonged to this family-focused, locality-oriented Irish world, expecting it to act in their favour in Australia in matters of employment and casual accommodation. They put back into it what and when they could. They fed it with news and gossip from home, exchanged in the evenings or on long Sunday walks, and circulated home newspapers — the *Northern Whig* in the Maxwells' case. And they acted as repositories and clearing houses for home mail, holding letters for new immigrants not yet arrived, or those up-country, or those moving about with no fixed address. But this was a migrant culture which, while strong, was crumbling fast under the solvent of rapid job changes and constant movement within Australia. It was also losing its hierarchical character. Those who had merited the title 'Mister' in Ireland were often to be found in Australia in ordinary employment, and respect for their former status quickly diminished, though it seldom quite disappeared. Others who had retained wealth and position in their transition to Australia abandoned or qualified pretensions to social superiority: they called on those once beneath them, conversed amicably, offered and gave them hospitality — and offered them jobs. Loneliness, the search for familiar society, and the need to get labour in a situation of short supply acted as great levellers. In Ireland the upper social orders could find ample congenial society and could draw as they wished on an oversupply of deferential labour: in Australia the opposite applied.

On 22nd October 1884 Hugh Maxwell described his own employment situation in a Melbourne drapery. His stay in this position had been, by comparison with other immigrants he knew, unusually long — by then about a year — and he had received a 5s. rise (to 35s a week) in August just before he was going to ask for it. Yet even he was restless — no doubt affected by the constant comings and goings around him — and was thinking of farming:

> You ask in the letter to John what kind of men my employers are. Well one is an Irish man from Newry and the other an English man. Craig the Irishman mostly attends to office affairs. It was he engaged me and indeed engages all the hands, of course with the other's opinion on the matter. He is liked better by most of the hands that I have heard expressing an opinion. The other is a whimsical old fellow and as some of the hands say, you don't know when you have or when you haven't him; is rather hard to please at times and sometimes get[s] through a good many strange hands. There has been many come and left since I went there. I often think of turning to the farming when bothered or annoyed about something or other but dearie knows I might turn farmer along with John some time; hard to say what's before us.

The work was tiring, a reason Hugh gave on 13 November 1884 for delay in writing home, and one probably explaining a good deal of migrant neglect of correspondence, especially among those who had a busy social life in Australia. Solitary bush dwellers often turned to letterwriting as a social outlet and depended on mail to keep them happy, but those in the city, with friends close by, could often survive emotionally on little mail, particularly at a time — such as the 1880s — when new immigrants were arriving frequently with inputs of fresh Irish news. Hugh wrote:

> I put off writing this day week as I was very tired. Although we have not a long day we have to work pretty hard and constant while we are there. This is now the busy season coming on to the summer, so we have not many idle minutes from we go in until we come out. Add to that the bustle, fuss and confusion and it makes a heavy enough day's work, but it is ever so much better to be busy than have too little to do.
>
> One has to be pretty particular about one thing and another as there are often mistakes occur. It is a very complicated kind of town to send parcels in as there are so many names of suburbs and so many ugly long-spelled native names one has always to be on their guard; at least that is my experience.

John had gone up-country to stay with his friends the Barron family at Murchison, for the good of his health. He took a keen interest in their farm (2 November 1884). The family in Ireland had reported farming prospects as dismal. John put this down to heavy rent and the uncertainty of the seasons, contrasting it with the Australian situation:

> The wheat crop will be very poor this year hereabouts owing to the dryness of the season in this district. I am greatly surprised to see the crop looking so well when I consider the dryness of the past few months. There is one thing, if they have a bad crop they have no rent to pay and no landlord to fear and they can live for one season without any return from their own land as they could go and work in other districts where crops are good, that is supposing they never had saved anything from former years . . . the land up here is very good being very well adapted for growing wheat and it's grazing capabilities are very good.

So much for farming, but there was more to life than that and there the comparison with Ireland was not so favourable. Their brother James now had a job in Bangor; occasioning a wry remark from John to Hugh:

> It will be much better for James's health to be going up and down to Bangor and Mr. Peters will be good company for him. He will be able to go home every Sunday and to see his girl as often as he had a fancy. You know it is a grand privilege to have such a luxury which [n]either you nor I have had the pleasure [of] indulging in since we came to the colony. Perhaps you have for all that I know.

Hugh had not: their present society was almost exclusively male. John was a firm advocate of emigration. He wrote to Hugh (4 December 1884).

> I wonder if William is still in the notion of buying a farm. I think the money would be better laid out here on a bit of good land than to buy a farm at home and still have to pay a rent for it. A man to select in this country would have more [than] he could call his own in 10 years than he would have in 20 [years] at home. I am quite sure. I see evidence everywhere I go. There is still land to select and under not more difficulties than in earlier times. Mr Barron used to have to cart wheat from here to Melbourne before the railway was made up this far.

Hugh disagreed, as he made clear when he sent John's letter home (1 December 1884):

> . . . there is one part of John's letter with which I cannot agree in which he says that "there is still land to select under not more difficulties than in earlier times". Well the first difference is the best of the land is selected. What is left is covered with wood and under-growth. There is less of the public domain to select from and more difficult to get a selection or farm. Then if the farmer had to draw his wheat a long way to market he had surely a better price than 3s. 9d. per bushel. If I was farming here I would not go heavily into crop growing as I believe stock would pay better at present, with less labour.

Who was right? Both. The best land was gone — or at least that easiest cleared — but the prospects for the would-be farmer with little money remained far better in Australia. Hugh was a town dweller, never out of Melbourne; John had spent most of his time in the country. But the difference in their judgment related not to economic or agricultural facts, but to temperament. Hugh was consistently sceptical about the grandiose plans and visionary schemes so readily entertained by the Irish immigrants he knew. They were wonderfully free with brave advice — get a land selection, bring out the rest of the family — all without security or experience themselves. Hugh was a worrier. As John saw him, he was liable to fret and unable to take things easy: 'had I fretted', wrote John, 'I would have been under the sod'. From his viewpoint, Hugh thought John rather too ready to resort to various manoeuvres to secure that easier life. According to Hugh (24 December 1884), 'John must soon draw his visit to a close at Mr. Barron's or his welcome may soon be worn thread bare'. Appreciating this, John had 'written to Mr. Robert Reid Jun. if a Mr. Henry who lives beside him would require a hand', but the real purpose of this enquiry was to contrive an occasion for an invitation from Reid himself. The differences between the brothers also related to matters of health. John was a refugee from consumption who thrived on the country life and who disliked Melbourne: 'there is a tremendous dust every [where] that would both blind and choke you'. He was sensitive about his health, remarking to his sister (11 December 1884):

> I have been feeling my liver a little out of order lately. I got a bottle of medicine from the chemist last night which I think will be of some good. This is said to be a very bad country for liver complaint indeed the worst in the world not excepting India. I suppose it is partly the heat but it is hard to say what are all the causes. I hope father and mother are keeping free from it. I would suggest to you as a possible preventative of headache to pour some cold water on the back of the neck first thing every morning; it won't do any harm at any rate . . .

But this concern was nothing unusual or obsessive: various ailments and possible (or impossible) cures formed a large part of the family correspondence in that hazardous and uncomfortable age before modern medicine and drugs.

On 29 March 1885 John reported home a reversal in the locations of himself and Hugh. Hugh had left Melbourne for the country while he had come to the city suburbs. After one job where the hours were too long (giving him no time to write earlier) he had found something suitable:

> I am now working as assistant gardener at a gentleman's place out at Kew (about 4½ miles from Melbourne) I am getting a pound a week and found. Hugh has left Craig's and is going up country to a place called Heathcote. He will have £2 2s. a week. I see by yours that you have taken a situation as landsteward at a pound a week. If you are found it is very good wages but, if not, it is not worth having. If my health keeps good I expect to have a bit

more wages before one twelve month comes round; that is as a coachman. The sound of coachman will jar in your ears I suppose but servants in this country are never so much looked down on about gentlemen's places as they are at home and you are not obliged to do flunkey so much or touch your hat or say yes mam or yes sir, simply yes or no, I will or I haven't time. If you are civil and obedient is all that is required but they will not have anyone who drinks. I find although my hand was so long out of practice that I can do work as well, and as much of it, as any other man that I ever wrought beside here. I find that although I have not perhaps quite so much physical strength as some I can handicap most of them in quickness.

And John had firm advice for his sister Susanna who, like himself, had chest problems:

Susanna: you must be very careful and not catch cold again. You must not get overheated. You must not put your hands in cold water. You must not be out in the night air and "yous" must take outdoor exercise, say weed potatoes when the ground is quite dry but perhaps there would be too much bending over your chest. Drink plenty of warm milk from the cow. Drink nothing else neither water nor tea and it will make you like it better. Be sure and take my advice for I have had experience.

On 15 April 1885 Hugh wrote home of his new situation in a Heathcote drapery store:

. . . I am over a fortnight in my new crib. It is a very quiet little town. I am getting along pretty well for so far. The hours are from 8.30 to 6 and 10pm. Saturday. We have not too hard to work, there not being a great rush of customers. They seem to get a good profit so that makes up.
There is a young man came up a week after me for the clothing department. He is a new "chum" from Magherafelt, Co. Derry.[9] His name is Vance. He is fine company for me. We are the only two assistants and we stop in the same lodgings. Our lodgings cost 20s. a week; we are very comfortable. Of course there is no other lodgers here.
The governor of our drapery side is a Presbyterian, so is Vance (there is also groceries kept but next door). Vance and I had a long walk up the mountain about three miles from here. Away on the other side of the mountain we could see the valley of the Goulburn River. This place is a little south of the Goulburn. From Melbourne we came about 40 miles by train and 30 by coach. It is a wonderful journey through the bush. The road is not the best; some parts of it is only a bush track. It is something strange to hear the "morepork" (the Australian cuckoo) calling at night. It is quite a different bird. The call is something like *mo-pork* and is not so sweet as the cuckoo and much slower . . .

A further letter, of 13 May 1885, made clear just how intensely Irish — indeed Ulster Irish — was the economic and social environment in which Hugh Maxwell lived and worked in Heathcote:

I am getting along pretty well in my new quarters . . . We have got a new hand in the grocery store Mr. Calthcart. He has been in New Zealand for a few years. He served his time in Beatie's in Ballymena where James Maxwell served his. The other drapery assistant Mr. Vance is from Magherafelt Co. Derry. Our bookkeeper Mr. Brown is a Belfast man; he has been 18 or 20 years here. The miller Mr. Grant is from Co. Armagh and the engine man his nephew Mr. Walsh is from Tyrone. The senior governor Mr. Moore is from Co. Down; he is always in Melbourne. Mr. Christie is a Scotchman; he looks after the grocery and grain store. Mr. Spinks is from Dublin; he is a Presbyterian also Mr. Moore. Mr. Christie goes to Church (English) rather odd for a Scotchman. Mr. Spinks is in the drapery store so he is the man we have to look after. He is very agreeable and not too hard to put up with.

The lady we stop with is a widow with two daughters an Irish woman from Co. Clare and an R[oman] C[atholic]. One of the daughters teaches music and she often gives us a tune in the evening which helps to pass the time. Mr. Cathcart does not board here but sometimes comes down a little while in the evening and we have a bit [of] chat and chaff.

Mr. Vance and I have joined the Mechanic's Institute (where we can see the newspapers every evening). There is a debating club in connection with it which holds a meeting every fortnight. All the members of the Institute who like, can debate. It is always worth hearing and one always learns something . . .

The store owners and workers were predominantly from Ulster counties — Down, Tyrone, Armagh, Derry — and Presbyterian in religion; but not entirely so: there was a Church of England Scotsman and a Dublin Presbyterian. And Hugh Maxwell's lodgings were with a Catholic Irishwoman from Co. Clare. All these matters of common geographic origin and shared religious allegiance were important to Hugh: the days of any Australian merging of identities and cultures into a general indifference to anything but a person's immediately experienced character lay in the far distant future. Placing oneself in the midst of a known and familiar human context in this faraway and strange land was much more than mere convenience, or even sentiment. It was to affirm, to family and to self, that one was home away from home, still part of the old world, not to be accounted somehow lost, to have become a stranger. But the old world had been significantly, indeed radically, widened. Its core and focus remained, but it had broadened from a small place and a county — the Bangor district of Co. Down — to a region and a religion. Even that was not rigid or exclusive, stretching to embrace a Scotsman and a Southern Irish Catholic as part of a Celtic cultural totality, a stance towards life, as intangible and as difficult to define precisely as it was real. Hugh Maxwell's Heathcote world offered familiar ground, in which the presence of those traditionally defined in Ireland as outsiders or enemies were as important to his sense of belonging as were friends: the accepted contradictions, eccentricities and oddities of the Irish cultural mix were somehow in harmonious place on the other side of the earth. No wonder Hugh was happy: briefly, time had stood still. He sought to preserve the old ways, joining the local Presbyterian church: 'we are not like some people that come to Australia and never go to church'. He enjoyed the 'fine company, more so on account of being from home' (12 July 1885) — 'home' now being the wider concept of all Ireland.

Australian experience changed the concept and connotations of home. Whereas in Ireland 'home' meant family, close friends, stability, a situation of little and slow change, in Australia its connotations were those of the dwelling of the moment, of constant mobility, people coming and going, the circle of family and friends making way for, by way of inclusion, dilution, a wide range of acquaintances, people one knew at a casual, less intimate level — 'mates': John Maxwell used the word in July 1885, defining it as 'friend' for his Irish family, but he meant something less, or at least different. The weaker, less demanding Australian concept of home is evident in his letter of 6 August 1885: 'Australia has become to us more of a home and we feel at home having made a lot of acquaintances'. Australian circumstances fostered a much more superficial sense of belonging than the Irish, but it was none the less real, and Hugh contrasted it very favourably (18 August 1885) with his experience in England. In Australia, criticism of the Irish did not preclude friendliness. The Irish were good mixers and Australians welcomed them:

> . . . For my own experience I like the country full as well as I expected to — indeed quite a different thing to the time I was in England. Although the Irish are always hard spoken of everywhere, I find that an Irishman takes as well with the people generally as any other countryman. One great thing is never try to hide it; I never do. Everybody is friendly with the "new chums" as we are called when we come out first. It is a bit different to England where everybody is English. Here you meet people from every part, of course more English than anything else . . .

But the process of integration could be viewed too simply. Living in a substantially Irish world in Australia bred a consciousness of others being outsiders to that world: the Maxwells long harboured suspicion of colonial girls. And from time to time the word 'strangers' leaps out in their correspondence, pointing to their consciousness of embarking on an encounter with an unknown foreign world, potentially hostile or threatening, not to be trusted, with which a considerable degree of caution and reserve was automatic. One could be oneself with family, friends and neighbours: outside these categories one was on constant guard. The meaning of 'stranger' fluctuated with the circumstances: it could be as narrow as not immediate family, as wide as not Irish. 'Strangers' were not necessarily people unknown, but rather those whose names, background and social position could not be securely and appropriately placed and called upon by reference to the known foundations and rules of a familiar traditional world. Emigration launched the Maxwells on a sea of 'strangers', a disconcerting experience requiring courage and adapatability. And it left behind their ageing parents to fear that eventually they might pass into the care of those whom they, and their children, also regarded as 'strangers' and not family members. Whatever emigration offered in regard to prosperity, opportunity, enhanced human development, its unsettlement of the old order of human relationships and affinities of place brought with it a gamut of emotions, pain, disturbance, worry. What is remarkable is how well most immigrants mastered the destruction of their old world order and the building of a new.

In Melbourne John had taken to the study of horses. He had bought a book, for 20s., on their diseases and treatment only to find he knew nearly all of it. At this time he tended to pass the evenings reading his copy of Armitage's *Horse Doctor and Cattle Doctor*, with an occasional visit to the Kew Temperance Lodge of which he was a member. In asking the family (14 May 1885) to send copies of all the recipes they had for horse treatment, he gave his news:

> I also got a dictionary at 4s. and an alarm clock at 12s. My expenses since I came here have been pretty high. I bought a pair of trousers at 20s., a pair of fine boots at 22s. a pair of every day boots at 14s. a good hat at 10s.6d. and I have joined the Good Templars which cost me half a crown and a devil of a lot of medicine, for let what come or go I have always to have a good supply of it. You must not think because I am using a good deal of medicine that I am worse. If I can pass the winter as well as I have done for so far I will be satisfied.

On 28 May he squashed rumours of marriage, fed back from home:

> The people need not be dreaming such nonsense about me being married for I can tell you the colonial heifers are a kind of cattle. I like to keep at a respectful distance. You know we "new chums" have a very bad opinion of the colonials.

John's references to marriage (n.d. 1886) tended to be highly unromantic and ruefully practical:

> James [Hanna] is now sitting on a box about a yard from me sewing on a button on his breeches. It's a terrible want, the want of a wife. He wants to know if Mary has mind of the time when she used to learn him to knit in the gallery in Ballymaconnell. He says if she had learned him to sew it would have been of more use to him now.

John Maxwell was a man of forthright opinions. If these had not been formed by colonial experience, they certainly found a congenial home there, as was vigorously clear in a letter to his brother David (11 June 1885):

> . . . I see by the paper that there has been a great fuss made about the Prince and Princess. I would like to know what the Prince ever done for Ireland that merits such an enthusiastic welcome. Undoubtedly the Princess has done what she could to forward Irish manufactory by patronizing the Irish lace and poplin. The Belfast people are always making fools of themselves. What is royalty? What good do they do for the middle and lower classes of Great Britain? They are the people who live by the sweat of their subject's brow. They are the people who think themselves made of better clay than their subjects. They are the people who mean people [to] bend their heads and knee-for what? For thinking themselves better than they. The aristocracy do well to look down on laity or democracy.
>
> Surely people will see through such nonsense by and by. They have not learned the lesson which the United States have been teaching them these many years past; but I believe the aristocracy has nearly seen its day in England. They have had to cave in a good deal the last few centuries. I believe the franchise has been a blow which will be felt by them at the next general election. It is hoped that the people of the Co. Down will have learned some sense and will look better after their own interests. In fact they, like most of their North of Ireland neighbour[s], do not quite understand politics and always keep mixing it and religion up together. They seem not to know that politics and religion are two things as widely different as the[y] can be. Politics belong to this world and religion to that which is to come. The one our temporal benefit and the other our spiritual welfare.
>
> The Orangemen have been a great hindrance to the advancement of civil liberties of the people at home. But poor men, the[y] know not what the[y] do and are simply guided by the aristocracy who use them with great dexterity to suit their own ends. There is no shout about loyalty, no waving of their filthy flag over people's heads here.

Comments such as these, mixing strong affection for Ireland with impatience with its condition, and its apparent acceptance of servility, were remarkably common among expatriate Irishmen, though perhaps not often to the degree or of the kind exhibited by John Maxwell. It would be astonishing if such insights had been born in the year and a half since he had left Ireland; equally evident that such views would be difficult to voice openly in the loyalist atmosphere of

Bangor, Co. Down. Probably John had long held such opinions, but only in the atmosphere of Australia was he able to develop and express them. But he did this seldom: Ireland was too far away to be often bothered about. The same went for the denigration of Australia being disseminated in the Maxwell's home district by the returned migrant, Hugh Sheils. John observed (9 July 1885):

> . . . he cannot be considered by any means a criterion. You know Hugh has simply made a mouth of himself. He therefore will have to blame his return home so soon on the country instead of homesickness but I expect he will [be] back in about a year or perhaps sooner.
>
> A man cannot well complain of a country where he can earn 25s. a week and found but I suppose Hugh will attribute his high wages to his superiority or I presume his father will, as he is a *bit of a blow*.

On 25 August 1885 John reported that he intended to take up bee farming.

> . . . the gardener here is a "new chum" who has been out in the colony about the same time as myself. He understands the management of bees and he and I have determined to start a small bee farm in spring. It will be carried on in a more scientific principle than I used to see you do it at home. There will be no destroying of bees for their honey. We will take the honey when they are at work, extract the honey from the combs and then place them back in the hive to be refilled. The hive consists of a square box which can be opened at the top. There are a number of square frames which are hung a little apart parallel to each other. In these the bees builds their comb and they can be removed when filled or at will without very much disturbing the bees.

Hugh, who had moved from Heathcote to Corowa, was putting some money into the venture (15 October 1885):

> . . . I left my situation in Heathcote rather more than a week ago. There was no chance of a rise "screw" there. I got another crib yesterday wages £2 15s. The name of the place is Corowa. It is on the Murray River, New South Wales side 184 miles from Melbourne, railway all the way. I should think it is not more than 40 or 50 miles from Yackandandah across the country but much more by rail. I don't know that the crib will be very permanent as it is a new firm and the[y] cannot tell what trade will be done. However the screw is pretty good and when that crib gives up something else may turn up.
>
> John looks very much stronger then he did six months ago. I believe he could do as much work as any other man. The cough is not quite gone, but is not very severe now. I do not know that he mentioned in any of his letters that he was going into bee-keeping along with another young man (who understands the scientific principle of working bees). He was the gardener where John is working. They each put an equal sum of money down and get equal shares of the profit. They make "Quinby" hives in the evenings (moveable frame hives). I think John will give up his crib in a week or so so that they can push forward hive making before the summer sets in, thereby securing the advantages of the best honey season. Mr. Amey the partner works 3 days in the week, the other 3 he devotes to collecting swarms and hive making etc. etc.
>
> I am going to put £10 worth of bees which will be about 16 or 18 swarms into the business. John and Amey will supply the hives and other appliances, look after the bees and sell the honey, for half the amount realised and the young swarms, the other half of the amount will be my share. I expect it to realise 100%.

You understand the bees have not to be destroyed under this principle, which is a great savings. If the undertaking proves a success I will go into the business next year. By that time John will know something about the workings of the bees etc. John will be able to give you fuller particulars by Christmas. It will save John from having to work so hard in the warm summer weather. Mr. Amey and John have taken a little house near Kew. They have got a tenant for half the house keeping two rooms and a workshop for themselves. They have ample sitting room for their bees in the little garden in front of the house; they will cook for themselves etc.

If I am not mistaken bee farming could be made one of the best paying occupations in Victoria for a man with small capital.

. . . it will be two years tomorrow since John and I left home. It does not look like it looking back. We have not made much money but if we get along as fairly, considering circumstances, the next two years we cannot complain. I enjoy very good health myself . . .

Hugh's next letter home (11 November 1885) was from Echuca, Victoria. He explained the circumstances:

When I wrote to William four weeks ago I was engaged to go to a situation at Corowa New South Wales. Well I went and when I went into the shop Mr. McLean, the governor, said he was sorry I had come up so soon as he thought he would sell the business over again if he could make a profit off it. I asked him to let me know as soon as he found out what he was about to do as I did not want to be wasting time there, so next morning he said he would either sell to a draper on the other side of the street or by auction but would pay all my expenses and give me a week's salary, which he did. I returned to Melbourne and found after paying expenses that I was £3 in pocket.

I got this situation a week ago arriving here on Thursday evening 5th November. I am getting 50s. a week and premiums which will make it about 55s. or 60s. I can count on the former at any rate. I am in the dress department.

Echuca which is a native name, means the meeting of the waters. It is built on the Victorian side of the Murray, the longest river in Australia (3,000 miles) at the junction of the river "Compaspie" which is a Victorian river. There is a half holiday on Wednesday afternoon. Prince of Wales birthday was on Monday last which is always a holiday. Well arrangements were made to take the *whole* day on Wednesday and work on Monday and have an excursion in a steamer 20 miles down the Murray. We started about 9am this morning and had a very pleasant run down the river, stopped on the New South Wales side and had a picnic, that is some of our own shop hands and my landlord and lady; he is our book-keeper. There were all the other shopkeeper's assistants on the steamer also, and everybody else that was willing to pay their half crown in all about 250 or 300 people. We started on our return trip about 4.30pm and after a pleasant run arrived here shortly after 6 o'clock.

The river is very crooked but deep and a good width say 130 yards wide. I believe it is much wider further down where some other large rivers join it. There is a large shipping trade done in wool and grain from both New South Wales and Victoria sides, and Echuca is the chief port as the wool and grain can be transferred from the barges to the train for Melbourne. The barges are towed by steamers which are also loaded, the load of both if in wool 2,100 bails, if in wheat 4,500 bags — some money's worth I wish I had it.

> Echuca is lit with gas and supplied with water from the Murray which is pumped by steam into two large tanks about 100 ft. high which gives it pressure in the pipes. The water is good and wholesome, much better than in Melbourne and the supply never runs done. I like the place so far as I have seen of it. I believe it is hot at times, sometimes as high as 120 in the shade. We had it 102 in the shade in Melbourne ten days ago.
> John is very busy about the bee keeping and making hives, so he will have not time to write this mail. They had got 20 swarms when I left town. They were likely to get orders for some hives (boxes) which would pay them well for their work. John is in high hopes about the undertaking and thinks it will pay. He was very well and improving when I saw him . . .

Enquiries from home — prompted by a curiosity stimulated by his brother William's thinking about emigration — elicited from Hugh a letter (26 November 1885) describing wages and conditions in Australia as he viewed them through his own and his friends' experience:

> . . . in reference to the Hanna brothers; James' wages are 10s. a day or £3 a week (the same as Mr. McDonald's etc.). There is no doubt that Samuel has £2 15s. My own wages at present is rather better than that being £2 10s. and "spiff" (which is worth from 5s. to 10s. a week); of course I want little said about what wages John and I have as people form their own ideas about those things.
> In the matter of wages all classes are better off than at home. Of course there are difficulties to be put up with in most departments of labour. I do not regret coming to Victoria in the least (although home is always where the heart lies) "the heart has many a dwelling place but only once a home". I feel that I can make a "dwelling place" anywhere now and be contented with it. At the same time I would not use any influence on any individual to come to the "land of the golden fleece". I am inclined to let folks please themselves as I did and then if things turn out different to what they expected (as it sometimes does) they will not turn round and say to me "you misrepresented the state of affairs to me and I blame you thatever I came here". We all have to run our chance of being out of a "billet" another name for "crib" and may go without one for a considerable time. It is at such a time we are apt to think that the new country is no better than the old. However when the tide turns and one gets in again his wages are such as will allow of saving something. I must agree with you that there is very little to be *saved* at home and most departments of industry are tarred with the same stick.
> You mention the price of wheat 5s. 9d. That is indeed exceedingly low. I think I mentioned about last harvest that there would be very little hope of wheat ever rising to the old prices. It is the foreign competition, not the home produce that brings down the markets. The Australian colonies produce a great deal more wheat than is required for consumption here; the surplus is sent to London. India can now produce as much wheat as the United States. The United States cannot use anything like her own produce. England or rather the United Kingdom is up to the present the best market in the world and of course the great surplus is shipped thither. Things must find a level and the result is low prices rule in the United Kingdom as well as other places. If I were farming at home I would give up wheat growing as a bad game, go into live stock more and feed more on the farm. So much for my ideas of agriculture . . .
> I am liking my crib for so far. Echuca is a much more important place than

Heathcote and farther north, therefore warmer. Some of the people here where I lodge, bathe in the River Murray, but for my part I prefer a shower bath. There is one here and I have a shower nearly every morning.
Yesterday was half holiday so some of the hands 3 besides myself went to the junction of the Goulburn with the Murray about 5 miles from here and had an afternoon's fishing. We drove there in the governor's parcel van. I enjoyed it very much but you know I am not much of a fisherman.

Perhaps not, but the strangeness of the Australian bush scene provided Hugh with constant interest. It impressed and moved him. As to its alleged inferiority to 'home' scenery, he made the perceptive point (6 October 1886) that the Australian natural environment had not yet been illuminated by art. Here was a shop assistant practical enough to be saving 30s. of his weekly wage against sickness and unemployment, yet profound enough to be aware of the complexities of experiencing an unfamiliar visual world:

The Australian bush impresses new comers very much on their first run up country. It is so different from the scenery at home. The evergreen forests of Australia are so very different to the home woods (when one does at home come to a wood which is so very seldom) then the dead trees which have been run to let the grass grow have such a weird desolate appearance. The scenery here does not come up to the home scenery generally, as far as I have seen at any rate. Of course art has done more for that of the home countries than it has yet accomplished for Australia . . .

John Maxwell also had strong views on the superiority of Australian life to that in Ireland, despite the personal reversal occasioned by the absconding of his partner in bee-keeping, Oscar Amey. He put these to his brother James on 19 January 1886:

. . . I have observed by several of your last letters that there is very little coin to be made at home. Indeed I am surprised that people in health and strength should stick so closely to the old country. Had I the health and strength of some people I believe I could make a very good living but unhappily I am never sure of having permanent good health. At present I had to give up my situation owing to not being strong enough to hold out, but indeed I had two good reasons that is very hard work and bad tack (food). I have determined on taking a couple or three weeks "spell" (rest) I intend employing my leisure at painting the roofs of our hives and making a few section trays. I have to make a hive for a man for which I will get 32s. 6d.
My partner Amey has absconded, nobody knows where. He left me to pay both my own and his share of some accounts which was against us and also took with him over £10 in cash. I am very glad to be rid of him and although he has taken a slant at me, yet he left me the art of beekeeping which I will be able to use to advantage.

We purpose holding on the *very few* stocks of bees which we possess and increasing their number next spring and going into a heavily timbered district which is the best for bee culture. The[re] is nothing which yields so much honey is this country as the gum trees (eucalyptus). The bees in this country depend more on the blossom of the trees than on the field flowers as clover and other good honey plants do not thrive in every district, yet they thrive very well and even better than at home in some portions of Gippsland. Gippsland is a great agricultural district. There is always a good and bad honey

year alternatively; this is the bad year. Some of our stocks have over 70lbs. of honey stored notwithstanding so that gives encouragement. There is one stock in particular which has 16 two pound sections but all filled. I believe if we had 200 hives we could make £600 a year . . .
Susie speaks of bad times and difficulty of making anything at home. Indeed I am surprised at people grumbling about hard times. What would the times be if like Hugh or I with no home and without capital? But the answer is people at home cannot make the money at home they can in Australia. Why then complain? There is many lines of splendid steamers plying between Australia and home? Whose blame is it if home people with means to alter it, cannot live as well as people on this side of the globe? The want of courage to face 13,000 miles of sea. The want of courage to depend upon the sweat of their own brow. These are part of the reason of people enduring and putting up with difficulties. They starve lest they should starve. They think it is better to starve in Ireland than to run the risk of starving in Australia. They prefer half [a] loaf and idleness to work and plenty of bread.
Everybody who comes here without a capital has to work or the[y] will starve or run the risk for Australians will not keep idlers. The only way to get out of it is to get into jail which is not a hard job. The most of the loafers spend most of their time there and the other part stealing. Some end the debate on starving or working by throwing themselves into the Yarra. But this is bad logic.

Safe in the arms of the policeman
Safe in Pentridge jail
18 months hard labour
For cutting off an old cow's tail

The above is better. I would prefer hard work any day to the Yarra . . .

The behaviour of his partner had both taught him a lesson and strengthened his resolve:

A great many people were disappointed in me. They thought that because the other fellow cleared that I would be disheartened and throw the thing up and that I could not manage them without him. However it happened that I held on to my purpose and the bees have done better under my own separate care than when he was with me. There is a man in Kew who was talking to me today. He was very anxious for me to join partnership with him next year *but no more partnerships for John.*

John learnt the lesson but harboured no bitterness. Three months after absconding his partner was dead. John told Hugh (28 March 1886):

You will be surprised to know that Oscar Amey departed this life on the 20th at the Alfred Hospital Melbourne (South) he died of typhoid fever and congestion of the lungs. Linch (Kitchen's gardner) Fraser and I undertook to bury him in Kew cemetery in a private grave, the deeds of which will be sent home to his father. It will cost me about £1. He was buried on Tuesday last.

As Hugh commented in sending the news home to Ireland (31 March 1886), "Although Amey's conduct was not what it should have been, John's humanity is too great to be set aside by broken trust".

But John's bee-keeping remained a sideline to a quick succession of gardening jobs in suburban Melbourne. On 4 April 1886 he described his situation and plans to his sister:

About ten weeks ago I knocked off work for about three weeks but this was through being over worked and want of nourishing food but I must say that within the last month I have not had better health since I came to Australia. I am at present at work in a nursery about a mile and a half from here and as I work by the day I start work at 8 every morning and knock off at 6 — one hour too long but as I am going to work in a neighbouring nursery in about ten days or when I have done where I am at present, I will work only till five. I have 6s. a day. In the spring I will be able to get 6s.6d. or 7s. Last week I got 2s.6d. more than my wages so you see I am able to do my work . . .

I intend going into the bees next spring with all the capital I can muster and give it a good trial. It will likely to be some part of Gippsland which I will select for the apiary. I would like to establish about 50 or 60 hives. The 14 which I have got will give off a good swarm each next spring which will mean 28 and with purchasing all the swarms I could get in the district I could likely raise the remainder.

Had Amey done right we ought to have had 50 now but he acted the rogue and the worse for himself for had he remained about a healthy place like Kew he would not have caught the fever.

Meanwhile Hugh was writing from Echuca to his brother James, to give him advice on emigrating (17 March 1886):

. . . I daresay if you do come out to Victoria you would be less troubled with cold in the chest etc. I think it would be advisable for you to give it a trial if you don't get things to your satisfaction in Belfast. You would be more at home, at any rate, than John and I were when we came. You know something about where you are going; we did not.

One thing you would not have much trouble in bettering your wages here although you need not expect to start with as much as you will get when you are a little time here. There is a little advantage taken of the "new chums" that way.

McVicker is getting along pretty well although he was hardly pleased at the first. However he has got a couple of rises of screw. Perhaps a few remarks would not be out of place in case you do decide on coming out.

A few good suits of clothes, fashionable made are never out of place; white shirts, socks, good boots and things much the same as we brought; a common suit (old) for aboard ship and a soft hat (light colour). Hard hats and clothes generally are worn much the same here as at home (bring John and I a "blackthorn stick" each).

Provisions for Voyage

Butter is useful especially if the ship's butter is bad (it is sometimes very good); a tin of biscuits, tea, coffee and milk gooseberry and currant jams to be kept till the warm weather when the home butter is done; butter should not reach the hot region but [be] used at the early part of the voyage or it will run to oil. If you are fond of cheese a little one would be no harm (this article I would say please yourself). Note a "panikin" is a common pint tin such as used at table but a mug is better for the hot tea; have nothing to do with cups and saucers; they are too easily upset. Do *not* bring ham; you might find trouble in getting it cooked (at least I would not). A £1 or 30s. given to the steward and cook is well laid out, *in little instalments*. Don't give much at first but often and they will get to know you. I think the enclosed cabins are better than the open berths which is sometimes a rough ground. There are

> four people in an enclosed cabin. Of course they are dearer than open berths. Choice of boats; Austral, Orient, Liguria, Iberia are the largest and best; the others are all much alike. The Austral will save nearly a week on some of the smaller boats.
> Don't stow away fruit in your box it will only rot. Leave your gloves behind you; they would spot on the voyage. A dozen nice neckties are safe "four in hand" shape or "windsors" according to taste; collars, stylish shape (John and I wear 16); pocket handkerchiefs, only if good and cheap.
> Do not burden too much with anything. Some people make a mistake in bringing too many things.

A couple of weeks later (31 March 1886) Hugh was telling his sister Susanna (with the cooler weather he was finding the mosquitoes less troublesome but the girls more so) that if James did decide to come to Australia, he should

> take a run in the bush the length of Echuca and see what it is like. I think he would do very well here and the dry climate might suit him better than home. I must say for myself that I like the country well although it is rough and wild looking in places. Indeed I would not like going to Belfast and taking a situation there at the wages I could get. I always hold up the name of Belfast here but still wages are small . . .

This last comment was revealing. Some of the Irish sentiment voiced in Australia was a matter of form, pride rather than preference: it would not do to renounce publicly allegiance to one's place of origin, even if, privately, practical considerations favoured Australia. Irish migrants lived at several levels, and in the grip of various degrees of conflict and contradiction. The superior economic realities of Australia competed with affection for home: the excitement of the new and strange vied with the remembered attractions of the known and familiar. Not many such migrants were as candid or as articulate as Hugh Maxwell and his brother: most preferred to leave such conflicts unacknowledged and unresolved.

John's reaction to James' proposed emigration (4 April 1886) was to suggest that the whole family should think of coming:

> I observed by James's last letters that he is in half a notion of coming to Australia. I say half a notion for I never take a great deal of notice of people coming to Australia until I see they have taken their passage. However as James is so much troubled with coughs and colds I believe it is the best thing he could do.
> In fact I have been inclined to think, but perhaps I am mistaken, that the whole family would do well to come out and take up land. They could select about 2,000 acres and as good horses sell at a good price (as high as at home) about Melbourne there could be a better living made out here at breeding horses. A good draught horse trained to harness will bring about £40 and a very good one more. Good carriage horses bring full better prices than at home but bits of saddle and spring cart-horses are not worth rearing.

By the following month (12 May 1886) Hugh was of a similar mind:

> I'm beginning to think that if times does not improve next season it would not be a bad thing for the whole family to try their fortune in the land of the "Golden Fleece". It is not such a big thing coming to Australia as home people generally think. Hoping to have your opinion on this subject . . .

Hugh followed the Irish political news in the Melbourne papers. The big issues were land reform and Home Rule,[10] and although Hugh followed the Presbyterian small farmer view, his stance was moderate. So on 17 March 1886 he observed:

> . . . I see by the paper that Gladstone proposes to raise a loan of £200,000,000 to buy out the landlords. There certainly needs to be something done. People could never pay high rents at the ruling price of produce. What is your opinion at the prospect of Home Rule? The North seems to be as much against it as the rest of Ireland is for it.

And on 28 April:

> I notice by the Melbourne papers that the Protestants of the North of Ireland are arming themselves with all possible haste, in prospect of the Home Rule Bill passing. I suppose it is the Orangemen principally who are making this "ado". I don't think the Home Rule Bill can possibly be passed. I am sorry Mr. Gladstone made such a mistake. I believe it would be a bad thing for the Protestants if it was to become law.

When the Bill was defeated Hugh remarked, more in sorrow over the whole matter than in righteous anger, 'I think it is better that it should be so . . . ' John, however, was prompted by the Home Rule issue to a vigorous critical comparison between Australia and Ireland, and to another denunciation of Orangeism (23 June 1886):

> Regarding Home Rule, it is most extraordinary how people differ at home from people out here or rather how they are situated and how they act. Every man who is over 21 and has his name registered has a right to vote at [the] time of Parliamentary elections. Every man votes for the candidate who he believes will look after his interest, irrespective of religion (save the Catholics who are greatly influenced by their ecclesiastical dignitaries, as they are in Ireland).
>
> Our present government is formed of a coalition of conservatives and liberals who act and work very well together, attending to the making and amending of laws with far greater dispatch than your English parliament. Your parliament is made too much a debating society. Its members are too fond of their own aggrandizement to look after the interests of the people who the[y] govern. Our parliament is made up of members who are paid £300 a year for making our laws and if a member returned by an contituency does not endeavour to forward the interest of their constituents, he is not re-elected and his place is taken by a candidate who will. Our parliamentary term lasts only three years not seven like yours.
>
> It is a grievous thing to think that Irishmen's bigotry should stand between men and their own interests. The only part of the Irish community who, as a whole, look after their own interest very closely and make use of every means in their powers is the landed proprietors. They have used with great dexterity — at the same time deceiving the world most surprisingly — the Orangemen of Ulster who unfortunately are too ignorant to perceive how they are made tools of by those who, if it did not suit their interest, would not strike a blow in the defence of the cause which they [the Orangemen] make such boast.
>
> The majority of those Orangemen who talk of upholding Protestantism and Protestant Ascendancy are men who may see the inside of a church once in twelve months and though the[y] may be strict church goers what Christianity can there be in their hearts if they persist in upholding unjust laws. If injustice

Presbyterian Church, Bangor Co. Down. (Courtesy: National Library of Ireland)

> is a part of Protestantism it is high time there was an indepen[dent] body of Christians. Injustice was the cause of Protestantism and now to uphold the same said Protestantism, injustice, its origin, is again practised. It is evident those kind of people are of a very similar type to those who persecuted the heretics. There are a great many people who think they are fighting for God and Christianity when in truth they are fighting for their own bigoted opinion. It is so with your Orangemen. Christ did [not?] teach us oppression — quite the reverse. Then how can it be Christian to oppress.

Such outbursts occasioned by Irish affairs were rare, even with the more volatile John: the demands of the Australian scene normally took precedence. Hugh reported on 28 April 1886 that he was beginning to fit in well locally. Evidently there were Irishmen who did not, or who let their conviction that they were superior to the rough colonials (an estimate earlier shared by his brother John) become obvious. Such provocative behaviour caused them to be shunned, but Hugh found he was increasingly accepted on his own terms:

> Last Monday was Easter Monday. On Good Friday which is also a general holiday there was a picnic for the children of the Sunday School in connection with the Presbyterian Church. It was held in the Echuca park. I went down to it and joined in the fun. There was a picnic arranged for Easter Monday for teachers choir and bible class; I am not in either, although I very often attend choir practise on Friday evening. I heard that I was to be invited about a week ago — I was invited on Sunday afternoon.
> We all gathered at the church on Monday morning about 9a.m. and started off in 6 traps for a drive of 10 miles to the selected picnic grounds. It was a splendid day, neither hot nor cold. We reached our destination all right, unyoked our horses and tied them to trees and began to enjoy ourselves in real earnest. We had all sorts of games, refreshed ourselves twice on the nice things the ladies had provided. We yoked up and started for home as it was beginning to get dark. There were three young ladies in our trap good singers. We sang all the way home songs, hymns and all sorts. I enjoyed the day's outing immensely . . . I find the colonial lad and lass friendly, agreeable, free and easy and kind hearted. I have always been treated with respect by all and never got the cold shoulder because I am an Irishman. It is people's own fault if they get treated with disrespect and their conduct the cause. I think I might safely say that Easter Monday was the most agreeable day I have spent this side of the "line" . . .
> I'm still attending the singing class and beginning to make some improvement. It is a very good way of spending one evening of the week. I have got another iron in the fire now. I was elected on the committee of the early closing association; it meets once a fortnight.
> I am getting along pretty well in my crib. We have a very nice kind of a governor. I have not heard him growl at any of the hands yet. I like Echuca better than Heathcote. It is much larger and [I] prefer it to Melbourne. One does not get to know many in a large town like Melbourne . . .

Hugh's preference for Echuca emphasises a salient feature of Irish immigrant social life. In the big cities — Melbourne and Sydney — Irish immigrants grouped together, not so much in anything that could be properly called ghettoes, but in close social networks, living with or close to each other, exchanging visits, working together, spending leisure time with each other, to the inevitable exclusion of 'outsiders', non-Irish, colonials: when in Melbourne, both Hugh and John Maxwell stayed with Ulster people and were constantly visited by Ulster friends. This was a situation generated naturally by the size, geography and anonymity of the city and chosen by many immigrants deliberately or instinctively as a protective environment against the strangeness of their new world. Hugh's own initial reaction to Australia had been exactly this — to join an Ulster world set in Melbourne. So had John's — although his chosen Ulster world had been segregated by distance at Yackandandah. When Hugh had moved from Melbourne to the small township of Heathcote, he had at first thought the tiny Irish enclave represented by the drapery-store society enough, but he soon found it as isolated as Melbourne, though for different reasons: in Heathcote, social life was small, established and segregated and it was not easy for a newcomer to join existing groups. By this stage Hugh had become sufficiently acclimatised and adjusted to colonial life not to need the constant and unvaried society of fellow-countrymen, indeed to regard them as a constriction on social possiblities. And they were exactly that in one very important respect: they were overwhelmingly male. The middling township of Echuca was sufficiently large, open and mobile to offer interesting female companionship and to absorb a personable and enterprising immigrant without difficulty or discomfort. Other Irish men and women made the transition to moving into a wider colonial society, in multifarious circumstances of city and country, with various degrees of ease or difficulty. For Hugh Maxwell the environment of Echuca provided both the opportunity and stimulus to move out of his older narrow world.

Such progress, such integration, often seemed to its participants fluctuating and unspectacular, even non-existent. Summing up his situation on 23 July 1886, John Maxwell considered that, mainly as a result of his indifferent health, he had 'not made very good headway at all' in Australia: he felt his 'little plans of life' had been thwarted. It was an uncharacteristic capitulation to depression, perhaps aggravated by his being out of work:

> At present I am out of work and has been for the past two weeks. However I have utilized my time as best I could. I had heard that there was a very good job to be had on the new cable tramways once one could get on. I applied and was informed that I was the sort of men they wanted and if I could get a good reference from some respectable person they would give me a trial. So Mr. Agnew my old benefactor furnished me with a character that would have pleased anybody. I went for training on last Monday week and passed on my seventh day's practise. I got my certificate and was told they would send for me when the new lines opened, as there are several under construction at present. It will unfortunately be three or perhaps six months before I will get on. I will be what is called engineer (a rather big word for what I will have to do). It is commonly called gripman. The tram-car is drawn by an endless rope running on underground pullies driven by a stationary engine of great power. The cable runs underneath the pavement between the runs and is caught by a grip wrought by a lever which passed down through a groove about two inches wide. The rope never stops but slips through the grip when the car is at a standstill. There are as many as 20 of these cars all on the rope at once . . .

John took the opportunity of his enforced leisure (and cheap excusion rail fares) to visit Hugh in Echuca, observing of him (4 August 1886):

> Besides enjoying perfect health he seems to be enjoying life better than he ever did at home. However that is not to be wondered at. At home he had

long hours, low wages, and few holidays. Here he has good hours, good wages and half a holiday once a week besides all other public holidays. To this I may add that he has formed a great many acquaintances some of the feminine gender who he has introduced me to are the finest I have the honour of being acquainted on this side of the "line".
Echuca is a quiet country town occupying about five times as much ground as it ought compared with the number of houses and the population. It has been designed for a large town but its progress was stopped and it has greatly decreased since the railway passed over the Murray and on to Denilquin, up till that time it being the terminus and a great emporium of the cattle and horse trade of New South Wales, the stock being transported across the river in a boat.
The country surrounding is quite flat, not as much as a mountain to relieve the eye in the distance. Although the climate is very dry there is a little tillage farming, the soil being admirably suited, being very rich.
Doctor Graham a medical practitioner in this town has been giving a number of lectures instructing how to attend patients in case of accidents or otherwise when a surgeon is not at hand. Hugh attended them all. They have formed a St. John's Ambulance Society. The Doctor will enter into instruction more minutely and each student or member will be furnished with a handbook with instructions how to deal with accidents etc. etc. . .

By 15 September 1886, Hugh was writing home on the firm assumption that his brother James was coming to Australia:

. . . Well as far as I can see it is a wise step and one which I think he will not regret. He will have a better chance of getting along here once he gets a start made. He will have a better chance of getting a good "screw" than he would in R[iddell?] and Co's. If he comes away before the winter sets in at home he will have two summers so he will have every chance to escaping cold this Christmas.
. . . you will all have a much easier mind about James coming away than you had about us as you now know something about the place and you had very little knowledge of it then. Besides he will feel it different, having someone here before him, to what we did having, I might say, no-one. Now John and I are both in work. Then we did not know how we might fall in as to work and one of us not very able to do work of any kind. We have indeed a great deal to be thankful for. Our welfare has not consisted in abundance of riches but in the fewness of our wants which have all been liberally supplied. I hope you will all look on the brighter side of the matter. Father and mother can at least feel that they are sending a living message to their two younger sons 13,000 miles away.
It is possible that James may have started before this reaches you so that any remarks or information I could give him would be too late. However I would advise him not to burden himself too much in bringing a lot of things but to leave room in his box for a couple of tins of good biscuits, a few pots of jam etc. which he will find very nice on board ship. If he is fortunate enough to have any money I would recommend him not to bring it on his person but send it to one of the Melbourne banks. That can be done by going to any of the Belfast banks and depositing it and then lifting it out here. I cannot tell you how to go about this banking business but he will probably know something about it himself or can get the desired information from some of the banks.

No doubt one could bring a considerable sum of money about his person in safety. Still there is some risk of losing it. When one has not the money about him (but sent on by the banking company) he has not the care of it on his mind. Of course one must carry enough to meet all expenses on the journey which often runs up more than he first counts upon. It is not wise to leave oneself bare as that sort of thing would be most awkward for one could not borrow from his neighbour when he is amongst strangers.

A soft felt or tweed hat would be the best during the entire journey. He should wear the worst suit of clothes he brings. Never mind appearances he will find many less tidy than himself on board. By the way Mary don't let him forget the "sprigs of scheilleagh". I want a stick badly.

John has not had any word about his crib on the trams yet. However he is doing garden work and can wait a while. Of course the wages will be better on the trams than he now earns. He is keeping strong and now that the winter is over he will get along nicely.

. . . I have not made up my mind about going home to get an Irish wife yet. If I had been half up to snuff I would have had one on the "triste" and brought her out at any time. However what can't be cured must be endured so I had better look out for a Colonial I think; that is the only thing left me. By the way the Colonial girls are not to be despised and they are not half so scarce as you people at home think.

I met Miss Christy of Bangor. She lives about 15 miles from here with some friends, an aunt I think. She was in the shop getting something and happened to find out who I was. We had a long chat in the course of which I could see that she lacks the polish and refinement to be found in most of the Colonial girls. However she seems to be a nice kind of young lady all the same, free in her style and manner etc. etc. . .

On the matter of a prospective wife Hugh was obviously in some indecision and confusion. With half his mind he retained the prevalent Irish assumption that colonial girls were both inferior and scarce (and that the prudent man would import a wife from Ireland); with the newer aspect of his experience and thinking he was granting such girls superior polish and refinement.

James Maxwell emigrated to Australia on the *Lusitania* in October–November 1886 with a group of four or five friends from the Bangor district. It seems that James's passage money of ten pounds was borrowed from a friend, his father acting as guarantor: within three months James had repaid it. (John remarked that if James had asked, Hugh would have sent the money). The Bangor group had a lively time on board ship: James was particularly popular, being a good dance violinist. In Albany, Western Australia, a railway contractor, desperate for labour, came on board, offering hands 10s. per day for two years engagement. In Adelaide James, to his agreeable surprise, received a letter from John giving instructions on what to do on arrival in Melbourne: Port Adelaide, was in great excitement and activity following a gold discovery inland.

In Melbourne, John was working and thus could not meet the ship. But a friend of John and Hugh — Mr McDonald — took the day off to do so. John commented (13 January 1887): 'His benevolence was far beyond what could have been expected from a stranger for Mr Mc[Donald] was not personally acquainted with James'. Mr MacDonald was not a 'stranger' to John and Hugh: they had lodged at his house. Again the strict old-world concepts of the boundaries of appropriate behaviour and the expected duties of relationships are obvious.

From Melbourne on 30 November 1886 James wrote to his mother. First he reported on John, then detailed his variant on the usual Irish immigrant round of calling on relations and friends, and of job-hunting: James had been an assistant in a hardware shop in Ireland. He found that John

> is not the delicate looking "scobe" he was when he left home; he is hardy looking in the face and muscular in limbs. He tells me he was something weightier some time ago but I expect he will soon pull it up again as he has got a situation with the Cable Tramway Company which is very light. He passed the examination some time ago (which he informed us). His post is engineering (as it is called) of the brakes — a very responsible position indeed and composed of the most respectable young men in Melbourne. He was changed off the dummy or engine of the tram to what is called time-keeper; this post he has had for the last week, this he may be at for a fortnight a month or perhaps more. He can do with this as long as it does with him; has got nothing to do but walk up and down a footpath and see that the buses are started in proper time and that they are not overloaded. The only objection I see to the time-keeping is that the hours are late (viz. 11.15) but not long as he gets it in spells. He commences at 9.30am relieved at 2pm on again at 5 is allowed time for tea between that and 11.15. He (John) is still lodging with Mr. Fisher of Kew where he keeps his bees. He wants me to start and hive a lot of them for him as he has not much time at his disposal. I wanted to start right off but he insists on me going up to Echuca (pronounced Etuca) tomorrow morning Wednesday (I don't know how long I may be there perhaps until the Christmas holidays. Hugh intends taking [doing?] a run down then to see his friends in Melbourne).
>
> John came here and slept with me. He lay and talked until 4 this morning. He is troubled a little with his cough yet but nothing to signify. He is very thankful for the different nice presents sent him by his friends . . . he will write you by next mail or so; his time for writing is limited now. I went round along with John and saw Mr. Agnew and Mr. Purce his brother-in-law and partner yesterday. They were very friendly and asked me if I intended looking for a situation right off I told them I didn't mind dropping into a situation but that I intended going up country to see Hugh. They advised me to do that and not to be in too big a hurry. Mr. Purce told me that he would introduce me to Mr. Cullen the hardware partner when I returned from country and he Mr. Cullen might be able to put me on a good track. He in the meantime would keep me in his memory. This he proposed without soliciting. Of course Mr. Purce had sounded my business capacities, while Mr. Agnew was engaged chatting to R. and J. Hanna who had called before us. We of course, in business like manner, made our visit short, with promising to call when I return from Echuca.
>
> Called with Mr. F. Crickard and delivered his stick and parcel. He was very busy and took my address and came round to Mr. McD[onald] and spent the evening with me. He is a fine chatty fellow and not the stuck up man I took him for. I am to call with him when I return as he wants me for dinner some Sunday.

On 14 December he wrote to his sister Susanna that

> . . . John gave me a trial overhauling some bee frames. He has a job that will keep me going for a fortnight if I don't get another in the hardware line. I purpose calling with Mr. Agnew tomorrow as promised. He may have an opening or know of one. I would just as soon not take crib for a fortnight

> but will not refuse a good thing if it turns up. I am most anxious about the bees. There would be more go to loss than I could gain out of a month's screw. John dropped into this billet (our situation) (as mentioned in last letter) a month too soon but it would not wait on him . . .

James was impressed by Kew, where John had lodgings, as 'the most aristocratic place about Melbourne' (far superior to Echuca) and continued:

> . . . we purpose staying at Fisher's convenient to where the bees are or taking the house connected with the gardens the bees are in. The only inconvenience in connection with the latter is we would have to keep a housekeeper and that I would not like to risk in the hands of a stranger. If we had some trustworthy friend it would suit well.

On 27 December 1886 James informed his parents that he had employment, in the hardware section of Mr Agnew's shop, work so strenuous that he had severe pains in his shoulders. It happened that he had called again on Mr Agnew who asked him if he could start at once:

> Agnew then had a short conversation with the Company partner (Mr Cullen). I was brought forward and introduced to him. Of course I soon saw that I had been talked about before as Mr. Purce another co-partner (brother-in-law to Mr Agnew and a country man of ours) had sounded me the first day I was in. They then made me an offer viz. £2 per week to begin the following morning and I would have charge of a department after the holidays when stock would be taken, so you see I have been assisting the man in charge up to Friday 24th being the day before Christmas and when I was getting paid (being only a week past on Thursday previous they paid me for a week and a half viz. £3 wasn't bad for a start was it?) Mr. Agnew fully initiated me as charge of the hardware side of that flat to commence after the holiday viz. 28th December. He told me the better I made it pay the better it was for myself and for them.
> The holidays commenced on Saturday (Christmas day) and continues until tomorrow Tuesday. We will have another holiday on Saturday being the New Year. I spent Christmas quieter than usual, went over to Kew and had dinner with John as I was invited by his landlady but unfortunately John had to go on duty at 2pm until 8pm. He is now on the grip (or engineer) as extra man. He had 8 runs yesterday (Sunday) and 11 for today which means about 1s. per run. He is in great spirit since he got on the dummy was dull enough at the time-keeping; the hours were too long and there was not enough of go in it for Jack. You must excuse him for not writing as he has been kept rather close to duty since I landed . . . [He] told me you always got most letters when he was not in the best of health or when he was off for spells so from this you may conclude he is in good health when he is not writing. I did not see him yesterday but went on foot to Fitzroy this afternoon (a distance of about 2 miles) and met him on his engine a little way from the terminus and had a ride to the other end of the line with him. He could only talk to me occasionally as it is forbidden that the engineers should talk to passengers in case their attention is drawn off their duty. John says *quite coolly* they have to watch and not kill any of them (meaning the people. You would think it was bees he was talking about). He (John) intends taking a run round this week to try and get suitable lodgings for us both convenient to the bees. They have been neglected lately . . . you will be glad to know that all the Bangorians except George Smith [have got jobs] and he may be into a good job but we

have not heard of him. R. Hanna is in a store in Paran (I think is the name) convenient to Melbourne. John Hanna is in the same house as myself. D. McClintock is in one of the stations I think Spencer Street station. S. Cullough went away last week to a crib near Sydney; so far we have been fortunate.

That this was very fortunate Hugh fully agreed, but he claimed to have thought beforehand that Mr Agnew would employ James (6 January 1887):

> I had half a notion all along that he would get a start there even before I advised James to come here. No doubt you will all think this is a fine flowery land, this Australia, when one can get into a situation so soon. Well all that I can say is that some people are not so fortunate in falling into a crib as James has been. You will also be made aware of the fine "screw" that John now gets. Things were not always so bright. A great deal is owing to dogged perserverance . . .

It is possible that the intention of Hugh's dampening letters was to dispel any impression in Ireland that the boys in Australia had money to spare. Neither he or John had sent money home, but early in 1887 their mother directly asked. Certainly the family in Ireland appear to have then been in some degree of financial difficulty, but this was abnormal: the prevailing family circumstances seem to be those of reasonable comfort. Mrs Maxwell's request may have been to test the response of her sons in Australia, in a situation where remittances from emigrants to family at home were common and had become a matter of comparative prestige within Irish society. The boys' reaction was dutiful but not enthusiastic: they had plans for their money themselves.

On 2 March 1887 Hugh wrote to his sister Mary:

> I am very sorry to know that things keep so dull and the prospect so bad. However I hope you will be able to tide over the bad times if all goes well etc. In compliance with mother's request I forward a little money to James which he will forward from Melbourne when he writes. It is all I can spare as we have had a lot to do with our savings. I need not begin to enumerate them but they have been greater, I daresay, than you would naturally think. Our bee scheme has incurred a great many necessary expenses and up to the present we have had no return. I hope however that that will go all right bye and bye.
>
> We would like very much to select a farm (that is an unimproved piece of land in the natural bush) as the tram work may or may not suit John's health for any length of time, so that he would have something to fall back on in the case of being unable to carry on the tram work. However at present funds will not allow of that so we cannot venture it yet a bit. I hope we will eventually be able to carry out our plans in that direction.
>
> Tell Susanna I am very sorry that I can't undertake to do any collecting or even give a subscription to the funds of the bazaar of which the gentleman Mr. Coates (I think the name is, I don't happen to know him) speaks of sending out collecting books. The people have to give a good deal to local churches, hospitals and charities and some of them do not get their money as easily as Mr. Coates may imagine.

James sent this money on, with some comments from himself:

> Enclosed please find Post Office order of £7 which Hugh sent me to forward to you, payable at the Belfast Post Office same as the last which I hope went all right. I would [have] liked to have made it out £10 but neither John nor

I had it to spare. John has not been working on the trams since the second week in January so you see money is not as flush with us as it would have been had it been otherwise.

John had to give up the time-keeping owing to the hours being long and late. Then he was on the tramcar for a fortnight the time of the holidays which ended his work on the trams until a new line is opened up, which may not take place for another month or so. He is going into town tomorrow to ascertain if there is any new hands wanted. You will be glad to hear that John and I are stopping together since 1st February . . . tell Susanna I will not be able to do anything in the way of collecting money for a bazaar. I need not tell you that collecting money is a thing I don't care for and besides I have little to spare myself. The church that John is in connection with is building a new one so they can do with a subscription from both of us.

Robbie Hanna was here spending the day with us last Sunday. He told me he had got a [collecting] book sent by Mrs. Furey. He has been round with Mr. Agnew and Mr. Purse. They gave him £1 each. He has several other pounds.

As James had remarked, at this stage James and John were staying together (changes of address were frequent) in Bell Street, Glenferrie, and John added a postscript to James' letter:

. . . I was very sorry to see by Mary's letter that things look so bad at home. It has ever been Hugh and my great [ambition?] to try and take up some land with the hope of bettering our position and perhaps opening a way for you all out here seeing things do not improve at home but unfortunately it has not been our luck. It requires capital and we have not that at our disposal owing to ill-health and other disappointments but we hope 'ere next year to be able to take up an allotment so as to enable us to establish bee-farming on a very extensive scale to which could be added other industries . . .

By April the situation of the family in Ireland was improving economically. Prices of cattle had improved and, despite dogs worrying the sheep, there was a good number of lambs. (Nevertheless, John later observed 'young horses of a good class seem to be the only thing which pays at home'). But the work was hard, particularly for the girls. James was sure Mary had too much to do, and he disliked Susanna's confining herself to flowering — intricate lace-making work of great delicacy — to supplement the family income (27 December 1886).

it would appear it is paying well; if I were her I would not confine myself at that sort of thing; it is quite too confining for her constitution . . . it is right enough for the two old people and it may be right enough for her providing she works at it to rest herself from other work. I am sure Mary has too much to do . . . I fancy I see her "sluching" about the back-door in mud and water.

Susanna suffered from neuralgia as well as a weak chest.

But the general family atmosphere in Ballygannah was perhaps more disturbing to the Australian boys. Their father was a good horseman and often rode in hunts, but their mother was inactive and experienced indifferent health: she fretted and worried about her sons so far away. Although the boys wrote regularly and at great length, their letters were never frequent enough. To complaints, they answered that letters must have been delayed or gone astray, but they arranged among themselves to write more often. As the most recent away from the family, James was most sensitive to this air of unhappiness and worry — did they live near a church, did they keep warm? He wrote to his mother (25 May 1887).

> I ask you to rejoice to know that we are in a country that we have a show (a chance) to make men of ourselves. I know I feel a better man today than ever I did within the last three years.

He had got rid of his indigestion and sported a beard. His brother John had let his beard grow to protect his throat, a health procedure, but James was anxious to diguise his youth — 'it gives me a senior appearance' — though he too was to confess later (the winter of 1887 was very severe) of being 'very frightened of his chest and throat'.

When John next wrote home (25 May 1887) he excused his failure to write more frequently by explaining that leaning over gave him chest pains. He was still with the tramways.

> Tramcar engineering is a pretty difficult job and requires a good deal of care, strength, quickness and judgement but practise has made me pretty proficient in the management of my little train. There was at least one accident a week these last three or four [weeks?]. The other night a drunken man was knocked down and crushed; he almost died immediately. I have been pretty lucky [in] not having hurt or killed anybody for so far. However I had one accident by a horse shying and running against the front of my dummy.
> The trains consists of a dummy and large sized tramcar very similar to the ones in Belfast only they are better got up. The dummy is the car which is in front and to which the car is coupled. It has seats all round very much like an Irish jaunting car. There is a seat across in front and behind exactly the same (either ends being front or rear according to which ways it is running — if it runs east the end which is the front was the back when running west). The side seats sit over the wheels exactly the same [as] an Irish jaunting car. The grip space inside of which are the levers for starting and stopping the motion of the train, there is room enough for a dozen persons to stand but nothing but the engineer is allowed in it except the conductor when collecting fares . . .
> It is pleasant work along clear streets but where there is much traffic it is very troublesome . . .

Life was proceeding much the same with Hugh in Echuca (12 July 1887):

> . . . since the last time I wrote home we have had uncommonly wet weather. The roads in this district are like ploughed fields. There is no gravel within 40 miles or more of here. Therefore the roads are merely beaten tracks fenced in. They do very well in our dry climate in the summer time and dry weather but when we get much rain like what we have had the last 4 weeks the[y] are almost impassable.
> . . . on Wednesday evening next there is to be a social ball in connection with the Half-Holiday Association. It is expected to be a very nice turnout. All the shop people who are interested in the half-holiday movement turn out to it, besides a great many of the general public. Of course there are any amount of nice young ladies in Echuca so one has not much difficulty in getting a partner. Echuca is very dull without something of this sort to enliven it up.
> . . . we have great illuminations here on [Queen Victoria's] Jubilee week. There was a bullock and three sheep roasted whole in the park and the meat was divided among poor people.

Hugh had become increasingly involved in the local Half-Holiday Association of which he had become secretary: his motivation seems to have been substantially social if his description of the Association's Ball (4 August 1887) is any indication:

> . . . the affair came off with great "eclat". The young ladies many of whom are subscribers to the Association's funds, turned out in full evening dress, and I must say that I have not seen anything to equal the style even at home. You must understand that the Victorian young ladies are, as a rule, highly accomplished and well educated. They also know how to dress with taste and to advantage. Neither is there any scarcity of them as is generally supposed at home. I might say that at our social we had more ladies than gentlemen . . .

Hugh, approaching thirty, had acquired a 'young lady' about whom he was initially very reticent. His first reference to her was when she left Echuca later that month, something which depressed him but on which his comment to his sister (1 September 1887) was merely a wry 'hard lines isn't it'. In November he told his mother that he seemed destined to become an old bachelor.

But now, in mid-1887, the Maxwell's eldest son, William, aged forty, married, with wife and infant daughter, was thinking of emigrating to Australia: he was working as a breadman in the nearby town of Newtownards. The newly arrived James put his view (20 July 1887):

> William again asked my opinion regarding his coming out here as he is frightened to risk another winter on the breadcarts. You can see by the already mentioned that we have got cold weather here as well as at home but the atmosphere is much clearer. I would rather not give any advice to William further than what I have done as there is a second party interested in the matter viz. Sarah and that is my reason for not advising him for or against. If I did it would simply be a repetition of what I have already told him in a former letter. If he came out here or any other person they have to run the risk of getting a situation to suit them. Some are very fortunate and others are not, but a man or woman that is willing to take a turn at anything for a time has never any reason to cry want. Although times are dull here at present, yet there is always work for a man with a willing mind. But men of capital have a better chance here than a man that is depending on his work graft.
>
> I believe if we had enough money to give us a start in a store up country that we could do well yet I have no reason to grumble and I may here mention that I don't regret coming out as regards money matters. Of course the mind often wanders back to the old home and home has always its "tighes" [ties]."

John was not particularly encouraging either: William should be under no illusion that Australia offered an easy life (15 September 1887):

> If he comes he must come with the intention to rough it for a bit and at any rate. I earn £2 12s. a week but if I do I work sixty hours a week for it and has only one holiday every three weeks — at it both Sundays and weekdays. Another thing William could not get a job like mine for he is too old; 35 is the age you must be under but he could earn from a pound to 25s. and board at ploughing.
>
> Of course a man like him would get plenty of work with the farmers at about £1 a week and board all the year round but he would have to be like any other serving man.
>
> The climate up country (that is inland) is much better than in and around Melbourne. The Melbourne climate is very changeable. We have spring,

summer and winter weather all in one day sometimes. The heat is very great in some parts except the cool parts of Gippsland . . .

Besides, John took a pessimistic view of the employment situation (20 July 1887):

Times seem pretty bad at present all over the world. Melbourne although much better than the adjacent colonies has at present a great slackness in almost every branch of business. There have been great meetings of the unemployed these last few days. Of course all first class men get employment pretty easily but the country contains a good many who if knocked out of their usual way have not the aptitude to turn their hand to something else. Besides there are a great many "good for nothing" sort of folks. These folks expect to have work at as good wages as others who are worth their wages. Last winter the unemployed of Melbourne were given work by the government. They were quite insulted on being offered 4s. a day for breaking stones. Probably something like that will be done for them this winter. You see our government looks better after the working man than they do at home.
As every man has a vote in this country and as our members of parliament are paid £300 a year, the members of parliament are very careful to keep the favour of the working men. You see the unemployed receive a good deal of sympathy with their fellow working people, consequently the above result . . .

James filled his parents in (15 August 1887) with news of his and John's doing and plans:

. . . I'm glad to inform you that John has got changed into another line. It goes out to Clifden Hill a very nice and healthy suburb. We will be able to live together there if we can get our ideas carried out. Mrs. Welby the woman whom I am staying with has sold this cottage and purposes taking a cottage at Clifden Hill to suit us. John is anxious for this and so am I as she is a very nice person and *tuckers* well (*tucker* food) I may here tell you that I have eaten more flesh meat since I came to the colony than I did in two years at home. I have a plate of nice porridge and new milk every morning except Sunday and a nice chop or fresh fish or rabbit with tea and toast . . .

He and John shared the same bedroom, but with single beds: it was evident that this was a substantial improvement on their Irish sleeping situation. As to John:

he gives the landlady the extra 2s. so that he can have anything he fancies such as a couple of raw eggs beat up in tea, coffee or milk when he is going to bed or working late. He has been on the late shift this week and has not done till 11.30pm; pretty late isn't it? But again he does not start until 11.00 o'clock when on this shift. I generally take him in a good plate of porridge and he has that in bed. Then he has a snooze, rises at 10, has breakfast and goes to work and knocks off at about 4 or 4.30 for a spell (rest), has dinner returns to work at 6.30. The night work is not good for him. I am surprised to see how he stood the winter and a pretty severe one too. I believe if he had only to work during the day that he would get rid of his cough . . . We three are trying to save what money we can as we purpose investing in a farm or select. We have been getting information from a young man from Derry (Ireland) who has taken up a selection and I intend when on my holidays going to see the country where land is available and convenient to

> where this young man has selected. If it was a good bee country they would be a good industry.
> I shall not dwell further on the subject as I cannot say much about it until I see the place. John intends sticking to the tram company until he runs a bit of a cheque together. If the land already mentioned is not selected or taken up the opportunity slips and in a few years good land will not be to [be] had in a reasonable distance from a railway or township.
> The already mentioned regarding land we wish to be kept among yourselves *strictly secret.*

The instruction emphasises the strong sense of family privacy and solidarity still operative. Family business was confidential, not so much by nature, but because it held together and differentiated a traditional identity. It also involved pride and status. If the Maxwells' ambitions to get an Australian farm were known outside the family, and then came to nothing, it would entail public humiliation, some degree of personal disgrace hard to endure in a close-knit society. And it was still close-knit: family, relations, neighbours, friends, acquaintances might be dispersed across the world but the traditional relationships still went on, with news and gossip, competition and rivalry, concern and caring, inquisitiveness and scandalmongering, stretched to an international scale. In Melbourne as elsewhere the members of the home Irish families exchanged frequent visits. These were governed by the etiquette brought from home: one waited until one was asked; no casual 'dropping in'. It was a matter for comment, and for concession to the more free and easy Australian ways, when the Hannas, whom James and John Maxwell visited often, said they should not wait for an invitation but come when it suited them.

James ended his August 1887 letter by recalling that it was a year since he had left home, four years since John and Hugh had done so:

> . . . I hope and speak the sentiments of the others when I say we hope that you look on yesterday a year ago and yesterday 4 years ago with joy and not with sorrow. We ask you all to rejoice to know that we are spared to prosper in the land of our adoption notwithstanding the little difficulties we have had to contend with. We feel thankful that our position is improved although the home "tithes" [ties] binds us to friends much dearer than any in this side of the globe.

But James was also well aware (15 September 1887) that other Irish migrants were disappointed and unhappy in Australia. One of the group that had migrated with him from Bangor was Sam Cullough, who was in fact thinking of going home:

> he says he is much disappointed with the country; there is many a one like him. Their idea of the country is that they have nothing to do but walk into a large store and ask for a situation believing that they have little or nothing to do and get a large salary. This is a very erroneous idea. Situations are hard to get especially in Melbourne being overrun with people from other colonies and when a situation is obtained you have got to work pretty hard, at least harder than Sam was ever used to in the old country. For my part I don't think I've got to work as hard as I did at Riddels. The only drawback here (or at least in Agnew's) is that the discipline is bad.

Reviewing his feelings, Hugh also had concluded that, on balance, he was better off in Australia (1 November 1887):

> . . . I am now in a position to state that I, in fact we, have no reason to regret coming to Victoria as far as prospects are concerned. I have not the least doubt that we all will get along better than if we had remained at home. Of course there are social disadvantages such as not being near the rest of you and not being able to see you all occasionally.

This growing sense of settlement among the Maxwell brothers was enhanced by the fact that most of the contemporary Irish immigrants they knew were settling down also. Some had turned their wandering restlessness into an employment, like Mr McVicker who had become a commercial traveller,[11] or put their constructive energy into the land as small selectors, or taken the initiative to set up shop, like Robert Hanna. Change and mobility of location and employment continued, but increasingly these tended to be within the perimeters of commitment to Australia.

In November 1887 the three Maxwell brothers in Australia were surprised to find that William and his family, together with another family from the district, were already on the way to Australia. James wrote (7 November 1887):

> . . . I feel sure that if the whole family could have come and taken up selections and used the same industry they have done at home that in the course of 10 or 15 years or perhaps less they would be worth a bit more money than they would be at home or I may say the land would be worth the money for in the course of 10 years land will not be to [be] had and in this way its value will increase.
>
> We don't know what William is likely to tackle first. Our idea is stock raising and if we can get things to our minds we will give it a trial. Of course it is up hill work for a year or two but if a man is able to hold his own for the first 3 years he may consider himself pretty safe and after that with the improvements that is put on, the land is worth a bit of money. You see the Government pays as high as £10 per acre for improvements.
>
> The great drawback here with farmers or people that pretend to be farmers or stock raisers is that more than the half of them knows nothing whatever about it; thus they are kept feeling their way for years. I firmly believe if William gave it a trial that he would succeed, unless he is much changed from what he used to be.
>
> I am sure you are all busy preparing for them starting. I have just been speaking to Mrs. Welby our landlady and making arrangements for William and Sarah. She Mrs. W[elby] shall be very glad to accommodate them. They will feel more at home with us than with strangers and Mrs. Welby will be nice company for Sarah and the little one until they get settled. I will write to Adelaide so that they will get instructions three days before they arrive at Williamstown, Melbourne. The Hanna family and us have arranged to go and welcome them.
>
> 10 November . . . we are glad that William is leaving Newtownards. I never liked the idea of him going round and serving the bread.

It was left to James alone to meet William. Hugh did not travel down to Melbourne and at the time of William's arrival, John had gone to Echuca to holiday with Hugh: perhaps they reasoned that James' presence was welcome enough, or that as older married brother he could look after himself. James's help at the wharf was indeed needed. A Miss McClintock had been put, by her sister-in-law, in the care of William and Sarah Maxwell for the voyage out. But in London they learnt from a neighbour of the lady that she had just been released from an asylum. As it transpired, William had great trouble in discharging the responsibility and had to watch over her like a child. He reported of their arrival in Melbourne:

> She should have never been out of the asylum. James and I went and got her fixed in a place at 8s. per week with a woman that kept boarders and we have not heard anything of her since. I have written to James to go and try and find where she is as she would soon go through her £5. I had to give her money when she landed and James paid her train up to Melbourne.

For the physically unfit or ailing, Australia was seen as a potential cure — and so it often proved. But it is evident that some relatives saw the colonies as a convenient way to dispose of unwanted or burdensome people of various kinds. Four years later (13 September 1891) James reported on this particular matter again:

> I had a letter from a sister of Mr. McClintock who came out with William. She is in great want and has requested me to write to her brother and ask him to assist her which I did but never had a reply. It is a shame for them to leave her like that in a strange country; besides she is hardly right in her mind.

In Echuca, Hugh, in search of a more homelike atmosphere, had changed his lodgings from a hotel to a boarding house (7 December 1887):

> The landlady Miss Reiley is North of Ireland, has lived near Carrickfergus and in Belfast; is about 7 years in Victoria. She is a music teacher as well as keeping boarders; is an old maid or at any rate a bit on the shelf; is rather peculiar looking but is very attentive to the boarders — that's the main thing . . .

In Melbourne, James was enjoying a lively time — a picnic on the Prince of Wales' birthday, a picnic on Melbourne Cup day, parties some evenings, and a group camping holiday at Fernshaw (23 December 1887).

> . . . it was arranged that two of our party viz. Frank and Eddie Beggs would start on Friday morning with a trap and convey the victuals and 3 tents one of which was large enough to accommodate 14 ladies and the other two were for the gents. Our friends did not get to the arranged camping ground until the following evening owing to the state of the roads. The remainder of the party went by rail to Lilydale, thence coach to Fernshaw a distance of 15 miles . . . the place selected for camping was on the side of the Black Spur Mountain.

Hugh observed of James (December 1887) that his spare time was taken up with his young lady — to which he added sourly that he was 'rather differently situated'. Without his girlfriend, he was finding Echuca a dull place. Time hung heavy in the summer evenings: he did a bit of fishing in the River Murray.

But early in 1888 Hugh joined John to look for a land selection, John having got leave from the tramways. Hugh explained (5 February 1888) that John

> had got leave of absence owing to not being very well; he was troubled with his liver and kidneys. I left here on a Wednesday morning and got into Melbourne at half past eleven same morning. John and me started for Sale Gippsland by the early train on Thursday; arrived there about 1 o'clock; took the boat which plys on the Gippsland lakes between Sale and Bairnsdale. There are three lakes which we pass through on the trip. We arrived a

Bairnsdale about 8.30pm stopped there all night and started next day at 7.30pm by coach for a small township called Bruthen; arrived there about 10 o'clock same evening. On Saturday morning we again started by coach at 5 o'clock and got to Tambo Crossing at 9 o'clock in time for breakfast. We were now at our journey's end. We soon found Mr. Wilson the young man that has taken up a block of land there. John and I started off to have a look at the lands available for selection. We were rather disappointed as we found it all extremely hilly indeed mountainous in some places.
I was obliged to return on my homeward journey on Monday afternoon so I had only Saturday, Sunday and Monday morning to look around but in that time we came across nothing sufficiently tempting. John stayed behind for a couple of days or so to have a further look but I am inclined to think he would come across nothing to suit.

In fact John had applied for a selection and paid the fee, but this was no guarantee of possession as many had applied.[12]

When John returned to his work on the Melbourne tramways he was immediately involved in a strike. James told the family what had happened (1 March 1888).

'Extremely hilly indeed mountainous in some places'. A view of a Gippsland dairy farm in the hills near Balook illustrates the terrain and clearing work faced by the Maxwells. (Courtesy: Port Albert Maritime Museum, Victoria)

There was a strike with the tram men and John of course was one of the ones that struck, but as the majority were not true to each other and went crawling back to work before they were three days out, the Company (or employers) has the best of it. The best of the men resigned and said they would not go back to work under the old rules, so John was one of these men that stuck true to his colours and true to his fellowman. He, John, did not intend staying longer on the trams than about a couple of months as the late hours seemed to knock him out of tune and the dust made him cough more than he would do otherwise. He has gone up to Yackandandah to Mr. George Reid's and will go on from that to Robert Reid's at Kiewa River. He purposes riding from that to Barnawartha to see William and his household being a distance of 15 or 20 miles I believe. He may drop into some sort of work up there for a few months that will suit him better than the trams. If he gets the selection he will have to go to it in about 6 months.

I had a letter from him a week ago in which he says he is in pretty good health. The few days the strike lasted he lost 4lbs. weight. He was one of the committee that was appointed to go through the wavering men and strengthen them. This was worse on him than his work . . .

Obviously, John's mixture of aggression and passion for justice were known to the family, and it was true that he had not thought of his tramway position as being permanent. It was also true that he disliked work that did not allow him evenings and public holidays free. In writing to his parents, John did not mention the strike: he had left the tramways because the job did not suit his health. There were some things it was better for parents not to know.

After some time unemployed, William and his wife Sarah got positions as farm help on the property of a Mr. Newson, Fassifern, Barnawartha, in northern Victoria 280 miles from Melbourne. The work was hard (Sarah complained of her legs in the mornings, especially after a previous day's washing and ironing), but as John was to note of William (28 March 1888):

. . . he does not complain; he knows he need not bother himself grumbling for if people get good wages they must work. I have to "graft" just as hard as him — there is [no] get out of it (please excuse slang for you will pick it up in spite of yourselves).

Like Hugh (who was 11st 11 lbs.) William kept a careful check of his weight: he was 12st 10 lbs., which he regarded as reasonable considering that he lost a stone on the passage out. The matter of weight was an item of constant interest. In September 1890 William was at pains to point out that information that the family in Ireland had given to a friend that William's wife Sarah was 12st was incorrect: the friend had written to William on the matter. She was only 11st 8 lb. (William was then 13st.). It was, of course, fear of losing weight which prompted this surveillance: weight was to be put on, and its increase was equated with better health. And William's health was better. The rheumatism in his knees was not nearly as bad as in Ireland. He found his work interesting and various. The novelty, adventure even, and the challenge of turning one's hand to whatever task or trade needed doing, was considerable compensation for the toil (28 March 1888):

. . . I was away with grapes today at Mr. Baumgarten's. He makes wine. He gets the grapes at 5 pound per ton; that is only a little over one half penny per pound. I have tasted the juice of them both sweet and fermented. If I had you here I could give you some of my own making. All it wants is age. We can make either white or dark wine and no adulteration in it. The local makers sometimes only gets one and sometimes 2s. per gallon when selling

> to large vintners. One ton of grapes will make from 120 till 160 gallons of wine. The picking is hot work and sore on the back but we have all ours away and is waiting for rain to start ploughing.
> I have two young horses under training at present. I intend to make a good job of them. The colonial when training thinks they are doing great things when they take a fresh colt and mounts him on the first or second day. How it is done is this way; when a young horse is brought in he is run into the crush (a small passage made of strong posts just the width of the colt and a pair of skakes [?] same as you would put a cow into. There is also two strong poles put across behind him so he can neither get up back or forward) then he is either bridled or haltered. Believe me they get rough usage. Well they are chased and beaten with a large stock whip until they cannot go any longer. Then he is mounted and ridden while he is able to go. The same is repeated for two or three days and then he is broken. After that when his owner puts him into either plough or cart he is sure to be a jibber or buckjumper. I have not seen a proper mouthed horse since I came to the colonies. A jibber is what we would call at home, ruster and sulky, not doing what they are able.
> Mr. Newson went to Melbourne today to spend his Easter holidays so I have charge till he comes back. The young man that was here has left and a young fellow from Tasmania is here to get colonial knowledge. He is not very smart but has plenty of presumption.
> We'll have a single and double furrow going also the disc harrow with 8 bullocks in it. When the ground is loose the disc can prepare the ground without ploughing. In the second turn with the disc we can sow the seed.

In addition there was shearing (wool cutting William called it) of 3619 sheep, pruning and grafting fruit trees, and — he thought his family would be surprised — castrating a horse. All of these to him unusual occupations, William discharged with enthusiasm and competence; quick and adaptable, enjoying the novelty of it all, he liked the colonial life. He was amazed that sweat should drop off his nose and beard and that he should be none the worse for this. He adopted the colonial habit of having a cool bath before sleep. The substantial Newson property gave ample scope for wonderment. The 1888 wool clip fetched £545. Newson was able to afford machinery William thought very expensive:

> Machinery and agricultural implements are very dear in this country. Mr. Newson bought [a] stripper at £50 a winnower at £25 reaping machine £30 with gearing to drive a chaff cutter; chaff cutter £15 and means to get a sheep shearing machine for next year.

William was also happy because he and his wife were occasionally able to visit (it was a three-hour drive) the Reids at Yackandandah, and the large number of Ulster Irish friends who lived in that district.

One aspect of life in Australia left them less than pleased. In their opinion, Australian clothing was both shoddy and expensive. William wrote to the family in Ireland, asking for stockings and slippers to be sent for his wife Sarah and small daughter Susie. He wanted boots, but did not wish them to be sent out, as, if they were discovered by Customs, a 25 per cent duty was charged; better to have them brought in by a friend as his own. In 1889 he wrote to his family:

> Sarah wishes you to send her the making of a black cashmere dress, buttons and body lining. A very poor black cashmere costs 4s. 6d. or 5s. 0d. There is such heavy duty here now that all the Irish people are sending home

William Maxwell's sketch plan of Newson's Barnawartha farm, in 1889

for dress goods. Also a white sunshade for Susie to go to church. What she wants is something with a puff in the crown with a ribbon across, either with or without; about what would fit Mary Johnstone.

Would James send me a black hard hat size 6⅞ at about 5s.0d. or 5s.6d., also a soft light grey for the summer. Send with James Colven if he is able to pack them. If not he could bring a small deal box about 18 inches by 24 inches. And she wants a few cheap silk handkerchiefs. Perhaps Mrs. Henry could help him to fetch them. Sarah has not a chance of wholesale prices here. Don't send them by post owing to the duty, only if J. Colven comes.

PS Please send the account of these things.

The prospect of their cousin James Colven coming to Australia led to a further request, this time for a veritable drapery emporium:

> . . . If cousin James was coming out along with the Henrys you might send a pair of buttoned boots No. 6 at about 10s.0d. and a pair of cloth slippers No. 6; also a print dress made skirt and jacket or some would call it a blouse with stringcase at the waist so as they will almost fit anyone. The same measure does her still. Make the skirt pretty plain as they are easiest washed. Also two or three aprons. Let some be checked linen and some spotted or checked muslin; more of a dress with lace, a pretty good size [?] also a pair of corsets 27 inches not too expensive. She gave 7s. 6d. for a pair and not very good at that. You might put in a few bits of lace and a few cheap handkerchiefs, imitation of silk to wear round our necks in the summer and a piece of Indian muslin or any kind of old fashioned muslin scarf to tie round my own hat in the summer. Mrs. Henry can tell you what we wear.
> Suzie will not need any dresses as Mrs. Newson is making some out of hers but you might send her some white pinnies with a good deal of Swiss work. Mrs. Watson's suited her very well only too short as she is 3 feet 5¼ inches long in her little shoes. She is in very good health and as good a colour as if she was at home.
> She has just minded about a black lustre apron a good size at about 14 or 16 pence. If James does not come it does not matter I would not like to trouble any other body. He could tell them that Sarah's things is the wife's.

On later occasions William was to complain about the meanness of some prospective couriers who would not bring out such goods ordered, *via* the family, but this was the exception: new migrants constantly delivered family parcels to migrants in Australia.

William and Sarah Maxwell had emigrated to Australia with their friends from the same locality, the large family of the McGiltons: the Maxwell brothers in Australia had anticipated that the McGiltons would have trouble finding work. Not so. Mr McGilton rented a piece of land (£1 a year for seven years) and all the adult members of the family got immediate work. Two of the girls went into domestic service, Annie with a gentleman's family; Aggie earning 8s a week with a gentleman farmer's wife. Another girl was a seamstress: her father bought her a new machine for her trade. A son took up cobbling, lucrative in Melbourne at 4s 6d for half soleing a pair of boots, and then got a job at £3 a week and found. Others who came on the same emigrant ship were also quickly employed — a goods van driver in Melbourne, a runner for a lodging house, others as station hands. The depression of the 1890s lay far ahead: for workers the situation was hardly one of boom — work was hard, hours were long — but jobs were not hard to get.

John Maxwell's application for a land selection succeeded (28 March 1888).

> . . . I am going to turn farmer in the course of six months. The land is not very good not as regards the nature of the soil but it is very hilly. It was the best I could get except the scrubby country which would take a man with a big capital, a stout heart and plenty of muscle. The first and last commodities I am a bit deficient in. I believe when I get (I should say we for the boys are finding the cash but the land is applied for and recommended in my name) the fences up and the timber killed it will be a good grass country. The block contains 800 acres. One half is very good but the other is almost valueless. It will be under a government lease for 10 years or 14 years from the passing of the Act, which came into operation at the beginning of 1884. Out of the

Shearing and wool pressing on Yanco station; photographs sent back to Ireland. (Courtesy; P.R.O.N.I. Belfast)

leasehold I can select 320 acres which will be excised from the leasehold and subject to a yearly payment of 1s. an acre per year for 20 years when it will be a freehold. The remainder of the land I will be paid for improvement up to the value of 10s. but not exceeding that amount, on the expiration of the lease. Then James has purchased four building allotments at £10 each. They will likely be worth a good bit some day for property about Melbourne is increasing in value very rapidly.
I have turned "gardner" again; the tram driving did not suit my health. My health has much improved within the last month. I was troubled with my liver and kidneys. I got examined by a herb doctor and am now drinking herbs or the tea of herbs. I believe herbs are the best as they have no injurious effect whatever. . .

John attributed his recent gain in weight (8lbs.) to this herb treatment.

Meanwhile James had been thinking of matrimony, though not for a little while yet. Not least in his mind was the fact that he could not get a button sewn on, or a stitch done without paying for it. According to him, his young lady was a 'true Christian', a Miss Maggie Ricketts: he sent home some verse she had written and recited at a surprise party at the Christmas camp at Fernshaw. And he was taking steps to build up some security, joining a friendly society and investing in land (19 April 1888):

. . . you will be delighted to know that I am a "Rechabite". Some of you will know what that order is. It is a very strong society here. First members require to be total abstainers and to be such for sometime before they are allowed to join. By paying about 1s. 3d. per week you have the benefit of a doctor without any further fee and after being joined a year members are entitled to £1 per week in case of injury or ill health that may prevent them from business or work.
You will also be pleased to know that I purchased a block of land containing 4 allotments. It isn't much but still it may be a good deal some day. It is big enough to build 4 cottages on. The Hannas bought some of the same. We got a chance of it cheap. . .
I am still with Mr. Agnew and getting along well. I am round the city every alternate morning taking orders. My health is pretty good but occasionally troubled with indigestion especially when I don't take enough exercise.

All the Maxwell brothers were keenly sensitive to the importance of health, particularly in the colonial situation. Life was precarious at any time, but in Australia one was without the protection afforded by family structures, and exposed to the temptation to overwork, given the opportunities to make money. Deaths among their friends the Hanna family prompted sobering reflections. On 11 April 1888, shortly before the death of Sam Hanna, John observed:

I have been [on] a visit to Melbourne to see poor Sam Hanna who is now very ill in consumption indeed too ill to be a long liver. I believe he has been dabbling a good deal in stocks lately. He has made a lot of money. I believe he is worth nearly £1,000 but if he has made money he has ruined his health. . . .

When Mrs Hanna died a year later, James was more outspoken (9 May 1889):

indeed I think she brought on her own death by overwork. They are all so anxious to make money that the work is over done. I don't object to people trying to make what money they can but I object to people making slaves of themselves for the sake of this world's gain.

The Maxwell boys in Australia had various schemes and plans, centering on the idea of building up a family farm. William wrote on 5 June 1888:

> . . . you will be surprised to know that John is up with us for a few weeks. Mr. Newson wanted a man so I wrote for John as the climate up here is better for him than at Melbourne or Lilydale. He seems and says he is a great deal better since he came up. I do not know how long he may be here. He never looked so well since we came to the colony as what he does now and is one stone heavier. I was surprised to see the change in him when he came here. He is still troubled with a cough in the mornings and if wet or close. I wish he had been here two or three months earlier when the weather was nice and dry, it having changed just a day or two before he came.
>
> He means to go to his selection as soon as the spring comes to get it fenced. James has made application for 740 acres just next to John's. If he gets it John will be able to look after both. They think that it would be healthier than in town. They mean to go in for cattle rearing and fattening bullocks. It will not be so sore on them as heavy work. Hugh says if it turns out anything well that he will quit selling rags. He is working hard for promotion. He is liked very well where he is and John says he is greatly changed. He goes to parties, balls and picnics and is very popular among the young ladies. We have never seen him yet but he is in good health. John had letters from him a few days ago making enquiries about his selection and also about some shares in mining that he (Hugh) has bought. Hugh wanted me to go in for some shares but I declined as I would rather put my money in house property or land as I think it would be the best investment.
>
> We will be here six months on the 16th of this month when I will have another instalment for the bank. James does that kind of work for me. This is the country to make money if you have your health.
>
> There is an old man that lives on a patch of 3 acres that he has taken from Mr. Newson at £2 per acre and [?] he sold £30 work of grapes this year, besides a lot of other fruit of all kinds.
>
> We will have our wheat finished in about another week. I am glad it is so near done as it has been a busy time. Do you think she [Susie] would venture out to Australia. She would have to make up her mind to stay and not be thinking long for home as bush life is quite different to what she has been used to. There is not so much company as at home nor what she would call home comforts. However if she would think of coming we would send for her. The boys would have sent home a present for mother only it will take all they can muster to pay for the survey fees and for fencing, but if they are anything fortunate they will do something after sometime. They do not want to borrow money as interest is high here.

James also had some news (2 August 1888). He had received a 10s. raise and had visited the opening of the Melbourne Exhibition in a procession of Rechabites. And he had discussed the matter of Susanna's emigration with Hugh. They both thought it

> better for her to take a *trip to Victoria if the doctor thinks well of it.* It is with much pain that I make the suggestion as, no doubt, you will think that she will not come home again. But we don't mean that, we simply mean that she could come away (as Hugh suggests) not later than the autumn early in October. By doing so she would escape the winter and land here about the

middle of November before the very hot weather would set in and then if she thought well of it could return before winter would set in here. In the meantime we have agreed (I mean Hugh and I) to send home £10 each or so which would make £20. With this you can use to her benefit as you think best. We cannot offer her much encouragement to come here as none of us has a home of our own and has to depend on the strangers for everything. But we are willing to do the best in our power for her if she comes. I don't know that she ever mentioned the idea of coming, but perhaps she was waiting until we would suggest it. This I did not like to do knowing what a trial it is for both parties.

I would give it as my opinion that there will not be much good health for any of the delicate members of the family while there is so much wet around the house. I am now speaking from experience. You all know how I used to whistle and cough during the winter months. Well I can tell you I never have a cough. I mean a cough that sticks to me. No doubt people will catch colds here but they can shake it off. I took a cold last July and also one this July with a sore throat but I blamed shaving and nearly everybody had it. I used a little eucalyptus oil and a piece of new flannel round my neck and was soon well again.

Hugh, in turn, had discussed the idea with John, and wrote to James (10 August 1888):

No doubt the voyage would be more likely to do her good if she travelled second as the accommodation and food would be much better. On the other hand if she came third it would very likely put her farther back than she would benefit by being here for the first 6 months. After all the difference in the passage money is not so very much when you count up bedding etc. and "tips" for better food etc.

I think I will be able to send you the money the next time I write to you. However it would be well to impress upon them at home the desirability of Susannah coming second class and we can send the money as soon as we find it convenient.

Hugh then wrote to Susanna herself (Autumn 1888) urging her to come: the dry climate would enable recovery from the illness associated with her weak chest:

In second class (I think) bedding and all table utensils are provided by the ship's company. Besides the bunks are very much more comfortable and the food is a great deal better (which is a very important item to a delicate person who has not a good appetite and cannot eat anything that may be given to them.) Let me here say that I would by no means advise coming by third class. I want to impress upon you the importance of this.

It is not necessary for you to bring a lot of clothes as you might not find them quite suitable to the climate but be sure to have something *warm* to wear in the *cold parts of the voyage* also some light to wear in the hot parts as you will find a great change of climate in the whole course of the voyage.

Decide at once about whether you are coming or not and when you have decided, take your passage in the earliest possible steamer. The best steamers are the Orizaba, Ormuz, Oroya, Austral, Orient, Liguria. These are the biggest, newest and swiftest steamers but any of them are swift and I think the second class accommodation on any of them would be pretty fair.

If you start soon you shall be in time to see our great exhibition. It is a very

> grand affair I believe. The building covers about 35½ acres. I would like to see it very much but shall put that off until you come when I can kill two birds with the one stone that is go down to Melbourne to meet you and see the exhibition. James will forward some money shortly which will help to pay for your expenses of travelling.

The boys arranged to send £35 between them — £10 each from Hugh, James and John and £5 from William. Susanna, however, did not wish to leave her mother and father, a sentiment perhaps in part springing from timidity but interpreted by William as dutiful affection (9 October 1888):

> . . . Indeed I would not advise you. It was the sorest trial ever I came across leaving them both in their old age when they both need my help most. But if God so wills it that we do not meet on this earth but on that land beyond not made with hands immortal in the heavens, but I trust they may both be spared and have long and happy days.

To cope with the situation left at home in Ireland, William had a practical proposal. A man should be employed to help their father in his old age: 'I believe the rest of the boys would help me to send as much money home as would pay him if we all kept our health'. But by Christmas 1888 Susanna had decided not to come to Australia.

Meanwhile William reported that his brothers were pressing on with their land schemes and arrangements (9 October 1888):

> John just left here on this day fortnight, the day after the harvest fair at home. He was in good health, only troubled with a little cough in the mornings or in foggy weather. I believe he is troubled with asthma but he takes great care of himself. We were very much vexed when he went away as we miss his company and it made it like home. He intends going to his selection very soon as he is making preparations for going. Yambulla is the name of the townland on or near the banks of the Tambo river Gippsland. James made application for a selection adjoining John's and met the Land Board at Bairnsdale on 17th of last month; had a letter from him last week saying he was trying to get a transfer to one on the other end of John's which it seems is better than the one he first applied for. If James gets either of these John will be able to look after both and James and Hugh will stay at their business and make a little money. John thinks he will be able to make a living from bees as they do well in the country and it would be easier looking after them than hard work.

Obviously the Maxwell brothers cooperated well together, with little tension in their relations. Nevertheless their personalities and temperaments were positive and distinctive in ways which allowed them to be self-critical as well as to appraise each other. The oldest, William, tended to be practical and matter-of-fact in his approach to life, with a capacity for good-humoured adaptability which led him to relate well to the variety of demands posed by colonial conditions. He was also sensitive and perceptive, and much struck by the remarkable personality change which had overtaken two of his younger brothers, James and Hugh (6 November 1888).

> James is greatly changed since he came here to this colony. He used to be gay and lively and Hugh the reserved old man but they seem to have changed places. James has joined some religious society which abstains from all strong drinks, reads a chapter in his bible at night before going to bed and asks a

blessing before taking food, this from keeping good company. . .

John — whose Australian experience had intensified his strong sense of independence and firm egalitarian convictions — had remarked earlier (1 August 1888) that Hugh was a changed man, much livelier than he had been at home, and much more sociable. Although Hugh claimed to be still 'a great home bird', this was because he found Echuca dull: his girlfriend, Miss Knubley, was in Melbourne. It was all very well, as he later remarked, that Echuca was so noted for its splendid winters that a great many delicate people wintered there every year; that hardly generated exuberant social life. William noted that Hugh was 'as quiet as ever and always takes a thinking fit as usual', but this was for home consumption: the family might not like to think that its distant members had too much changed. But changed they had. In addition to his membership of the Rechabites, James' serious pursuit of self-improvement took him into an attempt (a good thing too, his brother John thought) to improve his education and polish. On 23 August 1888 James wrote to his sister Susanna:

> . . .we have started a young man's mutual improvement society in connection with the church in which I am a member, also a committee man. This was one of the nights of the meeting and a lecture was rendered by a Mr. Morrow, one of the vice presidents and a North of Ireland man. In fact there were several north of Ireland people in it. The lecture was on gossip or Mrs. Grundy and her friends. It was very good and very instructive and one that any person could advise from. I am forgetting myself; this is not interesting to you.

A year later James was still striving towards improvement (10 October 1889).

> . . .Now dear Mary you will see by the enclosed syllabus that I am trying to come out of my shell. You will see that I am still on the committee (I sent one of these before) and have myself down to give a paper or essay on *Success* which I have been studying for the last month or so. It is a wide subject and requires a deal of study and contracting as we are only allowed twenty minutes. . .

Each one of the four Maxwell brothers had been changed by the experience of migration. In all of their cases the transformation had been positive. In the role reversal William observed between Hugh and James, Hugh had been liberated to develop his social potential, while James recognised the limitations of his intellectual and cultural formation and set out to remedy this. William had expanded to master with some zest the jack-of-all-trades demands of the colonial farming scene. John had thrived in a society where a man was as good as his master and where strong and independent opinions could be held freely and without fear. The Maxwells' reactions to migration — each one an instance of growth, of personal achievement — were not the only ones possible: there was a darker negative alternative which, as the brothers were well aware, a minority of migrants took. To use John's illustration of 19 January 1886, there was always the Yarra — Melbourne's river — or stealing, as ways out: 'safe in the arms of the policeman, safe in Pentridge jail'. For those migrants who could not cope there were obvious refuges and escapes — crime, madness, suicide.

The appearance in the Maxwell brothers, under the stress and stimulus of migration, of hitherto unknown or unrealised capacities is positive evidence of how the enormous challenges and novel difficulties of the Australian situation required confrontation and psychological mastering. The fundamental challenge was not that of hard work, though that was real enough for people brought up in the peculiar enervating stagnancy of an Irish economy. The main demand was for the will and perseverance to take charge of and responsibility for a hazardous and lonely pioneering life. James Maxwell summed up this requirement positively in a remark he made in a letter in October 1889 concerning his cousin Harry:

> He is a very energetic fellow. He is the sort we want here, people with push and courage to tackle anything and determination to overcome obstacles. . .

In the following month William made the point negatively. He had an Irish friend helping him cutting oats, but the man disliked heat and hard work: 'He is a soft fellow with no pluck in him. . . ' William had also firm views about the qualities necessary in female immigrants. When, in 1891, the mother of his friend J.A. Baird arrived in the colony, he thought her so fat as to be unlikely to be able to endure the heat. Besides, she lacked refinement and any cooking or household managerial skills. As William observed (27 December 1891):

> . . . we don't know what she will be able to do in this colony. She meant to take in boarders but the woman has no manners and knows nothing about cooking and lodgers would soon [eat] her out of house and home as she could not guide them and would give them far too much and waste food and besides it takes all that Jim has to keep himself.

In November 1888, John began the farming enterprise. Hugh reported this to his mother (13 November 1888):

> . . . John has made a start on his selection. He has got a horse and is now making ready to erect his little house. He stays at the hotel at Tambo Crossing where the Post Office is also, a kind of wayside hotel where the mail coach stops on its route. He has his horse to ride to and from the land. No doubt he will give you more particulars, some time when he writes, than I can. However you may not be surprised if he does not write very often as he will be tired.[13]

From then on John wrote seldom, but in February 1889, William who had gone to Melbourne to visit the Exhibition, returned *via* a visit to John's selection, and chose adjacent land for himself (13 February 1889).

> When down in town I went out to the Tambo Crossing to see John, found that he was well only a little cold he had got after a wetting he got some time previous. However I left him considerably better and in better spirits. When there, we had a ride over some blocks of land that he wanted me to buy. We settled on one. If John and the present owner can come to terms there is only one block of 550 acres between the boys and this one. There is quite a lot of kangaroo and wallaby. Anybody that was good with the gun could make a pile of money shooting them for their skin. John has got a splendid Martini Henry rifle that can hit a kangaroo at 200 yards away. He seems pretty comfortable only the cooking does not suit him as he does not care for too much heat. Bob Wilson and him are often together. He lives on the other side of the river from John. Sometimes he stops all night with John.

When he heard of it, James was sceptical of the seriousness of William's resolve to take up a land-holding, explaining (21 March 1889) that

> William seems frightened to tackle land as Sarah is more on for town life so I don't think he will mind it in the meantime . . . [John has] let by contract the ringing of the block known as mine viz. 450 acres. It is nearly completed and the men will soon start to do a contract of fencing. John has been looking

> after some cows as we purpose putting on cattle instead of sheep for a few years at any rate as there are wild dogs (or dingoes) in the district and we could not afford to lose any of our little flock.
> Speaking about John's house I can give little information on it only to say that the fireplace and chimney is just like a blacksmith's hob only the hearth is on the floor instead of being raised. The back and sides of the fire is lined with clay instead of mortar and stone to prevent the wood (with which the walls and chimney of the house is built) from catching fire. I shall not attempt to describe it further as I have not been there to see John's house. My description is what I saw of another house in the neighbourhood.

It was certainly the case that William's wife took every opportunity — there were in fact few — to get down to Melbourne, but far from being unhappy with this, his view was that she needed such a change. Nevertheless, in the general, James' point was well made: wives often swayed the decision of whether to seek work in the country or the city. On 10 October 1889 James made the point about a new immigrant from his home district who called to deliver a parcel from the family in Ireland.

> . . . I got the parcels sent with Messrs Graham and Barnes and forwarded them to William which I asked him to write you and acknowledge. Mr. Graham has got into a situation long since but I don't know that he likes the country. You know he is a married man and has a wife and two children which will no doubt make him home sick. However, let that be as it may, it should not be the means of giving him a bad impression of the country. We all have our home ties which is inseparable. At the same this country is not to be compared with home as far as business and in fact all industries are concerned.
> Mr. Graham called with me the next morning after he arrived. I had a long chat with him. He left me to go and see a second cousin, who came out with John and Hugh. This cousin (lives in Richmond about 4 miles from Melbourne) told him of a job which he went about and got. I advised him to go to the country but he preferred staying in Melbourne and suburbs.

When Hugh wrote home in March 1889 he had a wide range of family news, particularly about his girlfriend's illness and on James's marriage arrangements and intention to start his own business.

> . . . You will be sorry to learn that Miss Knubley and her three sisters have all been laid up with typhoid fever. They all had to take [to] their beds about four weeks ago. I am happy to say however that they are all on a fair way to recovery. I had a letter today written by Miss Knubley herself to the effect that the doctor said that the fever had left them all now and they were allowed a little change in their diet. Of course when the fever was on them they were only allowed liquid food such as mutton broth, chicken broth, water and milk and soda and milk. Miss Knubley is just able to sit up in bed and write a short note with a pencil. It is very shaky yet. It seems that they have not had the fever in its worst form but, even so, it is bad enough when four patients are laid up in one house. I hope however that the worst is over now and only time is necessary to restore them to health again.
> You will be glad to know that James is likely to start business on his own account in one of the best provincial towns of the colony, the city of Sandhurst on the line between this and Melbourne about 56 miles from Echuca and 100 from Melbourne.

All being well he is to be married about Easter, I think Tuesday 8 April. Of course that is as far as I know just now but no doubt he will have given you all particulars himself before this.
We have made arrangements that William and Sarah, John and myself will try and be in Melbourne on the date of the ceremony, all being well. It might be a long time before we would have a chance of all meeting together again so it would be well to embrace this event as a suitable occasion for a mass meeting of the Maxwell family in the Southern hemisphere. You know this will be the first time we have all met at once.
James wrote lately that it was their intention to invite Miss Knubley but I am afraid that she will not be strong enough to go. I would like very much that she could. We will see how things go before that.
The last word I had from John, a few days ago, he said that he had not been so bright for the last week or two. I attribute that to the extreme heat of the weather. It has been trying on strong people so he must feel it. I know that it pulled me down a good deal. In fact everybody is or rather was, complaining of exhaustion. The month of January and part of February was one continuous heat, said to be the greatest heat for continuity at a high temperature for the last fifty years. There has been individual hotter days by several degrees but not lasting more than two or three days.
John is getting on with his operations fairly. He has a ready market for what potatoes and vegetables he can spare, of which he can grow abundantly in his garden. The mare has foaled and it is a fairly good one.
When last I heard from William they were well but feel the heat a good deal. There is some talk of a woollen mill being started in Echuca on the limited company lines. I hope it may be a success . . .

Hugh also had some general observations about the colonial political and economic situation to pass on to his sister Susanna (13 March 1889):

Every man 21 years of age has a vote here. There is some candidates propose extending the franchise to women but it has not become a burning question yet. However I believe it will be extended to women before another 10 years passes over the politics of this colony. You will no doubt notice the tone of self content in regard to the prosperity of this colony as compared with the other sister colonies, in the papers from time to time. There is no doubt that Victoria is in a very much better financial state than either New South Wales or South Australia. Of course our papers do not forget to trumpet it forth to its admiring readers — the Victorians or those like myself, who have adopted it as our home. There is a great deal of truth in it all for Victoria is a favoured part of the world at the present time. The advantages of all classes have here compare or rather contrast to a wonderful degree with that of poor old Ireland . . .

John, Hugh and James corresponded weekly about the farm, at Yambulla, Tambo Crossing. John had begun organising the clearing and fencing of the land, employing the Madden brothers to help him, and set up several beehives. As James was the only brother living in Melbourne, he procured and sent on John's various needs — phenol and a syphon for disinfecting bees, bee keeping information, a trained sheep and cattle dog — and responded to John's proposals of complex plans and arrangements (1 May 1889):

The syphon can be had at a wholesale tobacconist and hairdressers in Bourke Street East, nearly opposite the post office only a little farther up. The barbers use them to spray your hair after cutting. I use it to throw a spray of solution of phenol and water over the combs and brood in a diseased stock of bees. They also can be had at the chemists but I think they charge more.

One of the young Maddens has been off with toothache for four days but he is now back at work. I got the wire put on the line yesterday but as the[y] have nearly all the piece of ground grubbed, and it will only take them a few days more to finish it, I think it advisable to let them work on till the end of the week and complete it. The trees were very hard to grub owing to having had a lot of tap roots running down and thus involving a great deal of extra labour. It is beautiful soil where the trees are worst to grub being [exac]tly chocolate.

The Madden's purpose going honey hunting after they get the wire in. I purpose trying to get Bannister's fencing for them. I could not take it with any likelihood of making anything out of it first because I would want a strong draught horse, second because I would not be able to pitch into the work myself. Had I both a horse and plenty of strength, there would be very little in it.

The reason I want the Maddens to get the job is this. It would give "Jima" work for a month or two, for we can do without him for a while from a pecuniary point of view and I would keep him, as it were, in my employment. Why I would like to keep him under my eye is this: he is a splendid worker and reliable. After Bannister's fence would be done we could finish the line between our two blocks before stocking at our leisure. I would not fence any more only the small paddock and would only carry a few head.

We will require 30 new hives next season so I think you would do well to send to America for a list of hives and bee appliances etc as if for Agnew and Co. I believe we could import them much cheaper then we could have them made in Melbourne. You could write to A. J. Root, Medina, Ohio, United States of America.

After you get the catalogue and list of prices of the bee hives and bee appliances we could then make up our minds how many to send for and get them through Agnew and Co or to yourself whichever would be best. You will have to send away at once as there will be no time to lose between now and the time they will be required and it would be a great loss if the bees would be inclined to swarm and us have no hives ready for them. If the bees get justice they will do us a good turn next season. If the[y] don't, of course we can expect no profit.

You could send the socks and the phenol and syphon by parcels post as on account of the car, the John and Elizabeth[14] is so uncertain. Be careful how you pack them. I would like to have the goods as soon as possible as I am now beginning to run short.

I will do as you desired about the cash. I paid for the carriage freight and commission. It, in all, came to £6 18s.0d.

If you can send the dog with Bannister so much the better for he could tie him on behind the coach. If you send him to Bairnsdale I think the best one would be Scott the draper where you sent the bags and I would get some of the bullock drivers to bring him up. Before you send him away send me a letter saying what day you intended sending him so as I could be on the look out for someone to bring him up and not have Scott keeping him long. You would do well to send Scott word before you send the dog so as he would know to expect him. The parcels man would take him to Scott from the railway.

The work involved in all this was arduous and costly — employment of three men for five months, fencing materials, beehives, provisions and much else. The brothers raised the money among themselves by various amounts of inter-borrowing. Perhaps James also borrowed outside the family on the security of the four blocks of land he had bought at Braybrook near Melbourne: building, including factories, was progressing in the area and land values increasing. He wrote to his mother on 9 May 1889 to describe progress on the farm:

> I forwarded John his [socks sent from Ireland] along with some other little articles he wanted. I also sent him another supply of groceries and some little ironmongery. The last letter I had from him he writes in good spirits and says his health is tolerab[ly] good. He has now all that little parcel of land of mine viz. 345 or 350 acre rung also about one and a half miles of fencing done. He had the men cutting down some trees and grubbing a bit of ground for an orchard and garden (when I say grubbing I mean clearing roots of trees and stones). He has had three men working since October or early in November. This means a lot of money, never speak of what the first cost of the land was. But I hope we will, if spared, be able to make the thing swim. No doubt it is a great undertaking but I have not the slightest doubt of its success.
>
> I was talking to a Mr. Thomas (who is a cousin to Mr. Wilson, John's neighbour) who is in business in Melbourne. He had been up paying his cousin a visit and he told me that he was surprised to see the vegetables John had grown, turnips that could not be surpassed, also French beans and vegetable marrow, the latter being the length of his forearm. The above did not get any manure and in fact very little rain as it was an exceptionally dry season. This report speaks well for the soil of Tambo Crossing. John also speaks highly of the appearance of the grass where the trees are rung. You see we have to ring the trees that is to cut a nick with an axe through the bark right into the pith so as to kill the tree, as grass will not grow under them on account of the sun being shut out and the trees use up all the rain. We have no stock yet but we hope to be able to put on some in spring. I am afraid we will have to put cattle on instead of sheep on account of the wild dogs. I am sorry for that as we could have stocked it cheaper with sheep and had a quicker return.
>
> Now dear mother with reference to John and his hut: I mentioned about it before but I know you like to hear something fresh. His house, some would call it a hut but I think the proper name for it is a house for it is big enough to accommodate three people to sleep in as Mr. Thomas and Mr. Wilson stayed with John all the time. Mr. T(homas) was up and Mr. Thomas says it is very comfortable. I sent John 20 yards hessian to line it with, which will also add to the comfort. I also sent him another pair of blankets to keep him warm during the winter.

After giving family news — he had heard from Hugh and had spent Easter with William and his family, visiting the Reids at Yackandandah while doing so — he regaled his mother with a spirited defence of the colony's young ladies. He told her that:

> the young ladies in this colony compared favourably with that of any other country. I was surprised to know that Mrs P[rotter?] held such a humble opinion of foreign country ladies and such a high opinion of North of Ireland girls. Well had I the option or privilege of giving my mind on the matter I could tell her that the young ladies of this colony compared favourably with

that of *any other* country (North of Ireland I speak from experience and other countries from what I read and hear). First their forefathers being of a most energetic class of people; this is proved by their action in leaving the old country; thus their offspring inherit it. Second because they have the quick activeness of the Americans whom they come in contact with every day. Third because the[y] pride in working when they work so that they are enabled to spend a sixth of their time in pleasure if they wish.

There is also many other reasons I could give if I did not feel I was filling my letter with something that was not interesting to you. Indeed I find I have often to put on a double quick pace to keep time with those in business around me although I do boast of discipline which is daily getting infused into them.

There is another idea I might have mentioned viz. that of education. Schools are kept by the State and according to the law of the country every father and mother must send their children to school where all the different branches of education is taught them free of charge.

Dear mother you will think that all this is a lot of stuff and that it is because the young lady of my choice happens to be a Victoria colonial. Perhaps there may be something in it but you will see that my argument has reason and facts. Speaking of the young lady I might as well (and I think it only my duty as a son to set your mind at rest concerning this matter) say that there is an understanding between us which is financial. Had I not undertook this land business I purpose getting married about September or October next but as funds are at a low ebb and likely to be for some time we thought better not to jump into such an undertaking until things were set agoing properly.

Her father Mr. R[icketts] bought a splendid cottage last week. It costs £1325. They purpose living in the old house for 6 months. The new one they are to receive 27s. 0d. per week rent from the party who sold it and built it . . .

Given the prejudice prevailing in Ireland, James felt obliged to justify his marriage to a 'colonial'. The suspicion or antipathy partly derived from the simple fact that the home family could not know, or approve, the prospective partner. By definition of circumstance she was a 'stranger', a person totally outside their frame of reference, whom it was proposed to admit to the intimacy of close family relationships. The situation excluded parents from the type of surveillance and control traditional in Ireland, and because it related to so central a social institution as the family, such marriages brought home with peculiar force how rapidly the hierarchical parental world was crumbling, how near to death were the practices and assumptions of the old order in Ireland. So powerful may have been this sense of threat of alien invasion at the heart of the old society, that the adverse image of colonial women was a simple reflex of that fear and hostility. How much that image reflected informed judgment is impossible to say. No doubt one factor influencing Irish appraisal was that implicitly countered by James: those at home naturally assumed that the best had stayed in the old world, and that Australia's colonial forefathers tended to be not so much energetic and enterprising as inferior ne'er-do-wells. But whatever such assumptions and feelings, home families were largely powerless to enforce them — and caught in a dilemma: their own children were immigrants, but in no way inferior.

From the Tambo farm, John was enthusing to his parents about progress (25 May 1889). But first he reported on his health. Generally he was much stronger, working when it suited him, and taking things easy when he did not feel so well. His chest was much improved — as little pain and coughing as he could remember — but there was another matter, to prove of future significance Hugh, James and himself suffered biliousness during the summer. John attributed this

> to sluggishness of the liver caused by eating meat during the hot weather Meat is an article of food that is on the Australian table at every meal. And it seems to me the longer you are in the country the fonder you get of meat and most people never think the table properly furnished unless there is meat However I restrict myself to eating it twice a day, breakfast and dinner, my third meal being generally bread and treacle and I find the treacle acts as a medicine and prevents any lodgement of bile.
>
> Although in Gippsland a land that might be said to be flowing with milk and honey, it is impossible to procure, for either love or money, a bit of butter and as I did not get any cows as I purposed on account of not having any land fenced in and it would have been great trouble to keep a cow in the open bush. As it is now in the middle of winter it would not be advisable to buy. We have an 80 acre paddock fenced in and expect to have the other 270 acres fencing by spring. Then we intend putting on a few head of young stock as many as there will be money to buy.
>
> I have about two acres with the timber grubbed, that is the trees are stripped at the roots of the earth and the roots are cut and thus the tree falls uprooted all save the very ends of the roots which are afterwards followed along as far as is necessary and cut out so as the plough or spade will not strike against them.
>
> I find the soil around my hut very productive (in fact all the block in James name and about the half of a block in my name is all very much alike with a rich black soil on the surface of a gritty clay subsoil) I having now proof of it in the shape of turnips cabbages and cauliflowers and vegetable marrows There are cabbages as big as my head grown without manure. When one compared this land with yours under the terms which they are held it seems a marvel that there is not even a greater amount [of] emigration from the old country.
>
> Undoubtedly a young farmer starting on a piece of new land has a great many inconveniences to contend with but there is one grand thing about it: the land is becoming your own and there will be no landlord craving you for the rent.
>
> I am now over helping Mr. Wilson with his sheep. They are now lambing and we have had great trouble guarding them every night on account of the dingoes which has killed no less than 14 or 15. They are a great pest to sheep owners . . .

In addition John had planted a small orchard and established his bees. His mare had foaled. He had put in some potatoes. And he was busy splitting timber for the next run of fencing. Later in the year (10 October 1889) James brought the family up to date with John's progress:

> He has engaged a man to help to do some splitting of posts for fencing. He has not put on any cattle yet. He wants the grass to get well up. It requires a year or so to let the grass get a "closs" bottom after ringing. John left here for Gippsland a year ago tomorrow. It seems but half the time. He has ordered a lot more groceries, also his honey extractor (this is a machine for taking the honey out of the bar frames without damaging the combs). I purpose

going to see him at Christmas at same time inspect my *estate*. In a letter some time ago John mentioned that a man the name of Johnston (our neighbour) had sold his block of land for £800 I think he, [John], said if Johnston's was worth that the block in my name was worth £500. I am inclined to think that John is over valuing it but we will suppose the half of that amount. It ain't bad is it?

You will all be pleased to know that I got my title deed for Braybrook a month ago. It is not very large. You will understand it is for building purposes. The frontage is 120 feet by 120 feet deep which is large enough for 6 cottages. There has been some lands sold convenient at one pound per foot. Robbie Hanna advises me to hold to it. He believes it will be worth two pounds per foot in another year or so. However I may be obliged to sell sooner as I would like to put as much steam into Gippsland as possible. And another thing I would like a little of that money so that I would be able to make a little home in case I thought of getting the better half.

From Tambo, John complained of being lonely, but James was reluctant to spend money visiting him: it would be better invested in the farm.

William and Sarah were doing well on Mr Newson's farm at Barnawartha. The work was hard, but reasonably lucrative (10 December 1889):

. . . I am in good health myself only a little tired drafting sheep and weaning lambs. I believe we will be stripping wheat next week. There is plenty of bulk but the rust is on the straw of both wheat and oats. We threshed the oats when Mr. Newson was in Melbourne, had the steam thresher and engine which threshed 162 bags of oats in 7¾ hours.

We are digging new potatoes now. There is not many grown here in this part of the colony as it is too warm. Mr. Newson has done well with his wool this year. He had 52 bales which brought £730 2s.2d. . . .

PS We will be here two years in six more days when we will have £40 to lift and does not know when we will be leaving. Mr. N[ewson] is trying to get a girl to help in time of harvest. . .

Newson was generous to employees he valued (14 January 1890):

. . . We have got the harvest ended. Sarah had Maggie McGilton up for 4 weeks helping her. She and I are going away tomorrow to Murchison where I am going for my holidays. You will be proud to know that Mr. Newson has just given me a present of £10 to defray expenses and told me that he was more than satisfied with both me and my wife and to take a fortnight's spell but I will only take a week . . .

William had asked his father to put a few grains of best Irish oats and wheat inside one of the Irish newspapers the family regularly sent, so that he might make a comparison with Australian grain: on arrival he pronounced them 'miserable'.

With James' wedding imminent, on 14 January 1890 William supplied information to the family in Ireland about James' intended wife. William also provided some details about Miss Knubley, Hugh's girlfriend. Miss Knubley

is head milliner in a good house; has about £3 or £4 per week. . . She seems a fine woman and, as far as I can learn, has got a good principle.

James's young lady is very quiet and reserved but very clever. She matriculated at the Ladies College in Melbourne intending to go for governess but her health began to fail with too much study so her father and mother thought better and brought her home so she has learned dressmaking and makes for her own family and teaches her younger sisters music . . .

Writing about the same time, James conceded that his wife was no beauty but he had learned to admire character more than appearance:

Maggie is just the woman to make a poor man's wife. She is very saving and can manage well.

The wedding took place in April. Hugh, John (plus his young lady), William and Sarah attended, the first time they had all met together in Australia. William provided the family in Ireland with a very masculine account of the presents (13 April 1890):

We gave James a splendid *"cruit"*, John a tea pot, Hugh curtains, Agnews employees a black marble clock and Robert Hanna a cake basket. The rest I took no interest in. Sarah bids me say that the bride was dressed in white with a wreath and veil. . . The bridesmaid wore cream, trimmed with black ribboned velvet . . .

James had made his marriage the occasion of launching his own hardware business in Sandhurst (renamed Bendigo in 1891). In this he had the financial backing of his employer Mr. Agnew to £500 or £600 though he did not need all this. This venture had considerable repercussions on the financial resources of the joint farming venture at Tambo: James was no longer able to help. When Hugh spent Queen's birthday weekend with them (he found James's wife Maggie 'quite a housekeeper') he noted (16 June 1890):

trade is not very brisk in Sandhurst at present. However he is getting a very fair share. It is satisfactory to note that his takings are steadily increasing week by week. James expects a hard fight with the other hardware people but he intends sticking to them and get the best of them if possible and I believe he will succeed.
I had a letter from John about a fortnight ago. He expects to get the fence finished that will enclose a total of about 350 acres about the middle of July. He has let the grass of it to a neighbour for 12 months when we hope to get a little cash together to put on some stock. It takes a lot of money to put up so much fencing. On account of James starting business he cannot help now with the money matters for the farm so it makes it all the stiffer for John and myself. However little by little we hope to get things into working order bye and bye.

Meanwhile the family in Ireland sought advice on behalf of their cousin James Colven. After twenty-four years in America, he had returned with the idea of going to Australia. William was unhelpful. Colven was in the boot trade and William professed ignorance of its Australian operation — 'only that they charge very high for an inferior article . . .' Hugh was much more willing to commit himself (28 April 1890):

One thing will be a great advantage to him, I think he is a man that will adapt himself to circumstances. Indeed that is what a fellow must do when he tries his fortune in a new country like this.
Perhaps he may be disappointed in Australia after his experience in that splendid land where he has spent a good part of his lifetime for there can be no doubt that America, especially the United States, is one of the finest countries in the world for its natural resources, social advantages

> and material prosperity.
> This is even a more baby country. America is now a full grown man. It is certainly true that there are better chances for the individual for "getting on" in a new country than there is in an old country — to wit the scion of the Maxwell family that has been transplanted to the land of the Golden Fleece. One thing I think we have an advantage over America in, that is climate. We may have as hot summers but our winters are not severe as the American winters undoubtedly are. I have often mentioned the autumn weather here. Well we are now in full enjoyment of weather that might please anybody. We could do with more rain in this part of the continent. In the interior, in New South Wales and Queensland, they are having some terrible floods at present while here we could do with the surplus water and not hurt . . .

Their cousin's intentions were of relatively minor importance. What was of major consequence for the entire Maxwell family were developments in relation to the youngest son, David, the only one of the five boys remaining in Ireland. Following bitter disputes, David had made what his aged parents regarded as a most unsuitable marriage, in defiance of their wishes. David worked the farm, and, since the other boys had emigrated, expected to inherit. But such was the intensity of the rift — and the vigour of their reaction to what his parents regarded as a dreadful disgrace — that they decided to rid themselves both of him and his unacceptable wife by paying their passage to Australia. News of this banishment prompted an urgent family conference, by letter, of the brothers in Australia. William wrote home first (15 June 1890). He sympathised with that part of his parent's motivation which related to the disposition of property, a vital consideration in Irish farming society: William also had no wish to see property on which he had worked long and hard eventually passing, *via* grand-children, to a family with whom he wanted no connection. But he was most unhappy about what had been done:

> Your letter containing the news of David's marriage to hand last week. We were sorry to know that he had been so unwise as to make a country's talk of himself by the mean way he got it done, especially as it will grieve both father and mother. If I were you all I would not make too rash a decsion about send[ing] him out here as father is not so able to look after things as he used to do. Of course I should not like all the time I wrought hard and sore to go back to any of Henry McClintock's grand-daughters.
> I have had letters from both James and Hugh stating that if the girl is decent and bears a good character, that David is of age and ought to make his own choice. I believe the better way would have been to have let him have the farm at a valuation and let him marry Miss Jennings sometime ago. However that opportunity is lost now so we will have to make the best of a bad job. If he comes out here either by himself or with his wife we all shall join in giving him all the help and advice that lies in our power as he is our own brother. I think it would have [been] wiser to have let James Colven come along with him if he comes as it will be very lonely and awkward for him to come by himself, he being not over quick and not having travelled much.
> If he comes, we, Sarah and I, will help and I am sure the boys will do the same, to pay for a good man to assist father in the farm work.

Hugh had even stronger views, but put them in a restrained manner (16 June 1890). He regretted that David's marriage

> was not such as would meet with the approval of all, but I must say, in all

> fairness, that I cannot commend the action taken in the matter. After all this is a matter in which a man must please himself and in pleasing himself it is just very likely that it will not please other people. I think a less arbitrary course should have been taken, which I think would eventually have brought about more desirable results to all concerned. Leaving all sentiment aside a "fit out" and passage paid to a foreign country can hardly be said to be a fair remuneration to one who has always been acknowledged to be an industrial main stay to the place.
>
> David will be more missed after he has left home than you are at present inclined to think. I consider with an impartial mind that a big mistake has been made, that if a more lenient course had been taken it would have been much wiser . . .

But long before these opinions reached home, his brothers were informed by the family in Ireland that David, together with a pregnant wife, was about to land in Melbourne, consigned to the care of John at the Tambo farm. Their parents had informed and not consulted them and obviously took John's housing to accord with their own experience, and not to be what it in fact was — a remote and primitive one-roomed bush hut.

None of the brothers could meed David at the wharf. In a somewhat confused and incoherent letter, a generous but agitated William reported home his efforts to organise his brother's reception (14 July 1890)

> I wrote to him to Agnew's and Co giving him all instructions about how to act but I have had no reply from him which cause the delay of this letter. I suppose he is not going to write to me. I question if he has written home yet.
>
> We could have given him [David] work here and had written to him telling him so if he could get her [his wife] into some place in Melbourne or if she had any friends with whom to stop with for a while. He could have done better to have left her at home and sent money home to keep her.
>
> I had word through a letter from Mr. Newson's that they were looking for a situation as a married couple and is stopping in Mr. Hanna's. I suppose it is with the old man out at Mitcham. I think you were wrong to send them to John as he has no accommodation for a married couple. He would have to put up a partition wall and board the floor. He could have done with David single handed as we could [have] given him fencing and ring barking of timber and besides it is 30 miles off a doctor where John is which might make things rather awkward in case David's wife would need one.
>
> Hugh also wrote to James to try and meet them but he says he could not leave the business as he had nobody but a little fellow of 14 to look after the shop so you see it would feel very awkward for them and John has no money to spend on training 180 miles while I am 178 miles and Hugh about the same, James 90 miles.
>
> James wrote to the ship at Adelaide giving him instructions how to act and also sent one to John Hanna asking him to assist David with his boxes etc. I do wish he may be successful in getting a place. I should have liked very much to have seen him. Perhaps I will at a more convenient season. Who paid for the wife's passage and how much money had they. Let us know who seen them off by the boat and if any of her friends were there . . .

John, however — the unconsulted host nominated by his parents for David and his wife — had ample time and opportunity to brood in the laborious solitude of Tambo Crossing. His anger at what had been done exploded in a letter of 29 July 1890, a rising crescendo of protest which ended with remarks about his parents' judgment, motivation and conduct which left some enduring wounds.

He began with something of an apology:

> Perhaps the remarks which I may make, may not be as smooth to your mind as the[y] ought to be but you will excuse me for my rude way of addressing all of you, knowing that all my surroundings are in their wild — or almost so — primieval state it is natural that I would borrow a little of their wild roughness. . .
>
> David and his wife did not come here for I have no accommodation for married people. The house I am living in is all in one room and has to serve the threefold places of kitchen dining room and bedroom. Had I enough money I could put a partition and make a pretty comfortable little place out of it but as I am very scarce of that much desired commodity, cannot afford to do it now.
>
> In truth since James started storekeeping we have had a hard struggle to get ends to meet. If we had had about another £100 it would [have] been different but James withdrew his help when we had almost reached a position which a little more would have made the place keep itself. You know 345 acres of country fenced and covered with a good coat of grass will not make you any money without you can buy stock to grow, increase, and fatten. We are just like a cart without a horse.
>
> Had David been a single man we could have found "tucker" for him till he got a job or had I had a proper house the[y] both could have come here provided she was not too heavy footed. In that case it would have been great folly for the nearest doctor is 40 miles away which would have to be traversed by coach or horse back and a visit of a doctor would cost £10. Of course you have no idea of what back bush life is in Australia, therefore thought they would be all right if they were here.
>
> Always when you think of Yambulla, fancy you are in the midst of a big forest, thousands of square miles in extent with the trees growing as thick as they are in Portavoe and that you are looking down from the top of a very big hill, very steep on the side you are looking down, that you see a creek (a burn) flowing in towards the big hill and when it runs right up against it, it bends round at right angles to your left and flows about half a mile then joins the waters of the Tambo. In front of you is another nice hill which slopes gradually back for about half of a mile; about a hundred yards up this sloping hill from the creek, imagine you see a very little house with walls built of small trees laid parallel with one door one small window about the size of the window above the slop trough, looking out on your back grounds. This little house has an iron roof. Not far from this little house imagine you see a shed about 20 feet and 15 feet wide built of bark. When you do this you will form a better idea of how new "selecters" are housed in Australia.
>
> Although I live in this humble way I have no reason for complaint for we have got on very well in the time, this being the most improved block of land in the district. It can boast of what no other can about here, a garden. But you all have had enough about this place so we will speak of something else. Well I must say that it is now you will perhaps deem me a little bold in my remarks. Those remarks bear reference to your action with David (perhaps I should say father's action but I now speak to all of you). In the first place for

> your own sakes it was unwise. Remember I quite agree with you that David did what was not much to his credit, but it was an unwise thing for father to send away his last son. It was like taking the last prop from the family. You must undoubtedly fall for what is to prevent you. Father is an old man and who will take his place and attend to the management of the farm when he is no longer blessed with strength and energy. I say it was absolute madness. Do you girls imagine for one moment that you are capable of managing the farm? If you are it will be one of the exceptions for I never saw a well managed farm that was managed by a woman. I do not mean to cast discredit on women but when a woman is out of doors she is like a fish out of water. Another thing father did very wrong by sending David to Australia without giving him what he has worked for. It is height of injustice to expect a man to work the best days of his life in drudgery and when he commits an error to kick him off to Australia with only his passage money. The law may justify you but the law of justice will not. And another thing is you had no right to throw your refuse on our door. We have a little self respect as well as you and you must not think that our acquaintances in Australia do not know as much about it as we do ourselves. By sending them here you did not hide your disgrace one bit and you have threw it on us more than otherwise it would have done. If instead of rushing at things headlong and after you had made up your minds to send him to Australia . . . you had first asked for advice, you could have kept David on the farm for a bit and if you found you could not endure his wife you might have made arrangements with him about the working of the farm. I am very sorry for all parties concerned. I will draw this disagreeable letter to a close with the sincere hope that none of you will suffer from your imprudence and that you may enjoy better health . . .

However disposed his brothers were to be helpful or sympathetic, David and his wife remained unco-operative. William had written several letters. James wrote inviting them to Bendigo. There was no reply, although it was known from friends that the new arrivals were staying with the Hannas in Melbourne as William had arranged (3 August 1890):

> They are stopping at Mr. R. Hanna's at Mitcham. I suppose it is the wife that has prevented him from writing. But she need not begin with any of her nonsense as no[ne] of us cares or will take any notice of such stuff.

William also responded to a home enquiry occasioned by his casual remark that John's girlfriend had been at James's wedding — the only reference the family in Ireland had to her existence:

> Mother would like to know about John's young lady. I believe he met her after he left Fassifern. Her father was a ship merchant now dead in India and an uncle was executor for the widow and family and he robbed the orphans and they had to go out as governesses. They being able to read music and two or three languages; one of them is master of five different languages. She is a very nice quiet girl with dark eyes and brown hair plump cheeks and always a smile playing about face and seems healthy looking. She is a great favourite of Sarah's.

Earlier in the year (30 May 1890) William had conveyed the news that he had acquired some land near John's:

> . . . Had a letter from John yesterday wanting Sarah to take up the grazing area beside the block that I have got. You will be surprised to know that we

> have got 780 acres. I applied for a block about 3 months ago and got notice to attend on the 23 April at Bairnsdale and I had the good luck to meet John at the Princes Bridge station and he stayed in Bairnsdale till after the court was held and I got it recommended to me. There is a block alongside that John wishes Sarah to take up but I do not know whether she will do so or not . . .

By August Sarah had taken this step in John's plan for an extensive landholding by the Maxwell family in Australia:

> Sarah made an application for a block of land beside mine. It will turn in useful for us to sell or perhaps give to David as he could not make an application for land until he has been in the colony one year . . .

The idea of including David was probably no more than an expression of kindness: Hugh had made it clear (25 August 1890) that David could not be usefully involved:

> As far as I can gather John has got the fencing of the 350 acre block completed and has let the grazing of it for 12 months to one of his neighbours for at present we have not capital to put the necessary stock on. John has reserved the right to run 2 cows the mare and foal on the grass. He is busy now getting his garden ready for crop vegetables etc which he gets ready sale for at the Crossing hotel.
> I don't think there would be much good in David going up to John unless John got a contract for fencing some of his neighbour's land. In that case there would be work for them both but not otherwise. Besides the accommodations are not very great for John's is only a one roomed logged hut about 20 feet by 12 feet.

As to David, on 20 September 1890 William supplied news of him, and also of John.

> David is helping the Hanna family to do some work at pruning and clearing [an] orchard beside them which they had took a contract for. D[avid] has £1 and his wife has 10s. 0d. per week.

Soon David and his wife were to go to Bendigo, to stay with James and Maggie. William continued:

> . . . Sarah Susie and I went to Beechworth on last Friday to take her affidavit concerning a block of land that adjoins mine. It will save her from having to go to Bairnsdale. She has a good chance to get it. I have got notice to pay my first half year's rent and survey fees; will pay it next week as I have it ready. If nothing better turns up I will be able to give David work for a spell. I sent John some vine cuttings last week which will be useful to stock both places. I sent him a lot last year and they are doing well. His fruit trees is looking well now and expects a good crop from them. He intends planting two acres of potatoes along with his other vegetables which he is very proficient at. John intends keeping a few pigs to use up refuse vegetables milk etc. He sold half [a] ton of melons and vegetable marrows. All he wants now is enough money to put on a good stock of either sheep or cattle and I suppose he would need a wife too.

William and Sarah looked upon their land acquisitions as investments rather than a potential farm for themselves (26 October 1890):

You will be surprised to know that Sarah applied for a block of land (700 acres) adjoining mine which she has been recommended for but awaiting the approval of the Minister of Lands. I have paid my survey fees making our lease and first half year's rent in all £20 11s.10d. for 742 acres of which I can select 320 acres and then keep the remainder in leasehold. Sarah's is leasehold but I can get somebody to dummy it and get 320 of Sarah's to put along with mine and make 640 which will be useful some day. I believe it will be good interest for our money as we can either let it or sell it.

Besides, William had become heavily involved financially in supporting John's farming venture. James had had to withdraw in order to launch his ironmongery business in Bendigo, and it was suffering the indirect effects of the 1890 strike: he had no surplus money. But John, in order to hold his land, was obliged to effect a legal minimum of required improvements. William financed most of these, explaining this in a letter home (30 November 1890) but finding it difficult to make it intelligible in Irish terms:

. . . We are thankful that mother is still able to knit and sew and hope that we may be able to repay her yet. Sarah having got a block of 700 acres she has been noticed to pay part of her survey fees now and with James getting married and going into business he was not able to assist John so I have been helping them to get theirs rung and fenced as if not done in three years they would have to forfeit and lose your improvements. You see although we have so much land it is all bush, or you would understand it better by looking at the inside of Mountstewart or Lord Dufferin's demesne only the trees are box and gums from 12 to 36 inches in diameter. Many gentlemen at home would be proud to have such bush. Of course we can sell our rights at any time as this is the way we are investing our money. We had a letter from James last week in which he mentioned that David's wife had got a son three weeks old but supposed we had heard of it. They have been very kind to both David and her and brought up Mrs. Ricketts to attend her to save paying a nurse which costs from 25s.0d. to 30s.0d. per week. But he says she is very ignorant like as if [s]he had come out of the moss.

Like as if she had come out of the moss: it was a colourful and vividly telling Irish phrase, whose use conveys the very real class or cultural differences the Irish found among themselves; not differences of religion or allegiance but a distinction within those categories — the gulf between the sensitive and cultivated, and the ignorant and uncouth, matters of civilisation. For the Maxwell family, David and his wife epitomised such problems. James reported to his sister on his experience of them (22 December 1890):

. . . With reference to poor David you will all be pleased to know that we had them for some time especially his wife. On going to Melbourne to see them sometime after they arrived I then found her in such a state of health that would necessitate the abandonment of house duties in a very short time. I then purposed to David for them to come and stay with us until she got over her trouble. This offer was solely on his account and as a brother I could not think of them staying with strangers. They came here about 29th September. David knocked about for 8 or 10 days until I procured him a situation with a farmer about 21 miles from here. Time passed on and a baby boy was born early in November. They are both doing well. They remained here for three weeks, are now living in a nice cottage on the farm where David is working. I do pity David poor fellow, he is badly mated but he has made the choice and will have to submit to the consequences. It is to be hoped they will stay where they are for a long time. I assure you I don't want her company here again. You are quite right when you say she talks and tells things she has no right to and things that never happened. She had the cheek to tell me that you were all offended because I married. I asked her what grounds she had for saying so but she would give me no reason. However in the course of her talk and story making she told Maggie or Maggie's mother that you were all offended at us all for thinking of marrying, that you wanted us to remain single so that you would get our earnings, thus classing David. She need not have made up any such yarns for I knew to the contrary.

Without doubt David has been stuffing them (the Kyles) with information to suit himself. On hearing him talk I could see that it was all a one sided story from beginning to end. Despite all this I could not see them homeless and gave them the best I could afford and put them on square footing for themselves. I hope he will make the best of it. I don't want to have her here again I have been cut to the bone repeatedly. I do not wonder at the steps father took although I thought it hard at first but it is evident that David has played the part of an undutiful son as well as doing that which is injurious to himself. It was no little that made father part with his last son now in his old age just when he wanted help. I was just saying to Maggie the other day if I had not been stuck up with this business I would not have thought twice about going home to work the farm. It is an awful thing that father is so badly situated.

William wrote to me some time ago asking my advice but I reserved it. However as I am writing to headquarters will venture to give my advice although not asked for. My advice is for father to put the farm in crop and sell it on foot and then dispose of the land stock and implements. He will surely be able to get as much for it as will keep those at home comfortable the remainder of their days. What is this life to mother and him if they cannot take it easy when they are old and infirm. I feel sure you would all have your health better if you were to live privately in some nice healthy little cottage.

Now dear Susannah this is now the last Sunday in 1890. I began my letter a few days ago but have been kept so busy that I could not get time to finish it. However as my work is cut out for every night to the end of the year I thought I could not spend it better than stay at home from church and finish this epistle.

Another Christmas has gone. Who will be spared to see the next. God alone knows. We have been thinking about sending some little thing to mother and poor aunt as Christmas presents but things are so very tight and money scarce that we have not been able to afford it. However it is to be hoped that we will be able before long to send some little thing.

The strike has been pretty hard on me owing to my business being cash. However it is to be hoped that business will stir up after harvest.

From then on, James wrote home seldom: his evenings were taken up with his business correspondence. William tried to write home at least once a month. The reduction in postage from 6d to 2½d helped, and he seemed to find the time to convey the basic family news. James' gross turnover in his hardware shop was a little over £20 a week. He had his Braybrook property and his block of land in Gippsland all fenced. William thought his situation was such that he could survive the business recession. John had taken a fencing contract in order to make money for expenditure on his own farm. David was working for a man from Ballynaskeagh, Co. Down, whose sister had once been courted by the

Maxwell's uncle in Ireland. And in March 1891 William took a holiday to visit Yackandandah to see his many Ulster friends who now lived in that area. It was a veritable grand tour on horseback. He saw the Reids (several families), the Cunninghams, the Manns, the Styles, the Henrys, old Robert Tanner, the Moores, in ten days riding and talk: 'Nothing I get as medicine [is] as good for me as the outside of a horse' concluded William. (Hugh was the one for medicines, recommending to his sister 'Dr. Churchill's Hypophosphites of lime and soda, one bottle of each using each bottle alternately every few days'.) William's letters were full of gossip, Irish and Irish-Australian — marriages ('they get on like a pair of fools'), who had bought or sold or got what (a hotel, an inheritance), who was sick ('Old Robert is getting very much bent and one of his loins is knocked out') and who had got jobs (J. Glover 'got a billet at drawing a milk cart in Melbourne at 17s.6d. and tucker if he keeps it'.) Nobody had heard from David. As to James in Bendigo, he had told Hugh, who passed it on to William, that he and his wife had moved house 'owing to bad smell arising from essence of offal from a butcher's shop that got into the cellar and was affecting both their healths.' Hugh also told William that John had asked him to be best man at his wedding to Miss Wilton in Melbourne at Easter. Hugh, who could not get off work, suggested May. It was the first William had heard of this and he was writing home on what was in fact Easter Sunday (28 March 1891) 'but it is not recognised more than any other Sunday.'

John died on 6 April 1891: he was twenty-nine. His wedding had been arranged for 21 April. He was busy with fencing. William wrote to Susanna in Ireland (11 April 1891):

> ... please break the following news to mother and the rest as gently as possible... I received a telegram of Robert Wilson stating that John had died suddenly that morning (Monday) and to come at once. James was nearest the train and he got away at once and Hugh was a little later and as the train was the last one, when I got the telegram I was unable to be at the funeral. When James arrived after travelling night and day he found everything done as we would wish except the death of our brother, having been washed and dressed and the coffin ordered from Bruthen. I shall give you the particulars. In the first place he had two young men working for him who slept in the house. One of them named Jock Anderson had been away on his holidays and came back on Sunday afternoon. He asked John if he had got his dinner and John replied he had not as he had taken a drink of sweet milk. So Anderson said he would put the kettle on and make the tea for all and John took a hearty meal and remarked with a little laugh that he was nearly dead since he (Anderson) had went away and he thought he had burst a small blood vessel and was spitting a little blood. Well Anderson said to John that he must be making fun as he never saw John look better for John had just took off his beard that same day before his departure to Melbourne to get married to Miss Wilton on April 21st. The invitations were sent to the friends to attend the ceremony (on Monday morning before James told her). On Sunday evening he had a chat with the boys and said that they would not go to the fencing on Monday as they would take a ride and see how much of a fence our blocks would take as he wished to leave work for them when he was in Melbourne. He then filled his census papers with perfect correctness and went to bed fairly well considering the spitting of blood. On Monday morning the boys lay long being tired with their journey when about 8 or a quarter past 8 o'clock Anderson heard John vomiting and jumped out of bed

and John called him to come as he was dying and that his hour was come. Anderson cleaned his mouth and held him in his arms and asked John if he had any messge to leave to any of his brothers or friends and if he could do anything more for him but John answered him no "all you can do is to pray for me".[15]

John's death distressed and saddened not only his fiancee but his brothers — save for David who, when informed, seemed little interested: within a few weeks he had moved on to New Zealand. The other brothers were linked, not only by strong ties of affection, but by a complex set of financial transactions and property understandings. William (who seems to have inherited or raised some Irish money) had lent James £160 (at 4 per cent and 6 per cent interest) to finance the ironmongery venture. He had also lent small amounts to John and Hugh. But Hugh, and also James before he started in business, had put money into John's farming enterprise. William, despondent and disheartened, told his parents of some of these complexities (26 April 1891):

> . . . James and Hugh went to a solicitor about poor John's affairs. I have a paper to sign stating that I had no claim on John's property and effects. The boys did not know whether my name would do as they might have to send one paper for you to sign. Of course I told the boys that I did not want anything off the land as I thought Hugh had a right to all that was in John's name. The land was taken out in John's name but in reality they were partners, Hugh giving money and John labour and experience.
>
> We settled for them to keep the land for another year and appoint Bob Wilson as agent to look after some fencing, letting of grass selling cattle and horses etc for which he is to be paid a percentage. I also gave him power to sell Sarah's block and mine as I have not the heart to go there now since John's decease. We would have been there before this only waiting to gather a little money together before we could go as the boys had all we had before this. However if we had known there was anything the matter or that John was in delicate health we surely would have been there. I am extremely sorry that I did not spend my holidays with John instead of going to the river but was keeping the money to send to him.

Added to this disaster, the situation on the family farm in Ireland was becoming increasingly difficult and precarious. Their cousin James Colven had been helping their father on the farm since shortly after David's departure. But he had emigrated to Australia, and for the first time in twenty years Mr Maxwell Senior had to sow the oats. The sons in Australia discussed this situation when they met after John's death. William reported (24 May 1891):

> I was talking to James and Hugh when we last met, that we thought we should go home as it would be only right to do so as father, mother and aunt was getting not so able to look after things as they used to and they said without doubt it would, as it was our duty to look after the old people but financially speaking that we were better here. But owing to the way that David had acted it changed the programme of affairs in many ways.
>
> I had a letter from James last night stating that David, his wife and her child had left where they were and had gone to New Zealand and they never thought worthwhile to let him know that they were going. David's wife wrote a note and sent it by a neighbour asking for the price of a small basin stand that they left there, at same time remarking that if he had not time to send a reply by bearer, not to write until she would write to him again. James

wrote me on 20th and said they had left on Tuesday week which would be May 12th. After all that James and Maggie has done for them she has not forgot to speak her mind pretty freely about Maggie especially and not in her favour and James also remarks that he is not all sorry that they left as her scandalous tongue would have done him a lot of harm in his business. . . I expect if they do not succeed in New Zealand that you will have them home with you soon. . .[16]

By September 1891 it had been decided that William and his family would return to Ireland. He, James and Hugh accepted responsibility for their parents and the farm. While they had sent home little money — presumably because it was not really needed by their parents — they retained a strong sense of obligation when it came to the care of parents and property. They had little respect for anyone they knew — such as J. A. Baird — who could be said to have repudiated such obligations (7 May 1891). William wrote of Baird:

He has sent no money home since Christmas and I doubt if he has anything worth to send as he has bought a horse and is very fond of dress and spent a lot of money. . . I don't think he spends his money in bad company. He says he will not go home and that they may sell the farm as he had written home to that effect.

In the wake of John's death, Hugh was thinking of leaving the drapery store in Echuca, and going on the land — his and John's block at Tambo, which he had moved to have transferred to his name. He explained (5 July 1891):

. . . trade with James is as good as can be expected. Things in general are very dull all over Australia. There seems to be a depression in trade of all kinds at present. There are a great many people out of employment and the tendency of wages is downward.

There has been a great many strikes in various classes of labour which have done a great deal of harm. In Melbourne the shopkeepers have a great deal of surplus stock left on their hands after their winter trade which they are now selling at very low prices in order to clear stocks which of course shows that trade is dull and money scarce.

I had a letter from Mr. Wilson last week. He thinks that Mr. Johnston will re-take the grazing of the paddock for another term. We left the garden and beehives to Mr. Wilson at a nominal rate as the things — fruit trees, beehives, etc, will be better looked after than they otherwise would be. It is just possible that I may go on the land about this time next year. Things would be better looked after and seen to besides there is not much sign of a rise in the drapery trade and I might be better off in the long run on the land. I will wait the development of circumstances and weigh carefully the best course to pursue.

With a concern no doubt heightened by John's death, Hugh was increasingly free with advice on medical and diet matters. Sweet milk should only be taken in little sips as larger quantities could cause indigestion. He lectured his sister Mary (2 August 1891):

. . . be careful to keep the bowels open, eat wheaten bread and as much fruit as possible. Do not drink much tea or coffee. A little new milk with hot water in it will be a good substitute. I don't think oatmeal or wheaten meal porridge would do you any harm. It is easily digested and keeps the bowels open.

Speaking of myself I have given up drinking coffee altogether and only drink one cup of tea in the day sometimes only half a cup of tea. I eat a plate of porridge every morning except Sunday when it is not made in the hotel. I usually take a light tea and do not eat later than half past six o'clock in the evening. Late suppers are not good for either man or woman. Do not wear tight stays. Suspend the skirts and petticoats from bands over the shoulders — if possible — instead of buttoning them *tight* round the waist.

William had announced to the Irish family that he would return to work at the Ballygannah farm — but not without some guarantees (20 September 1891):

> . . . we are satisfied to go home to help father and mother now in their old days. But I think it right to one and all that father should settle his affairs. It will not shorten his days one hour but rather lighten them as he would be more content . . . David and his wife have been keeping a lot of talk about us going home and is angry that they did not get the farm so they would give all the trouble that they could. If he had got some decent respectable woman for his wife I would be only satisfied that he should have got the place as it means a loss to us of about £70 per year besides sacrificing our land. But for father, mother and aunt Grace's sake we would, as you say, sacrifice something for them.

And sacrifice it was. Despite his references to his Australian land as an investment, what he really wanted was to buy a small farm. They had made many friends in Australia (although such friendships tended to amount to closer ties to Irish emigrants known before to some degree from home). He again urged the Irish family to come to Australia, where, he argued, their health and wealth would be enhanced. To his sister Susie, who had been ill, he continued to insist that she in particular would be better in Australia. To his suggestion that she take cod liver oil and port wine he added (10 January 1892):

> as for port wine if you were here you could get plenty of it at 4s. and 6s. per gallon for the best quality and 2s. 6d. for light wine or what you call sherry at home. We have not the slightest doubt but if you had a change of air that you would be the better from it.

All this to no avail. His mother claimed that her health would not allow emigration to Australia. William wondered the reverse: would his health stand a return to the cold Irish climate? For William to return was, in James' view, 'a noble act'. But William persevered and put in train the sale of the land he and his wife held in Gippsland. It was slow selling, and meanwhile his father struggled on with the Irish farm, sowing a little wheat, while aunt Grace drove the threshing machine. William continued to insist that his father make a will to clarify ownership of the farm in the event of any dispute from David: his father took no action. Nor would William leave Australia until not only had his land been sold, but he had actually received the money: both his Irish and Australian circumstances filled William with the fear that unless he was careful he might be cheated.

It was a bad time to sell. From Echuca Hugh reported the town continued to decline. The river wool trade had been tapped by the railways at a point further down stream, and in ten years the population had dropped 1300 to its 3419 in 1891. These were particular circumstances, but Hugh's report on the whole Victorian economy was pessimistic (4 April 1892):

> . . . rain is very much wanted as grass is very scarce in this northern district of Victoria. Besides ploughing cannot well be carried on till the ground has been softened by a good fall of rain . . . times are very dull in Australia at present. Melbourne in particular is in a bad state and things are expected to

> be worse during the coming winter. There has been a season of prosperity but it was not quite real prosperity. There has been over-speculation in many ways especially in land and building. Then there was the great strike and there has been many failures of financial institutions. Indeed things will be in a bad state for some little time to come.
> This would be a very bad time for anyone to come to Victoria for one has to know the ropes to get along or obtain employment. There is to be great retrenchment by the new government which will shortly be elected as the governments of the last six years have been spending money far too fast. In fact the whole family of the Victorian people are on the saving lines at present or in other words are whipping the cat.
> Well it is natural after all for a country any more than an individual cannot spend more than it earns and at the same time keep its head above water . . .

At last, in April 1892, William was informed that his father had made a will. In June he and Sarah made a tour of the district to farewell their friends. They left for Ireland on 9 July. James remarked (31 October 1892) on the changes in farming practices William would bring back to the Irish farm:

> You will think it something new that the men should do the milking. You will find William will have a lot of new ideas which will be a great improvement on the home ones . . .

The intensifying colonial depression was gradually squeezing the circumstances of Hugh and James. James was happy enough in Bendigo. As he reported home on 13 September 1891 he had added to his hardware business what amounted to a backyard farm:

> We have quite a farm here now 3 cows, 8 or 9 calves and heifers, horses, ducks, geese and fowl. It is a fine healthy place here. We have both had better health since we came here. In fact I have not had so good health for many years . . .

He had also joined the military volunteers (13 March 1892), probably not least because it brought in a little extra money:

> . . . we have joined the cavalry or as you would call it the soldiers but I may tell you we are high class. We are volunteers and are drilled two nights per week and two hours during our half holiday which is on horseback. The government provide us with uniform which is blue with yellow stripes. We provide horse, saddle and riding boots. I might say this is the only recreation or amusement we have and we are paid for it. . . I have completed my second year here and am just taking stock. I hope it will turn out well. I have every reason to think so although business in general has been very quiet.

But by Easter 1892 James' and Hugh's efforts to stock their land at Tambo Crossing were running into difficulties. They needed £30 to buy twenty eighteen-month heifers at 30s. each, but as James explained (5 June 1892),

> . . . Hugh was down here on Easter Monday. He and I had hard scraping up to get as much money as would buy 20 store heifers. Our land would carry a good number of cattle now but we cannot stock it; will have to be satisfied with re-letting a portion and stocking part. I am sorry I cannot do my share towards stocking it owing to all available cash . . .

Hugh was also feeling the pinch at work (15 August 1892):

> . . . the usual dull times are felt in Echuca as well as other parts of the colony. There has been changes at our place lately. Mr. Scott a man who has been in the establishment for over 12 years; the millinery saleswoman who has also been there about 12 years and the milliner about a year have all got the "swap" owing of course to dullness of trade. Mr. Scott will not be replaced and a milliner and saleswoman combined will take the place of the two ladies. The rest of us that were getting anything of a screw have been reduced 5s. a week. However it won't be much loss to me as I will have a greater run of sales owing to getting first sale in the department Mr. Scott left besides my own department as usual. We get premiums of many things we sell so you see I will have more work and possibly more premiums.

Worse still, there were problems with the Lands Department. On 28 August 1892 James wrote:

> . . . I had a letter from Hugh yesterday. It contains rather bad news about his land as the lands department decline to take the improvements already effected as sufficient to comply with the Act. However they have given him three months to complete same. It will put him about a bit as he is not financially in a position to comply with their request. It has been a source of trouble and worry from the beginning up to the present. However, I hope it will repay us later on.

Their cousin James Colven had taken up what had been Sarah Maxwell's selection, next to that of Hugh and James. This allowed him to be employed to do necessary work on it: Hugh bombarded him with instructions and advice (3 May 1893).

> I herewith enclose £3 which will carry you over for a little. I will get some rape seed and also some peas tomorrow. You will find the peas useful for table use before Christmas. I think they will grow well enough on the ground where you had the potatoes last year as they are a different kind of crop. I want you to dig round the fruit trees and sow the rape a few feet round; then when it has grown 8 or 10 inches dig it down for manure. If there is any part of the garden where you do not want to plant other seeds or crop throw a few seeds of the rape about and when growing down it is a splendid green manure.
>
> We have decided not to charge you anything for the garden for last year nor for the incoming year. The only conditions are that you dig around trees and sow rape as above stated. A few peas sown among the rape also makes a good manure but you had better keep the peas for use. Try some new ground for a few potatoes. Throw wood ashes where you plant the peas also horse dung if there is any. . .
>
> You are right in boarding your man. Then you have any little benefit there is from the milk and the garden. But I would advise you to make arrangements with him to pay him only for the [time?] he is working. You cannot afford to pay him for wet days when he is loafing about the hut. It is quite enough for you to feed him on such occasions. *Be sure you make these arrangements before he starts work with you.* If he does not like that let him go. You could keep on the young fellow for a little while at any rate but should the weather set in wet I do not think you would be wise in keeping him as there would be too much broken time. Keep up your heart the block will come in useful to you yet. Don't ring every tree it takes too much time; leave a good few here and there; at some future time you could go through them . . . besides you make

a bigger show for your work. Leave the good straight trees.

You will be glad to know that I am to be married on the 31st of this month God willing. If the journey was not so great we would go the length of the Crossing . . . are there any neighbours to erect half of your dividing fences. I mean those on adjoining blocks and yours . . .

Hugh was anxious to get married. When he went to Melbourne in November 1892, he thought his fiancee overworked — finishing millinery orders for Melbourne Cup Day — and looked forward to the time when she could give up business for housekeeping. And he admitted (13 November 1892) that, quite selfishly, he was tired of being a bachelor. He was married on 31 May 1893.

Hugh's farming property had been financed, in part, by William, so he reported occasionally to William in Ireland on progress both on his selection and that of James Colven adjoining (18 June 1893):

I shall be glad should James Colven need more money than what is now due to him in wages to hand him over an amount equal to your year's interest as your letter sanctions. At the same time I will be careful only to advance such money in case it should be absolutely necessary to carry through the necessary improvements thereby conserving your interest in the block for as you have a sum of money against the block it is necessary in your interest that the improvements should be made complete so that the land may be worth some rent for grazing.

As far as I am concerned I will render him any assistance that may be in my power and as I know the rape a bit my advice may come in useful. There is some further work to do on our own front block and of course I will give it to him to do so that he may have some ready cash. The use of the garden he will also have free for keeping it in order.

I am glad to say that I have at last got the half year's rent which was due in February but it was only yesterday that I received a post office order for the amount.

I hope to have a better man to take the paddock next term. The letting has not been taken out of the hands of Mr. Wilson therefore he has a perfect right to the commission and as it is only 2½% I consider he earns it.

James has moved to his new home in Bendigo . . . trade is keeping up very well with him considering the dull state of the times . . .

PS The Lands Department have passed my block as satisfactory. The improvements on it now amount to £228 odd.

A year later (3 June 1894) he passed on the information through his sister Susanna:

Tell William that James Colven has been granted five months from about a month ago to complete the improvements. The last word I had from him he was busy getting up posts and pushing on as fast as possible with the work. He seems to have taken more heart again in the prospects of the land. It is pretty well certain now that a butter factory will be started at Ensay and possibly a creamery at the Crossing. Should it be so it will be good for James as well as for ourselves.

Everything is very depressed here at present, the price of wheat being so low leaves the farmers with very little money to spend. Wages have fallen in every department of industry and thousands of men are out of employment in Victoria alone.

One good thing gold mining is reviving a good deal at present. Some mines that have been in working for a long time are yielding better now than ever they did. Besides there has been a lot of new discoveries both surface diggings and quartz mining. The new discoveries are owing simply to the fact that men both with money and those who have little but their labour to put in it are giving much attention to gold mining and digging. When people are out of other employment and can get none they turn their attention more to the search for gold and the result is very satisfactory so far. It will help to pull the country through the bad times. There has been a find of a "deep lead" near Barnawartha which is expected to turn out well. There has also been some finds near Bairnsdale in the county of Dargo and also at Omeo. This will help on Gippsland a bit.

Within a fortnight of this Hugh, now married with a newly born baby, was writing to William from his mother-in-law's home in Melbourne: he was now to become a compulsory farmer (14 July 1894):

I suppose it will not be a matter of great surprise to you to know that I have left Echuca — further retrenchment. They are filling up vacancies with cheap young hands from Melbourne. Just now young fellows are willing to take anything over and above what will pay their board, anything from 25s. to 35s. a week and very few get the chance of the latter wages.
Trade has been slow in Echuca for a considerable time and the outlay was greater than the income so the largest salaries must go. However I have had a good innings in Echuca and as I put a bit of money into Tambo Crossing while I had a good salary it will come in very useful now.
I am not going to lose any time looking for a billet as they are too scarce and the wages now offered I would not accept (having the land to fall back on).
I will therefore be off to Tambo Crossing next week and help J. Colven with his fencing and then get his help to get a better crop into the garden. Fannie, the little one and myself have stayed over a fortnight at Bendigo. Fannie will stay here for a while at her mother's till I get things a bit fixed up at the Crossing. Besides she will be just as well here for a little while till she gets stronger and the baby is a bit older.

By the middle of 1895 Hugh was doing well enough at Tambo Crossing. He, like others had trials and uphill work to contend with' as James put it, but his report to William on the potato crop and other farming matters was determined and positive (1 June 1895).

J. Colven and I have been lifting the potatoes this week. The early planted ones, the "pink eye" variety did not turn out very well. They were a splendid seed 5cwt. and we did not lift much over 10cwt. of marketable potatoes. They were planted rather early and got dry weather at first then rain later on which gave them a second growth. The later planted crop were "Brown's River". We had 8 cwt. seed from Mr. Davidson. They were indifferent looking seed. The ground was very dry when planted so there were a good few misses. However they got the little rain that was just in the nick of time and they now turn out a good average crop, are very good to eat. We only sold a few of the "pink eyes". Mr. Wilson bought half a ton of "Brown's River" at £3 10s. per ton. Mr. P. Johnson, Mr. Simpson (Mr. Johnson's father-in-law), Mr. Sand (?) and Mr. Somerville (Mr. Wilson's new neighbour on the north side) bought a few in cwts. at 4s. per cwt.
Potatoes like everything else is very cheap at present in Victoria, "Warnam-

bools" and "Colacs" from 20s. to 22s.6d. per ton. I saw it stated in the Australian that they had been sold as low in one district on the ground as 10s. per ton. I think Bruthen price is about from 2s. to 2s. 6d. per cwt. but we have the advantage of the extra price paid for carriage from Bruthen to the Crossing for 1s.6d. per cwt. Besides the Bruthen potatoes are not good this year.

J. Colven and I divide the profit after paying for the seed. The house supplied and the small ones for the hens against rent for garden.

We have been burning off the dead wood in the 80 acres for some weeks back. It is slow work. It is our intention to drag the ashes down to the garden and use that as manure for next year's potato crop.

Grass is likely to be scarce during the winter. Often rains have been very light and late in coming. Frosts have been bad a few nights the last fortnight. Splendid weather through the day for working but that does not bring the grass.

Mr. Wilson is away at present at Bairnsdale with 130 old ewes (in lamb most of them) having too little grass to carry all his stock through the winter. He had in all nearly 900 head of sheep. He expects to get about 2s. for the ewes. If I had a paddock at my command I think I would have speculated.

It is my intention at present to make a big effort and stock after next shearing unless I deem it advisable between now and October to change the programme.

I consider the re-ringing of the big paddock in the front block and the burning off the dead wood in the 80 acres will increase the grazing capacity at least 30 per cent.

With a fair season the 800 acres ought to carry 1,200 sheep. Of course, we could not stock that much but will try one block and letting the other. There are two cows milking at present. The old cow has been again turned out. Grass was getting scarce in the McDougall paddock and the cow had been in about 7 months. There is now 13 head of horned stock counting calves . . .

On 15 December 1895, Hugh reported that his wife Fanny was about to return home after the birth of their second child;

only she has to have Violet Grace and possibly John Hugh Lupon (which she has decided on as a name for our boy) vaccinated with calf lymph before leaving town. We, neither of us, believe in vaccination but it is against the law in Victoria not to have it done. Therefore their mother will get it done with calf lymph and may thus avoid many of the diseases consequent on the ordinary vaccine . . .

In the course of 4 or 5 weeks I intend trying to get about 250 four or six tooth cross bred ewes and putting Lincoln rams with them, about 3 rams. I got one ram from Mr. P. Johnston. If they should do well on the back block (the only paddock in the district there is green feed at present owing to being lightly stocked lately) it is my present intention to try and sell again about July, then stock with wethers for shearing but should prices be dull at that time we will keep the ewes, take crop of lambs and shear. I hope to be able to buy the above number out of the money I got as surrender value of my life policy £57 12s. 8d. It went much against my inclination to surrender my policy but there was no help for it and I may be able to assure again some time.

It is a matter of the utmost economy and a big effort to try and get a start with stock. Hitherto James Colven has been boarding with us and we took out the board as far as we could in work (after of course the days were squared for that I worked on his block), one week's work squaring three of board but as we have no work to do now except extraordinary improvements we would be obliged to charge for board which we offer at 8s. 0d. per week. I think however that he will try baching again and it is likely he will camp at the hut at our garden as being more convenient to possible work. An extra mouth to fill (a man's) in our present pinched circumstances means something and we cannot do it without some remuneration. I will therefore plod along doing what work I can by myself besides looking after stock, and what I can't do must stand.

I have been many years together with the other boys scraping and saving what made the place what it is, with the help of your loan, and I must try hard not to let it slip out of our fingers even if the struggle, in hard times, be a big one.

Produce with you is very low indeed but hope there may be an improvement in prices soon. Here, that is to say in Victoria generally, crops both of grain and hay will be *very very* poor. Prices have gone up, wheat 4s.0d. bushel and so on, but the rise in price won't make up for falling off in yield. Wool as you no doubt know, is much better in price than last season, so that sheep is about as safe a thing as a man can go for.

Flour is more than 50% higher than this time last year, an article which of course we have to buy. Unfortunately the rise does not go into the pocket of the producer but the middle man get[s] it. However we cannot growl at the man who invests his money as a speculation in wheat for he keeps up the prices to some extent when they are at low level.

The Bendigo folk are well. The bad season for the farmers of that district has had its effect on the town trade so James has had a pretty stiff pinch lately. However he writes me that it would have been worse in the old shop than in the new, as the old was more of a farmer's trade, while the new is more of a town trade. I have had to call on him twice for money to which he loyally responded but it went hard with me to ask it from him knowing how things stood. He like myself is hopeful and together with retrenching and frugality hope to pull through till better times come.

It is perhaps not surprising that you have not had many letters from him lately for a fellow has not much heart to write unless he has good news.

Six months later (12 April 1896) it was still a hard struggle but Hugh's report to William carried a sense of progress and some achievement:

You will be pleased to learn that we bought 200 four tooth merino ewes from about 10 miles above Ensay. They cost 6s. 0d. and as sheep are not dear at present you may conclude they are a fairly good class. There are two Lincoln rams with them at present. I hope the lambing may turn out well for we will need it much. It was a struggle to keep money enough together to pay for them, but they are paid for at any rate. The Lands Department noticed for two years rent in February but did not get it; they must wait and the store keeper is also a bit troublesome for his account. However I can give him some soon for I expect the half year's rent for front paddock soon. Had I squared off these I could not have bought the sheep. But the sheep will increase and I may be able to bridge the grocer and the "Lands" over for a little bit but it is uphill, very uphill.

Now we have the sheep I feel that we *have* something. If I can manage to finance the othe things for a little the sheep, with good luck, will steadily

The Ensay district, where the Maxwells bought sheep, twenty kilometers (about 12 miles) up river from Tambo Crossing, in 1911, showing E.J. O'Brien's property 'Fernlea'. (Courtesy: East Gippsland Historical Society)

grow into a larger flock. They will have plenty of feed as the paddock (back block) is much under stocked with that number and the few head of cattle. Besides, the severest drought (for the time it lasted) that has been for a long time, broke up in February and now the hills are green, where every blade was bleached or trodden out of the ground. There is now the prospect of a good autumn and winter. I am also careful to keep them constantly supplied with salt, so they seem to be doing very well so far.

I have not heard from Bendigo for about 4 or 5 weeks. Maggie has not been very well and had gone to Melbourne. Of course James would be busy stocktaking lately.

The wheat harvest was very poor in Victoria, averaging only about or slightly over 4 [million?] bushels. The price is at present about 5s. 1d. per bushel. Flour is more than double what it was a year ago being now in Bruthen 27s 6d. a bag. This is "stiff" when one has to buy. Many farmers and storers are holding but if they are not careful they will hold too long. Should the season keep good there will be, I think, a fall about October to much lower prices. By the way wool is expected to be a good price next season. About *nine millions* of sheep died during the late drought in New South Wales.

The garden potato crop is next thing to a failure, being merely a small potato fit only for the fowls and those are very second growth. In this district potatoes are worth about 8s. 0d. We won't have to buy but don't expect to be able to sell. Warrnambools are quoted about 70s. 0d. to 80s. 0d. per ton.

The fruit was fairly good but owing to the dry season vermin was more destructive than usual. I poisoned many opposums but still they came so we got very little fruit as our share. Grasshoppers were also *very* bad, eating the parsnips and carrots and cabbage as soon as they were fairly above ground so we have had little vegetables this summer, but we have now a few turnips, carrots, parsnips, cabbage sown since the rain which are coming on grand.

A further letter from Hugh to William on 26 July 1896 confirmed this trend of gradual expansion and improvement:

Since writing last I bought 84 cross bred two tooth wethers from Wilson (having obtained a small loan £12 from a friend of Fannie's) as we were [in] plenty of grass, which will add to our little clip.
As Wilson was likely to be scarce of feed he proposed sending over 59 cross bred two tooth ewes to graze till shearing, agreeing to give us half the wool. As this was a good bargain for us I agreed. Unfortunately during the last week the dogs (tame ones I believe) got amongst them with the result we have lost 3 viz. one merino ewe and 2 cross bred wethers. Wilson has also lost 3 of his cross bred ewes. After poisoning the carcases we interviewed neighbours who keep dogs for wallaby hunting and talked very plain as to consequences in case they were seen hunting in that quarter.
Simpson, Hamilton's man and myself had around the back well poisoned for dingoes, but hunters and tame dogs are mostly "inside" not "outside". I think however there is not much likelihood of a recurrence of this sort of thing for sometime to come.
The sheep look splendid otherwise and I expect lambing to begin first week in August. We have had heavy rains last month and the Tambo was in flood for a week. Since the weather has been more or less leaky the ground has had a thorough soaking and a good and early spring is looked forward to.
The potato crop turned out very poor, but with such a season as we have passed through it is not to be wondered at. Mr. Somerville, Mr. Davidson and Mr. Wilson planted also and only Wilson dug a very few. The rest of seed never germinated. Mr S[impson], Mr. D[avidson] had not a single "spud". So we are the only people on the Crossing eating our own potatoes *now.* We won't have any to sell but expect to have a few to spare for seed. I consider I can beat anybody around here in potato culture and I bar *none.*
Mr. Somerville is the man who has started cheese and butter making in P. Johnston's old place. He makes a fairly good article in cheese but the butter is not A1. Mr. Johnston has removed to the block north of ours and has taken that paddock into his own hands again (Hamilton had it) and intends going into sheep once more after shearing. Hamilton now holds only 970 acres on the Crossing so I would not be surprised should he throw this lot up also as it is less than half he had a year ago while he has still a man's wages to pay all the same. Should he not require ours I intend having a big try at fattening the lambs and putting them on the market and get a few more ewes to stock the front block also.
I have not had any word from Bendigo for over a month. They were well then but trade was terribly bad and prices have been greatly cut . . .
PS I have to again recommend you to try the leghorn fowls. Ours are white. They are a big improvement on commons birds; even the first cross is much better than "barndoors". I can assure you it means the difference between profit and loss. We have proved it beyond doubt. They are also hardy and good foragers. Kill off the common rubbish, keep a few leghorns or at least first cross; feed them well in winter with oats and wheat for the evening meal, potatoes with or without "pollard" or wheatmeal for mornings — warm

and they will give it back again every penny. Common birds won't.

While Hugh was slowly building a successful — or at least not unsuccessful — farm at Tambo Crossing, James' situation in his Bendigo hardware business was becoming increasingly precarious. His letters home were always cheerful, and his comments on the state of his business either optimistic or non-commital. The truth came from other sources. On 3 April 1893 his wife Maggie, who occasionally wrote to Sarah in Ireland, remarked that James had got thin worrying about the business:

> He has just finished stock taking. Trade was never so dull. Our boasted Melbourne is in a shocking state. You may have seen all sorts of accounts in the papers. Hundreds and thousands of people who became rich at a bound have as suddenly lost all just through this land panic. Consequently hundreds are out of employment. "Retrench" is the Government cry and taxes are heaped upon us poor unfortunates. We hope that this state of things will not last long. Some of the more hopeful tell us it will not . . .

James' own story, in October 1894, was that while business was generally bad, he was personally pleased with his own performance:

> . . . things generally, in fact everything, has been very bad during the last winter. The Government is in a bad state financially, hence retrenchment has been the order of the day right and left; this with the Bank failures has affected everybody, directly or indirectly. However I am pleased to say that with all I have been able to keep up my returns. Indeed I shall be very much disappointed if this year is not as good as last, so far it is better.

Early in 1895 James moved into a new shop which drew on the Bendigo town trade, rather than that of the indigent farmer. Hugh told William (1 June 1895):

> . . . the last letter I had from James, about Easter, he had been then a short time in his new shop and was pleased with the prospects. He had been working hard and worrying about [it] and had knocked himself up a bit having an attack of diarrhoea. Maggie was well.

Little of this worry surfaced in James' own letters, though he conceded — in relation to newly arrived migrants they knew — the grimness of the colonial economic situation. And he always had advice on diet (24 November 1895):

> I am not surprised at Mr. and Mrs. Graham going home. They came out in a very bad time consequently never got a good start. Willie Trotter was equally unfortunate; am pleased that he has got a good situation in America. He was with us about a week and enjoyed himself very much. I recognised him at once, thought he looked "Johnie". When he left us he intended going to America if he did not drop into a situation of some kind in Melbourne; did not hear from him until he was on his way to America . . .

James provided a cure for Mary's indigestion advising her not to eat ham or bacon and seldom if ever corned beef; tea should be used as little as possible and the less liquid taken with food the better:

> . . . you cannot take too much fresh fish or fowl; never take salt fish or herrings. Never be tempted to eat potatoes and salt or potatoes and herrings when going to bed. This used to be a favourite dish in Ballygannah, enough to give a horse indigestion.
>
> . . . Maggie is just home from Sunday School. I am relieved of that now,

having the leadership of about 40 young men who meet in class every Friday night at the Church. We are enjoying good health although I suffered a good deal from worry and anxiety after moving into the new shop . . .

But on 5 July 1897 James reported home the failure of his business, using (it was a common emigrant device) a response to dismal home news — a catalogue of Irish illnesses, misfortunes and low farm prices — to introduce his own bad tidings:

. . . according to your letter things are not much improved; [I] am sorry at that but you are not alone in this. I expect before this reaches you that the news of my having to give up business will have reached you or Bangor at any rate. However the deficiency was not a great deal only £32 19 shillings. The last two years has been very trying on everyone in and about Bendigo owing to the severe drought. Farmers in Bendigo and Northern districts are simply in a state of insolvency, consequently shopkeepers suffered, as they had to give credit with the hope that things would improve after the first year but as things did not improve and I was one who gave a little credit, I could not make sufficient return and could not get my money in when wanted to meet my bills and as the prospects for the districts mentioned are very black and not much hope for the next twelve months.

At the present time there is not a blade of grass in the Northern districts. Sheep have died by the thousand, cattle by hundreds and are dying daily. In the face of this I thought it would be simply putting off the evil day. Had I sufficient capital I might have pulled through until things righted themselves again, but as this was the state of affairs, was compelled to go under after 7 years hard struggle. However such is life. This is what makes up the world and I should and am thankful that my health is good; am also pleased to say that Maggie is enjoying better health now than she has for some time. The heat at Bendigo was very trying on her besides she shared with me in my worries about business. The doctor told us some 12 months ago that she should go away from Bendigo, that it did not suit her and one thing after another has been pointed toward a change.

About 2½ years ago I had a great longing to go [to] West Australia but being tied to Bendigo could not carry out my wishes and satisfy my longings. However the day has arrived when Bendigo and its cares have ended. By the time this reaches it[s] destination I hope to [be] about 3 weeks in Fremantle or Perth West Australia.

To the ever-optimistic James, in the midst of the defeat of his dreams of success, independence and prosperity, Western Australia seemed the last great frontier, a land of hope, 'a new country and room for all comers' as his wife put it, where a great number of his friends and acquaintances had gone, and, by all report, done well. And he was not going to be discouraged by Hugh, who did not like the idea. Hugh's farm was progressing well (5 July 1897), according to what he told James:

Feed he says is simply luxuriant. He is putting on as many sheep as he can manage to buy; thinks prices will advance owing to the scarcity of sheep in the Northern districts caused by the drought. He is not very favourable towards my going West having had bad reports. These reports were principally from miners who simply rushed the place and when exemption set in (mines stopped work for say 3 to 4 months for want of water which has been gradually overcome through people making dams and sinking for water) they

> were thrown out of work.
>
> I see by today's paper that the gold yield for Coolgardie has been splendid. Coolgardie is about 200 miles from Fremantle. The latter is a shipping port for the former as well as Kalgoorlie and other gold fields so you see there is bound to be a good deal of traffic.
>
> Young Rankin who used to be at Agnew's when I was there (I think you met him) went to Coolgardie about 18 months ago. He has done remarkably well. The little fellow Woodward who was with me for 5 years left and went to Fremantle, got a situation second day after he landed; is still in the place in a large ironmongery store besides numerous others that I know have done well.

James wanted to make absolutely clear to his family in Ireland that he was in no way ashamed of the collapse of his business: he had nothing to be ashamed of. The members of the Presbyterian church in Bendigo had organised a big farewell function. But someone in Australia had seen in the incident at least the potential for scandal or family disgrace and had promptly passed back the news to the Bangor district so that his family were made aware of it indiretly before he had chosen to inform them himself: obviously the gossiping mentality of the traditional small farming community still existed, transferred onto an international scale. James wrote from Fremantle (2 September 1897) from his new position in Union Stores:

> . . . strange how news of that kind travels. However I am pleased to say there was nothing dishonourable about it. It was caused by that over which I had no control. If anyone is asking about me you can truthfully say that I sold out (*which I did for the benefit of my creditors*) and went to Western Australia. The words bracketed and underlined need not be mentioned. [I] am exceedingly sorry I did not come here 2½ years ago. However must make the most of things now.
>
> You will be pleased that I have got a start in the already mentioned stores. It is the largest place here being the retail shop for Bateman and Sons who own the largest wholesale place in Western Australia. I did not get [the senior] position I wanted or was qualified to fill but hope to get to the top most rung of the ladder. They are few and far between who can give me a point here. The department I am now in is the furnishing and I have already made myself felt although I have just completed my third week last Saturday. The manager of the builder's ironmongery wants me badly as second sale. This will come off as the manager of the firm has promised that I should go there after stocktaking which is now on.
>
> Fremantle as you know is on the sea and is much healthier than Perth although the latter is the best business place. The wages are not as good as I would like viz. £2 10s. and overtime with a promise of 5s. to be added in a few weeks. I could have got better wages if I had gone up country but I prefer staying here even at the lower wages. I think this place will suit Maggie first rate. She is going to Hugh's place for a month before she comes over here. She is going up about the end of this month. I don't expect her here before the middle of November. The sooner she is here the better . . .

His wife arrived early in 1898. The strain of the previous two years had turned James' beard so grey that he found it 'necessary' to shave it off: its appearance aged him to his disadvantage. But his health was better and his wife liked the cooler climate. Yet as he made clear to William in Ireland (16 January 1898) their situation was not what he would have wished:

We have a spare room which is occupied by boarders and in this way we are able to put a little in the bank every week, although rents are very high; imagine 20s. per week for a five bedroom cottage. This makes a hole in a fellow's screw to begin with.

I forgot the mention that I got the promised rise of 5s. but is not likely to be able to get another for sometime owing to a standard wage being the ruling of the firm which in my opinion is a very bad idea. There is no encouragement for further advance. However my purpose is to stick to it and save what I can as I intend someday going squatting. It pays better than being behind the counter providing one has a little cash to make a start with. This was my only reason why I did not go to Gippsland when I left Bendigo; [I] would not be afraid to make it pay if I only got a fair start and we did not wish to be any encumbrance on Hugh. He had a hard beginning and struggles through honourably.

Sunday 23. During the week I was offered another situation in one of the largest houses in Perth (William Sandover & Co.). The salary is the same but there is promises of a rise according to ability. As I have already mentioned there was no further prospect of a rise in the Union Store having reached the standard wages. This is not so in Sandovers. I prefer living in Fremantle to Perth. However we will not move from here until the summer is over.

A little over a year later, in March or April 1899, James and his wife joined Hugh and his family on the farm at Tambo Crossing. No doubt they had used the intervening time to save sufficient not to be a burden on Hugh. At first the brothers worked well together as Hugh described to William (14 August 1899):

. . . We have determined to go in for a little cultivation, so with that end in view we started grubbing a piece of ground of the ridge that runs in front of the old hut, only about a quarter of a mile further back in the paddock. We have about 5 acres now grubbed and the posts for the fence up, and expect soon to have all ready to plough. We shall put part of [it] in early potatoes and the rest in oats for hay. The piece we have chosen is a nob with a broad spur running north from the main ridge which runs east and west. As it was one of the highest points in the front block it was a very favourite camp of the sheep so it should be fertile for a few years at any rate and being on high ground all we have to do is open the gate, when crop is taken off, and the sheep will again make it a camping ground.

We bought a little one horse plough, strong built but handy, which we work with 2 horses. James went down to the sale at Bairnsdale and bought a useful half bred mare unbroken, fit for saddle, buggy or plough work for £9. She has turned out very well and now works very quietly in plough or harrow (we also got a light harrow).

The grubbing was very slow, tedious work as the ground was very heavily timbered. However, I think it will give a good return for labour and expense. The ewes are nearly all lambed. They are earlier this year having started lambing 10th July which is at least 3 weeks earlier than is usual in *this* district. That I hope will have the effect of giving a better *grown* crop of lambs, as heretofore the later lambs were somewhat weedy and small. The lambing I think will be very fair.

We have had a wet winter which keep[s] us back in many ways. Dingoes have been very bad in the district for the last 12 or 14 months. We had one visit from them in April but have got off much easier than any of our neighbours. On the whole our paddocks are considered the safest in the group, but at the

same time we are all liable to a visit from the dingoes at any time. Again the heavy rains have risen the river several times so that we could not cross for a few days at a stretch. This is a great bother to us.
If we can manage it after shearing we will try and build a four roomed house in our own paddock. Then we will be nearer the stock in case of danger and also handy to our work in the way of cultivation. All being well we intend doing some more clearing as there are two more favoured spurs with the north by east aspect.

The only major drawback of their remote situation was the absence of schooling for the children. Hugh's wife explained (7 November 1897):

. . . we have no school here now it was closed last Christmas. The attendance was so poor. The people did not appreciate it when they had it. Now they are making a great [fuss] I don't know what [to do] about our children. A week or two ago I commenced to teach them their capital letters . . .

Pioneer housing in North Gippsland. (Courtesy: East Gippsland Historical Society)

It was a problem serious enough to prompt Hugh to consider leaving, but he did not do so.
By the end of 1901 the projected house was almost habitable. Hugh described it, and the state of the farm, on 20 October 1901:

. . . We are now living in our new cottage in our own paddocks. It is a four roomed building in the body of the house and a wide back verandah with one end serving as a kitchen and the other, which is not finished yet, will be a little room which will serve as a store room or maybe a bedroom when quite enclosed. It is built on a "nob" or "rise" on the main ridge which runs right through from the Tambo valley road to our back fence on back block. So we are quite on a hill and all drainage water runs away by any of the four points of the compass, but least fall to front and back and a big fall from either gable.

The principal part of the building work was done by James and a handy man named McCallum (who also shears for us every year) with what help I could give them when not attending to the stock. A good deal of the square timber joists, studs rafters etc. were split on the paddocks from stringy bark trees and dressed by McCallum. The weather boards are red deal, roof corrugated iron. The structure is very staunch being well angle braced.

Carriage plays a big part in the cost of a building material here so we saved a good deal by using split stuff instead of getting sawn timber from Bruthen mill. The wood shed which "Johnie" McGilton built, is at the back of the house, about 120 yards further along the main ridge and close to the milking and sheep yards, which had also been kept well on the saddle of the ridge when built some years ago, so we have insured dry footing except, indeed, when the rain pours, but 15 minutes after the heaviest rain one may walk to the woodshed or yards in a pair of slippers.

Expenses have been heavy with us owing to so much building etc of late and tested our resources considerably, consequently we have been quite unable to send William any interest lately, but I am in high hopes that after the sale of next wool clip there will be a good margin and we will send something then and make it as big as possible.

We have cleared and enclosed with rabbit proof netting a piece of ground about one and a half acres running length ways to the front of the house and have a dozen young fruit trees just in front. The remainder is planted in early potatoes. This may sometime be all planted in fruit trees and will hold 60 or 70 more trees. The fences extend backwards also, so as to enclose the house at the back, to keep out the fowls and give room for vegetables, and will have the advantage of cutting off any grass land from the house in case of a bush or grass fires.

Just now feed is good for all classes of stock and sheep and cattle are picking up in condition, but they have passed through a very trying winter. Cattle especially had a hard time of it. A great many cattle died in the more mountainous parts of Gippsland.

Rabbits have become so plentiful here in this district that it has been declared rabbit infested country and every land holder is compelled by law to lay poison for rabbits. When I came to Gippsland 7 years ago there was no such thing as a rabbit in Gippsland. They began to put in an appearance a little over 4 years ago, gradually becoming more plentiful. There is no hope of ever getting rid of them now. There is too much rough country for breeding and cover.

The prices of livestock are good but the stock tax has been removed since we have got Federation but stock are still scarce in New South Wales and Queensland owing to the prolonged drought. When New South Wales has had time to breed up again prices are nearly sure to fall.

However when things get so bad that we can't make a living we had better sell out and try what luck elsewhere possibly near a school for whatever comes or goes I intend to try and get the children a fair education, without which they will be what the Yankees call "left". At present Aunty Maggie teaches them and they seem to be getting on fairly well. However the prospect is not quite good enough I think for the children to remain here always so a change will likely come about sooner or later.

Writing to William on 2 August 1901, James had a somewhat different angle on the same developments and situation:

> We are now settled in our own house (I mean Hugh and family and us) I did all the particular work myself. The house is situated on the highest knob on the main ridge in my block about 100 yards from the dividing fence between Hugh or what was John's block and my block. The wool shed, cow and sheep yards are on Hugh's block 100 yards distant. We have just finished clearing about ploughing about 2 acres of ground in front of the house for an orchard. We are putting up rabbit proof netting around it, as rabbits and hares are getting very plentiful:. [We] are able to keep them in check by poisoning.
>
> I am nearly two and a half years here now and the work and improvements done in that time is remarked by all of the neighbours. I get the name of making things hum but I know what for as it is telling on me. I must take things a little easier in future or I will be an old man before the time.
>
> I don't intend writing a long letter as I have been swing[ing] a mall[et?] all day splitting posts for orchard . . .
>
> . . . I am personally very sorry that we have not been able to send at least the interest on loan and at such a needful time. But you will see by what has been done the last 2 years or so that our hands have been full, what with the wool shed a year ago, and the house this year it has used up all the money that was raised from wool stock potatoes etc. besides between £60 and £70 of mine being amount of surrender value of my life policy. We did the wrong thing first. The *shed should not have been built for another year or so.* We could have put up with the trouble of driving the sheep to Davidson's shed to be shorn. But Hugh was bent on a shed and a shed was built. Consequently are unable to let you have the needful but we hope before long to do something towards reducing interest at least.
>
> This brings up a very important item viz. that of loan. You accepted from Hugh and myself a written acknowledgement. Such acknowledgment is not worth the paper it is written on in case anything happened to either of us (I mean death) I don't think this will startle you, for I am sure the thought has often occurred to you. It was very good indeed of you to accept it and be satisfied with our written promise which is honourable and our intentions are still so. But you know as well as I do no one has a lease or guarantee of life. In the face of these facts a mortgage is the proper thing (the land won't die) and for the protection of you and your family I am agreeable to this. It was I that borrowed the money, and therefore I am responsible for it and to simplify matters it is best to have it on my own block, which is good security for £1,000 itself never speak of the house. Hugh is also agreeable to this as it would enable he and I to get matters settled legally.
>
> As Hugh is a bit slow in getting such matters fixed up, write me asking for a mortgage on my block giving reasons etc. as if the idea had originated with yourself. It may tend to have the thing fixed up much sooner than would otherwise [be] *Don't mention that you had any communications about it from me whatever.*
>
> By the tone of this epistle will think I have made up my mind to die soon. Well I don't know how soon. This I do know I am striving by God's help to live the life that would merit the well done good and faithful servant and enable me to face death sooner or later. I must finish as my hour is up long since.
>
> This I would like to add that Maggie is enjoying good health and looks as

young and fresh looking as when you saw her first. Of course she gets a bit tired occasionally with the extra work lately. For myself I have had not better health for the last 20 years. That is something to be thankful for. I said I had been working hard and that I feel the results but a day's spell (rest) will make me kick up my heels like a foal.
Hope the children are getting on well at school and that they are strong and healthy. Hugh's children have not been to a public school but Maggie teaches them at home. They are bright and intelligent nippers sometimes too smart . . .

Tambo Crossing in the early 1900s. (Courtesy: East Gippsland Historical Society)

Obviously, the seeds of discord were present in these fraternal differences and mild abrasions. There were too many disparate factors affecting the close proximate relationship of the brothers, differences of temperament and style, of farming seniority and experience, and the ordinary minor conflicts of families living with each other. When their father died in Ireland in May 1902 aged eighty-six, Hugh took the opportunity of his response to this news (20 July 1902) to explain that James had left their partnership on the Tambo Crossing farm, to take the rental of an independent property of his own:

> You will have learned before this that James has rented a sheep farm in Lindenow district near Bairnsdale. He stated in his last to me that he had written to you. He reckons that he can make more money and do better for himself than remaining at Tambo Crossing. Time will tell. However he expressed himself that he might have gone on here for the next 10 years and when my children were reared and educated there would be nothing for him. He did not consider the children much three years ago when he came to recuperate his fortune. He has now got a fresh start in life and we will see

what use he makes of it. One thing I consider: should my children live and have health they in ten years will be the best spokes in the wheel.

As the lease of the front block will be transferred to me at an early date, you must in the future look wholly to me for your money, both interest and principal.

As the price of sheep has been low lately owing to the general drought up north, and James need money, I preferred not to sell any but obtain a stock mortgage on the sheep, but this I expect to be able to lift bye and bye when sheep go up a bit as they are almost sure to do as rain brings on the grass in other parts. In fact there is an upward tendency at present. The stock numbers at present are 840 sheep 42 head of cattle and 1 horse.

A typical Ulster farm house of the period c. 1880s. (Courtesy: Ulster Folk and Transport Museum, Holywood, Co. Down)

From this point, the Maxwell correspondence between Australia and Ireland, already shrinking, rapidly grew thinner and less frequent. The threads that had held together the old world were fast disolving, terminated at the one end by death and by lives growing apart, at the other by increasing absorption with children and the multitude of local matters consequent on a settled family existence. Hugh continued to remit money he owed back to William. Their sister Mary died in June 1903 aged forty-three, after a long and painful illness: there was no more call for Hugh's dietary advice. In April 1896 he had exhorted her to treat her indigestion by eating food as dry as possible. New milk (always from one particular cow) was better than tea or cocoa. Tomatoes (when obtainable in Belfast or Bangor) were good for digestion either raw or stewed. Some light boiled mutton . . . Both Hugh and James received £30 under their father's will.

Within twenty years the Irish Australian world of the Maxwell family had been born, flourished, and had fallen apart. John was dead in Australia, Mary in Ireland, David vanished in New Zealand — though he was eventually to return to Ireland. William had returned reluctantly; Susanna had considered emigration but never left. Hugh and James — estranged — had settled in Australia and seldom wrote to Ireland. Indeed, by 1906 a second generation had taken over the correspondence: the brothers' Australian children were writing to their Irish cousins and aunts. The elements of that strange twilight world of intermingling cultures and lifestyles that had held the Maxwell family together in brilliant focus from 1883 to 1903 had now separated out into its constituent parts, Australian and Irish, though each had been changed by their period of interaction and amalgamation.

Changes in Bangor; Ballymagee St. about 1914. (Courtesy: National Library of Ireland)

The traditional emigrant introduction system still worked, though the flood had slowed to a trickle. The immigrants of the 1880s were now among the established employment contact points for the new generation. At the end of 1910 William wrote to James (whose farm was named 'Ardoyne' at Stratford) about young men emigrating from the district. James was keen to help, but only on his terms of employment, which offered some security, but low wages (17 January 1911):

> . . . Am sorry you did not mention what boat young Lowry came by or some address. However I wrote by return post to Mr. Agnew on the chance that he might call on him. I told Mr. Agnew that I could put him on, if he preferred coming to the country and this life.
> He would come in handy for me now providing the wage will suit. Of course

we can't pay the wage for my class of work that an agriculturalist will pay. At the present time we can get young men from 10s 0d. to 15s. 0d. per week. I have a big strong able chap now; he has been with me over 6 years and wishes to make a change. Therefore there would be a vacancy for young Lowry.
I could have put young Lowry on but he was advised by the Hannas to go down Warrnambool way and take on farming which he would get from 20s. 0d to 22s. 6d. per week but it might not be permanent.

In replying he took the opportunity to make a few remarks about his farm. He was

> . . . holding close on 1100 acres all freehold or as we call it Crown Grant. Had over 2000 sheep on for the last 3 months; sold 540 lambs at 10s 0d. each; have still 20 to sell. These were all bred by myself since July last being the lambs from 608 brood ewes. This year I have 760 brood ewes. I got 9d. per lb. for lambs wool.

And, after ten years, he supplied his version of the breach with Hugh:

> PS I very seldom hear from Hugh. He has only written to me once since we dissolved partnership. Have met him two or three times in Bairnsdale. We hear of them through neighbours who correspond with Maggie . . .
> Hugh took offence at me leaving him; has never forgiven me since. It became impossible for us to tolerate the children. Hence we were forced to let him have the place at his own price with 3 years to pay it free of interest.
> Since then we prospered with leaps and bounds and he [I] am sorry to say has done little more than hold his own.

James's was a reasonable summation of Hugh's situation: he was hardly prospering. On 2 August 1914 he told William he was pulling through despite the patchy Gippsland seasons. It was a typical farmer's lament, down to his comment on the forthcoming Federal elections:

> . . . If things go on as they have been lately the man with a stake in the country will have little to do in the ruling of it. Trade unionism and socialism will run the show.

Hugh still followed the Irish news: it was the time of Ulster's determined campaign against Home Rule. Hugh sided with the Ulster position, but his brief comments suggested sentiments proffered for appearances, and in family sympathy, rather than any genuine or substantial commitment.

Irish migrants of the First World War period found a very different situation in Australia from that of the 1880s. Charles Lowry, about whom William Maxwell had written to James, eventually arrived in Melbourne early in 1915. He wrote to Susanna on 4 April:

> I remained here for a week trying to find employment. The one universal answer that met me by *everyone* I spoke to was you have arrived here in the worst time in the history of Melbourne. They have had no rain for one year. I had a letter from your brother James stating he would like to see me. I immediately went up to his country. He met me at the station. He and his wife received me in a most hospitable and friendly manner. James has been very successful. He lives in a nice part of the country. He owns 1076 acres a nice house a good wife and a very happy home and everything points towards him being more successful as he is improving his farm every year. He told

The Lower Tambo River area, 1915. (Courtesy; State Library of Victoria)

> me that he sold last year between £500 and £600 lambs and wool. It appears that Gippsland is the only part of the country that has suffered least from the drought. Any number of farmers have been completely ruined.
> You could have no idea how barren the country is.
> Millions of sheep have died; horses and cattle in correspondingly large numbers have died.
> The Lord Mayor told me that the drought had cost this country over 20 millions. In fact he said the war was nothing to it.
> Your brother James is a very much respected and influential man in his neighbourhood; takes a great interest in his church and important office bearer.
> After returning to Melbourne I met Mr Agnew. He has taken the greatest possible interest in me and introduced me to the most influential and business merchants in the city and up to the present have been unable to find employment. Thousands here have enlisted solely for want of employment. It would appear to me that this country is either a feast or a famine. I have unfortunately arrived in a famine time. Had I any idea the state of things in this country [I] would never have been here.

In 1917 Hugh's son Jack joined the Australian Army. Sent overseas to France, on an early leave he visited the Irish family at Ballygannah. His cousin Susie wrote to him in France, sent him socks and food parcels. He wrote frequently in reply, sending Australian news, telling her about farming matters at Tambo Crossing, complaining of the boredom of war; he did not leave France for home until July 1919.

James died in Sale Hospital, Victoria, on 26 August 1920, of double pneumonia — he had been planning to visit Ireland. Hugh conveyed the news to William on 5 September. Hugh had visited James in hospital and spent some time with him before his death. The brothers had been reconciled. James' death led to the disposal of his farm and the dispersal of his family. Hugh remained his usual crusty self. He lamented for poor old Ireland,

> a good country spoiled by a lot of fanatics. But here in Australia we have our share of fools. People that are never content no matter what the conditions may be. Indeed the whole world seems topsy-turvy. I suppose it is the result of the war . . .

Tambo Crossing in 1983. (Photo by author)

In Ireland, Susanna died in 1925, aged seventy-two, William died in 1928 aged eighty-two. Hugh died in 1929, aged seventy. He got a splinter in his foot which became poisoned. It was lanced, but pneumonia had set in. His wife Fannie died of a heart attack on 6 July 1938 aged eighty. Both were buried in Bairnsdale.[17] His son Jack continued to work the property until 1961, when he sold it and retired to live in Bairnsdale. The Maxwell family of Ballygannah near Bangor, Co. Down, had wrested laboriously from the wilderness a tiny part of North Gippsland and, across a variety of modest, inconspicuous employments since 1883, had contributed with hard work, decency, and a fund of ready humanity, to the creation of the ordinary Australian world.

NOTES

1. Introduction

1 The material for this book has been selected from just under 800 letters coming from nearly seventy correspondents. One of the principles of selection has been to include only correspondence conducted within the intimacy of families. Thus, for instance, the hundred or so letters of 1850-3 written to Lady Monteagle by emigrants whose passages she had assisted (National Library of Ireland, MS 13400) have not been drawn on here. There is already an excellent discussion of the special value of emigrant letters in an Irish context in E R R Green 'Ulster Emigrants' Letters' in E R R Green (ed) *Essays in Scotch-Irish History* London 1969. The points made in this introduction build, in some cases, on those already made by Professor Green

2 Professor Green's reference is American, and not all his conclusions fit the Australian situation. There is also specific discussion of the 'Amerikay letter' in Arnold Schrier *Ireland and the American Emigration 1850-1900* New York 1970 reissue pp 39-42: Schrier collected and used such letters as a major source for this book

3 See David Fitzpatrick 'Irish emigration in the later nineteenth century' *Irish Historical Studies* Vol. 22 No 86 September 1980. In relation to Irish emigration generally, the weight of evidence indicates that if the destitute of the poorest regions did find the resources, opportunity, energy and initiative to emigrate — and they usually did not — they tended to get no further than England. Many of those with the qualities, enterprise and perseverance necessary to take them farther afield were undoubtedly poverty-striken, or on the verge of becoming so had they stayed in Ireland, but this did not necessarily mean that they were culturally impoverished or lacked education or were inept

4 The favourable impression conveyed by such Australian immigrants is strikingly similar to the 'characteristic' American Ulster emigrant as perceived by Green p 94

5 It should be noted here that the sex-ratio of Irish immigrants to Australia was remarkably well-balanced (Fitzpatrick pp 136-7), but that there was

an occupational and educational imbalance of a kind which significantly favoured men as letter writers. This is a conclusion supported by the very slight Irish reference in A. James Hammerton *Emigrant Gentlewomen* Genteel Poverty and Female Emigration 1830-1914 Canberra 1979. However, various references in Una Monk *New Horizons. A hundred years of women's migration.* London 1963 suggest that a significant element in Irish female immigration to Australia were neither 'fine ladies' nor women 'of the rougher class', but 'useful, companionable women', 'the daughters of clergymen, officers in the army and merchants who had suffered reverses of fortune' (pp 8-9). This Irish female immigrant 'middle class' (presumably mainly non-Catholic), awaits research attention. Irish orphan emigration to Australia — mainly female — is treated by Joseph Robins *The Lost Children. A Study of Charity Children in Ireland 1700-1900* Dublin 1980 Chapter 9.

6 Clerical correspondence is one of the major primary sources in my *The Catholic Church and Community. An Australian History* rev.ed. Sydney 1984

7 The historical neglect of the Protestant Irish as emigrants is discussed — with some provocative suggestions as to explanations — in relation to Canada by Donald H Akenson 'Ontario: Whatever Happened to the Irish?'in Donald H Akenson (ed) *Canadian Papers in Rural History* Vol 3 Cananoque Ontario 1982 pp 217, 240-1

8 The available Irish figures support a graph with a marked peak in 1882-4, (see W E Vaughan and A J Fitzpatrick (eds) *Irish Historical Statistics* Population 1821-1971 Dublin 1978 pp 264-5) but returns from Irish ports give no true indication of Irish emigration: the Maxwell family, for instance, the subject of the largest section in this book, embarked from London

9 The general thesis of that book, which is planned for 1985, is prefigured in my article 'The Irish in Australian History' *Quadrant* December 1978. Brief overviews of that history may be found in my 'The Irish in Australasia' in J J Lee (ed) *Emigration; the Irish Experience* Cork 1984; 'The Irish in Australia: Some aspects of the period 1791-1850' *Descent* Vol 7 Part 2 March 1975; (with J J McGovern) 'Australia' in P J Corish (ed) *A History of Irish Catholicism* Vol 6 fasicule 6 Dublin 1971; 'Emigrant attitudes and behaviour as a source for Irish history' in G A Hayes-McCoy (ed) *Historical Studies* (Ireland) Vol. 10 1976

10 This is to prefer the conservative estimate (39 percent in 1881) given by Robert E Kennedy Jr *The Irish; Emigration, Marriage and Fertility* Berkeley 1973 p 27. J A Jackson in *The Irish in Britain* London 1963 p5 puts this proportion of Irish born who were resident outside Ireland at *two*-thirds

11 This matter has been raised (rather than investigated thoroughly) in relation to the Irish in American society in a brief but stimulating essay by Robin Winks 'The American Exile' in D N Doyle and Owen D Edwards (eds) *America and Ireland, 1776-1976)* Westport Connecticut 1980 pp 43-56. However his observations do not necessarily apply to Australia

12 Despite the enormous importance of emigration in Irish life and history its impact on Ireland itself has been little studied until recently: see Kerby A Miller with Bruce Boling and David N Doyle 'Emigrants and exiles: Irish cultures and Irish emigration to North America 1790-1922' *Irish Historical Studies* Vol 22 No 86 September 1980. The bias of such study toward emigration to the United States is understandable, but generalisations erected on an American urban base are often unsatisfactory or misleading when applied to Irish emigration to Australia, which offers its own problems and insights to the historian

2. Convicts and Emancipists, 1825-1847

1 See A G L Shaw *Convicts and the Colonies* London 1966 p 89; J B Hirst *Convict Society and its enemies* Sydney 1983 p 105. For contemporary reference see e.g. *Sydney Gazette* 1 March 1817. The Irish letters quoted in this section support the general positive reinterpretation advanced in Dr Hirst's book, which argues that convict society in New South Wales was a much freer, happier and humane one than traditional judgments have allowed.

I am grateful to Professor Brian Fletcher of the University of Sydney for reading this section. Note the contrast between the standard of spelling, grammar and punctuation, and the choice and use of words associated with a high degree of literacy. That the spoken word of the educated and official classes was the basis for imitation by the less literate is strikingly obvious in the case of Thomas Fallon (quoted later) whose spelling clearly reflects the apparent sound of spoken words

2 The letters in this section are taken from the Free Settlers Papers 1825-47, which form only a small part of the material held by the State Paper Office, Dublin, in relation to Irish transportees to Australia. A section of this material has been photocopied (Convicts 1836-1840) and is available in the National Library, Canberra, and Mitchell Library, Sydney, but this was merely the beginning of the project, begun in 1972-3, which did not progress far beyond initiation. Fortunately, the present Keeper of State Papers, Mr Breandan Mac Giolla Choille subsequently began work, which is currently proceeding, towards a comprehensive dictionary of Irish transportees year by year. This aims to make available, eventually, the substantial individual documentation which has been preserved, a project whose dimensions may be gauged from the fact that over 20000 Irish people were sent to Australia in the period 1836-57 and a substantial file exists for many thousands of these cases. For a selection from these state papers, see Breandan MacGiolla Choille *Transportation. Ireland-Australia 1798-1848* facsimile documents State Paper Office, Dublin 1983. In addition to facsimiles, this publication provides illustrative and explanatory material relevant to the operation of the transportation system from Ireland to Australia.

3 Alexander Berry (1781-1873) and Edward Wollstonecraft (1783-1832) were two prosperous merchants and landholders who entered into partnership for various pastoral and commercial ventures centered on Sydney in the 1820s and 1830s. Berry in particular was noted for being solicitous about the welfare of his assigned convict servants — such as was Mahony — though his views had hardened somewhat by 1825. Both Berry and Wollstonecraft have substantial entries in the *Australian Dictionary of Biography*

4 Dennis Mahony arrived in Australia on the *Earl St. Vincent* in 1823 and had a wife and four children in Dunmanway Co. Cork. Every effort has been made to confirm the identities and personal details of these letter writers, but available records are often inadequate, incomplete and contradictory — and at times inconclusive in the case of those with common names. This is further complicated by the existence of variants of convicts' names, not only in regard to spelling or the addition of 'O', but in regard to the use of quite different names for the same individual — as in the case of Timothy Regan whose name was rendered not only 'Egan' but also 'Ryan'. Add to this the convict's own mistakes or uncertainty — Mahony dated his arrival in 1825 when he meant 1823 — and the possibility of error and confusion becomes substantial.

5 John Macarthur was the most prominent of Australia's early landowners. For a biography see M H Ellis *John Macarthur,* Sydney 1947 and *Australian Dictionary of Biography,* Vol 2 pp 153-9. For descriptions of the Camden property see Hazel King *Elizabeth Macarthur and Her World,* Sydney 1980

6 It is possible that this is a copyist's error for Thomas Blake, listed as a convict servant of Macarthur's in the 1828 Census. Blake, aged 23 in 1828, had arrived on the *Hercules* in 1825 with a life sentence. Hirst *Convict society,* p 105

7 These Egans cannot be distinguished readily from the many of that surname then in the colony

8 Brogan had been transported in 1829. He had six children. His 35 year-old wife Ellen, together with three daughters and one son (the other two sons, aged twenty and eighteen left on a later ship) left Cork to join him on 22 October 1835 on the *Roslin Castle*

9 Boyce (also recorded as O'Boyce) had been transported for seven years on the *Sophia* in 1829 and had been on ticket of leave since 1833. His wife Elizabeth had been granted a free passage in 1832, but before embarking, and unknown to her husband, she died in 1833. His 1835 letter (quoted here), written under the assumption that she was alive, led to his daughters then aged seventeen and nine being offered passages. They were then living at Carnmoney Co. Antrim. They first replied they were unable to take up the offer as they were convalescing from illness. To a later offer they responded that they were unable to get to Cork and must decline. On being granted assistance, in February 1836, to enable them to get to Cork, they still declined to go

10 Literacy rate investigations among convicts are few and suspect as to accuracy, but analysis applied to Irish 'protestors' sent to Australia 1800-52 suggests a rate of 38-48 per cent. See George Rude *Protest and Punishment,* Oxford 1978 pp 243-4, 249. It may be assumed that around a third and certainly less than half of Irish convicts could read and write. The proportion who might be able to compose a letter of reasonable complexity was probably significantly less — 20 per cent? The estimates made by James Waldersee (*Catholic Society in New South Wales 1788-1860* Sydney 1974 pp 59-60) are somewhat more generous for men — 60 per cent could read, 40-50 per cent could write — but suggest that less than 10 per cent of women could write.

11 Regan had been sentenced to seven years transportation for sheep stealing, arriving in the *Marquis Huntly* in 1828. His wife and their three sons, aged fifteen, fourteen and ten, left Cork for Australia in August 1836
The case of the convict David Moore led to charges of serious administrative incapacity. Promised passages to New South Wales for his wife and family, Moore returned to Ireland when they did not arrive, to find them wandering around the country, unaware of the available passages, his wife having meanwhile had a child by another man. He accused the Dublin administration of not pursuing proper enquiries to locate them. The whole family was eventually granted passages to New South Wales during 1837.

12 This James Atkinson is not to be confused with his more famous English-born namesake, author of the 1826 *An Account of the State of Agriculture and Grazing in New South Wales.*

13 The story of the wreck of the *Neva* is recounted at length in Charles Bateson *The Convict Ships 1787-1868* Glasgow 1959 pp 228-232

14 Hammon had been transported for life for highway robbery, being sen-

tenced at Trim, Co. Meath, in 1827. His wife Mary, two sons (aged eighteen and fourteen) and one daughter (fifteen) left Cork for Australia in 1836

15 William Cox (1764-1837) arrived in Sydney in 1797 as a lieutenant in the New South Wales Corps. He became a substantial landowner and a magistrate, acquiring in both roles a reputation for humanity above many of his contemporaries (see *Australian Dictionary of Biography 1788-1850 Vol. 1*). As in the case of Berry's convict servant, it is obvious that the favourable disposition of the master assisted such convict petitions

16 Fitzgibbon had been sentenced at the Ennis summer assizes in 1832 to transportation for life for being engaged in disturbances connected with the Terry Alts, one of the numerous agrarian secret societies endemic in Ireland at this time. He had a daughter aged eight and a son of five. The decision on his application was that no free passages could be made available to his family until he had a certificate of good conduct from the governor

17 This appears likely to be the Thomas Connors listed in the 1828 Census as then aged thirty-seven, who had arrived on the *Medina* in 1823 with a life sentence

18 Honora Moore of Corofin, Co. Cork, left Clare for Australia on 19 August 1836 with their four daughters. John left a few days later. The local clergyman described the family as wretchedly poor, and offered to provide clothing for them — for which he sent the Dublin administration an account for £30 4s 2d, plus £4 3s 6d for the trip to Cork. William Moore was granted a free pardon, dated 1 September 1836

19 William Lithgow (1784-1864) was a prominent public-servant and colonial auditor general in NSW. He built up substantial private estates and financial interests and was known for his liberal principles. See *Australian Dictionary of Biography*

20 Helion had arrived on the *Cambridge* in 1827, with a seven-year sentence. His wife Mary (aged forty-eight in 1836) together with their three sons and two daughters, had been granted a free passage in 1830 and again in 1834. They eventually left for Australia in August 1836

21 This seems likely to have been the Patrick Byrne recorded in the 1837 Muster as being then aged nineteen, having arrived from Dublin in 1834

22 Mally's wife in Co. Roscommon was told to apply for a passage for herself and two sons (aged seven and five) on a female convict ship

23 Boyd had been transported for life for burglary. His wife and three children in Carrickfergus, Co. Antrim, were not granted a passage, as Boyd had not provided the necessary Governor's recommendation

24 Montgomery had been transported for his part in 'the battle of Macken'in 1829 — apparently one of the disturbances common in the year of Catholic Emancipation. His wife Bridget (they had two daughters) initially accepted the offer of a free passage, then declined under pressure from relatives, and eventually agreed to leave for Australia in November 1840

25 Halloran (or Holleran) was a labourer from Ballinarobe, Co. Mayo, serving seven years for stealing timber and transported in the *Middlesex* in 1839. His wife had given birth to twins after he had left. As he lacked the Governor's recommendation, no passage was provided.

26 Certainly other documentation on the "Free Settlers" scheme exists which indicates that the number of applicants in the period was significant — over five hundred between 1828 and 1848. In these cases correspondence from convicts may have been received but not attached to the file, or it

may not have been conducted through official channels.

3. The Voyage Out: 1838-1884

1 For portrayal of passengers and conditions on voyages to Australia during the era of sail, based mainly on shipboard diaries, see Don Charlwood *The Long Farewell* Melbourne 1981 (Penguin 1983). This contains few specific references to the Irish, but conveys the general picture of life on the voyage. For academic treatment see Chapter 9 'The Voyage Out' in F K Crowley 'British Migration to Australia 1800-1919' D. Phil Thesis Oxford 1951.
Excerpts from the accounts of Ulster emigrants to both Australia and New Zealand, taken from papers held by the Public Record Office of Northern Ireland, are given in Grenfell Morton 'Ulster Emigrants to Australia, 1850-1890' *Ulster Folklife* Vol 18 1972 pp 111-120. This article also gives extracts from some of the collections used in chapter four. Substantial unpublished work has been completed, and is still proceeding, on the individual detail of Irish immigration to Australia, particularly in regard to assisted immigration, where fuller details are available. In 'Australian Immigration With Special reference to the Irish Migrant' *Irish Ancestor* Vol IV No 2 1972 pp 83-6, Majorie J Morgan refers to work proceeding then, and continuing, particularly in Victoria. Since then Mrs Morgan, with Rev. H W Coffey have published *Irish Families in Australia and New Zealand* in four volumes (Melbourne 1978-80 rev ed 1983+). The Society of Australian Genealogists in Sydney have an index to Irish Assisted Immigrants to New South Wales and similar projects are in various stages of progress or completion in other states

2 Burke's *Landed Gentry of Ireland* (p 505) gives the family history of the Stewart Moore family, minor landlords at Ballydivity near Dervock, North Antrim. Captain James Stewart-Moore (b 1793) had served in the Peninsula War, at Waterloo, and in India. Two of his grandchildren settled in Australia

3 Port Phillip Bay contains the port of Melbourne

4 H. Morton's Log 1863 kept on the voyage of the *Fiery Star* from London to Brisbane. I am indebted to Mr. J. L. Morton of Maroubra NSW. for the use of a typescript copy of this log

5 For discussion of some of the questions posed by the more primitive comprehension of their religion held by some Irish Catholics in Australia, see my 'In Search of the Hidden Ireland' *Journal of Religious History,* Vol 12 No 3 June 1983 pp 322-330, which investigates some of the Australian implications of S J Connolly *Priests and People in Pre-Famine Ireland 1780-1845* Dublin 1982

6 Further extracts from Shaw's account of the voyage are given by Morton 'Ulster Emigrants' p 115

4. Cameo Portraits 1838-1920

1 For a biography of Bourke, see Hazel King *Richard Bourke* Sydney 1971

2 Noah Dalway of Bellahill near Carrickfergus came from a family of Scots that had settled in Antrim during the reign of James I. John Dalway, founder of the family fortunes, married a grand-daughter of Hugh O'Neill, Earl of Tyrone, and built himself a castle in 1609. Noah Dalway's grandfather (after whom he was christened) was famous for his exploit (around the time of the 1800 Union with Britain) of riding his horse into the castle, up the stairs and into his bedroom. Noah had been a bank clerk before his emigration to Australia. See Morton 'Ulster Emigrants', pp 111-2, 115-6. The value of letters and diaries of gold miners, as both basic source material and presentational structure, is

vividly illustrated in J.S. Holliday's remarkable reconstruction of the Californian gold rushes, 1849-51 *The World Rushed In.* The Californian Gold Rush Experience London 1983

3 Further quotations from William Carlisle's letter may be found in Morton 'Ulster Emigrants', pp 112, 116

4 There were ten Lawrence children, eight surviving infancy. The writer of these letters, Sampson, was a deaf mute, born at Coleraine on 11 October 1810. He went to the Deaf and Dumb School in Edinburgh, probably in 1822, remaining there for at least five years. Nothing is known of his movements over the next twenty years, but as the family milling business had failed, and all his brothers had left Ireland, it seems likely that he joined his older brother Charles (born 23 May 1808) in the West Indies until they came to Australia in 1853. In 1860, before the correspondence quoted here, Sampson Lawrence was quite severely injured when attacked in his tent at night by a Chinese who attempted to rob and murder him. It is not known when Sampson Lawrence died, but it appears to have been in America, not Australia

5 The careers and pastoral empires of Sir Samuel McCaughey (1835-1919) and Sir Samuel Wilson (1832-1895) are briefly reviewed in Coffey and Morgan *Irish Families* Vol 3 pp 344-5 and Vol 4 p 626

6 Although there were violent confrontations and ugly scenes, this is a highly dramatised and exaggerated account of the 1890 strike. Quinn's account of events in Broken Hill is, however, substantially accurate. For life in Broken Hill in this period see Brian Kennedy *Silver, Sin and Sixpenny Ale. A Social History of Broken Hill 1883-1921* Melbourne 1978

7 Extracts from John Sayers' account of his voyage to Australia in 1875, with his wife, daughter, and some relatives and friends, are given by Morton 'Ulster Emigrants' p 113

8 In 1909 Lewis Twigg in Toowoomba (to his father 11 February) made a similar complaint of anti-Protestant sectarianism in Queensland: 'It is very hard to get anything doing out here. A lot is done by favour. If you are a R.C. out here you can get on. They are very strong out here and the feeling is nearly as bad here as in Ireland.'

5. Love Letters: 1880-1883

1 The salient facts of Crawford family history are reviewed by A. T. Q. Stewart in *The Ulster Crisis* London 1967 pp 89-90 as a background to the career of Alexander's younger brother Major Frederick Hugh Crawford who, after a colourful career as a wanderer, in the army, and in various schemes to frustrate Home Rule for Ireland, organised and led the famous gun-running schemes from Germany to Ulster 1911-14. Crawford's own account of this venture is given in his *Guns for Ulster* London 1947. Substantial extracts from his diaries are included in Patrick Buckland *Irish Unionism 1885-1923. A documentary history.* Belfast 1973

2 The present family understanding is that Alexander Crawford came to Australia because, while at Queens University, he developed a complaint which, in his doctor's view, necessitated his living in a warm climate.

3 The immediate occasion of Alick's return to Australia is explained in family tradition as follows. His father (who had met John Wesley) had started a Methodist girls' Sunday school. He decided that it was time his son married a good Christian girl and certainly not one of his cousins. Consequently, he invited the entire Sunday School class to afternoon tea with his son. The

tradition has it that this was too much for Alick, who, rather than face the bevy of school-girls, fled back to Australia.

4 Crawford's letters contain other references to this song, composed by the best known of Ireland's nineteenth-century song writers. Moore (1779-1852) was enormously successful as a composer of drawing room ballads, notable for their romantic Irish atmosphere. This particular song reflects a mood and sentiment very close to some aspects of the relationship between Alick Crawford and Lillie Mathews.

Oft, in the stilly night,
Ere Slumber's chain has bound me,
Fond Memory brings the light
Of other days around me;
The smiles, the tears,
Of boyhood's years
The words of love then spoken;
The eyes that shone,
Now dimmed and gone,
The cheerful hearts now broken! Etc.

5 It is not among the purposes of this book to evaluate white conceptions — more often misconceptions — of Aboriginal beliefs, customs, and society. The classic works on these subjects are A.P. Elkin *The Australian Aborigines* and R.M. and C.H. Berndt *The World of the First Australians,* but it is an area where there has been both progress and controversy. For a recent overview, see Kenneth Maddock *The Australian Aborigines. A Portrait of their Society* Penguin Books 1982. A general history of the relations between Aborigines and Europeans is given by Richard Broome *Aboriginal Australians. Black Response to White Dominance 1788-1980* Sydney 1982 The best brief overview is given in the series of entries under Australian Aborigines in the *Australian Encyclopedia* Sydney Fourth Edition 1983 Vol 1

6 The word 'gentleman' has a range of imprecise meanings. Here, Crawford's usage suggests that he meant a person of leisured affluence who stood apart from and above the rough practicalities of life: he did not profess to be one of those. The 'gentry' as a class, or social group, regarded the commerce and industry which constituted Crawford's family background as vulgar middle-class pursuits. They were themselves distinguished by landed wealth, British public school education, addiction to hunting, shooting, fishing and polo as sports, and loyalty to a set of imperial values. There were some points at which a very few Irishmen — mainly Anglo Irish — measured up to this definition of 'gentleman', but in the main it was a narrowly English rather than a broadly British preserve: see Patrick A. Dunae *Gentlemen Emigrants; From the British Public Schools to the Canadian Frontier.* Manchester 1983. However, viewed from below, and within an Irish context. Crawford would have been taken to be a 'gentleman' on the basis of family position and assets, education, and various matters of personal style and stance. The term is used by James Hamilton Twigg (Chapter 6) whose background was professional, to indicate not so much social position or class, as individual qualities of culture, sensitivity, honour and bearing, to which he could easily relate.

7 The report in the Melbourne *Age* 11 July 1883 read as follows:

NATIVE OUTRAGES IN WESTERN AUSTRALIA [By Electric Telegraph] [From our own Correspondent] Perth, 10th July

The natives continue troublesome in the upper Murchison district, a number having killed a native boy for cannibal purposes. They also destroyed several dogs on Dr. Hope's station in order to get caul fat for the preparation of their horrible repast. The manager of the station, Mr. Crawford, while engaged in tracking them, was suddenly assailed by the natives; one sprang on him, and another speared him in the arm. He was then knocked down, 19 more blacks rushing him. He drew his revolver, which, however, missed fire, but he clubbed two blacks with the butt end, and the others decamped.

6. Success and Defeat in Western Australia: 1891-1907

1 The standard history of Western Australia is F K Crowley *Australia's Western Third,* London 1960. For a larger, more recent, collaborative approach, see C T Stannage (ed) *A New History of Western Australia* Perth 1981. There is also the fourteen volumes in the Sesquicentenary Celebrations Series, published by the University of Western Australia in 1979

2 James Hamilton Twigg was born at Killybegs in Co. Donegal on 28 August 1873

3 The term selector refers to those who selected Crown Land made available to the public under various colonial Selection Acts from the 1860s. These Acts were designed to make land freely available to small farmers under various conditions of development, end land speculation and promote closer settlement — objectives which were only very partly realised by the 1880s

4 Dr Collis Browne's chlorodyne is still available

5 All the West Australian poison plants kill only beasts that chew the cud

6 According to their descendant Mr Stewart Twigg, Lewis was 'never properly educated' — an observation borne out by Lewis's spelling and grammar, but irrelevant to the sharp and shrewd intelligence that lies behind Lewis's lively correspondence to his father and brother Richard. In Ireland he lived for much of the time with his elderly aunts at Clogher and was spoiled by them. He emigrated first to New Zealand and lived with Twigg relatives there. In April 1902 he joined his brother James in Western Australia, leaving him for Queensland in late 1902 where he married a Frenchwoman and had ten or twelve children. Writing to his father from Australia on 16 August 1904 he described himself as 'your wild son . . . of a roving sort wanting to see the world . . . You can forgive me for once for being what I am, but you will find worse than this chicken in jail.'

7 Batteries were large mechanical devices for crushing quartz to allow removal of gold. The story of Western Australian goldfields is the subject ot two books by H H Wilson, *Westward Gold!* Sydney 1973 and *The Golden Miles* Sydney 1977. For an account directly contemporary with Twigg's prospecting see N K Sligo *Mates and Gold* Reminiscences of the early Westralian Goldfields, 1890-1896 Victoria Park WA 1980

8 Lewis, writing home to his brother Dick from New Zealand (8 December 1898), had a very different view of his situation relative to James's '. . . everyone tells me that Australia is an awful hole and if you do happen to strike good wages you have to pay so much for food as you won't get good wages unless you go up country. So I have come to the conclusion N.Z. is the best. Jim was foolish to buy land especially where he is . . . you would not catch my buying government land in Australia. In Australia it is acres to the sheep and not sheep to the acre like N.Z. Poor old chap he will find that out soon'

9 James's brother Lewis had something of an admiration for colonial crudity. Living at Paeroa in the Thames goldfield district he remarked of the miners (to Dick 8 December 1898) '. . . you should see them come down and spend

£5 a day on drink. I saw one chap wipe his back-side with a £5 note. He was a bit drunk and very hard cases they are'

10 Geoffrey Wright had also written to Richard Twigg in Ireland (13 February 1902) without James's knowledge, to stress the seriousness of James's financial situation and the likelihood that he would lose the property unless help was forthcoming: he suggested £100 would be sufficient. Wright stressed the improvements James had made and that he was the victim of a broken promise.

11 In fact Lewis had much more 'gumption', and held more critical opinions than James appreciated. Writing to his father from New South Wales shortly after he had left James (16 August 1904), Lewis supplied a scathing indictment of James as a farmer, much as he otherwise loved him: 'Jim is a hard working chap and deserves credit in the way he had got on, but he was a fool to settle down on a place like his. I have seen country, like others, both good and bad, but Jim's beats all I ever saw; the people tell him it is good land; so as not to disappoint him, but ask them yourself and you will here [*sic*] different. As I have said Jim is a good work[er] but as for being a judge of stock a bigger fool was never born. Harry Wright told me that Jim always got the worst of the deal. I saw him on sheep and he fell in heavily and on horses he has no idea whatever. He is as bad a judge of a horse, as he is at riding one. If he does not improve on these points, he will always be the same as he is, for his ground would never be any use for the plow [plough], it is too hilly. He has a few acres of flat and a fair orchard if he would only look after it, but he has too many irons in the fire and being no plow man he would be better on stock. Pastoral is the only thing that pays in Australia'

12 Lewis was critical of his brother's matrimonial choice: 'Geoffrey Wright made a good match as regards to a woman. I dont think she had much money, but is a lady, well brought up and very pretty, a different girl to what Jim is going to marry. People are wondering he took to her. If all was put together she is a nobody only a servant: used to teach a dancing class at Donneybrook [Western Australia], used to go under the name of the dancing juddies. Well everybody must please themselves. So far as I am concerned I wish him good luck from the bottom of my heart. She will make him a good wife and that is all a man wants now adays' (Lewis Twigg to his father 16 August 1904)

13 The workers had a different perspective on the realities of their own situation. For an intimate glimpse of poverty and hardship in the same period and in an area of Western Australia not far from the Twigg property, see 'Starting Out 1894-1905' and 'Bush Schooling 1905-1908' in A B Facey *A Fortunate Life* Fremantle WA 1981. Facey's account is remarkable not only for what it reveals of pioneering life at its most primitive, but his positive attitude to it as an enriching human adventure — a fortunate life.

14 Lewis Twigg was also critical of the Wrights. Of Geoffrey he remarked to his father (11 February 1909): 'He seemed to be a fool of a chap, all for dress and high living when he had nothing'

15 Despite their essentially labouring status, small farmers such as James Twigg were consistently hostile to labour governments. That this derived at least as much from traditional self-image as from real economic interest is evident from the case of Lewis Twigg. In Queensland he worked on stations, in sawmills, as a trapper, and coach-driver and was occasionally out of work, but saw himself as having nothing in common with the labour movement. He observed to his brother Richard (14 August 1919): 'The Ryan [Labor] government have got a good holt [hold] on Queensland and

look out for their own class.' It did not occur to him that he qualified as a member of that class.

7. The Fortunes of a Family: 1883-1929

1 The farm was over sixty acres, with a house, outbuildings — a poultry house and tool shed — and walled orchard, occupying over an acre. The house was furnished with items later to be valued as folk antiques e.g. ladder backed chairs. There was a stable for three horses. The family dealt in horses, kept a horse at stud, and was even, as in the case of son James, skilled in coachbuilding: he built a trap of fine craftmanship before emigrating to Australia. The daughters and their mother were skilled needleworkers, not only in the locally traditional fine lace, but in patchwork quilting

2 See Robin Walker 'The struggle against pulmonary tuberculosis in Australia 1788-1950' *Historical Studies* Vol 20 No 80 April 1983 p441

3 The Reid family were among the first settlers of Northern Victoria in 1838 and became associated with the Yackandandah district in 1844. This area, centering on the Ovens River, developed rapidly from 1852-3 with gold discoveries in a variety of adjacent places. See Leo Lane *The History of the Parish of Beechworth 1854-1978 with Ovens Goldfield Background* Beechworth 1978. The Maxwell family contact was with George Reid, presumably a relation of the pioneer family. He had come from Ireland in February 1855 and after goldmining for two years, settled in Yackandandah as a butcher and storekeeper, acquiring land holdings of 1700 acres. See H W Coffey and M J Morgan *Irish Families in Australia and New Zealand 1788-1981* Melbourne 1980 Vol 4 p511. For the historical geography of north-east Victoria in the 1870s and 1880s, with emphasis on the poverty of most selectors, see John McQuilton *The Kelly Outbreak 1878-1880. The Geographical Dimensions of Social Banditry* Melbourne 1979

4 The standard history of the city of Melbourne at this time is G Davison *The Rise and Fall of Marvellous Melbourne* Melbourne 1978. For Victoria as a whole, see Geoffrey Serle *The Rush to be Rich.* A History of the Colony of Victoria 1883-1889 Melbourne 1971. A three volume history *The Victorians* to commemorate the 150th anniversary will be published in 1984-85: the immigrant experience will be the subject of volume one *Arriving* by Richard Broome

5 Andrew Agnew, born in Bangor 18 November 1839 had emigrated to Melbourne in 1859. Originally an apprentice in the sewed muslin manufacturing trade, in Australia he went into hardware and coach building, starting his own business in 1868. By the turn of the century he was among the best known of Melbourne's businessmen. See *The Cyclopedia of Victoria* Vol 1 p505 and *Australasian Hardware and Machinery* 1 September 1903 p 403. The Freeholders Registers for Co. Down 1746-68, 1769-1795, indicate that the families, or some branches of them, were neighbours

6 Malone Road was the wealthiest residential district in Belfast

7 The term 'selection' is defined in Note 3 to chapter 6. The operation of Victoria's Land Acts under which people such as the Maxwells made their selections is discussed in Serle *The Rush to be Rich* pp 50-4

8 It is not suggested that this phenomenon was peculiar to the Irish in Australia. Half a century ago the relocation in America of the basic elements of the Irish village community was noted in W F Adams's pioneering and classic study *Ireland and the Irish Emigration to the New World from 1815 to the Famine* New Haven 1932. Recent market research, in relation to attracting

Americans to Ireland through a 'roots' and 'heritage' program, has shown that even in large industrial cities, when third- or fourth-generation Irish have lost their sense of particular Irish locality, they retain the knowledge of at least the county from which their ancestors originated

9 In the nineteenth century the normal usage in relation to both county and city, for Irishmen of all traditions, was 'Derry'. The official title of Londonderry was not commonly used at this time

10 There are numerous histories of Irish affairs in this period. For a general overview see F S L Lyons *Ireland since the Famine* rev. ed. London 1973. For the present author's treatment of Anglo-Irish relations see, *Ireland's English Question Anglo-Irish Relations 1534-1970* London 1971, and *England and Ireland since 1800* London 1975

11 Apparently he was successful in this employment. By the mid-1890s J. McVicker was a committee man of the Commercial Travellers Association of Victoria. See *The Traveller* 17 October 1896.

12 On today's viewing, the judgment Hugh made that the land at Tambo Crossing was 'extremely hilly indeed mountainous' seems entirely accurate, even after a century of habitation. Since John shared Hugh's disappointment with the locality — again, it is a reaction easy to understand even today — his application may seem surprising. Perhaps he was attracted by the sharper highland climate — but his selection was made in summer. More likely it was the simple fact that he was determined to buy land and this was the only area available within the brothers' financial resources. For the general circumstances of John's tramway employment, see Alsion R. Churchward 'Attempts to form a Union: The Employees of the Melbourne Tramway and Omnibus Company, 1882-1898' *Labour History* No 42 May 1982

13 The most recent and comprehensive history of the general area is John D Adams *The Tambo Shire Centenary History* Bruthen 1981, which has a substantial bibliography. In 1886 the Shire boundaries were changed so that Tambo Crossing thereafter fell within Omeo Shire.

The buildings referred to in John Maxwell's letters no longer exist, and there is now no settlement at Tambo Crossing. The hotel to which he refers as a stopping place for mail coaches — the Sir Walter Scott Hotel — was the second hotel of that name, and subsequently burnt down in 1962 and its site covered by realignment of the road.

Reminiscences of life at Tambo Crossing itself are given by W H Davidson *Tales of the Tambo Valley* Sydney 1981. The Davidson family owned the hotel and the central farm at Tambo Crossing from 1889/90 to 1960. Mr Davidson's memories — spaning ninety years — give the background and flavour of farming and life in the immediate area of the Maxwell's property, during their occupancy. I am indebted to Mr Davidson's son, Dr Bruce Davidson of the Department of Agricultural Economics, University of Sydney, for assistance in relating the present landscape at Tambo Crossing to the features mentioned in the Maxwell's letters.

There is also a history of the country town to which the Maxwells most closely related — Hal Porter *Bairnsdale. Portrait of an Australian Country Town* Sydney 1977 and a sensitive essay on the ethos of the region as a distinctive zone of historical settlement — Patrick Morgan 'Forgotten in the Fertile Crescent. The Settling of Gippsland' *Quadrant* No 195 Vol XXVII No II Nov 1983

14 The schooner *John and Elizabeth* was one of a number of small vessels used

to transport heavy goods on the Tambo River. Adams *Tambo Shire* p147

15 It seems most likely that John Maxwell was buried in the small cemetery that seems to have then existed at Tambo Crossing itself. No trace of this cemetery now exists, but former residents can recall wooden tomb markers standing in the 1930s, though there is no recollection of that of John Maxwell being among them. Cemetery records of both Bruthen and Bairnsdale indicate that John Maxwell is not buried there. I am grateful to the Shire Secretary of Tambo Shire at Bruthen and the Town Clerk of Bairnsdale for assistance in this matter, and to Dr. Bruce Davidson.

16 In justice to David's wife, the highly critical judgments of the Maxwell brothers made in these letters should be balanced by the present affectionate recollections of one of the family's descendants. To him, his grandmother was not 'like she had come out of the moss', but, in an equally telling Irish phrase, 'the heart of corn' — a person who was strong, exceptionally kind, and welcoming to visitors. She had a talent for folk medicine: her cure for erysipelas involved application of butter. And she had been deeply hurt by the treatment she had received from her husband's family, to the extent of insisting that she be buried, not with him in his family grave, but in the grave of her own family. Seen from the vantage point of her grandson in 1983, William's judgment was prejudiced and very unfair, made by someone recollected as a hard old man, very bossy and a pusher. Prejudice on William's part would certainly be consistent with a reaction to David's wife as seen as mainly responsible, if indirectly, for circumstances which eventually compelled William's unwilling return home to Ireland from Australia.

17 Hugh Maxwell was buried in the Presbyterian section of the Bairnsdale cemetery, the grave being reopened to admit the burial of his wife.

SOURCES

State Paper Office, Dublin

Free Settlers Papers 1825-1848

Public Record Office of Northern Ireland, Belfast

(Entry refers to correspondence, except where noted otherwise)
Adams 1847-9, T1555/1-3
Anketell, Elizabeth, Journal kept during a voyage to Australia, December 1865-April 1866, T1769/3
Armstrong, J N (New Zealand), 1859-65, T1978/1-3
Barton, 'Charlie', Journal of a voyage from England to Australia starting October 1884 in the form of a letter to his mother, D718/4
Bates, 1857-1912, D1414
Bates, Rev. William, diary, 1858, D1414/2
Bell, William H, 1893, T1542/3-4
Brisbane, Thomas, Account of New South Wales, 1823, D207/67/58
Butler, 1838-40, D1908/2/Bundle 2/1-3
Carlisle, William, 1856, T1790/3
Cherry, William, 1865-8, D1560/1-7
Crawford, Alexander, 1881-4, D1913/3
Crawford, Alexander, 1880-1884, D1700/8/1-3
Crawford, Alexander, 1884-1935, D1700/6/1/1
Crawford, correspondence 1921-1936, D1700/6/1/X, 3, 4-29
Crawford, Alexander Jnr, 1948, D1700/9. 1-2
Crawford, Rev. T, 1857-66, D1913/4/6
Cromie, John, Rathfriland, Co. Down, A log of the voyage from Melbourne, Victoria, Australia, to London, England in the clipper ship *Norfolk* . . . commencing on 13 April 1861, T2902/2
Dalway 1854-7, T1701/17-18
Dempsey, James Dempsey to Capt Stewart Moore, Co. Antrim, 1838, T1935/1
Doody family, 1844-1857, D1384/5, 7, 10, 11, 17-21
Dysart, William, 1877, D2035/4/7

Elliott, Charles, Log kept on board the ship *Prince of the Seas* bound for Melbourne (Captain Brown) 1861, D957/3
Flemming, Mrs, Log Book kept on a voyage from England to Melbourne on board the *Fearnought* [c1870s], D1944/9/1
Gardner, Daniel R, 1875, D1099/7-9
Gass Family, 1896, T1396/1 and 8
Getty Papers, 1853-7, T2052
Gilmore, 1829-1903, T1611/2-7
Greenfield, Charles C, of Belfast. Extracts from the diary kept during a voyage from London to New Zealand and back 1879, D2794/6/1
Huey Journal, 'The Voyage of the 73rd Regiment of Foot', 1909-10. Daily Journal of Ensign Alexander Huey, 834/1-9
Hume, Hamilton, 1824-72, D/2765D/1-35
Lawrence, 1825-80, D955/69-93
McCorkell Family, 1891, D2035/7/1
McDonald 1833-42, D1003/1-4
McLean, George, 1870, T2680/2/14
Madill, 1874-5, T1488
Maguire, 1852-92, D1420/1/117A-126
Marks, James, 1871, T3115/1
Marsh, Francis, 1848, D856/D/92
Martin, John, fragment of diary in Van Dieman's Land, September 1850, D560/4
Martin, John, Young Irelander, Journal of Voyage from Ireland in the convict ship *Mountsteward Elphinstone* to Australia, June-September 1849, D560.2
Milliken, James, 1884-7, D985/4-6
Moody, Abraham, J H, of Magilligan and Coleraine, Co. Londonderry autobiographical memoir, 1809-1899, T2901/4/1
Moody family, 1851-1875, T2901/3/1-17
Moore, Thomas, 1845, D22763/1-4
Motherell, R, 1890, T1504/3
Nicholson, J S, 1861-1927, D1626/6.14A
Quinn family, 1890-1907, T1552/1-15
Patterson Biography, typescript Biography of Dr John Patterson of Strabane, Co. Tyrone, 1789-1853, T1280/1-2
Robb, Frank R, 1878, T1454/5/17
Sayers, John, 1887, T1917/2
Sayers, John, Diary of a voyage to Australia from Belfast, 1875, T1917/1
Shaw, Samuel, An account of a voyage to Australia in a sailing vessel in the years 1877-78, T1923/1
Raeburn Ms Book, 1852-3, T634 (Pillow brothers' journal)
Rea, Hugh, 1905, D965
Sloane family, 1892-6, T2663/9-24
Simpson, George Bamber, 1862, T2551/13
Tailor, 1874-75, T1488
Twigg, 1891-1907, T3219/1-67
Vogan, 1845-49, Thomas Vogan, Goulburn and Melbourne to his brother Richard C. Vogan, Co. Armagh, D268/5-6
Von Stieglitz, Memoir of the 1830s, T1937/1A-1C
Waugh, William, 1857, D1004
Wilson, James, 1880, T1370/3
Witherow, Joseph, 1898-1900, D2587/3A

INDEX